Collected Works of Northrop Frye

VOLUME 4

Northrop Frye on Religion

Excluding *The Great Code* and *Words with Power*

D1738140

The Collected Edition of the Works of Northrop Frye has been planned and is being directed by an editorial committee under the aegis of Victoria University, through its Northrop Frye Centre. The purpose of the edition is to make available authoritative texts of both published and unpublished works, based on analysis and comparison of all available materials, and supported by scholarly apparatus, including annotation and introductions. The Northrop Frye Centre gratefully acknowledges financial support, through McMaster University, from the Michael G. DeGroote family.

Northrop Frye on Religion

Excluding *The Great Code* and
Words with Power

VOLUME 4

Edited by Alvin A. Lee
and Jean O'Grady

UNIVERSITY OF TORONTO PRESS
Toronto Buffalo London

Toronto Buffalo London

Printed in Canada

ISBN 0-8020-0957-3 (cloth)
ISBN 0-8020-7920-2 (paper)

Printed on acid-free paper

Canadian Cataloguing in Publication Data

Frye, Northrop, 1912–1991
Northrop Frye on religion excluding The great code and Words with power

(Collected works of Northrop Frye ; v. 4)
Includes index.
ISBN 0-8020-0957-3 (bound)
ISBN 0-8020-7920-2 (pbk.)

1. Bible – Criticism, interpretation, etc. 2. Church and the world.
3. Frye, Northrop, 1912–1991 – Sermons. I. Lee, Alvin A., 1930–
II. O'Grady, Jean, 1943– . III. Title. IV. Series.

BR85.F79 2000   230   c99-931768-7

This volume has been published with the assistance of a grant from the
Lilly Endowment Incorporated.

University of Toronto Press acknowledges the financial assistance to its
publishing program of the Canada Council and the
Ontario Arts Council.

University of Toronto Press acknowledges the financial support for its
publishing activities of the Government of Canada through the Book
Publishing Industry Development Program (BPIDP).

Canadä

For Eva Kushner

Blake's *Illustrations of the Book of Job*, plate 13.
From the copy in Frye's library (Methuen, 1903).
Courtesy of Victoria University Library (Toronto).

Contents

Preface

This collection assembles a wide variety of Northrop Frye's writings on the Bible and religion, including essays, editorials, addresses, sermons, and representative benedictions and prayers. They have been divided into two groups. The first, "On the Bible and Human Culture," consists of Frye's scholarly writings and addresses exploring the Bible as text. The second, "On Special Occasions," shows Frye's activities as a minister, grouping together his public utterances in services and his writings on the church and its role in society. Within these two series the items are arranged chronologically.

These pieces were written over a period of fifty-seven years. "The Freshman and His Religion" (no. 13, 1933) was produced when Frye was twenty-one, newly graduated from the Honour Course in "Philosophy (English option)" at Victoria College and just starting his studies in theology at Emmanuel College. *The Double Vision: Language and Meaning in Religion* (no. 12) was written in 1990 and published in 1991, following Frye's death in January of that year. Altogether the forty-three texts edited and presented here illustrate the complete chronological range of Frye's adult life as a thinker centrally interested in the Bible and religion. The earliest of these writings is contemporary with the materials included in *Northrop Frye's Student Essays, 1932–1938*, edited by Robert D. Denham as volume 3 of this Collected Works edition. The latest, *The Double Vision*, comes after the two major books *The Great Code: The Bible and Literature* (1982) and *Words with Power: Being a Second Study of "The Bible and Literature"* (1990), but coincides in time with Frye's final changes to the text of *Words with Power*. A relatively short book, *The Double Vision* sets out in a distilled form and easily accessible style what Frye decided to say for publication as he approached the end of his quest about his own personal understanding of language, nature, history, and God.

The text of these writings offers few puzzles for the editor. The practice of the Collected Works is generally to use as copy-text the first edition, which was often the only one carefully revised and proof-read by Frye himself. Frye did sometimes revise essays for inclusion in his own collections, such as *The Stubborn Structure*, which then become the source of the authoritative text; but none of the Bible writings was so revised. Some of them were included in collections edited by Robert D. Denham, such as *Myth and Metaphor* and *Reading the World*, but these volumes were set from Frye's original typescripts, and minor changes generally derive from the editor rather than from Frye. Headnotes to the individual items indicate where the work was first published (with explanation, if necessary, for an anomalous choice of copy-text), list all known reprintings in English, and also note the existence of typescripts and their accession number in the Northrop Frye Fonds of the E.J. Pratt Library of Victoria University. These typescripts have been consulted, particularly when the printed text appears corrupt. All substantive changes to the copy-text are included in the list of editorial emendations at the end of the volume or in notes.

In preparing the text, we have followed the general practice of the Collected Works in handling published material from a variety of sources. That is to say, since the conventions of spelling, typography, and to some extent punctuation derive from the different publishers' house styles rather than from Frye, we have regularized them silently throughout the volume. For instance, Canadian spellings ending in "-our" have been substituted for American "-or" ones, commas have been added before the "and" in sequences of three, and titles of poems have been italicized. Sometimes, where editors have added commas around such expressions as "of course" and "too," these have been silently removed to conform with the more characteristic usage in the typescript.

Notes identify the source of all quotations that we have been able to find; in the case of straightforward references to Classical works, the section number, from the Loeb edition, has been placed in square brackets in the text. Notes provided by Frye himself are identified by "[NF]" following the note. Authors and titles mentioned in passing are not annotated, but life dates and date of first publication are provided in the index.

Acknowledgments

We express our gratitude to Victoria University which, under the leadership of Eva Kushner as President, initiated the Collected Works editorial project; we are pleased to dedicate this volume to her. We are grateful also to the late John M. Robson, the first General Editor; to Roseann Runte, President of Victoria University, and to Ann Lewis in the President's office; to Robert Brandeis, Chief Librarian at Victoria University, and his staff; to Jane Widdicombe and Roger Ball, executors of the Northrop Frye estate; to Brian Merrilees, Director of the Northrop Frye Centre; to members of the board of management of the Centre: Ruth Alexander, William Callahan, Edward Chamberlin, Eleanor Cook, Roger Hutchinson, Heather Jackson, and Jane McAuliffe; to Thomas Adamowski, Brian Corman, and the English department of the University of Toronto; to the editorial committee; to Ron Schoeffel, Editor-in-Chief of the University of Toronto Press, and to William Harnum, Vice-President, Scholarly Publishing, and Anne Forte, Managing Editor of the Press. We owe special thanks to Marc Plamondon, our graduate assistant, to our editorial assistant Margaret Burgess, to the late Rea Wilmshurst, and to Carrie O'Grady. Robert D. Denham has been a rich and steady source of knowledge and help. The following have provided information and other kinds of important assistance, both direct and indirect: Joseph Adamson, Gisela Argyle, Johan Aitken, John Ayre, Scott Bader, Warren Cariou, James Carscallen, Tristanne Connolly, Gillian Cooper, William Cooper, Nella Cotrupi, Lawrence Dewan, Michael Dolzani, Jeffery Donaldson, William Fennell, Robert C. Fisher, Glen Gill, Don Goellnicht, Eleanor Gow, Michael Happy, Patricia Howard, William Closson James, Carrie Hintz, Douglas Jay, Kingsley Joblin, Brian John, Julia Kristeva, John Mentek, John O'Connor, Wallace McLeod, Clover Nixon, Robert Rae, Richard Rempel, Evan Simpson, Michael Sinding, Ian Singer, Antoinette Somo, Leon Surette, Francesca Valente, Joseph Velaidum, Sarah Wolch. We express our gratitude to the Michael G. DeGroote family, the Lilly Endowment Inc., Victoria University, and the Social Sciences and Humanities Research Council of Canada for essential financial support.

A.A.L. and J.O.

Credits and Sources

We wish to acknowledge the following sources for permission to include works previously published by them:

Bulletin of the American Academy of Arts and Sciences for "The Double Mirror" (1981).

Columbia University Press for "History and Myth in the Bible." From *The Literature of Fact: Selected Papers from the English Institute,* ed. Angus Fletcher (1976).

Shenandoah for "The Dialectic of Belief and Vision" (1985).

Sydney University Arts Association for "The Bible and English Literature." From *Arts* (Journal of the Sydney University Arts Association; 1986).

University of Calgary Press for "The Bride from the Strange Land." From *Craft and Tradition: Essays in Honour of William Blissett,* ed. H.B. de Groot and A. Leggatt (1985).

University of Toronto Press for "Crime and Sin in the Bible." From *Rough Justice,* ed. Martin L. Freedman (1991).

With the exception of those listed above, all other works are printed courtesy of the Estate of Northrop Frye/Victoria University.

Abbreviations

AV   Authorized Version

CW   The Collected Works of Northrop Frye. Toronto: University of
      Toronto Press, 1996–.

EAC   *The Eternal Act of Creation: Essays, 1979–1990*. Ed. Robert D.
      Denham. Bloomington: Indiana University Press, 1993.

GC   *The Great Code: The Bible and Literature*. New York: Harcourt Brace
      Jovanovich, 1982.

MM   *Myth and Metaphor: Selected Essays, 1974–1988*. Ed. Robert D.
      Denham. Charlottesville: University Press of Virginia, 1990.

NF   Northrop Frye

NFF   Northrop Frye Fonds, Victoria University Library

RSV   Revised Standard Version

RW   *Reading the World: Selected Writings, 1935–1976*. Ed. Robert D.
      Denham. New York: Peter Lang, 1991.

SE   *Northrop Frye's Student Essays, 1932–1938*. Ed. Robert D. Denham.
      CW, 3. Toronto: University of Toronto Press, 1997.

TS   Typescript

WP   *Words with Power: Being a Second Study of "The Bible and Literature."*
      New York: Harcourt Brace Jovanovich, 1990.

Introduction

I

The twelve lectures or addresses presented here under the subtitle "On the Bible and Human Culture" were written in the eighteen years that saw the publication of *The Great Code* and *Words with Power*. Predictably then, there are approximations in the lectures to matters that are dealt with, sometimes more fully and sometimes more briefly, in those two intellectually massive works, but there are also substantial bodies of thought, commentary, and brilliant insight in these lectures that do not appear in the more extended publications. Much, for example, of what Frye says about the Genesis myths of creation and fall in *Creation and Recreation* (no. 4, 1980) and in the two later talks "The Mythical Approach to Creation" (no. 8, 1985) and "The Bible and English Literature" (no. 10, 1986) does not appear in *The Great Code*, where it could have appeared. Parts of the two talks are recycled in *Words with Power* but *Creation and Recreation* is a largely independent text. The hauntingly beautiful essay-poem about the Book of Ruth, "The Bride from the Strange Land" (no. 7, 1985), was first presented as an address in Holy Blossom Synagogue in Toronto. Its discussion of harvest imagery is carried forward into the "Garden" part of *Words with Power* (210–12) but Frye lets most of the address stand by itself, outside both the big books about the Bible and literature, in spite of the fact that he saw in these five short chapters, tucked away between Judges and 1 Samuel, two things important to *The Great Code*, *Words with Power*, and *The Double Vision*: a vision of nature as something identical with the human, something to live in rather than to dominate; and the larger mythical structure of the Bible itself: exile, return, and redemption.

In contrast to Frye's final disposition of the essay on the Book of Ruth, two other of the texts become important for *Words with Power*. "Repetitions of Jacob's Dream" (no. 6, 1983) and the substantial section of "The Mythical Approach to Creation" which deals with the ladder as a spatial metaphor for the *axis mundi* reappear with full force in *Words with Power* where they provide important content and the organizing structure of the second half of the book. "The Meaning of Recreation: Humanism in Society" (no. 3, 1979), a lecture given at the University of Iowa, is a somewhat informal, discursive trial run at what becomes chapter one of *The Great Code*. Like its later recension this essay takes its start in the observation that the Bible, although written in Hebrew and Greek, has had most of its influence in Latin and vernacular languages. To begin to understand this large cultural fact, Frye selects, from Giambattista Vico's theory of three ages of history and language cyclically repeating themselves, what he needs to construct a schematic account of three distinct phases of language, present in each period of history but with one of them in any given epoch having cultural ascendancy over the others. Frye rejects the cyclical or, in his words, "failed spiral" part of Vico's theory. Eleven years after the lecture and eight years after the publication of *The Great Code*, the fundamental idea of a historical sequence of phases of language (*langage*, not *langue*) is still at work but in the significantly altered and more refined (and so more useful) scheme of five modes of language in the first chapter of *Words with Power*. Three others of the Bible lectures became the shorter book *Creation and Recreation* and another three, supplemented by a fourth written essay, constitute *The Double Vision* (no. 12, 1991).

Each of the twelve texts in this group is the product of a scholar-critic intent on trying to articulate what the Bible is as an interrelated structure of words, how it has worked historically as the major shaper of Western culture, and also how it might still exert transforming power in the multicultural interrelating contemporary world. Although all these texts sooner or later made their way into print, in a wide assortment of places, they were conceived first as lectures or addresses and they were given at academic meetings (nos. 1, 2, 5, and 8), at universities other than Frye's own (nos. 3 and 10), at nonacademic institutions (nos. 6 and 11), in an established ongoing lecture series (no. 4), in a special lecture series that included other lecturers (no. 9), or, in the case of *The Double Vision* (no. 12), in a special series designed for the purpose. This last was at Emmanuel College and took place at the initiative of its principal,

Douglas Jay, to provide a forum in which Frye would present his thinking on spiritual subjects that he had long considered but about which, on the whole, until relatively late in his career, he had been notably reticent, both within Victoria University in the federated University of Toronto and in the wider public realm.[1]

Most of the texts in the second group in this volume show Frye writing and speaking somewhat meditatively, though often still in his customary rigorous dialectical style, studded with arresting gnomic utterances and culminating in what, in old-style clerical compositions, would have been anagogic conclusions; for both the group and the individuals being addressed, Frye's pastoral conclusions point inward and outward—to the possibility of a transformed here and now—not upward according to an anachronistic other-worldly cosmology and eschatology. He carefully chooses passages from his broad reading in both religious and secular texts and brings them to a sharp intellectual and spiritual focus on particular occasions in the life of an academic community. In still other texts, the ones pointing outwards from the academy (nos. 14, 15, 16, 17, 18, 19, 20, 21, 26, 37, and 39), he assumes the role of cultural critic and social and political reformer, shaped by a religious vision that was spacious in its verbal and cultural range but concerned with the human need for loaves and fishes, and for freedom, in a world rampant with injustice and cruelty. Among the inward-turning texts, in the prayers Frye uses—traditional, composed by him, or a combination of the two—there is nothing subjective. There is no grovelling of the human creature before a deity thought to be transcendent, nor is there any suggestion of an individual ego asserting itself. Always there is a sense of what Frye referred to as a real presence, and a reliance on the power of imaginative language to transform the particular occasion by giving it heightened meaning. In his sermons, Frye used his customary flat vocal style. He did not preach or declaim, but there was extraordinary power in the words uttered, and a palpable impact on those present. The homilies were given in the Victoria College chapel, at other chapels and churches in Toronto, or in chapels at Merton College, Oxford, and at Harvard.

As a religious visionary at once erudite and articulate Frye fulfilled a special role as an intellectually conscious pastor in specific university settings. Over the decades he made it possible for thousands of individuals to hear, in the symbolic verbal language of their culture (and at times of other cultures), expression of some of their deepest desires and frustrations. In the extant pastoral texts—many such texts did not survive—we see Frye engaged with the lives and deaths of students and others (weddings,[2] funerals, memorials), with the rituals of his university on special occasions (baccalaureates, convocations, an institutional anniversary), and with delivering trenchant critiques of the churches and contemporary society. He called on these institutions to get beyond their habitual preoccupations with doctrinal and moralistic issues and concentrate instead on diminishing the hell on earth which, as he saw it, is actual lived history for vast numbers of people. He was a member of the United Church of Canada's Commission on Culture, appointed to investigate points of tension between culture and contemporary Christian faith, and contributed to its report entitled *The Church and the Secular World* (1950).[3]

In the years 1946–50, we see Frye writing editorials on religious subjects (nos. 14, 15, 16, 17, 18, and 20) for the *Canadian Forum*, a high quality journal of left wing political thought and cultural criticism. His association with the *Forum* had started in 1936 and involved reviews about the function of literature and the arts in society as well as commentaries on political changes and events during World War II and in the period leading into the Cold War. In 1952, at the age of forty, for another publication, he wrote "The Analogy of Democracy" (no. 21). This is an important essay in political science by a major thinker. In it Frye states that democracy is not the name of a specific form of government but an informing idea, at once traditional and revolutionary. It is a devourer of states, the central revolutionary process now transforming the world, and it will reach its limit only in a worldwide federation. The view of human nature implied by democracy, says Frye, is a secular form of the conception of original sin: no one, good or bad by nature, is to be entrusted with secret or autonomous power. The dynamic of democracy—continuous opposition, criticism, and reform—and the basis of its hope, is not that human beings are good, but that neither they nor their institutions are ever as good as they could and should be. Members of the churches are in the world from the start and must come to know and understand it. No religious body, Frye thinks, should have secular power.[4] Much of the saving power in the modern world is outside religious institutions, and it would only be through the rule of charity, as lived by their individual members, that these institutions might sufficiently revolutionize themselves to play a genuinely redemptive role.

II

Northrop Frye was not a theologian; he had, however, read, understood, and been influenced by many specific theologies.[5] Neither did he "have a theology," in the sense of a body of doctrines that he articulated and held to creedally. He was deeply involved throughout his life in an intense process of imaginative and spiritual creation and recreation, though the essentially religious character of this process often was obscured, for his readers and for those who knew him, by his unwillingness to use overly familiar and exhausted or dead verbal formulations about religion, and by his wide-ranging and profound engagement with what many believers think of as "the world" or secular culture. Above all, Frye was an exceptionally conscious inhabitant of verbal language. It was his heightened awareness of the powers and failures of words, and his perception that the central issue of humanism is language and how a society uses it, that ensured his lifelong fascination with the Bible.

A reader coming new to Frye's lectures, articles, and books about the Bible immediately encounters a conception of verbal language that radically contradicts one of the most deeply embedded assumptions of our culture, that the primary and main function of words is to describe realities beyond themselves. That this descriptive use of words is important, and probably always has been as long as human beings have been uttering words, Frye never questions. But he spends a large portion of his energies throughout his career, with increasing intensity in the last two decades, showing the radical limitations of the assumption and setting out for consideration other uses of verbal language. In Frye's view, expressed at length in the texts in this volume, as well as in *The Great Code* and *Words with Power*, the Bible throws into sharp relief the inadequacy of the reliance, by believers and Biblical scholars alike, on the view that the Bible is composed in descriptive language and conveys its main truths by pointing to a history and a deity external to itself. In Frye's terms, the much discussed "crisis of faith" in modern times, discussed that is by those who have not simply abandoned the matter as no part of serious inquiry, is a crisis in understanding the language of faith.

Frye found that to begin to understand the language of the Bible, as the basis for an explanation of the book's spiritual and imaginative power in the cultures influenced by it, it is necessary to consider the Bible as a whole. This is partly because that is the way it was seen and used until the eighteenth century. It is also partly because that is the way it seems to have been put together by a host of anonymous compilers and editors over several centuries, and by those who established its canonical contents and shape. The Bible is a gigantic story or myth (*mythos*) beginning with creation and ending with the apocalypse, the story of humankind symbolized by Adam (Israel) and Christ (the church).[6] Frye sets out several of his key ideas about the Bible in the first text in this volume, "*Pistis* and *Mythos*." Approached from the perspective of a literary critic, the overall Biblical narrative is a comic romance, a *commedia* with its recognition scene in the Gospel and a romance that polarizes its characters and has a divine hero or protagonist killing a dragon. The recurrent patterns of imagery are polarized and the principle of metaphor—things closely associated tend to become identified— is pervasively at work. One pole has images of the world transformed into a human shape by human work and the other pole is demonic, a verbal projection of a world that human desire rejects.

These large contours of the Bible—outlined in *"Pistis* and *Mythos,"* present in several of the other texts in this volume, and elaborated in detail in *The Great Code*—do not emerge in the books of the Bible, in Frye's considered view, by means of descriptive language about nature and history. It has been known for two centuries that the actual physical universe did not begin as indicated in Genesis and it is no longer expected by informed thinking people that the history of the world and of humankind will end in a final act of judgment by an avenging deity, even though there is a growing awareness in the twentieth century that as a race we have the potential to destroy ourselves, and that we have shown some willingness in that direction by annihilating in this century alone many millions of our species. The creation myths told in Genesis are increasingly isolated from everything the sciences tell us about the origin, evolution, and nature of the cosmos and of human beings. Unlike literalist and semi-literalist champions of the Bible, Frye takes these advances in knowledge fully into account and accepts them as the best provisional understandings of the physical universe now available. Following William Blake, he recognizes that the old mythology derived from the Bible—about an all-powerful Creator, a perfect creation, an errant Adam and Eve, and a subsequent history culminating in doomsday—has been destroyed as an authentic representational account of what has happened or ever will happen. His approach to the "truth" or the welcoming and commanding rhetoric of the Bible, then, points necessarily to linguistic means other than the descriptive uses of words and to purposes quite other than a scientific understanding of nature or history.

Frye takes the traditional idea of the Bible as "literally" true and turns it inside out. The old view, still accepted in some quarters, was that since the Bible is true it must be a nonliterary counterpart of something outside it, Derrida's absence invoking a presence, so to speak, or the word of God as a book pointing to the word of God as a speaking presence in history (84). Frye says, rather, that the Bible blocks off any world of presence behind it. To use his metaphors, it functions not as a windowpane through which something external is seen but as a double mirror reflecting only itself to itself. If this way of thinking is not to sound excessively tautological, a pointer to complete irrelevance for the Bible, it is necessary to let the speculum metaphor do its work, and see where it leads. To begin to understand its implications, as Frye uses it, involves recognition that almost every page of the Bible employs figurative language and that certain principal figures or metaphors recur again and again throughout the books of the Bible. The cumulative effect is that of a unified text and, despite a host of inconsistencies and tendencies to fragmentation, it does "hang together" overall. This is what words do once placed together and it is the fundamental reason that the heterogeneous collection known as the Bible has traditionally been read as a coherent story as it moved into various cultures, including shaping in a major way the Western one that is Frye's main but not exclusive focus.

The recurrent figures and metaphors pull the text away from centrifugal or external references—which originally were working in some parts of the Biblical narratives—in favour of an internal word-ordering and myth-making associative process. We see this aggregating and synthesizing activity going on within the Bible itself, as the historically later texts are identified by their writers or editors with earlier ones, and as the New Testament in a host of places presents itself as a mirror image of the Old, but seen from a different perspective. Because of this constantly recreating process a multitude of identities get established and form major symbolic patterns within the overall creation to doomsday mythology. Frye was aware, though he did not often dwell on the fact, that the Greek and Latin fathers in the first four centuries of the common era spelled out and greatly elaborated the same identities that he focuses on, and many others as well. They did this whether the correspondences and connections were already explicit in the Bible or simply implicit waiting to be found. In so doing, in their commentaries and interpretations, the fathers facilitated the Bible's enormous impact during the next millennium and a half as a single "authoritative" account of God's dealings with human beings, as an earlier manifestation, we might say, for the prescientific medieval culture and its transcendental religious assumptions, of the Bible as the great code of life and art.[7]

Although, in Frye's words, the Bible is "literature plus," its many literary qualities mean that, like works of literature, it turns its back on referentiality. Watching *Romeo and Juliet* we do not say, "Is this what was really happening in Verona in the time of the Montagues and the Capulets?" Neither should we say, reading of the birth of Isaac to the hundred-year-old Abraham and his aged wife Sarah, "The narrative about Abraham and Sarah becoming father and mother of a multitude is useless or untrue because we know that men and women of such advanced years do not produce babies." As with literature, so in reading the Bible, the reader is meant to be more than a sceptical outsider. He or she is invited by the figurative language and the commanding rhetoric also to be an active co-creator with the story-tellers, writers, compilers, and editors. The "otherness" to be grappled with is the literal (which is to say, the literary) order of words that is the text itself, not something behind the text.

III

In both parts 1 and 2 of *The Great Code*, Frye comments extensively on the Biblical myths of creation and fall. Proceeding there as a comparatist, a myth critic, a close reader of texts, a structuralist, a deconstructionist, and, especially, a sophisticated literary critic with a polysemous approach, he explores the deep ambiguities, contradictions, and ideological biases of the Priestly and Jahwist documents in the first chapters of Genesis, and also their shaping impact on the rest of the Bible and, to some extent, on subsequent culture. The shorter book *Creation and Recreation* was published two years prior to *The Great Code* and is a rich and much fuller account of one important aspect of Frye's thinking about the myth of creation: the later cultural influence, both positive and negative, of the myth. There is much more here than in *The Great Code* about the harmful effects which historically have accompanied the acceptance of the Biblical account of creation.

Frye gave the Larkin-Stuart lectures which constitute *Creation and Re-*

creation on 30, 31 January and 1 February 1980 under the auspices of two
Anglican institutions, Trinity College in the University of Toronto and
St. Thomas Church. The stated purpose of this book is "to look at certain
aspects of the conception or metaphor of creation, as it applies to both
its divine and its human context," and also to see how the use of the
same word "creation" in speaking of both divine and human action has
affected our habits of thought (36). Here Frye distinguishes himself
sharply from the neo-orthodox modern Protestant theologian Karl Barth
(1886–1968), an exile to Basle from Nazi-dominated Germany, for whom
only God was a creator while man was a very lowly creature. Frye's distancing himself in this 1980 text from Barth's thought has an immediate
social context. For many years he had been present and conversationally
alert, though far from loquacious, in the social life of Victoria University, with its arts college Victoria (where he taught) and its theological
college Emmanuel. His almost daily habit was to eat lunch at the high
table in Burwash Hall along with faculty members from both colleges.
He had many opportunities to hear about and discuss not only the work
of Barth but that of numerous other thinkers about religion. He was well
aware of the competing traditions and changing fashions, including the
trend in the postwar years away from liberal theologies to what was for
a time called neo-orthodoxy, with its renewed emphasis on doctrines
and dogmatic formulations, including in the case of Barth, from 1925
onwards, a heightened interest in orthodox Calvinism. Frye's own fundamental humanism and willingness to learn extensively from secular
culture, along with his preference, when speaking of spiritual and imaginative matters, for the language of myth and metaphor rather than for
that of doctrines and creeds, assured that he had little in common with
Barth's conception of *das Ganz Andere* ("the Wholly Other" or "the
Wholly Different") God who rigorously calls into question everything
made by human beings.[8] As Robert Denham has pointed out in "The
Religious Base of Northrop Frye's Criticism" and in the introduction to
Northrop Frye's Student Essays, 1932–1938, the German theologian whose
ideas on religious and aesthetic experience most closely parallel Frye's is
Friedrich Schleiermacher (1768–1834).[9] As Denham notes, Frye does not
cite Schleiermacher in any of his publications, though in four of his student essays he does mention him as an influence on his own thinking
about art and religion. Frye's acquaintance with Schleiermacher may
have come about because of the strong intellectual and personal presence of John Line as a faculty member at Victoria University, beginning

in 1929, Frye's freshman year, and ending in the mid-1950s. Line taught philosophy and the history of religion at Victoria College, where Frye majored in philosophy between 1929 and 1933, and systematic theology and the philosophy of religion at Emmanuel, where Frye was a student from 1933 to 1936. Line introduced the work of Schleiermacher to successive classes of students for many years. Beginning in 1939 when Frye became a member of the English department at Victoria College, Line was also a faculty colleague of Frye in the Senior Common Room and at the Burwash Hall high table.[10]

In the three lectures in *Creation and Recreation*, Frye concentrates on the Blakean and Viconian conception of human beings not as creatures of a transcendent and external Creator but as themselves creators, as beings who, according to Vico's *verum factum* principle, understand only what they themselves have made. In *The Great Code* (164) he judiciously adds "and that only up to a point." It is only by coming to understand their cultural conditioning, including for Westerners the large influence of the Biblical myth of creation, that knowledge becomes possible. "Traditionally," says Frye, "everything we associate with nature, reality, settled order, the way things are, the data of existence that we have to accept, is supposed to go back to *the* creation, the original divine act of making the world" (41). The journey of the pilgrim Dante, for example, is back to this creation and its Creator. The initiative impelling Dante does not come from within himself but from the energy and grace of the descending movement of the divine Word, through intermediaries like Beatrice. Even in the revolutionary Milton as late as the seventeenth century, there is no real human initiative to function freely as a being responsible for reimagining and recreating the world. For Milton, liberty is not something that human beings naturally want. It is something God is determined they will have. In Frye's reading of the history of Western culture the decisive shift away from the traditional acceptance of the Genesis creation myth, as a model, began in the eighteenth century. By the time of modern culture it had totally disappeared. Now, he writes in 1980, "the humanly creative is whatever profoundly disturbs our sense of 'the' creation, a reversing or neutralizing of it" (41). Human creations, including all the arts and technologies, initially are "decreations," attempts to break free from the givens of existence in nature, and in history as it has unfolded so far, and then to recreate the world in ways more in accord with human needs and desires. Without decreation, there can be no waking from what Joyce's Dedalus called the nightmare of history nor can there be recognition of the indifference of "created" nature towards humankind that is revealed to Job in the form of the mighty Leviathan—in order that recreation can take place, including transformation and remaking of the old mythology.

Consideration of what is wrong with the creation story in the old mythology, as Frye sees it, brings us back to the mirror metaphor. Human beings live within a cultural artefact that insulates them from nature. The mythology which is the embryo of literature and the arts, not of the sciences, is a major part of that cultural insulation. It is this mythology and its cultural products that we see in the mirror, not the objective world that is the proper study of the sciences. Whether we are conscious of it or not, these artefacts visible in the mirror embody our cultural heritage and are the great dreams that we are born into. They condition us and reflect us back to ourselves. Like all cultural expressions they themselves are in part socially conditioned, and so must be deconstructed prior to their being made new through imaginative recreation. Both in *Creation and Recreation* and in *The Great Code* Frye does deconstruct the Biblical account of the origins of the world and of humankind, by bringing out its peculiar characteristics as a myth.

The Biblical myth of origins, especially in Genesis 1, tells of an artificial not a natural creation. It is carried out by a sky-father deity who looks down, not by an earth-mother who looks up. The creation imagined here suggests conscious intelligence and planning by a Creator intent on fashioning a hypothetically perfect world with which he can be pleased. This model world, brought into being by divine fiat, unlike the more natural or existential one presented in the Jahwist account (starting at Genesis 2:4), has in it no death or decay or disease. It is so good that the Creator spends the seventh day contemplating it. Frye cites Hegel's view that this creation myth is the symbol of absolute thought passing over into nature, nature being both the contrary and the dialectical complement of thought. Frye suggests that in the creating Word in Genesis 1 there are glimpses of a divine consciousness descending into experience and that "In the beginning" symbolizes waking from sleep, awakening to consciousness, as in Milton's *Paradise Lost* and in the near-meeting of the fingers of God and Adam in Michelangelo's ceiling fresco in the Sistine Chapel. This particular view of creation, Frye points out, is part of a larger mythological structure, evident in the Bible itself but intensified in patristic, medieval, and later cultural uses of the Bible.

Part of the symbolism at work in the structure is that nature as such is not really part of the contract between God and humankind. Nature has no law of its own; it has one bestowed on it by God. This is in contrast, says Frye, with Greek paganism as seen in the *Oresteia*, where there is a contract between the gods, humankind, and nature.

The Priestly conception of an artificer God, the patriarchal Creator of a perfect creation, becomes a major liability, Frye suggests, for all three Bible-based religions, Judaism, Christianity, and Islam, in each of which historically there have been deep prejudices against representational art, against female nature, and even against nature itself. As long as nature was thought of as the second book of God (after scripture), that is, as the Art of God, the merely human writer or artist was in a hopeless competition and could at best try to imitate what God had already fashioned perfectly. Similarly, in relation to the prejudice against women built into this mythology, Frye finds indications of a repressed earth-mother myth underlying parts of the Genesis creation, especially in the feminine Hebrew noun *adamah*, meaning "earth," "ground," or "land." This layer of meaning was largely excluded when Eve was assigned a subservient role both in Genesis itself and in most later traditions derived from the Bible. The myth of a special, unnatural divine creation, at least in its more rigid forms, also has worked against the scientific understanding of nature, including human nature. In its giving to Adam the custodianship over creation, the Biblical account has been used extensively to justify the "view of nature as an unlimited field of exploitation" and, in further Christian rationalizing, has been instrumental in developing the persistent idea that the true home of human beings is in a nature higher than that of the animals, to which law, religion, morality, and all genuine education are meant to raise the human creatures.

Hence Dante, like all human beings in the old tradition, is understood to have a goal placed before him. In order to ascend the Mount of Purgatory he must drop one of the seven deadly sins at each turn of the spiral upwards, until he reaches the Garden of Eden at the top, from where he can be led into the heavenly Paradise. The end of his journey is the beginning of the human journey, Biblically speaking. He is a creature within a mythology in which both the work of creation and the work of redemption are the work of God; he, the human exemplar, has a very limited actor's role. As Frye puts it, Dante performs in "a drama within the persons of the Trinity" (67). The doctrine of the Trinity, in both Catholic and Protestant traditions, in its historical settings, was "designed primarily to prevent man from slipping out of the grip of the church" and was part of an authoritarian structure which, from the eighteenth century, has been hammered by major revolutions in thought (67). Frye, deeply schooled in the thought of William Blake, sees Blake as the "first person in the modern world who understood that the older mythological construct had collapsed" (69). It wore out because it repressed human autonomy. An awareness developed, in the Romantic poets, artists, and philosophers and in a host of later, modern thinkers, that there are more things within human beings than any religious institution or government can recognize or accommodate. In the world of the "Tyger," that is (in Frye's use of Blake's metaphor), in the world that our adult minds inhabit, the conception of a divine Creator "makes no sense" (70). It does make sense in the world of the lamb but that is not the existential world we live in. There is now no longer any functional place for a divine creation myth at the beginning of things. There is only human culture.

In *Creation and Recreation* Frye is unequivocal that Blake destroyed a mythology derived from the Bible and that he himself accepts that the destruction had to take place, two centuries ago. But it is important to realize that it is the mythology derived from the Bible not the Bible itself that is dead. Blake was an intensely Biblical poet, reading the scriptures in what he called their infernal or diabolical sense, in which the creation of the world, the fall of humankind, and the deluge of Noah all are metaphorically and mythically the same event: a fall in both the divine and the human nature, into existence, into the world, into history. What traditionally was thought of as the creation was in fact a ruin and there is no creation except human recreation, the work that Blake and Frye see as already in process in the paradisal, pastoral, agricultural, and urban imagery of the Bible itself. This vision of a new "creation" now points not backwards to a Paradise that never existed in time and space but forwards to the end of what Frye calls "a long journey to somewhere on the far side of the tiger" (70). The main thrust of *Creation and Recreation*, then, is away from the conception of a Wholly Other deity—and "the impoverishing qualities of the myth of a special divine creation" (66)—towards the counter-movement of creation established by human vision and work. In other texts in this volume, in particular "Crime and Sin in the Bible" and the sermons in the second section, Frye draws extensively on post-creation, pre-apocalypse parts of the Bible—Exodus (revolution), Law, Wisdom, Prophecy, and

Gospel—to explore some of the ways in which a life informed by the "unnatural" virtues of faith, hope, and love can be lived, in a world in which heaven and hell are active principles in human existence, not absolute, extraterrestrial realities to be called on to repress and tyrannize over human creatures.

Creation and Recreation is an account of why the human arts and sciences are essential radical breaks with the givens of nature and history, and of why the old Judaeo-Christian idea of hearkening back to an original perfect creation called into being by a patriarchal sky-god had ceased, in the eighteenth century, to have functional cultural value, even though large numbers of believers and thinkers about religion, as Frye was well aware, have never come to terms with the fact. Two years after these lectures, after a long gestation, *The Great Code* appeared. In it Frye again deconstructs the Genesis creation myths but in this much more comprehensive and slightly later study he goes on to delineate a significantly more positive symbolic function for the ancient mythical materials, by reading the creation as the first of seven typological phases in the narrative of upward metamorphosis that he sees as the overall Biblical revelation.

<h2 style="text-align:center">IV</h2>

Ten years after *Creation and Recreation,* and coincident with the completion of *Words with Power,* Frye delivered three more lectures—this time at Emmanuel, a United Church theological college—on the subject of language and meaning in religion.[11] In at least two important respects the Emmanuel lectures, followed by a fourth written essay that completes *The Double Vision,* are a sequel to the Trinity lectures of 1980: they are a continuing exploration of the ways in which human creativity makes possible a cultural envelope with which human beings try to free themselves from the determining forces of natural existence in space and time, and they carry further, and more openly than ever before, Frye's story of his personal quest for the humanized God, the human form divine that, in his words, "has created all our works of culture and imagination, and is still ready to recreate both our society and ourselves" (82).

Like other texts in this volume and like many of Frye's other writings, *The Double Vision* is an occasional work. This does not mean that it is in any way superficial or slight, or that it was easily done, however erudite

Frye had long since made himself and however experienced he had become as a writer, as he now reached the age of seventy-eight in July 1990, the month in which the book was completed. *The Double Vision* is Frye's carefully considered (even tormented) response to an invitation from Emmanuel College and it was formulated over a period of seven months: the five months between the time of the principal's request and the actual dates of the delivery of the lectures—14, 15, and 16 May, followed by another two months in which he wrote the last chapter—called "The Double Vision of God." In this same seven-month period Frye was putting the finishing touches on *Words with Power*, he was still teaching, and his health was failing. But it was for reasons deeper than these that the assignment was formidably difficult.

The subject of language and meaning in religion can be addressed easily, one supposes, on some level, by the culturally unconscious, the intellectually underdeveloped, or the ideologically overconfident. But Frye was none of these. To speak, late in the twentieth century, in an academic setting, while also simultaneously writing for a worldwide educated readership, about the meaning of language, nature, time, and God is no trivial matter. Frye had done this before, of course, but never without prodigious mental effort sustained over a period of years. His writings, especially *The Great Code* and the earlier *Anatomy of Criticism*, had been widely both acclaimed and condemned. Often, gratifyingly, they had been understood, valued, and used creatively. Whatever the response and even though Frye knew that he had major achievements behind him, he was seldom if ever content with what he had done and was constantly pressing on to another project. In Notes 53, paragraph 85, for example, written in 1990 as *Words with Power* was about to appear and while he was preparing the Emmanuel lectures, he speaks of being "haunted by the feeling that even WP needs a few extra paragraphs about the imaginative universe."[12] He senses a "warning" that "the axis mundi is an exceedingly arbitrary choice from a whole complex." As if receiving instruction from somewhere else, he suggests that the feeling haunting him is "perhaps a hint" that the writing of an account of "the whole imaginative (or imaginary) cosmos," may be his "next big job, with these Emmanuel lectures the transition between them." Then he asks, "How long do I have, angel?" What was different this time was that he had to go further in crystallizing his thoughts on these substantive matters and also, at least with the last of the four subjects, "The Double Vision of God," as he realized before finishing the book, he had finally to tell his own "double vision," to an audience and readership many of whom did not know for sure that he, the towering literary critic and philosopher of culture, had such a vision. He also had to do so in a very particular set of circumstances.

Almost a half-century earlier Frye had been a student of theology at Emmanuel, albeit an exceptional one, with a good background in philosophy, a wide cultural range of experience, and the intellect and imagination of an emerging prodigy who would go on to produce some of the twentieth century's most influential and most frequently cited writings in the arts and humanities. While at Emmanuel he had not locked himself into the theological disciplines in any narrow or conventional confessional sense. Instead he had spent much of his time reading, thinking, and writing about literature, the other arts, cultural anthropology, comparative religion, and psychology, while also reading church history and various theologians. He had also pursued his study of the Old and New Testaments, but from perspectives quite unlike those of the Biblical scholarship (historical, linguistic, form criticism) practised at Emmanuel in the 1930s. In this period of its history, Emmanuel was theologically a rather liberal Protestant school with most of its faculty members and students interested at least as much in the practical social implications of Christianity as in the finer points of either scholarship or theological doctrine. The institution was liberal enough to accommodate him but not intellectually or culturally exploratory enough to engage actively with his ferociously energetic mind. One indication of the lack of engagement is the brevity or absence of any real comment by his professors on the student essays that have survived. It seems that, as at Merton College later, at least some of Frye's teachers were thoroughly intimidated by the prodigy in their midst.[13] As the years passed and Frye became a faculty colleague in the Victoria University community, collegial relations between Frye and faculty members in both colleges were warm and cordial. But the intellectual gap widened, as Frye, a few metres away from Emmanuel in his office and the classrooms of Victoria College, became a powerful magnet for a host of students over the years, not only in his English courses on Renaissance literature, Spenser, Shakespeare, Milton, Blake, the development of the drama, nineteenth-century thought, and the principles of literary symbolism but in his constantly evolving course on the Bible. This last course ostensibly was a kind of primer for Biblically illiterate students of literature but it quickly became a major intellectual force that shocked into consciousness generations of students and shaped their thinking, not only about the Bible but about the culture derived in large part from it.

For many years at Victoria University, then, with its college of arts and its college of theology, there existed a large institutional paradox, so far as Frye was concerned: Biblical scholarship and the related theological disciplines were centred at Emmanuel, where Frye himself and many other men and women prepared for ordination as ministers in the United Church of Canada; meanwhile, the really revolutionary thinking about the Bible, religion, Christianity, and the churches was taking place at Victoria in the mind of Frye, who sometimes referred to himself as a "fifth column" and who, although a minister of the church, was following his own critical path in spiritual matters as in others. Early in the three lectures, Frye identifies with his fellow alumni of Emmanuel and with the United Church (in its sixty-fifth or superannuation year) but this metaphorical and existential reaching out by one member of two larger bodies embraces numerous personal and institutional tensions and differences, as well as a genuinely charitable giving of himself to the task in hand. The occasion of *The Double Vision* is the culmination of a great deal in Frye's autobiography. In the event, it also became a book of passage or transition, though not in the sense hoped for in his note about his next big book, referred to above.

The still larger historical context in 1990, beyond Frye himself and the institutions in which he was directly involved, is also part of the occasion for *The Double Vision.* That was the year in which the Cold War was ending and "state capitalism" known as "Communism" or "socialism" appeared to have collapsed. Frye makes good use of this historic change to remind his listeners and readers not to fall into the same kind of naive optimism about the apparent triumph of the capitalist West that had been pervasive when he came to Victoria as a freshman in the fall of 1929, just before the Wall Street crash. Part as well of the larger historical context, the *Weltgeschichte*—this becomes a major preoccupation throughout the four chapters of the book—is what Frye sees as the ongoing fundamental "lack of spiritual vision" which has kept most societies throughout history in a "primitive" state and has allowed the nightmare of history to unfold again and again, denying the satisfying of primary human physical needs: for food and drink; sex and companionship; property, or what is "proper" to one's life as an individual, starting with clothing and shelter and perhaps territorial space; freedom of movement. The primitive society precludes as well any fulfilment of these needs in their spiritual dimensions: the focus of sharing goods in a community; love and companionship; scientific discovery and the production of poetry and music; freedom of thought and criticism.

The Double Vision, in this editor's view, is a little masterpiece of compressed, vital prose writing, easily accessible but filled with brilliant perceptions and resonant with knowledge and wisdom. When the book first became known, it surprised many of those who had read Frye's previous works, and thought they knew the main workings of his mind and imagination. The book was a surprise because of the degree to which it reveals, without becoming subjective or self-absorbed, the individual man Northrop Frye as an imaginative and spiritual visionary. Certainly there had been preparation for such a book, in most of the other texts included in this volume, in the chapter entitled "The Word within the Word" in *Fearful Symmetry*, and in *The Great Code* and *Words with Power*. *The Double Vision*, as Frye says in the Preface, is "a rest stop on a pilgrimage," not a retraction by him as if he were considering his previous works as worldly vanities. On the contrary, one of the main themes in *The Double Vision* is the enormous importance of imaginative literature, because it is literature more than any other kind of human cultural expression that reveals over and over what the primary needs of human beings are. Literature shows people "in the throes of surviving, loving, prospering, and fighting with the frustrations that block these things." The world of literature is a hypothetical world "where even the most terrible tragedies are still called plays," a world that "does everything that can be done for people except transform them." Moreover, the literature whose criticism had occupied most of Frye's life "creates a world that the spirit can live in, but it does not make us spiritual beings" (178). Now, in *The Double Vision*, he talks of how this metamorphosis can take place. In his writings and his life Frye was a superb ironist, often leaving unpublished or unsaid much of what was on or in his mind. It is that other Frye who now is becoming known, at least in part, from his previously unpublished diaries, notebooks, notes, and correspondence, from this last published work of his spiritual autobiography, and from a careful reading, now becoming possible for the first time, of the overall body of Frye's works.

Each of Frye's numerous books is organized according to a schema that he constructed through a protracted process of starts, stops, and reshapings and into which he then placed, while simultaneously searching out the narrative links that would provide the "argument," whatever materials from his rich store of observations of the world and from his reading and thinking and imagining were suited to the subject at hand. In the cases of his big books *Anatomy of Criticism, The Great Code,* and *Words with Power* this strategy resulted in complex structural architectonics necessary for the containment, integration, and presentation of a wealth of learning and insight. We now know as well, as the implications of his long-standing fascination with the "ogdoad" become clear, from his previously unpublished writings, that there was an even more complex, diverse, and constantly changing visionary structure behind even the most spaciously and intricately designed of his publications.[14] In this overall context of encyclopedic work realized and of work envisioned but not completed, *The Double Vision* is relatively simple in its organizing schema, though not in the range of its potential meanings. The title is from a Blake lyric composed in 1801, included as the epigraph of the book. The stanza from the lyric quoted by Frye is filled with imaginative implications and it is these that are explored as he delineates his double vision of language, nature, time, and God.

Each of the four chapters is divided into three parts with subtitles, giving twelve units, followed, in the case of chapter 4, by a thirteenth part which is different in kind and is entitled "The Humanized God." Each chapter proceeds dialectically, exploring the contrast signalled in the Blake lyric between physical or natural vision and spiritual vision, in relation to the historical crises precipitated by "natural" human beings uninformed by vision and redemptive imagining: the confusion and perversion of verbal language; the exploitation and degradation of physical nature; the nightmare horror of time-bound human experience throughout history; and, finally, the appalling record of the history of religion, including Christianity, and the ways in which religion has been used time and again to repress and destroy human beings rather than fulfil them. Each chapter of *The Double Vision* sets against the crisis delineated a redemptive vision informed by Frye's long absorption in the works of a host of thinkers and writers, including, as important elements woven directly into this culturally resonant book, ideas and insights from the following: Anaximander, Pythagoras, Sophocles, Plato, Aristotle, Lucretius, Virgil, Seneca, Ovid, Plotinus, Augustine, Joachim of Fiore, Aquinas, Dante, Erasmus, Luther, Shakespeare, Milton, Marvell, Hobbes, Browne, Vico, Rousseau, Burke, Kant, Keats, Blake, Hegel, Coleridge, Kierkegaard, Marx, Dickinson, Arnold, Morris,

Newman, Nietzsche, Freud, Whitehead, Jung, Eliot, Auden, Foucault, and Pynchon. There are others, referred or alluded to in passing, as well as nonliterary artists and composers of music. Above all, however, given the main subject of *The Double Vision*, the lifelong interest of its author in the Bible, and the mainly clerical composition of the book's original live audience, it is Frye's responses to the stories, metaphors, and kerygma of the Old and New Testaments that serve as the main visionary elements feeding into the record of this quest for a *Heilsgeschichte*. It is with these elements and others like them—he is always inclusive—that he would have his listeners and readers imagine and existentially realize, on an individual and perhaps even at times on a social level, the redemption of language, space, time, and conceptions of God. In the case of the last of these, the conceptions badly need, in Frye's words, to be "cleaned up."

Frye is modest about his expertise as a Biblical scholar, but it is clear that he knows in general, and often specifically, what this scholarship has been over the last two centuries and what its main preoccupations are in the latter half of the twentieth century. In *The Double Vision*, as in *The Great Code* and *Words with Power*, he brings to the Bible a multidisciplinary experience so rich and varied that it beggars most contemporary academic efforts to carry out such work. In *The Double Vision*, in addition to important things learned from literary criticism, philosophy, and history, there are "revelations"—this is how he thought of what is learned from the human arts and sciences—from comparative literature, literary history, literary theory, and the history of language, from Biblical scholarship, theology, the philosophy of religion, and comparative religion, from anthropology, psychology, and political theory, from the history of philosophy and of science, and from cultural, feminist, and environmental studies. The disciplinary range, the correlating and identifying of this fact or cultural element with that one (while also differentiating them), and the overall synthesizing that are embodied in *The Double Vision* would be an absurdity, in an age of specialist scholarship, were they not the product of fifty years of intensive intellectual work and imaginative (including spiritual) openness, in one of the most active and powerful minds of the twentieth century. In his late Notebook 44 (paragraphs 270 and 448) Frye says, regretfully, in the context of thinking about the discipline and practice of meditation, "In all my life I've never known an instant of real silence." It is a credible statement.

At the beginning of chapter 2 of *The Double Vision* Frye explains what he thinks is happening in the four lines of Blake chosen as epigraph to the book. In a general way, the "thistle" seen by the poet's outward eye and the "old man grey" visible to his inward eye indicate that simple sense perception and detached observation of nature are not enough. But "Blake is not recommending that one should try to awaken from the sleep of single vision by seeing two objects instead of one, especially when one of the two is not there." This is what literalist reading might indicate but imaginative literalism would understand that the "old man grey" is an aspect of Blake himself and that what Blake means is "that the conscious subject is not really perceiving until it recognizes itself as part of what it perceives" (183). Here we have a poet's succinct rendering of the way Frye himself thinks, and of the way this last of his books holds together and takes its identity. Beyond the formal or schematic organization of four chapters, in twelve plus one parts, the real organizing principle of *The Double Vision* is Frye's interpenetrating, metaphorical mode of thinking. Each part of the book is present in all the others, as Frye's mind flows freely into and out of a host of observations of the actual world and of texts and other cultural products, perceiving each one, communicating with it but not violating it, and then using it in a recreation meant to transform and expand the vision of his listeners and readers.

Alvin A. Lee

On the Bible and Human Culture

1

Pistis and *Mythos*

1 June 1972

From Annual Proceedings of the Canadian Society for the Study of Religion *(Montreal, 1972), 29–33. Frye's offprint in NFF, 1988, box 50, file 5 has two substantive corrections in his hand which are adopted here. This is the summary of the argument of a talk given at the annual convention of the Learned Societies of Canada, McGill University. Frye distributed this summary beforehand and then spoke extemporaneously, using it as a guide. A tape recording of his speech, in NFF, 1991, box 63, includes questions from the audience but is of poor quality. Pistis is the Greek word for "faith."*

1. The question of the "crisis of faith," which is really, I think, a crisis in understanding the nature of the language of faith, has emerged for me as a by-product of an undergraduate course on the typology and symbolism of the English Bible, which I have been teaching for some years.

2. To explain the impact of the Bible on Western thought and imagination, it was necessary to deal with the Bible as a whole, as a book beginning where time begins, with the creation, ending where time ends, with the Last Judgment, and telling the story of mankind in between, under the symbolic names of Adam and Israel.

3. The *narrative* of the Bible, from the literary point of view, is a comic romance. Comic, because it begins with Adam-Israel in relative prosperity, sends him into exile and bondage, and restores, or rather renews, the original state. Cf. Dante's term *commedia*. Comedies often reach a climax in a "recognition scene" where something previously concealed is brought out, often the identity of the hero or heroine. Similarly the concealed hero of the Biblical narrative, the Messiah, is identified as Jesus in the Gospels, which constitute the Biblical recognition scene. Romance,

because the narrative polarizes its characters into heroes and villains, with a story of a divine hero killing a dragon deeply embedded in its structure.

4. Hence the story of the Bible is a myth (meaning *mythos*, narrative or story). In primitive verbal cultures myths are distinguished from folk tales or legends, not by their structure, but by a specific social function. Myths are the *serious* stories: they are the ones that really happened or explain what is of primary importance to their society. Hence (a) they take root in a specific culture, whereas folk tales remain nomadic, and (b) they stick together to form a mythology, a network of shared allusion and imaginative experience which literature inherits. The Samson story, for example, has analogues in folk tale of the same general structure, but Milton writes *Samson Agonistes* because the Biblical version is part of his central mythical heritage.

5. The *imagery* of the Bible is polarized between images of relative peace, prosperity, and independence, and images of their opposites, exile, humiliation, or bondage. The principle of metaphor, that things closely associated tend to become identified, applies both to literature and to the Bible. The garden of Eden, the Promised Land, Jerusalem, and Zion, consolidate into a single body of imagery; so do the wilderness and the sea, Egypt, Babylon, and Rome.

6. The imagery in the former group consists mainly of (a) oasis imagery, trees and rivers, (b) pastoral imagery, of flocks and herds, (c) agricultural imagery, of corn and grapes, (d) city and building imagery. Note that these are the images of the world transformed into a human shape by human work. In the New Testament Christ becomes the metaphorical key that identifies all these images. He is (a) the tree and river of life, (b) the Lamb of the sheepfold, (c) the bread and the wine, the vine of which his followers are branches, (d) the temple is his body and the city his bride. Similarly with demonic imagery: Egypt, Babylon, and Rome, the Pharaoh, Nebuchadnezzar, and Nero, the waste land and the sea, beasts of prey and dragons, including the sea-serpent Leviathan who is both the sea (i.e., dead as opposed to living water) and the demonic kingdoms, are all metaphorically identified.

7. Questions from my students at first took the form: is it all just a myth, only a myth, nothing but a myth? That is, is there nothing there but an aesthetic pattern that involves no commitment? Note the similarity here to the words "fable" or "fiction," which are also terms meaning literary structure, but have acquired a secondary meaning of "untrue"

because of the general conviction that literature is a form of socially permissible lying.

8. A deeper assumption underlying such questions points to the influence of the art of writing. Writing is of course older than the Bible, but is used for legal or commercial purposes for a long time during which everything we think of as literature is still oral. The Bible is always very close to the oral tradition, even in the New Testament. Note the independence of great religious or even ethical leaders (Jesus, Buddha, Elijah, Socrates, even Mohammed) from writing. Moses is an exception, because Moses is associated with the Law, the earliest type of writing to be made public.

9. Writing develops the notion (along with the continuous prose which it also develops) that the primary, or, as we often say, the "literal" function of words is to describe external phenomena. Hence if the Bible is "true," its words, on this assumption, must be simply descriptive of historical events or of concepts, and definitively accurate in its rendering of them.

10. Dealing with such questions drew me to explain that description is a late, subordinate, and second-rate function of words. Words don't describe external phenomena with definitive accuracy; they're too bound up with their own grammatical fictions, especially the fiction of causality. Myth is the language of the present tense, of "confrontation," of events assumed to start operating within the reader as he reads. The historian tries to place us in the past with what he describes; Biblical writers convey events to be "spiritually discerned," which we, had we experienced them, would have misinterpreted as ordinary experience. Myth and metaphor express what language is primarily equipped to express, and only myth and metaphor can evoke the deeper world of identity in which different things are one thing, and all men the same man.

11. Aristotle was the first to attempt to explain the role of the mythical or poetic function of words. The historian and the discursive writer make specific and particular statements or predications, and are judged by standards of truth and falsehood. The poet gives the "universal," typical, or recurring events of history, makes no specific statements, and is bound to no such canons. Similarly with discursive writing, though Aristotle is not very full on this. The poet gives us universal, typical, or recurring thought, including the metaphorical structures from which specific propositions emerge. Note that Aristotle's

basis is the sense of the "literal" as the descriptive and the poetic as a displacement of it.[1]

12. In the Bible pure myths (creation, deluge) shade off into folk tale and legend (Elijah and Samson stories), historical reminiscence (Exodus and the call of Abraham), and didactic and manipulated history (the Deuteronomic historians). As there is no boundary line, it follows that nothing in the Bible which may be historically accurate is there because it is historically accurate.

13. The same principle applies to the Gospels, which are so far from being biographies. The effort to treat the Gospels as roughly credible narratives with mythical accretions is dismally futile. The Gospels are myths, and any attempt to "demythologize" them will disintegrate them to nothing.

14. It is not difficult to show that myth is unhistorical and that the Bible, though its action goes on where history is and though it is consistently and very sharply aware of history, is not historical in the descriptive sense either. But one feels that the relation of myth and history is more specific than that.

15. History begins as chronicle: history in the proper sense begins when chronicle is realized to be the content or raw material of history. Question of shaping form: the simplest and most obvious is the one later (after Boethius) popularized as the wheel of fortune or roughly cyclical change. This is the tragic or ironic view of history, and is the one established by Herodotus, who saw the history of the world as leading up to the David-and-Goliath defeat of Persia by Greece. The moral is that the gods don't like big empires.

16. Hence there grows a sense of the divine will as a counterhistorical force, working toward the destruction of empires and against their indefinite power. This sense is often projected as "Providence," which is only recognized when you win—e.g., the storm that wrecked the Armada was providential to the English, but a natural event to the Spaniards.

17. In the Bible exile and bondage seem to be the normal condition of man in history: over against this is an ideal kingdom symbolized by imagery of the past (e.g., the Davidic monarchy in the Chronicles and Psalms) or the future (e.g., the Second Coming; the millennium). Here the divine conception of human life seems to be expressible only through myth and also opposed to the process of human history. Babylon will be destroyed, but not until after the Captivity.

18. The Augustinian vision of the church arising out of the chaos of history is a revolutionary view of history, but one which sees secular authority as fulfilled by spiritual authority.

19. Beginning with Hegel and Marx we get an immanent or donkey's-carrot view of history which sees history as containing within itself a counterhistorical force which is actually the real, though concealed, historical process. This is hitched on to some future epiphany, whether a classless society or the manifestation of God.

20. The contrast of Augustinian and Hegelian views is part of a larger shift in thought. Man lives in two worlds, the world given him by nature, and the world of culture or civilization he constructs. Down to about the eighteenth century, God was thought of as taking charge of the order of nature and also as the creator of the forms of human civilization (the city and the garden), hence the two worlds could not be separated.

21. For the last two centuries religious thought has been shifting to the world constructed by man, and away from the given world of the physical environment.

22. In the Bible human history (*Weltgeschichte*) makes no sense; only *Heilsgeschichte* makes sense, but *Heilsgeschichte* is a counterhistorical process concealed within the rise and fall of empires, and cannot be described in historical language. In contemporary terms it might be defined as the positive or genuine human activity, as distinct from making war and feeding parasites, which goes in the direction of the spiritual transformation of man, symbolized in Christianity by the Resurrection.

23. Now, can this view of myth as expressing the counterhistorical be applied also to discursive or conceptual verbal structures in science and philosophy?

24. Metaphor is the basis of imaginative presentation, and metaphor is certainly illogical to the point of being counterconceptual. In metaphor A and B are said to be the same thing while they remain two things, which is logically absurd.

25. Several of the central Christian doctrines (e.g., the Real Presence; Christ is God and Man; in the Trinity one is three) can only be expressed metaphorically. The effort to adapt them to conceptual predication afflicted philosophers with that unlucky notion of "substance" that they are still trying to wriggle out of.

26. In belief as ordinarily understood, experience is divided between

the involuntarily credible, or what we can't help believing (e.g., the data of sense experience, or some of them), and the voluntarily credible, which is accepted without confirming or supporting evidence. This kind of belief is a statement of one's adherence to a specific community; it's exclusive because of the formula "I believe that this is true" (implying that if you don't believe it you don't belong to my community); it shuts off academic discussion; and, like immanent history, its evidence is mostly referred to a future (e.g., you may not believe in a Last Judgment, but you just wait).

27. I notice in my students a strong willingness to come into contact with religion, along with an equally strong reluctance to go along with "dogma." This seems to have some relation to the fact that "God" has dried up as a conception, of no use to any form of scientific or, increasingly, philosophical construct. It looks as though, if belief is to be understood as the voluntarily credible, it cannot for much longer be regarded as a virtue. When we consider beliefs that others hold and that we do not, our feelings are increasingly those of a sense of freedom delivered from obsession. In short, the less we "believe" in the ordinary sense the better, and one comes to distrust believing in anything that has to be believed in.

28. Some Eastern religions (e.g., yoga in Hinduism and Buddhism) bypass belief in favour of direct experience. Similarly the uniquely dramatic element in the narrative of the Bible affords the possibility of an imaginative response in which the story of Israel and the life of Christ offer a narrative model for one's own experience. Faith thus becomes a course of action informed by a vision of human life, counterconceptual in the sense that all conceptualizings of it are limited to the assumptions in which they began. It requires the same kind of imaginative response as literature, though it differs from literature in demanding an existential or committed response as well.

29. Thus belief becomes less "I believe that," and more "I see what this means." This opens the possibility of indefinite (i.e., not closed off at the point of accepting an exclusive dogma) dialogue with other religions.

30. Faith is defined in the New Testament as the *hypostasis* of the hoped for, the *elenchos* of the unseen [Hebrews 11.1]. *Hypostasis* returns us to substance. But as the two worlds of the given and the humanly created separate, "substance" shifts its centre of gravity from the objective to the subjective. Possible translation: "Faith is the realization of human hopes, the dialectic of the invisible."

31. In some cosmogonies, e.g., Stoicism, the visible order of nature becomes the symbol of a hidden spiritual reality behind it. In the Bible "spiritual" always retains its metaphorical connection with air. Air is the invisible medium by which things become visible, hence the spiritual is the power of making things visible, the medium of creative energy. The spiritual life thus becomes something inseparable from human creativity, which gives the arts a central place as helping to define the form of that creativity.

32. Returning again to my course, in this whole process the emphasis gradually changes from the Bible as a literary work to the conception of the Bible as the work which enables one to understand, among other things, the social function of literature. It would not ultimately make sense to call the Bible a work of art, but it does make a good deal of sense to call it, as William Blake does, "the Great Code of Art."[2]

2
History and Myth in the Bible

1 September 1975

From The Literature of Fact: Selected Papers from the English Institute, *ed. Angus Fletcher (New York: Columbia University Press 1976), 1–19. A typescript with holograph corrections is in NFF, 1991, box 36, file 2, and clean copies are in NFF, 1988, box 5, files m and n. The talk was originally given to the English Institute in New York.*

We should expect to find the greatest imaginative powers among oppressed peoples. Strong and successful nations, like ancient Rome, Edwardian Britain, or contemporary America and Russia, tend to be somewhat earth-bound in their cultural products and to keep their real imaginative exuberance for their engineering. The intensity of Biblical vision has much to do with the fact that the Hebrews were never lucky at the game of empire. The Bible records only two periods of relative prosperity for Israel: the period of David and Solomon and the period following the Maccabean rebellion, and the reason was much the same in both cases: one world empire had declined and its successor had not yet arisen. This link between imaginative intensity and alienation is not confined to the Hebrews: in medieval Europe there seems to be a distinctive kind of creative energy among the Celtic tribes squeezed into the remote corners of Western Europe. The Arthurian legends might well have become, in a different cultural setting, the starting point of great apocalyptic visions of Celtic triumph and Teutonic or Latin disaster, paralleling the Biblical dreams of a fallen Babylon and an eternal Jerusalem. Even Yeats, writing in a Teutonic language, still finds enough vitality in Cuchulain and Oisin to think of them as part of a mythology that may be remembered in a future that has forgotten

Christ.[1] Yeats had, Eliot says, a "minor mythology,"[2] but so did the Biblical prophets and apostles on the periphery of the Roman world.

Religious structures tend to expand as their societies expand. Small communities live in a world in which most of the gods are local and epiphanic ones, the ancestors of the nymphs and fauns and fairies of a later age. Larger social units, big enough to have aristocracies, produce a set of departmental and administrative gods on the analogy of such aristocracies. The larger the social organization, the further the gods retreat, from trees and rivers to mountain-tops, from mountain-tops into the sky. When large nations become empires, whose rulers begin to think of themselves as rulers of the world, the notion of monotheism takes shape. Monotheism appeared in Egypt before the Biblical period, and more continuously in Persia and the later Classical world. This is imperial monotheism, in which the ruler normally is the representative, sometimes the actual incarnation, of one supreme god. Such a monotheism is tolerant of local cults, but expands into a sense of the order of nature, particularly the heavenly bodies, as the visible counterpart of the one invisible God. The most impressive form of this monotheism in history, probably, was the Stoicism expounded by Posidonius, which is reflected in a good deal of Manilius, Cicero, and Virgil.[3]

We can hardly overestimate the importance, for our own cultural tradition, of the fact that Biblical monotheism, the basis of Judaism, Christianity, and Islam, is a revolutionary movement, totally different in social context and reference from imperial monotheism. The story of Israel begins with God in the burning bush, informing Moses that he is giving himself a specific name and is about to enter history in a highly partisan role, taking the side of an oppressed people against their overlords. There even seems to be some evidence that the word "Hebrew" itself, back in Abraham's time, originally meant something more like "proletariat" than a conventional name for a people. Two features of a revolutionary mind are particularly important for us here. First, it is a dialectical and polarizing mind: whatever is not for it is against it, and it seeks to reduce or eliminate all middle ground, all liberal, eclectic, or "revisionist" attitudes. God consistently speaks of himself as "jealous," intolerant of any deviation in ritual or doctrine. Many gods are not different aspects of him: they are his enemies: like an earthly ruler, he can tolerate only subordinates. Second, a revolutionary mind is intensely concentrated on a reversal of the social order which is bound to occur in the future, a future which may be simply future time, or, as in apocalyptic literature, the end of time, but which is made, in the writer's expectations, as near and as imminent as he can get it.

Imperial monotheism reflects a strong and secure human order that feels able to come to terms with the order of nature. It expresses itself in visual symbols: its ruler and his god are usually associated with the sun, the source of visibility. A visual image of authority immobilizes the body, brings it to a respectful halt before a manifestation of loyalty or obedience. The revolutionary monotheism of the Bible develops a hatred of "idolatry," and an idol is essentially a visual image of something authoritative or numinous in society or nature. For Biblical monotheism there is nothing numinous in nature: all the divinities that have been discovered in nature are devils, and the chosen people listen to the voice of its invisible God. The shift from visual to aural metaphors, the stress on the hearing of the word, is essential to a revolutionary attitude. The eye was satisfied in the garden of Eden, and will be again at the end of time, but throughout history we depend on the ear. In the Old Testament there is never any difficulty about hearing God, but in even the greatest visions, those of Isaiah and Ezekiel, what is actually seen is much vaguer, and in the earlier books editorial redactions cluster thickly around anything that might be interpreted as a direct vision of God. The emphasis on a received canon of sacred writings, and the drawing of rigid boundary lines against the closest heresies, such as the cult of high places in the northern kingdom, are also aspects of a revolutionary mentality, and similar features reappear in Marxism in our own time.

The Hebrews seem to have been a rather unhandy people,[4] not distinguished for sculpture or building or even pottery, and the contrast with Greek culture is instructive. In a polytheistic religion one has to have statues or pictures to distinguish one god from another, and Greek culture was focused on two intensely visual emblems: the nude in sculpture, and the theatre in literature, the theatre being, as the etymology of the word indicates, a primarily visual experience. We notice how often, in the Christian tradition, movements of iconoclasm recur, associated with a dislike and distrust of religious painting, sculpture, and stained glass, as well as the theatre itself. Such movements are usually rationalized as a return to the primitive purity of Christian doctrine, and iconoclasm in Judaic and Islamic traditions is even more deeply entrenched.

The Biblical narrative runs from the beginning to the end of time, and the Old Testament presents a roughly continuous history from the creation of the world to the capture of Jerusalem by Nebuchadnezzar. After that, the continuous historical narrative disappears, but there are episodic indications of later history, such as the books of Maccabees. We start with stories of the creation and the flood, which most readers today would agree were myths, and myths very similar to other creation and flood stories over the world, except that they have been integrated into a religious vision of unique scope and power. We then move on to legend and folk tale, stories of Samson killing a thousand Philistines with the jawbone of an ass or of Elisha making an iron axe head float, which again belong to familiar patterns of story. The reasons for telling such stories, such as accounting for the name of the place where such an incident is said to have occurred, are equally familiar.

The accounts of Abraham and of the Exodus belong in an area best called historical reminiscence. They must contain some historical kernel, but it seems clear that Egyptian history knows nothing of any Exodus, just as Roman history knows nothing of the life of Christ. Eventually we move into what looks like actual history, to which we can attach some dates and supporting archaeological evidence. But it is didactic and manipulated history, which tends to be simplistic in its approach to facts. Ahab, for example, is portrayed as a kind of sinister clown, except for one episode from a different source which presents him as an able ruler,[5] so convincingly as to make us wonder whether the Biblical writer is not deliberately preferring less reliable sources, or distorting the ones he has.

In this narrative there is no boundary line anywhere clearly defined that separates myth from legend, legend from historical reminiscence, reminiscence from didactic history, didactic from actual history. The Bible, considered as history, is a baffling and exasperating document which the historian has to learn how to use, and it creates more problems than it solves. The inference we are interested in at the moment is: if there is anything in the Bible which is historically accurate, it is not there because it is historically accurate, but for quite different reasons. The reasons seem to involve what we may call spiritual significance. Historical accuracy has no relation to spiritual significance, unless perhaps the relation is an inverse one. The spiritual significance of the Book of Job, which nobody has ever thought of as anything except an imaginative drama, is obviously greater than the lists of names in the Book of Chronicles, which may well contain authentic records.

Being aware of history and being historical are different things. A hundred years ago, critics of Homer were inclined to minimize the historical basis of the Trojan War and assume that the poet made it up out of his own head. Schliemann began to provide some archaeological evidence (of a very equivocal kind, it must be said) that there was a city more or less where Homer said it was,[6] and since then scholars have acquired a considerable respect for Homer's sense of fact, in both history and geography. But no increasing respect for such matters will make Achilles' fight with the river-god or the hurling of Hephaestus out of heaven less mythical: those are as mythical as ever, and doubtless always will be. More simply, Homer's sense of history does not mean that he is writing history. Similarly with the Bible. The degree to which the Bible does record actual events can perhaps never be exactly ascertained. In our day a writer who has had a considerable vogue, especially among students, Immanuel Velikovsky, has written books to show that two of the most unlikely events recorded in the Bible, the sun standing still during a battle of Joshua's and the shadow of the dial going backward during the illness of Hezekiah, did take place in the way that they are described.[7] What is significant here is that the Bible itself does not appear to regard confirming evidence from outside itself as really strengthening its case.

History emerges from chronicle as soon as we have a writer who can see chronicles as material for some other kind of form, an organizing form which is not simply sequence but a *mythos* or narrative. The principle of narrative is the basis on which the material is selected and arranged. The story is familiar of how Gibbon sat musing among the ruins of the Capitol in Rome, and how the idea of writing about the decline and fall, first of the city itself, then of the Roman Empire, took possession of him.[8] Ahead of him was still a vast body of sources, but he had the essential thing, the *mythos* of "decline and fall," and the *mythos* was the magic wand that he could use to make this monstrous brood of mental chaos obey his will.

The historical narrative in the Bible is not really a history but a *mythos* or narrative principle on which historical incidents are strung. We soon realize that we are being told the same story over and over again, and that this story is U-shaped. Israel starts in a condition of relative peace, independence, and prosperity, disobeys or forsakes its God, meets with disaster, plunges into humiliation, slavery, and exile, and then a God-appointed redeemer starts it on the way back to its original state. This U-shaped *mythos* of fall into bondage and redemption to freedom is not confined to the historical narrative: the entire Christian Bible is enclosed by the story of Adam, who loses the tree and water of life on the first page of Genesis and gets them back on the last page of Revelation. We find the same pattern in the story of Job, who loses and regains all he has, and in the parable of the Prodigal Son—which incidentally is the only version in which the protagonist himself determines the point of his return. It is a *mythos* closely related to that of comedy in literature, with the same pattern of descent into threatening or actual complications reversed by some providential redemption. Directly opposed to it, and forming the background against it, is the *mythos* of the recurring rise and fall of heathen empires. This vision is tragic and ironic: the social unit, whatever it is, first rises and then falls, forming an inverted-U shape like that of a hero's role in a tragedy.

In a religious context there is usually a suggestion that there is something in the rising of great powers opposed to the will of God. This suggestion is not confined to Biblical writers. The tremendous panorama in Herodotus, for example, comes to a focus in the account of Xerxes' invasion of Greece, where all the emphasis is on the invincibility of the invader [8.83–96]. Many of the Greeks went over to Persia at the outset; those who resisted were hopelessly divided and mistrustful of each other; the great hero Themistocles was a grafter; even the oracles were bribed with Persian money. It was impossible that so demoralized a rabble as the Greek resisters could have stopped the mighty Persian machine, but stop it they did. The moral for Herodotus, apparently, is that the gods clearly don't like big empires. Something similar emerges from the Book of Daniel, written on the eve of the successful Maccabean resistance to the power of Syria. In Christian centuries the action of Providence, as a divine force intervening in human affairs, can be seen more clearly when you win: thus the storm that destroyed the Spanish Armada was providential to the English, but a natural event to the Spaniards. We notice that this sense of Providence is strongest in David-and-Goliath situations where, as in the battle of Agincourt, a big force is defeated by a much smaller one. In any case the rise and fall of Egypt, Assyria, Babylon, Persia, Greece, Syria, and Rome forms the historical background to the Bible, and is presented as a series of repetitions of what is spiritually the same event. In the Book of Revelation the approaching fall of the secular Roman power is identified with the fall of Babylon, and the author speaks of "that great city, which spiritually is called Sodom and Egypt" [11:8].

Biblical scholars distinguish what they call *Weltgeschichte* and *Heilsge-schichte*, world history and spiritual history. It seems to me that the essential *mythos* of *Weltgeschichte* in the Bible is the inverted-U or negative cycle, the rise and fall of aggregates of human power, and that the essential *mythos* of *Heilsgeschichte* is the U-shaped positive cycle, the fall and rise again of a representative of humanity itself, Adam or Israel or Job, whose period of exile is ended by a power beyond humanity. The symbol of the end of the rise is Moses on top of a mountain seeing the Promised Land, or Elijah going up in a chariot of fire, or Job contemplating God's Leviathan, or Jesus ascending into the sky. Nobody in history has ever seen the Promised Land: what we get in history is Joshua's conquest of Canaan, which starts the cycle turning once more. At the beginning of the Acts of the Apostles, Jesus ascends to heaven, but the Holy Spirit, the third person of the Trinity, comes down and begins the history of the Christian church. It looks as though it were the power to go beyond history that provides the energy for a new historical cycle: in any case, the U-shaped pattern never turns into a closed circle, with the end exactly identical with the beginning.

Man's inability to learn anything "from" his own history has often been lamented, and there is a recurrent desire to use history as a moral parable. But nothing ever repeats itself in precisely the same conditions, hence trying to learn from history is a precarious enterprise. Besides, history usually has to be arranged a good deal before it will fit the parable form, and, in general, historical parables are to history much what bestiaries are to zoology. The same thing is true of the cultural histories based on value judgments, which imitate the U and the inverted-U patterns of Biblical history, but are pseudohistorical constructs. The historical view of Renaissance humanism, which was close to that of Gibbon's *mythos*, saw Classical and more particularly Roman culture as reaching the height of a Golden Age under Augustus, then declining through less expensive metals until we reach the Dark Ages, where Latin develops rhyme and accentual rhythm and similar horrors, until the Renaissance began to complete the U-turn. Ruskin's *Stones of Venice* presents us with the opposite construct: here we have an inverted U, rising with the "servile art" of the pre-Gothic period to the height of Gothic itself in the thirteenth century, then declining through the "fall" (Ruskin's word) of the Renaissance to modern times. If we compare these two views with one another, our final conclusion has to be, however much we may have incidentally learned from them, that neither of them has any real content. Like everything else founded on value judgments, sooner or later we have to throw them away and start again with genuine data.

History conceived as parable can be applied to the present only very indirectly and morally, by the individual, not by a programme of social or cultural action. This is the old *exemplum* theory of the usefulness of history, in which, say, the stories of Esther and Judith supply us with models of patriotic heroism, which we may admire but can apply to our own behaviour only in the most oblique way. In such a moral and individual context Biblical history can be parable, with the parable's epilogue, "go thou and do likewise,"[9] or, more frequently, "go thou and avoid doing likewise." But, we are told by so many critics from Aristotle onward, this exemplary approach to history is more the concern of poetry than of history itself. The historical narrative of the Bible, which arranges everything with a view to bringing out its central *mythos* shape, along with the moral principles implied by that shape, is much closer to poetry than it is to actual history, and should be read as such. At this point the word *mythos* begins to turn into the word "myth," and we have to face the possibility that the entire Bible has to be read in the same way that most of us now read the story of Noah's ark.

The ordinary notion of myth and history is that history is what really happened; myth is what probably didn't happen, at least not in that form. The historian, we feel, tries to recapture the past in the present: if he is writing about Julius Caesar's assassination, he tries to show us what we might have seen if we had been present at the event. Truth, in this context, means truth of correspondence: a history, or structure of words, is aligned with a body of human actions and is judged true if it is a satisfactory verbal replica of those actions. But truth of correspondence is not the concern of the literary critic: he deals entirely with verbal forms which are not primarily related to external facts or to propositions, and are never true in that context. To paraphrase Duke Theseus in Shakespeare, the poet, like the lover and the lawyer, is incapable of telling the truth by correspondence.[10] So far as truth is involved in poetry, it is contained within the verbal form and provides no external criterion for it.

However acutely conscious I may be of my deficiencies as a Biblical scholar, I cannot be entirely unaware of the deficiencies of Biblical scholars as literary critics. Real literary criticism of the Bible, in the sense of a criticism that takes seriously its mythical and metaphorical aspect, has barely begun. Myth and metaphor are still often regarded as things to be apologized for, and scholars still speak hesitantly of "mythical elements" in Genesis or the Gospels, as though they were elements that could be, and therefore should be, removed. In Biblical terms, literary criticism is "higher" criticism, the criticism that is supposed to start after a certain amount of work has been done on establishing the text. But for all the to-do made about it a century ago, there has been no higher criticism of the Bible until very recently. Lower criticism, or genuine textual scholarship, has been followed by a still lower, or sub-basement, criticism, where the disintegrating of the text becomes an end in itself. Dozens of books tell us that the account of creation with which the Book of Genesis opens comes from the Priestly narrative, historically much the latest of the four major documents that make up the Pentateuch. If the scholar saying this were a genuine "higher" critic, his next sentence ought to say that this account of creation stands at the beginning of Genesis, not because it was written first, but because it belongs at the beginning of Genesis. The third sentence would land him in a full-scale critical analysis of the Book of Genesis, and eventually of the whole Bible, as it now stands. What one needs is a criticism that, instead of trying to cut away the myth as an accretion and retreat into some hypothetical embryonic stage of textual development, would tell us something about why the books of the Bible exist as they now do in their present form.

Such an obsession with disunity is a narrowly historical obsession, an inability to understand that there are forms of truth, meaning, and significance which are not dependent on correspondence with facts or other external criteria. The reason why the procedure is futile is that there is, quite simply, no end to it. If we start to "demythologize" the Gospels, for example, as some theologians urge us to do,[11] trying to throw out everything that seems incredible, or suggested by something in the Old Testament or contemporary Jewish ritual or teaching, in quest of some historical core of events of which we can say "this at least must have happened," we shall find that we have thrown out so much of the Gospels that not one syllable of any of the four of them is left. No advance is possible until we reverse the procedure, accept the whole Bible as an imaginative unity of myth and metaphor, and see what comes out of that hypothesis.

What comes out of it is, among other things, the entire structure of post-Classical European literature, for which the Bible provided a mythical and metaphorical framework. Another is the fact which, in the age of Heidegger and Wittgenstein, we are finally returning to: that poetic language is primary language, and that what words do with the greatest power and accuracy is hang together, that is, form mythical and metaphorical entities. Poetic statements are not distorted or secondary forms of so-called "literal" statements: "literal" statements are distorted and secondary forms of poetic ones. Words certainly have their descriptive uses, but these are of limited help if we are trying to investigate the kind of world that the Bible seems to lead us to: a world in which truth is a person or a personal God, and in which all men make up, not the aggregate "mankind," but a single man. The Bible, taking it at its own valuation, is far too important a book to contain any "truth," as that word is generally understood.

At this point we may begin to suspect that myth is not simply unhistorical event, and metaphor not simply a nonconceptual form of thinking, but that they are antihistorical and anticonceptual, and are being used in the Bible for that reason. How, we may ask, could a book regarded for so long, and by so many, as a sacred book, a divine revelation, ever have been supposed to be speaking any other language? Surely a myth, or self-contained verbal structure in which the recurring exile and return of Israel forms a counterpoint against the contrary movement of the rise and fall of heathen empires, is the only way of giving any sense of *Heilsgeschichte*, or history as seen from beyond history. Man is continually throwing up great intellectual anxiety structures, like spiritual geodesic domes, around his culture and social institutions. If a book is believed to originate from a source beyond the limitations of the human mind, and a benevolent source at that, one would expect it to speak the language of breakthrough, a language that would smash these structures beyond repair, and let some genuine air and light in. But that, of course, is not how anxiety operates.

We have to move, therefore, from the historical and doctrinal to the poetic and literary in getting a better understanding of the Bible. It is possible to stop there with great profit: if we are looking at the Bible without commitment, in the context, say, of "comparative religion," this is in fact where we have to stop. But the limitations of stopping here are equally obvious, so obvious that I have to make some comment on it even at the risk of going beyond the concerns of the English Institute. It sounds absurd to say that the Bible is a work of art or an epic poem like the *Iliad* or the *Mahabharata*, although the statement is really less absurd than it sounds. "Epic poem" is clearly the wrong classification, but the sense of absurdity comes mainly from the total critical ignorance of the literary and rhetorical issues connected with scriptures and sacred books. Still, there is unmistakably a sense in which the Bible transcends the poetic as well as the historical. Even Blake, for all his devotion to both the Bible and the arts, did not call the Bible a work of art: he called it the "Great Code" of art.[12]

For the historian, what is true is what is credible: the miraculous or the fabulous tend to get squeezed out of history even if the historian believes them. What is credible corresponds to what we encounter in ordinary experience. To adopt standards of credibility is a serious thing to do, and one can understand why the literary approach, which bypasses the issue of credibility altogether, should in some contexts come to be thought of as not very serious. The distinction between fact and fiction is essential to sanity; in reading a newspaper we want to know whether the stories in it are true or only made up, and if we had no means of knowing, the society we live in is, like the society in *1984*, deliberately trying to keep us mad. History tells us of real events that we can assimilate to our ordinary experience because they are more or less what we should have experienced at the time. Poetry tells us of events that are real, not in the sense of having happened just like that, but in the sense of being the kind of thing that is always happening. There is a third category: the actual event which is probably nothing like what we should have experienced if we had been "there." The assumption here is that in some events, at least, our ordinary experience does not tell us what is really happening.

In the last dozen years or so, with all the emphasis on separate realities, altered states of consciousness, and the like, we should be able at least to conceive the possibility of thinking in such terms. The Biblical prophets were usually ecstatics capable of going into trance states and speaking with what they called the voice of God. But it is clear that with, for example, Isaiah, this ecstatic power was not something separate from conscious intelligence, as it would be in a medium or the priestess of an oracle, but was simply an additional dimension of experience. Neither was it the same kind of thing as the creative imagination of a poet, even though it expressed itself in poetic language, as any language of such intensity would have to do. It was rather a description of experience as it appears to a higher state of consciousness. The word "higher" may beg a question, but the question certainly is begged in the Bible, or rather seized. Similarly in the Gospels, where it seems clear that the ordinary experience of those who were "there," including the disciples, took in very little of what the Gospel says was really going on at the time.

The danger of returning to square one still confronts us, for there is no going back to ordinary historical canons. A structure of myth and metaphor is what we have: it is all that we have, and it is no use trying to shake a residue of factual history out of it, even on a spiritual level. We may say, for example, that some Biblical stories seem to deal with really central issues, like the five versions of the Resurrection story, and that these may be the spiritual forms of real events. Others, like the stories of Samson, seem to be clearly folk tales, or at best allegories, while still others, like the story of Job, are explicitly poetical. But as long as we keep steadily looking at the whole Bible as a seamless web of myth and metaphor, this reductive solution becomes increasingly unsatisfying. If we want to go from the imaginative to the existential, we have to try to take a step forward from our literary understanding, in the opposite direction from the historical. Belief, as ordinarily understood, is a matter of credibility reinforced by credulity. But, as Tertullian suggested long ago, there may be such a thing as a belief which is the opposite of anything based on credibility.[13]

The real step forward comes when we see that the entire Biblical vision, from Genesis to Revelation (or Chronicles in Judaism), may be spiritually present in every particular event, and may be in fact the genuine form of that event. But the only particular events that we can apply this principle to are the events of our own lives. Our credible historical lives form a part of *Weltgeschichte*: they rise and decline; they end in death, and whatever successes or triumphs they may include, there is always more frustration than fulfilment in them, no less than in the histories of Assyria or Rome. We can imagine another perspective on that life, a U-shaped perspective in which the real progression is the reverse of this, beginning in Eden or a Promised Land and ending like the story of the returned prodigal or the restored Job. Once this is seen as a part of *Heilsgeschichte*, conceived as the spiritual reality in contrast to the natural reality of what happens, we have started to go beyond imagination. This view of life is incredible, especially in its beginning and its end, and the proofs of its reality are not given: they are what it is up to us to supply.

The world of *Weltgeschichte* is a series of repetitions within a framework of compulsion and fatality: it is the world of the Viconian *ricorso*,[14] and of Platonic *anamnesis*, or recollection [*Meno*, 81c–d], where we can know only by *re*-cognizing or seeing once again what we already know. In the world conveyed to us through the language of myth and metaphor, repetition is the power to make a new beginning, the power associated with humility in Eliot's *East Coker*, because he thinks of humility as the opposite of the pride that continually builds the tower of Babel out of a confusion of tongues. The Biblical symbol of this new beginning is the rebuilt temple which marks the end of exile [Ezra 6:16–22]. This is the kind of repetition that regains time in Proust, that delivers us in *Finnegans Wake* from the returning history that Stephen Dedalus in *Ulysses* calls the nightmare from which he is trying to awake,[15] that leads Dante in the *Purgatorio* upwards to his original identity in the garden of Eden, and that enables Eliot finally to describe history itself as a pattern of timeless moments.[16]

It is only the language of the imagination that can take us beyond imagination. Two inferences follow, for students of literature. First, the Bible demands a literary response from us, hence the study of literature has to expand a good deal beyond its usual limits. No book could have had the Bible's literary influence without itself possessing a literary form, however many other things it may also possess. There is also the question of the mythological framework which the Bible has provided for Western literature, already mentioned, and which is part of what Blake's phrase "Great Code of Art" means. Similar frameworks have been provided for other cultures by other sacred books: if one is attempting a serious study of Islamic literature, one has to begin with the Koran as a piece of literature. The second inference is that, as the mythical and metaphorical language spoken by literature is primary language, and the only means of reaching any spiritual reality beyond language, then, if such reality exists, works of literature themselves represent a practically untapped source of self-transforming power.

3

The Meaning of Recreation: Humanism in Society

12 April 1979

From Iowa Review, 11 *(Winter 1980): 1–9. Originally given as a lecture at the University of Iowa.*

I begin with the fact that my critical interests have always revolved around the Bible, not for doctrinal reasons but for reasons that had directly to do with my work as a literary critic. When I was still a junior instructor, I was trying to write a book on Blake and trying to teach Milton to undergraduates, and I complained to my departmental chairman[1] that I was having some difficulty in reaching my students because we could no longer take for granted the working knowledge of the Bible that we used to be able to take. And a student without that knowledge simply does not know what is going on in English literature. My chairman said the only thing to do was to draft a course in the English Bible and teach it. He said, "How do you expect to teach Milton to students who don't know a Philistine from a Pharisee?" I said, "Perhaps in the kind of society they are going into, that particular distinction won't be important to them." But I didn't often talk like that to my chairman, except in moments of stress, so I drafted the course and I'm still teaching it.

Recently I've become more and more preoccupied with what becomes of the Bible when it is examined from the point of view of literary criticism. I think the first question that confronts one, then, is in what language has the Bible been written? The factual answers are Hebrew and Greek, but they hardly do justice to a book which has exerted most of its cultural influence in Latin and vernacular translations. Hebrew and Greek are, to use a useful French distinction, only the *langue* of the Bible;

the *langage* is something else again.[2] The question then arises, is there such a thing as a history of *langage*, and does the Bible have an historical context in that respect which one has to take account of?

That question took me to the eighteenth-century Italian philosopher Vico, who was the first person to think seriously about such matters. Vico had worked on a theory of history according to which society goes through three different stages: a poetic age of the gods (a mythical age), an aristocratic age of the heroes, and a democratic age of the people.[3] In his day there had been no permanently successful example of a democracy, so Vico assumed that after going through those three phases, society went into a *ricorso*, and did the whole thing all over again. He said too that there was a language for each of these stages: for the age of the gods there was a hieroglyphic language; for an age of the heroes, a hieratic language; and for an age of the people, a demotic language. These languages were all forms of writing because Vico believed that people communicated by signs before they could talk. His theory is bound up with a rather curious mythology according to which the original inhabitants of the world before the flood were giants who carried on in a very unseemly manner until they were terrified by a thunderstorm, after which they dashed into caves dragging their women behind them. So began private property. Vico was a favourite author of Joyce largely because Joyce was also terrified by thunderstorms.

It seemed to me that Vico's distinction was something that one could adapt, although it would have to be a very free adaptation. I won't buy his *ricorso*, at least not in the form in which he gives it. I don't think that people communicated by signs before they could talk. At the same time I do feel that this conception of three phases of language which have some kind of relationship to hieroglyphic, hieratic, and demotic might make a certain sense. I'd like to try out the idea on you.

I am not at the moment speaking of literature; I'll come to literature later. And I'm not speaking of the use of ordinary language, which I take it has been much the same from the Egyptian Old Kingdom to our own day. I'm speaking of the language of cultural ascendancy, the kind that survives in religious and literary documents. It seems to me that the language of Homer, of early Greek literature, and the language in which the bulk of the Old Testament is rooted belong to a phase of language which has something in common with what Vico meant by hieroglyphic. Language in this phase is conceived as something which emanates from the speaker towards the natural world and expresses a kind of identification with that world. In other words, it is fundamentally a metaphorical language, metaphor being, in this phase, not an ornament of language, but the way of thinking about language. It is hieroglyphic not in the sense of sign writing but of sign thinking, or rather of sign *language*; the word evokes the image.

In a monumental study of Homer's vocabulary, a book called *The Origins of European Thought* by Onians, we are shown how intensely concrete Homer's vocabulary is. Words like "life" and "mind" and "soul" and "thought" and "passion," to say nothing of such terms as "time" and "space," have no genuine abstract reference at all. They are all concrete conceptions related to the action of the heart and the lungs and the brain. To be alive is to take breath into the lungs, and vitality consists of the sperm dripping down from the brain into the genital organs, or however Homer conceived it. Nor were these conceptions metaphors to Homer, though they are metaphors to us. We can only think of this kind of language as dominated by the metaphorical identification of subject and object. The core of the metaphor is "this is that," A is B; and the two things that are fundamental in the metaphor, the A and the B, are something in the subject—something in personality—and something in the object—something in the natural world. Consequently the central conception in this phase of language is the conception of the god with the small "g" because a god is essentially a metaphorical idea. You have sun-gods and war-gods and tree-gods and so on in whom some aspect of personality is identified with some element in nature.

In this phase of language there is a powerfully magical residue. In Babylon on New Year's Day, the epic of creation, a poem called *Enuma Elish*, was recited;[4] and the reciting of the poem of creation on New Year's Day obviously helped to sustain and encourage the operations of nature in bringing the year around once again. Similarly warriors would begin their battles with boasts because boasting is a way of acquiring the words of power that may make them stronger than their opponents. Gods take an extremely dim view of human boasting for the same reason. If man acquires the word of power, he may unseat them from their position. And there are various themes in folk tales such as the rash vow of Jephthah, who says, "I have opened my mouth unto the Lord, and I cannot go back" [Judges 11:35], expressing the feeling that the spoken word has already set up some kind of operation in the natural world.

In this phase of language, prose is intensely discontinuous. Prose consists of the kind of prose that you find in the Old Testament, broken down into kernels of law or commandment in the first five books, of oracle in the prophecies, of aphorism or proverb in the wisdom literature, of pericope in the Gospels. These sentences are surrounded by silence. You are not expected to argue with them; you are expected to brood over them and think about them. Similarly with Greek philosophy before Socrates; the Presocratic philosophers so called were really gurus, or spiritual leaders. They would utter various aphorisms like "you never step twice into the same river," or "all things flow," or "Don't eat beans," or something of that kind. When they were said by a Heraclitus or a Pythagoras, again you didn't argue because this was *ipse dixit*; this was what the master had said. You brooded and thought about it. Elsewhere in the world you find it as well. There are many books on yoga in India written in continuous prose but they all refer you to the yoga sutras of Patanjali, which are written in tight, gnarled epigrammatic aphorisms, each one of which could be a source of commentary in itself. And there are large vacant spaces between each aphorism.

This is the phase of language that seems to me to have been superseded in Greek culture by Plato, who began a second phase that dominated language down to the time of at least Kant and Hegel. In this second phase there is a stronger sense of individuality, words now being thought of primarily as the expression of thoughts, and to some degree as the residue of thoughts. The scholar Eric Havelock, who was a former colleague of mine, has written a book on Plato [*A Preface to Plato*] in which he associates the Platonic revolution in language with the development of writing. I don't question his scholarship, but I prefer to associate it with the development of continuous prose. That seems to me to have begun when Socrates approached the youth of Athens and said to them, "I don't know anything, unlike my predecessors, but I'm looking for something; come help me look." Those who responded found that they were moving along a linear trail of words, the trail that is known as dialectic. Dialectic is incorporated into Plato; in Aristotle it becomes the pattern of deductive and syllogistic reasoning. It's a ranging of verbal associations in a linear sequence so that they go marching like the Macedonian phalanx across reality. It's a sequential ordering of words in which the fact of sequential ordering becomes itself one of the primary elements of language. Descartes, you'll remember, began by saying, "I think, therefore I am."[5] The operative word is "therefore." Before he believed that, he believed in the connectability of words, in the cogency of "therefores," in the fact that an inference from a premise would not let him down. Doctrines like the ontological proof of the existence of God really reduce to the same formula: I think, therefore God exists. God is really an inference, then, from the power of therefores. That is where the residual magic of the first phase is still operative, in the sense that words are ineluctably linked together. The most bizarre notions, like God predestinating people to damnation before they are born, may still be clung to because of the intensity of feeling. If you accept this, then you must, etc.

This phase is, as I say, an age of words as the expression of thoughts; and just as the kernel of the first phase is that of the god with a small "g," which is a metaphorical identity of a personality with an element in nature, so God with a capital "G" is the central conception of this second phase. Instead of being metaphorical, it is rather what linguists call metonymic.[6] In metonymy, you don't have the formula "this is that," as you have in metaphor; you have "this is *put for* that." Among other things, this includes the form, called technically the synecdoche, where the part is put for the whole. The word God with a capital "G" is a metonymy because a name is finite and what it expresses is infinite, and it is therefore a part of a whole. In this phase of language we are in an age of commentary and, because of continuous prose, of rationalization. In continuous prose, the general principle is that when you are confronted with an inconsistency in something that you have to treat with respect, if you just keep on writing enough sentences, any statement whatever can be reconciled with any other. So you begin to get the encyclopedic thought systems of the Middle Ages and the Renaissance down to the age of Kant, which extend themselves and swallow everything like pythons swallowing sheep.

Occasionally you become aware of the tensions between the different phases of language. In St. Thomas's *Summa Contra Gentiles*, for example, there is a chapter with the title "God Hates Nothing." Well, that's fair enough; a perfect being obviously couldn't hate anybody or anything, so St. Thomas has little difficulty proving that God hates nothing. Then he is confronted by a long list of things in the Bible that God is said to hate. Because he has to take the Bible seriously, he has to take the first phase of language seriously, so he chalks that up to his old friend analogy, analogy being essentially the conception developed in St. Thomas to harmonize his use of language with that of the Bible.

This phase of language is the language of the post-Biblical Christianity, which is largely Aristotelian in structure; and it's been characterized as late as the nineteenth century by Cardinal Newman when he said that the Bible was not there to teach doctrine but to prove it.[7] What was taught, that is, was taught in continuous prose in a doctrinal structure and is then related by analogy to the metaphorical constructs in the Bible. Just as the first phase is hieroglyphic in an extended sense, so this phase is hieratic in the sense of being, as we should say now, elitist: it is taught by an educated minority to the rest of the human race.

Every phase of language tends to expand into an encyclopedic system, though the word "system" strictly applies only to this particular phase of language, for a reason which has been very well expressed by Wallace Stevens in one of his finest poems, *Description without Place*. There he says that man does not live directly in nature; he lives within his own constructed world in which nature is included. A parallel of latitude divides most of Canada from most of the United States. The birds and the buffaloes and the seeds and the trees don't pay any attention to this parallel of latitude, but, on the other hand, the world of birds and buffaloes and seeds and trees doesn't exist for us either except as part of a human construct which includes parallels of latitude. This is peculiarly, I think, the attitude of what I've called the hieratic or second phase of language. At least it's then that it becomes most obvious.

The Bible seems to me fundamentally a product of a metaphorical conception of language. This first phase is closest to its successor, the second phase, in the genre that we call oratory, because oratory is a highly figured form of speech. It is hieratic in the sense that it tries to draw its audience into a closer unit, but it makes use of the same rhetorical and figurative devices that metaphor does. The bulk of the Bible is really different forms of oratory, or what is sometimes called kerygma or proclamation; and there are many phrases in it like "he that hath ears to hear, let him hear" [Matthew 11:15] which suggest, again, the drawing of an audience into a tighter unit of belief and assent.

The third phase of language begins in English literature with Bacon, theoretically, and more effectively with Locke, this being a period in which the conception of language is fundamentally descriptive; that is, language is thought of as reflecting the facts of time and space in the outer world. Consequently its controlling figure is neither the metaphor nor the metonymy but a kind of suppressed simile—"this is *like* that"— "this" being a structure of words and "that" being whatever the structure of words describes. This third phase is the conception of language that completes the cycle from the first. In the first or metaphorical phase of language, the word evokes the image; in this phase the image evokes the word, and the word is the servomechanism of the things that the words are there to interpret. This conception of language depends on truth, in the sense of the truth of correspondence. A verbal structure is set up to describe something in the world outside it, and it is considered true if it is a satisfactory verbal replica of what it describes. This phase also uses continuous prose, like the preceding phase; the subject is still pursuing the object through a forest of predicates. But it is a nonfigurative kind of writing. The descriptive writer tends to avoid what he would consider merely verbal devices, tries to define things clearly and consistently, tries to collect facts that can be verified by others, and sets out his arguments in full. Ideally, such writing has the virtues of clarity and honesty and appeal to a demotic or democratic consensus. Elsewhere I have suggested that it is this conception of language, along with the principle of public access to its documents, that makes democracy a working possibility.[8]

If I am right, we have gone around a cycle of language in three phases, and if Vico is right, we go into a *ricorso* then and start the cycle all over. Well, I don't like cycles; I think the cycle is simply a failed spiral. I think that when we come to the end of a cycle we ought to move up to another level and proceed accordingly. Consequently I find it an extremely reassuring aspect of the contemporary scene that there should be so intense an interest in the resources and capabilities of language itself. Language has become a model for a study which has drawn together a great variety of humanistic and social scientific disciplines: linguistics, literary criticism, phenomenology, sociolinguistics, anthropology, and a number of others. It seems to me historically right that there should be this interest in the possible resources of language because obviously society would be at its most efficient if all varieties of language were recognized to have their own validity, their own place, and their own context in the linguistic scene. At the same time, I have a particular interest in this early phase of language out of which the Bible grew because the Bible is a logocentric document, that being one of the things which makes it so intensely relevant to our contemporary concerns. It is the book that presents the word as the fundamental image for the relation of God to man and for the destiny of mankind generally. It is interesting that its most sacred sentence, from many points of view, is the sentence, "In the beginning was the Word" [John 1:1], and that there have been interesting attempts to translate that in both the second and third phases of language. In the Renaissance, Erasmus translated it as *in principio erat sermo*.[9] That is, in the beginning was not the word but the interconnection of ideas or thoughts out of which words grow and of which they are the expression. That is a typical second-phase attitude to the first. Then in Goethe's *Faust* we have the character Faust, who claims to have studied theology but obviously doesn't understand much of it, attempting to struggle with the same verse from John. He finally winds up with *Im Anfang war die Tat*, the "act," of which the word is merely the record.[10] As soon as he says that, of course, he is fair game for Mephistopheles, who turns up and takes him over. And it serves him right.

Now it seems to me that it is the fundamental function of literature, and more particularly of poetry, to keep recreating in society that first phase of language, that original, metaphorical sense of immediacy, a sense of identity between personality and nature. That is why there have been so many arguments like Peacock's "Four Ages of Poetry" which demonstrate that the poet is a hopeless anachronism, or rather an atavism, that he has fallen behind in the race of civilization, and that he belongs to essentially a crude and archaic form of society. That is quite true; it is what percipient critics have always said. Elizabethan critics, for example, kept uniting the poet's function with the most ancient periods of society which they associated with legendary names like Hermes Trismegistus, and Orpheus;[11] and when Shelley said that poets were the "unacknowledged legislators" of the world, he was really calling on the same conception.[12]

Literature of course comes to terms with other conceptions of language. During the second phase it came to terms with it largely through allegory, in which the images and metaphors of poetry ran along in a continuous counterpoint against the conceptions and doctrines which had a higher authority than the images of the poet, as we can see very clearly in Dante. In the third phase, literature produces what is called realism, sometimes an almost documentary realism, where the words reflect events and social conditions and, again, attempt to tell the "honest truth" about what is going on in the world outside. All through literature there is, as one of its central principles, and perhaps its organizing principle, the principle of recreation. Every poet recreates previous literature in his own way and in his own form. And just as art recreates previous art, so criticism recreates art in a different conceptual framework. The Elizabethan critics adopted the maxim *ut pictura poesis*, poetry is a speaking picture.[13] By that they meant that something in the past is brought into the present and given the immediate, almost hallucinatory clarity of something in the present.

That brings us to a fourth figure of speech. I've spoken of metaphor where this is that, of the metonymy where this is put for that, and the simile where this is like that; but those are all figures in space. There seems to be no figure that is related directly to time, not at least in that group. In time we have a figuration in which this *anticipates* that and, in reverse, that *recalls* this. That is the kind of figure which obviously has to be connected with any conception of recreation in time. And that fourth figure, which we call typology, is the figure dominating the Bible, where everything that happens in the Old Testament, in the Christian view, is an anticipation of what happens in the New Testament. What happens in the New Testament, moreover, recalls what is done or prophesied or seen in the Old. But of course the Old Testament keeps recreating itself, as we can see if we compare the books of Chronicles, for example, with the books of Kings. It is partly this sense of figuration in time that gives to the Biblical religions, both Judaism and Christianity as well as, to some extent, Islam, an historical dimension, which, as it is a commonplace to observe, is different from that of other forms of mythology.

The conception of recreation, of course, can go further. Plato even went to the point of saying that all knowledge was, in effect, a re-cognition, a knowledge of something already known [*Meno*, 81c–d]. He tends to refer that to a kind of rudimentary reincarnation doctrine that what you know you actually remember from a previous existence. Whether that's true or not, it certainly is true that what you know is what other people have known, and it is a recognition for us in that sense. Even in the ordinary sense of the term, recreation, whatever is valuable or positive in it, has to do with recreation in a more specific sense. If you go out to play a game of golf or tennis, you are recreating your athletic skill; and if you go to a movie, you are recreating your knowledge of movies. It is that element which gives value to one's leisure activities. Certain elements of criticism which have preoccupied Harold Bloom, the conception, for example, of the "anxiety of influence" and the fact that every poet misreads and misunderstands his predecessors, and has to if he is to speak with his own voice, depend again on this matter of recreation.[14] The archetype of all that is in the Bible, at least in the Christian Bible, where the New Testament's conception of the Old is, from the point of view of Judaism, a preposterous and perverse misunderstanding.

This conception of language, as I say, tends to extend encyclopedi-
cally because of the Wallace Stevens principle that we live not directly in
the world but in our own construct of the world, or as I should say,
because I am not a poet, we live within a mythological universe. That of
course brings up the question of the word "myth" and what it means.
To me a myth means fundamentally what it means in Greek, *mythos*,
meaning a narrative or a sequential arrangement of words. I think that
anything which can be read sequentially, that is any book except possibly a telephone book, does have a narrative and therefore a *mythos*. In
the first phase of language, these *mythoi*, or narrative sequences, are for
the most part stories. They move through a concrete world of personalities and metaphors. In the second phase of language they become arguments or conceptions, but the important thing is that story myths and
argumentative or conceptual myths have a very strong family likeness
and are related by analogy. That is in my opinion a still unexplored
issue in criticism, one that I think will bear a good deal of examination.

Myth in this sense, of course, has no connotation whatever of the
untrue or the imaginary. If we look at Gibbon's *Decline and Fall of the
Roman Empire*, we can see that that was intended to be a work of historical scholarship. But if we look at the phrase "decline and fall," we can
see what Gibbon's *mythos* was, the principle on which he selected his
material and arranged his words in a linear sequence. That myth has to
be there whether the content is true or imaginary.

According to Aristotle, the historical narrative is particular and the
poetic narrative is universal [*Poetics*, 9]. Therefore the historical narrative is judged by whether it is true or false and the poetic narrative is
not. But I think that imposes an oversimplified duality on the situation.
In teaching the Bible, I am often faced with a resentful student saying to
me, "But you're saying that the story of the Gospels is just a myth, and
therefore that Jesus had no historical existence." It's a more intricate
matter than one would think to get all the fallacies in that statement
unsnarled. To me the statement that the Gospel is a myth and the statement that the Gospel tells a story are exactly the same statement, and it's
clear that the relationship between poetry and history is a midway one.
It doesn't fall exactly into either camp. The writers of the Gospels obviously assumed the historical existence of Jesus; they would never have
written a line if they hadn't. At the same time they were not writing
biographies. They were concerned with the life of Christ as a universal
event, falling in between the poetic and the historical. That in-between

area can only be the area of what I've called typology, the area where this anticipates that and that recalls this. Those writers selected for their account of Christ that which fulfils the Old Testament prophecies, and they were concerned with nothing else. Whether they were right or not, the distinction has proved very fortunate in our own cultural heritage. It means that the Biblical religions have a diachronic mythology, to use that term,[15] which moves in time and has an historical dimension, whereas the pagan mythologies are synchronic: they deal with elements in nature that recur cyclically but are the same thing every time. This historical element in the Bible is also a personal element. Jesus and Adonis are both dying gods; they have very similar imagery and very similar rituals attached to them; but Jesus is a person and Adonis is not.

This conception of recreation means that there are two major directions in criticism. There is a progressive, forward movement in criticism which is a continuous accretion of commentary which keeps wrapping up the original text in thicker and thicker wrappings. We can see that in the history of Biblical interpretation, where the centuries of commentary form a long tradition of their own. Then with the rise of the descriptive phase of language, we begin to get also a critical activity that moves backwards towards the genesis or origin of whatever it is engaged in studying. In the case of Biblical criticism, we have not only the advancing movement of commentary as it adapts the Bible to later phases of society and culture, we also have an archaeological and historical criticism that moves backwards from the Bible itself into the original rituals, into the earliest possible phallic or other symbolisms and mythologies out of which the Bible grew. There comes a point, of course, where the only thing we can reach that is sufficiently primitive to go on with is the investigator's own subconscious, and at that point scholarship has to turn psychological. If, for example, we take the familiar lines of the hymn,

> His chariots of wrath
> The deep thunderclouds form
> And dark is His path
> On the wings of the storm,[16]

we should say that if we were to take that literally (whatever literally means) we should be faced with about as crude and superstitious a notion as it was possible to put into words. But of course we don't take it that way; we take it as poetic metaphor. Like other hymns, its language is founded on the Bible, for the Psalms tell us that God or Jehovah rode upon the wings of a cherub and did fly [18:10]. But in the Bible it is still poetic metaphor. I doubt if you can go back to any society sufficiently bemused or bewildered actually to believe that when they heard thunder in the sky it was God riding around in some kind of private airplane. But what we do come back to is a point at which such a conception was the only way of expressing, in language, what was actually a quite authentic experience. And so the whole problem resolves itself into a linguistic problem rather than a purely historical or archaeological one.

The general moral of all this, I think, is that a myth—which may be a story in one phase and an argument in another, or keeps on being a story in literature—a myth means everything that it has in fact been made to mean. For St. John of the Cross, the sixteenth-century Spanish mystic, the Song of Songs becomes an allegory of the soul as the bride and of Christ as the bridegroom.[17] We can't say that that is a wrenching or distorting of the Song of Songs; it's an integral part of its development in culture. On the other hand an historical critic would trace the Song of Songs back to the wedding festivals and their rituals, to the erotic love songs out of which it grew; and again we can't say that that is something which the Song of Songs has left behind. It makes no attempt to leave it behind; it incorporates it with the greatest enthusiasm.

There is a continuous process, then, moving forwards and backwards, which literature expresses and which criticism takes account of. In revolving around as I have been throughout this paper the theme of humanism in society, I am isolating specifically what seems to me at the moment the central issue of humanism, which is the issue of language and the way that society uses language. This is an issue which, as I have said, nearly all of the humanities and many of the social sciences have converged on in our day. But it seems to me that it is literature and the study of literature which stands in the centre of all this activity and which is, to use a phrase of Blake, holding the end of a golden string.[18]

4

Creation and Recreation

30, 31 January and 1 February 1980

Toronto: University of Toronto Press, 1980. A preliminary typescript is in NFF, 1988, box 55, file 5, and the final typescript is in 1992, box 1, file 4. Originally given as the Larkin-Stuart Lectures.

Preface

These are the Larkin-Stuart Lectures, delivered under the auspices of Trinity College in the University of Toronto and St. Thomas Church, on 30, 31 January, and 1 February 1980. I am greatly obliged to Trinity College and St. Thomas Church for their hospitality and for the honour of their invitation to give the lectures.

The lectures draw on earlier material of mine, some of it now out of print, and, as the opening page suggests, they are also connected with an ongoing project of greater length, a study of the narrative and imagery of the Bible and its influence on secular literature. They will doubtless be made use of for the larger book, but form a unit which can be read by itself.

I

I am a literary critic, mainly concerned with English literature, and I have recently developed a special interest in the way that the Bible has affected the structure and imagery of that literature. The first word to attract one's notice in both fields is the word "creation." Page one of the Bible says that God created the world; page one of the critic's handbook, not yet written, tells him that what he is studying are human creations.

In this book I should like to look at certain aspects of the conception or metaphor of creation, as it applies to both its divine and its human context, and, also, at what effect the extending of the same word to cover these two different areas has had on our habits of thought. I know that many questions connected with the word "creation" are among the most hackneyed topics in both religious and secular culture, and I shall try to keep clear of what seems to me likely to have bored you already. On the other hand, I chose the topic because it is hackneyed, and is therefore easier to look at with a fresh eye. Through some closed-circuiting mechanism in the human mind, certain themes seem to get things said about them that are prescribed in advance, so that they are not really explored at all, but are simply talked out, in a way familiar to members of parliament who introduce private bills. If there are students of mine among my readers, they will often catch glimpses of charted territory, but I am not offering a rehash of lecture notes.

I want to begin with what is called "creativity" as a feature of human life, and move from there to some of the traditional religious ideas about a divine creation. It seems to me that the whole complex of ideas and images surrounding the word "creation" is inescapably a part of the way that we see things. We may emphasize either the divine or the human aspect of creation to the point of denying the reality of the other. For Karl Barth, God is a creator, and the first moral to be drawn from this is that man is not one: man is for Barth a creature, and his primary duty is to understand what it is to be a creature of God.[1] For others, the notion of a creating God is a projection from the fact that man makes things, and for them a divine creator has only the reality of a shadow thrown by ourselves. But what we believe, or believe that we believe, in such matters is of very little importance compared to the fact that we go on using the conception anyway, whatever name we give it. We are free, up to a point, to shape our beliefs; what we are clearly not free to do is to alter what is really a part of our cultural genetic code. We can throw out varieties of the idea of creation at random, and these, in Darwinian fashion, will doubtless descend through whatever has the greatest survival value; but abolish the conception itself we cannot.

A year or so ago, after agreeing to help teach an undergraduate course in Shakespeare, I settled down to reread one of my favourite pieces of Shakespearean criticism, Oscar Wilde's essay on "The Truth of Masks." The essay, however, was one in a collected volume of Wilde's critical essays, and I find it easy to get hooked on Wilde. His style often makes him sound dated, and yet he is consistently writing from a point of view at least half a century later than his actual time. He is one of our few genuinely prophetic writers, and, as with other prophets, everything he writes seems either to lead up to his tragic confrontation with society or reflect back on it. Partly because of this, he deliberately restricts his audience. He sets up a palisade of self-conscious and rather mechanical wit, which not merely infuriates those who have no idea what he is talking about but often puts off those who do. We may get so annoyed at his dandies waving their hands languidly at thick volumes labelled "Plato" or "Aristotle" that we may forget that Wilde could, and did, read Greek, and that his references to Classical authors are usually quite precise. So before long I was back in the world of the essay called "The Decay of Lying," now widely recognized to have said a great deal of what modern theories of criticism have been annotating in more garbled language ever since.

The main thesis of this essay is that man does not live directly and nakedly in nature like the animals, but within an envelope that he has constructed out of nature, the envelope usually called culture or civilization. When Wordsworth urges his reader to leave his books, go outdoors, and let nature be his teacher,[2] his "nature" is a north temperate zone nature which in nineteenth-century England had become, even in the Lake District, largely a human artefact. One can see the importance, for poets and others, of the remoteness and otherness of nature: the feeling that the eighteenth century expressed in the word "sublime" conveys to us that there is such a thing as creative alienation. The principle laid down by the Italian philosopher Vico of *verum factum*, that we understand only what we have made ourselves,[3] needs to be refreshed sometimes by the contemplation of something we did not make and do not understand. The difficulty with Wordsworth's view is in the word "teacher." A nature which was not primarily a human artefact could teach man nothing except that he was not it. We are taught by our own cultural conditioning, and by that alone.

We may see already that the word "creation" involves us in a state of mind that is closely parallel with certain types of paranoia, which may give us a clue to what Wilde means by "lying." Our envelope, as I have called it, the cultural insulation that separates us from nature, is rather like (to use a figure that has haunted me from childhood) the window of a lit-up railway carriage at night. Most of the time it is a mirror of our own concerns, including our concern about nature. As a mirror, it fills us with the sense that the world is something which exists primarily in reference to us: it was created for us; we are the centre of it and the whole point of its existence. But occasionally the mirror turns into a real window, through which we can see only the vision of an indifferent nature that got along for untold aeons of time without us, seems to have produced us only by accident, and, if it were conscious, could only regret having done so. This vision propels us instantly into the opposite pole of paranoia, where we seem to be victims of a huge conspiracy, finding ourselves, through no will of our own, arbitrarily assigned to a dramatic role which we have been given no script to learn, in a state of what Heidegger calls "thrownness."[4]

The cultural aura, or whatever it is, that insulates us from nature consists among other things of words, and the verbal part of it is what I call a mythology, or the total structure of human creation conveyed by words, with literature at its centre. Such a mythology belongs to the mirror, not the window. It is designed to draw a circumference around human society and reflect its concerns, not to look directly at the nature outside. When man finally gets around to doing that, he has to develop the special language of science, a language which becomes increasingly mathematical in idiom. Many things have to come together in a culture before science can begin, and when it does begin it does not descend from or grow out of mythology directly. Mythological statements about nature are merely grotesque or silly if they are thought of as pre-scientific explanations of it.

Early students of mythology, it is true, liked to think of it as primitive science, because that view implied such a flattering contrast between primitive visions of nature and theirs. Thus we have Frazer defining myth as mistaken notions of natural phenomena,[5] and Max Müller speaking of mythology as a disease of language.[6] If he had said that language was a disease of mythology, the statement would have been just as untrue, but considerably more interesting. However, this attitude was mainly a by-product of a European ideology designed to rationalize the nineteenth-century treatment of non-European peoples. Mythology is the embryo of literature and the arts, not of science, and no form of art has anything to do with making direct statements about nature, mistaken or correct. Similarly, as science does not grow out of mythology, so it can never replace mythology. Mythology is recreated by the poets in each generation, while science goes its own way.

There is a kind of painting known as *trompe l'œil*, which endeavours to render pictorial objects so accurately that the viewer might be deceived into thinking that he was looking at the real thing. *Trompe l'œil* is a quite legitimate form of painting, but the word "deceive" indicates the paradox in it. Returning to our figure again, when it comes to representing the outer world, no painting can compare with a window pane. This principle applies much more forcibly to literature, because there is no verbal equivalent of the window pane. Words can describe things only approximately: all they do with any real accuracy is hang together, in puns, metaphor, assonances, and the self-contained fictions of grammar and syntax.

All this is contained in Wilde's conception of the creative arts as essentially forms of "lying," or turning away from the external world. As long as we can keep telling one another that we see the same things "out there," we feel that we have a basis for what we call truth and reality. When a work of literature is based on this kind of reality, however, it often tells us only what we no longer want to know. For this reason Wilde makes fun of the careful documentary realism of Zola and others which had such a vogue in his time, of Zola settling down to give us a definitive study of the Second Empire at the moment when the Second Empire had gone hopelessly out of date. But the attack on realism is a side-issue of a far more insidious disease of writing: the morbid lust for what Matthew Arnold calls seeing life steadily and seeing it whole.[7] Recently a collection of early reviews of mine was published,[8] and on looking over it I was amused to see how preoccupied I had been then with two writers, Spengler and Frazer, who haunted me constantly, though I was well aware all the time I was studying them that they were rather stupid men and often slovenly scholars. But I found them, or rather their central visions, unforgettable, while there are hundreds of books by more intelligent and scrupulous people which I have forgotten having read. Some of them are people who have utterly refuted the claims of Spengler and Frazer to be taken seriously. But the thinker who was annihilated on Tuesday has to be annihilated all over again on Wednesday: the fortress of thought is a Valhalla, not an abattoir.

This is not merely my own perversity: we all find that it is not only, perhaps not even primarily, the balanced and judicious people that we turn to for insight. It is also such people as Baudelaire, Rimbaud, Hölderlin, Kierkegaard, Dostoevsky, Nietzsche, all of them liars in Wilde's sense of the word, as Wilde was himself. They were people whose lives got smashed up in various ways, but who rescued fragments from the smash of an intensity that the steady-state people seldom get to hear about. Their vision is penetrating because it is partial and distorted: it is truthful because it is falsified. To the Old Testament's question, "Where shall wisdom be found?" [Job 28:12] there is often only the New Testament's answer: "Well, not among the wise, at any rate" [cf. 1 Corinthians 1:19–20].

What Wilde calls realism, the attempt to base the arts on the recognizable, to find a common ground of reality with the audience, is, he suggests, a search for some kind of emotional reassurance. I hear an echo of this whenever I listen to complaints about the difficulty or obscurity of contemporary art, complaints which often take the form, "but I think a work of art ought to communicate something." The function of the recognizable in the arts is not aesthetic but anaesthetic. A painter of cows in a field is bound to be addressing some people who want to be reminded of cows more than they want to see pictures. The cows function as a tranquillizer, so that the more genuinely attentive part of the viewer's mind is released for pictorial experience. A painter may, however, get fed up with the compromise involved, as most painters today in fact have done, and say: to hell with the cows; look at the form and colour of the picture. If this is his attitude he is not withdrawing from "reality": he is seeing more intensely by means of his medium. The recognizable as such is, in human terms, the noncreative; it is the disturbing insight into it that we associate with the word "creation."

All this has become a commonplace in a time like ours when we are so much more heavily insulated against "nature" than we were even in Wilde's time. A glance out of the window of an airplane, to the patterns of the landscape or city lights below, will tell us why this is the century of Kandinsky and not that of Constable or Ruysdael; more important, it will also tell us that space for us has become a set of co-ordinated points: we do not live in a centred space any more, but have to create our own centres. In "The Decay of Lying" Wilde is, verbally, defending the romantic against the realistic, but these are only the terms of his age: the positive thing he is defending is not the romantic but the unmediated. His point is that what is called realism is not founded on nature or reality at all. We never see these things directly; we see them only through a prism of conventionalized commonplaces, outworn formulas within the art itself, the fossilized forms of earlier attempts to escape from nature and reality. Only a distorted imagination that breaks away from all this and sees reality as a strange, wonderful, terrible, fantastic world is creative in the human sense of the term.

We are now perhaps beginning to glimpse something of the complexity of the situation we are trying to look at in this book. Traditionally, everything we associate with nature, reality, settled order, the way things are, the data of existence that we have to accept, is supposed to go back to *the* creation, the original divine act of making the world. Now we find that if we apply the word "creative" to human activities, the humanly creative is whatever profoundly disturbs our sense of "the" creation, a reversing or neutralizing of it. The encounter of God and man in creation seems to be rather like what some of the great poets of nuclear physics have described as the encounter of matter with anti-matter: each annihilates the other. What seems one of the few admirable forms of human achievement, the creation of the arts, turns out to be a kind of decreation:[9] I might have called my lectures "Creation and Decreation" if I had not been afraid of irritating you beyond the limits even of your tolerance.

I turn the pages of my Wilde book to the next essay, "The Critic as Artist," and there I read near the beginning the wonderful passage about music:

> After playing Chopin, I feel as if I had been weeping over sins that I had never committed, and mourning over tragedies that were not my own. Music always seems to me to produce that effect. It creates for one a past of which one has been ignorant, and fills one with a sense of sorrows that have been hidden from one's tears. I can fancy a man who had led a perfectly commonplace life, hearing by chance some curious piece of music, and suddenly discovering that his soul, without his being conscious of it, had passed through terrible experiences, and known fearful joys, or wild romantic loves, or great renunciations.[10]

First, of course, we cannot restrict the scope of this passage to music; it applies to all the arts, though it may well be true that music has some special mystery about its evocations. Second, we see that Wilde is postulating two levels of experience, in which one level is remembered and the other repressed, though he gives repression a very different context from Freud. Our sense experience, our memories, our established habits and rituals, all act as filters: they screen out or accommodate whatever in our lives is disturbing or threatening. "Had we the first intimation of the Definition of Life," said Emily Dickinson, "the calmest of us would be Lunatics!"[11] It is only the arts that allow this screened-out emotion and experience to return in some bearable form, and make us realize that while we have been living our lives as "normally" as we can, we have also been, all the time, citizens of the lunatic country of Don Quixote and Captain Ahab and King Lear. That is why their moods and behaviour can be intelligible to us.

This principle of the arts evoking the real and repressed past is familiar to us from Proust, whose narrator Marcel perceives the pattern of his own real past through an accidental glimpse of it, so that he comes to the beginning of the imaginative vision of his life at the moment when his reader comes to the end of it. The implication is that what Marcel sees at the end of his experience is the possibility of looking at it in the way that the reader should have been looking at it all along. This opens up the issue of the creative reader and his role in literature, which is Wilde's main concern in this essay, and to which I shall return in the last chapter.

If we apply this principle to social and historical existence we get some simpler and more familiar data. Out of the general welter of human life, the great works of literature and music and the plastic arts have been born. There is no cultural development in the past which did not have in its background all the cruelty and folly of which mankind is capable; yet the works of culture themselves seem to be in a perpetual state of innocence. This is still true when the cruelty and folly are directly reflected from the art itself. The pottery and textiles and metal-work that we see in museums, when compared to the conditions of life that produced them, seem to float up from those conditions as, in Apuleius' story of *The Golden Ass*, the lovely fairy tale of Cupid and Psyche floats up like a soap bubble out of the sickening brutality of its context. But, of course, we have to take the whole book, brutality and all, as a cultural product of its time, and similarly we cannot abstract some of the works of man from others. It is a gross error in perspective either to detach the cultural from the historical past or to confuse the two.

Our cultural heritage, then, is our real and repressed social past, not the past of historical record but the great dreams of the arts, which keep recurring to haunt us with a sense of how little we know of the real dimensions of our own experience. As I have insisted so often in different contexts, such words as "classic" or "masterpiece" mean very little except that some recurring dreams from the past refuse to go away, and remain staring at us silently until we confront them. They are the reality behind all ancestor worship, and the part of our own identity that extends into the past. It has been said that those who do not learn history are condemned to repeat it: this means very little, because we are all in the position of voters in a Canadian election, condemned to repeat history anyway whether we learn it or not. But those who refuse to confront their own real past, in whatever form, are condemning themselves to die without having been born.

The contemplation of the ordinary historical past, however, suggests another kind of vision that seems to start with us and be independent of the arts. This is the vision of what humanity might conceivably do, and what human life could conceivably be, a vision that breaks with everything man has done and is projected on the future. This social vision of a future discontinuous with history as we have known it, turning history, in Joyce's phrase, into a nightmare from which we are trying to awake,[12] is really a vision of human redemption, though the redemptive power is not necessarily one outside ourselves. Mary Shelley records with some wonder, in her note on *Prometheus Unbound*, that "Shelley believed that mankind had only to will that there should be no evil, and there would be none."[13] But surely this is the kind of reflection that must occur to everybody at some time or other. It is particularly in youth, I suppose, that one feels most strongly the absurdity of ordinary human actions, and, even more, the absurdity or wickedness of believing that they are made necessary by fate or reason or nature or the will of God. Here again, in a different context, is the sense of the crucial importance of setting free something normally repressed in ordinary human experience. And here again is a sphere of creation, though social in reference rather than individual, linked to the future rather than the past, and with the imaginary rather than the imaginative.

Sometimes this feeling clashes with the claims of the past, however impressive. Black students reading a white man's literature, women bored by heroines presented as models of virtue because they conform to male codes, radicals of all persuasions, often develop an anticultural streak that wants to scrap the past, including its greatest imaginative achievements, in order to start doing something else and something better. A friend of mine travelling in China during the cultural revolution wanted to see some ancient frescoes in Peking: her guide took her there, but said impatiently that if she had her way she would cover them all up with posters explaining how exploited the people of that day were.

The difference between the actual and the cultural past was of little importance for this guide compared to the urgency of changing the direction of life entirely.

It is true that our course of action in life is guided, to an extent we seldom realize, by some underlying vision of what society could be. Such a vision has to be projected on the future, but it exists only in a metaphorical future. We do not know the future at all except by analogy with the past, and the future that will happen will not be much like anyone's vision of it. This gives our social ideals the intensity and purity of something that does not exist, yet they are born out of analogy with what has come to us through tradition. So all visions of a social future must be rooted in the past, socially conditioned and historically placed. I note a comment in Jacques Lacan, in an essay discussing the role of language in psychoanalytic treatment: "the effect of a full Word is to reorder the past contingent events by conferring on them the sense of necessities to come."[14]

Some reactionaries deliberately model their visions of the future on a return to the past, or what they imagine to have been the past; radicals, as we generally understand the word, have a vision of the future which is more of a break with the past. But all changes of direction in society, progressive, revolutionary, reactionary, or whatever, come to a point at which they have to establish continuity with what has gone before. Some rationalizing historical construct usually appears at that point, showing how certain tactical changes in the prospective future are outgrowths of certain trends in the past. But if we are dealing with the fundamental social vision which underlies all creative action, the only element in the past deep enough to call to that deep is the tradition of human creative achievement. It is on that level of social insight that we realize why the vision of a new social order cannot be disconnected from the forms of past creation in the arts.

Wilde attempted to deal with this aspect of creation too, in his essay "The Soul of Man under Socialism." He remarks there that "a map of the world that does not include Utopia is not worth even glancing at, for it leaves out the one country at which Humanity is always landing."[15] By "socialism," however, Wilde means apparently only distributing wealth and opportunity more evenly, so that all people can become pure individualists, and hence, to some degree, artists. He says that in his ideal world the state is to produce the useful, and the individual or artist the beautiful. But beauty, like nature and reality, is merely another of those reassuring words indicating a good deal of ready-made social acceptance. Wilde is preoccupied in this essay by his contempt for censorship, and is optimistic that what he calls socialism would bring about the end of the tyranny of an ignorant and mischievous public opinion. This has not been our experience of socialism or any other system since Wilde's time, and his prophetic vision in this essay seems to have gone out of focus. But, as usual, his sense of context is very accurate: he identifies the two aspects of our subject, the creation of a future society and the continuing of the creativity of the past in spite of the past. As he says: "the past is what man should not have been; the present is what man ought not to be; the future is what artists are" (48).

The issue of censorship, and other aspects of social resistance to creation, is a very important one, if we are right in regarding the creative as expressing what ordinary experience represses. You will perhaps not be surprised to learn that I have no use for the lame-brained hysterics who go around snatching books by Margaret Laurence and Alice Munro out of school libraries. I also resent the mindless cliché that the best way to sell a book is to ban it, which means that all its extra readers will be attracted to it for silly reasons. But I sometimes wonder whether the work of creation in society is really effective if it meets with no social resistance at all. The conventions of painting, for example, have become so tolerated that it is difficult even to imagine what kind of pictures today would go into the *salon des réfusés* to which the Impressionists were exiled a century or so ago. One applauds the tolerance, except that the public is so seldom tolerant about anything unless it has become indifferent to it as well. A world where the arts are totally tolerated might easily become a world in which they were merely decorative, and evoked no sense of challenge to repression at all.

What we see continually in the world around us is a constant and steady perversion of the vision of a free and equal social future, as country after country makes a bid for freedom and accepts instead a tyranny far worse than the one it endured before. There seems no escaping the inference that the real desire for freedom and equality is not only repressed too, but is in fact one of the most deeply repressed feelings we have. And if the vision of a social future is connected with the vision of the creativity of the past, which is our main thesis here, then there must be different layers of repression appealed to by art, some much deeper than others. At the deepest layer, if we are right, the enjoyment of the arts would be as strongly resisted as any other effort at freedom.

Human life consists of leisure and work, and these provide the bases for, respectively, our visions of past art and social future. To the extent that leisure and work have been represented by different classes of society, each has been fostered on a rather superficial level. The leisure class on top was supposed to enjoy the world of culture as a special privilege; the working class below was supposed to work without a vision of any social future of which they could form a part. It seems to me that this set-up is slowly rearranging itself: the phrase "leisure class" no longer means very much anywhere now, and the phrase "working class" would probably not mean very much either if it had not become a pious cliché. Work and leisure are gradually becoming different aspects of the same life, not two different classes in society. But the old class habits keep persisting, at least in our thinking. It has puzzled many people that it is possible for someone, the commandant of a Nazi death camp, for example, to have a cultivated taste for the arts and still be what he is. It is possible because the response to the arts can also exist on an aesthetic level, of the sort indicated by Wilde's term "beautiful," where they are objects to be admired or valued or possessed.

But the arts actually represent an immense imaginative and transforming force in society, which is largely untapped because so much of our approach to them is still possessive and aesthetic. There is a much deeper level on which the arts form part of our heritage of freedom, and where inner repression by the individual and external repression in society make themselves constantly felt. That is why totalitarian societies, for example, find themselves unable either to tolerate the arts or to generate new forms of them. During the Nazi occupation of France, the French discovered that one of the most effective things they could do was to put on Classical plays like *Antigone* or *The Trojan Women*, in original or adapted versions. The Nazis had no excuse for censoring them, but because of the intense repression all around, the plays began to mean something of what they really do mean.

As for the life of work, the more alienating and less creative it becomes, the more completely it becomes an observance of time, a clock-punching and clock-watching servitude. Leisure begins in the breaking of the panic of time, that unhurried commitment in which alone the study of the arts, which take their own speeds, is possible. On the aesthetic or possessive level there is still a preoccupation with time. We read at the end of Walter Pater's *Renaissance*:

We are all under sentence of death but with a sort of indefinite reprieve . . .
we have an interval, and then our place knows us no more. Some spend this
interval in listlessness, some in high passions, the wisest, at least among
"the children of this world," in art and song. For our one chance lies in
expanding that interval, in getting as many pulsations as possible into the
given time.[16]

The panic of the phrase "as many as possible" indicates that for Pater
the pursuit of experience has not yet broken free of the tyranny of time,
nor of the aesthetic level of response which is really a collecting of
impressions. In contrast, we have Marcel Duchamp, the painter of the
Nude Descending the Staircase, speaking of a picture as a "delay":

Use "delay" instead of "picture" or "painting"; "picture on glass" becomes
"delay in glass." . . . It's merely a way of succeeding in no longer thinking
that the thing in question is a picture—to make a "delay" of it in the most
general way possible. . . .[17]

This conception has been considerably expanded in our day by Jacques
Derrida and others, where distancing in both time and space becomes
central to the contact of text and reader.

To the extent that work becomes creative, it tends to incorporate and
be based on a vision of an ideal society projected on the future. If we
turn to Biblical imagery, we can see that the core of this vision is that of
the humanized creation out of nature that I spoke of at the beginning. So
far, in speaking of creation in the Bible, I have referred only to the somewhat confusing activities of God at the beginning, who creates the
world in Genesis 1, creates paradise in Genesis 2, destroys paradise in
Genesis 3, and destroys the rest of the world in the deluge of Genesis 6.
As a creator, the Deity seems to have had other things on his infinite
mind, or perhaps, as a poem of Thomas Hardy suggests, he had no real
talent for creation at all.[18] But there is also a partly human vision of creation in the Bible, associated with a future restoration of Israel to its
Promised Land. Man lives, we said, isolated from nature by his own culture, and this culture is partly a technical achievement and partly a
visionary one. At the centre of the technical achievement is his transformation of a part of his natural environment into a nature with a human
shape and a human meaning. In Biblical imagery we begin with the fruit

trees and fresh water of paradise, and then go through various phases of social development: the pastoral phase of flocks and herds, the agricultural phase of harvest and vintage, and the urban phase of cities, buildings, streets, and highways.

Similar imagery lies at the heart of every mythology and every development of the arts, and indicates that what man really wants is what his genuine work shows that he wants. When he is doing genuine work, that is, not making war or feeding a parasitic class, he is making a human artefact out of nature. Whatever the status of "the" creation ascribed to God at the beginning, there is another creation which involves human effort, and the idealized forms of this creation are again projected on the future. I call this "recreation," or the counter-movement of creation set up by man. The destructive activities assigned to God in Genesis provide the motivation for this, and his original creative activities, such as the planting of the garden of Eden, provide the models.

But while all cultures reflect similar patterns of imagery in regard to nature, the Bible is distinctive in its attitude to nature. I shall be looking at this in more detail in the next chapter, but the general principle is that for the Bible there is nothing numinous, no holy or divine presence, within nature itself. Nature is a fellow creature of man: to discover divine presences in nature is superstition, and to worship them is idolatry. Man, according to the Bible, has to look to himself, his institutions, and more particularly his records of verbal revelation, to find the structural principles of the creation he is entrusted with.

Further, and by the same principle, the solution of the major human and social problems has to precede the real recreation of nature. We are gradually beginning to realize that the exploitation of man by man is evil, and not merely evil but unnecessary. Human nature being what it is, the transforming of some of the natural environment into a humanized one has not been wholly a creative operation: there has been an immense amount of spoiling, wasting, destroying, and plundering as well. But only recently have we come to feel much uneasiness of conscience about this: our cultural traditions insist that nature was provided for the sake of man, and that the unlimited and uninhibited exploitation of nature has nothing to be said against it, except that we obviously have to call a halt after we have used up everything there is.

This view of nature as an unlimited field of exploitation is found in most human cultures, but with us is peculiarly a legacy of our Biblical and Christian inheritance. We notice that the prophets in the Bible, when they speak of a final restoration of Israel, also speak of a regenerating of nature and a reconciliation with it, but they emphasize that this can take place only after man has stopped the destructive activities within himself. Hosea says, for instance:

> And in that day will I make a covenant for them with the beasts of the field, and with the fowls of heaven, and with the creeping things of the ground: and I will break the bow and the sword and the battle out of the earth, and will make them to lie down safely. [Hosea 2:18]

The implication is that the regenerating of human society must precede, though it forms a part of, the regeneration of nature.

The Bible has little or nothing to say about man's cultural past, and to that extent is deficient as a guide to human creative perspectives. The traditions of the literary critic are of Classical origin, and for this aspect of our subject we have to depend mainly on secular literature. I began by referring to a course on Shakespeare that I had recently agreed to help teach, and in looking over the texts of Shakespeare I found myself once again absorbed, as I have been all my critical life, by the immense profundity and complexity of social vision in the final romances, *Pericles, Cymbeline, The Winter's Tale, The Tempest.* I noticed, as I had noticed before, that they resemble the earlier comedies, but differ from them in that they seem to contain a tragic action as well as a comic one, instead of merely avoiding a tragic conflict as the earlier comedies do. I had realized for a long time that the comic vision in literature is one which is very close to what I have been calling the vision of a future society. In comedy a certain drive to freedom, generally symbolized by the impulse of two young people to marry, is being thwarted by something foolish and obstinate in the social order which nevertheless has control of that order temporarily. But normally, at the end of a comedy, the drive towards freedom succeeds, its opponents or blocking figures are baffled, and the action ends with most of the characters together on the stage, suggesting a new society being formed at the end of the play. The ideals of this new society have to be left undefined, because its activities are assumed to begin after the play itself is over.

Sometimes, more particularly in *The Winter's Tale*, this comic action is associated or identified with the fertility imagery of a renewal of nature, as spring succeeds winter and new life emerges from old. In *The Winter's*

Tale the great sheep-shearing festival scene in the fourth act depicts the determination of two young people, Florizel and Perdita, to marry in the teeth of parental opposition, and in the background is the triumphant renewing vitality of "great creating nature," as spring in Bohemia follows hard on winter in Sicilia. But at the same time that Shakespeare gives us this vision of youth and spring victorious over age and winter, he puts as much or even more emphasis on the reintegrating of an older generation. It is the reunion of Leontes and Hermione, where the past folly and obsession of Leontes is cast out, that forms the final scene, and this scene is as closely associated with art as that of Florizel and Perdita is with nature. It takes place in a chapel, an alleged work of painting and sculpture comes to life, and the miracle is accomplished by music and poetry. It seems as though two things must happen if either is to happen: there is a vision of a happy social future, but there is also a vision of a reintegrated past in which dead things come to life again under the spell of art.

All the romances seem to have something of this double resolution, of young people forming the nucleus of a new social order and a new outburst of fertility, and of older people restored to their original lives through the arts, the arts often being represented simply by music. In *The Tempest* the young lovers, Ferdinand and Miranda, are shown by Prospero the masque which symbolizes their future lives, where the main characters are Ceres, Juno, and Iris, the earth, the sky, and the rainbow, deities of fertility and promise. They are then ready to encounter what Miranda calls a brave new world. At the same time Prospero, whose art is symbolized by magic, though it consists very largely of music and drama, is reintegrating his own past as Duke of Milan, transforming the society of his former enemies into a new shape.

In this play the reintegrating of the past through art and the renewal of the future through the energy of youth and nature are contrasted with the mere past and the mere future. The mere past, where everything vanishes into darkness and annihilation, is evoked by Prospero's great "end of the revels" speech; the mere future is what we see in Prospero's return to Milan, to be as absent-minded and ineffectual a Duke as he was before. The positive action of the play, therefore, where reintegration and renewal both take place, is not in the past or future at all, but in an expanded present where, as Eliot says, the past and the future are gathered.[19]

This present is a resurrection which is not the reviving of a corpse, and a rebirth which is not an emerging of a new life from a dying older body to die in its turn. It is rather a transfiguration into a world we keep making even when we deny it, as though a coral insect were suddenly endowed with enough consciousness and vision to be able to see the island it has been helping to create.

II

In the previous chapter I spoke of human life as contained within a cultural envelope that insulates it from nature, and said that the verbal part of this envelope is, or at least starts out as, a mythology. A mythology is made up of myths, and so I should first of all try to explain what the word "myth" means in the sense, or senses, in which I shall be using it. As a literary critic, I want to anchor the word "myth" in its critical context. Myth to me, then, means first of all *mythos* or narrative, words arranged in a sequential order. Every structure in words designed for sequential reading, which excludes practically no structures except telephone books, has a narrative, a *mythos*, a sequential ordering that begins, in our culture, on the top left-hand corner of page one and ends at the bottom right-hand corner of the last page. Naturally there is a great variety of myths or narratives: some are stories, some arguments, some descriptions, and so on.

However, the use of the term in so broad and general a sense would entangle us in a discussion of the different shapes that language and thought assume, which enable a myth in some contexts to take the form of an argument or a description. We have no time for that, so I shall restrict the word "myth" to its more familiar sense of culturally early narratives, which come from a time when concepts and arguments and abstractions had not yet appeared in language. Such myths are stories, or sequential acts of personified beings. Every culture produces a mythology of this concerted kind, and it is out of the story patterns contained in such a mythology that literature develops.

My own interest in myth begins with its literary development: to me a literary myth is not a contaminated myth but a matured one. In my perspective as a literary critic the "real meaning" of a myth emerges slowly from a prolonged literary life, and then its meaning includes everything it has effectively been made to mean during that life. What the Song of Songs "really means," for example, is not confined to the village wedding songs and late echoes of fertility ritual out of which it may have originated, but includes what it has been made to mean in Bernard of Clairvaux and St. John of the Cross, where it expresses the love of Christ for his people.[20] Theoretically, there is no analogy between a myth and a species: a poet can do what he likes with his myth, and can marry it to any other myth and still produce imaginative offspring. But what is theoretically possible and what poets actually do seem to be different: in practice, poets show a great respect for the integrity of the myths they treat. Samuel Butler remarked that a chicken was merely an egg's device for producing more eggs;[21] similarly, a poet often seems to be merely a myth's device for reproducing itself again in a later period.

Anthropologists, on the other hand, and others who are interested primarily in the immediate social and cultural functions of myths, find myths most useful to them at the earliest possible stage, before the free play of the creative imagination has begun to turn them into what we think of as literature. The distinction between myth and literature is strictly speaking impossible, as no myth can exist except in some sort of narrative formulation, but still it is possible to isolate, in some cultures, what is essentially a preliterary mythology. In the highly developed cultures surrounding the Bible the problem hardly exists. Myth and literature are already indistinguishable in the Gilgamesh epic, which is much older than any part of the Bible.

But the Bible is exceptional in having a strongly doctrinal emphasis, in its story of creation, which is clearly not intended to be primarily literary or imaginative. What it is intended to be will, I hope, become clearer as we go on, but we have to approach it first on the poetic level all the same. The status of the opening of Genesis as a factual historical record is no longer an issue for many of us, and to try to accept it as one is merely running scared. To go back to the argument of Oscar Wilde's essay on "The Decay of Lying" discussed in the previous chapter, it is only when the creation story is considered factually false that it can be of any conceivable use to us. The hero of Eliot's *Family Reunion* complains that his family understands "only events, not what has happened."[22] It is myth, and only myth, that tells us what has happened.

It becomes clear in many modern studies of myth, such as those of Mircea Eliade, that it is only when a myth is accepted as an imaginative story that it is really believed in. As a story, a myth becomes a *model* of human experience, and its relation to that experience becomes a confronting and present experience. The truth of the story of the fall of Adam and Eve does not depend on the possibility that an archaeologist may eventually dig up their skeletons. It depends on its power to convey the present sense of alienation in human consciousness, the sense of being surrounded by a nature not ours. Such a myth bears the same relation to the Law in the first five books of the Bible that a parable of Jesus bears to the teaching of the Gospel.

Milton's *Paradise Lost* is a poem about the creation of the world and the fall of man written by a poet convinced of the factual reliability of the Biblical story. Yet even Milton draws a distinction between the kind of instruction that the unfallen Adam receives from Raphael and the instruction that the fallen Adam receives from Michael. Raphael tells Adam the story of the fall of Satan, which except for an allusion or two in the Bible is entirely Milton's invention.[23] The implication is that teaching by means of parables is the only appropriate kind of teaching for a free man. Michael summarizes for Adam the story of the Bible, events which are future to Adam but will certainly occur, implying that man's freedom of will has been curtailed to the vanishing point. All Milton's reverence for the Bible as a book of promise and a charter of human freedom cannot conceal the fact that this kind of knowledge is debased and sinister knowledge: that is, knowledge of an already determined future is part of the forbidden knowledge that Adam should never have had.

Our next task is to bring out the peculiar characteristics of the story of creation in Genesis as a myth. The word "mythology" implies, by its very existence, that story-myths have a tendency to stick together to form an interconnected series of stories. It would be usual for such a mythology to begin with a creation myth, and there are as many varieties of creation myths as there are societies to produce them. In the early Near Eastern and Mediterranean cultures that we are concerned with, however, two types of creation myth seem to dominate. Perhaps it will be easiest to explain this by a creation myth of my own about creation myths. Let us assume a primeval myth-maker, standing alone in the garden of Eden, about to design a creation myth *a priori*, wholly detached from his social context and conditioning. No such person could exist, but we may learn something from postulating him. The kind of creation myth he will come up with, then, will depend on whether he is looking up or down at the time he is constructing it.

If he looks down, he sees the earth with its progression of seasons, the place from which all living things, animals and plants, are born and to which they return when they die. A creation myth based on these phenomena would be a sexual creation myth, assuming that the world took shape originally in the same way that it still renews itself every spring, or renews life in birth. In the beginning there was winter, and then came the spring; or, in the beginning there was a female body, and something got born from it. No feature is invariable or without many exceptions in mythology, but one very obvious figure for such a myth to focus on would be that of an earth-mother, the womb and tomb of all life. For such an earth-mother, from whom all living things emerge and to whom all dying things return, would be the direction of all death as well as the source of all life, and would consequently have a sinister aspect as well as a cherishing one. The cycle over which she would preside is what Plato might call the cycle of the different. Newborn animals are not the reborn forms of their parents; the flowers that bloom in the spring are not the same as those that bloomed last spring.

One immensely simplifying principle in such a creation myth is that death, along with the pain and solitude that go with it, would not be a problem. Death is built in to a myth which is primarily a myth about living things, all of which die. Life is unintelligible without death: there may be a continuous force that propels the birth of new life, but such a life-force merely uses the individual: it does not exist for his sake.

If our myth-maker looks up, he sees the cycle of the sun and the slower cycle of the moon. This suggests rather a cycle of the same: it seems to be unmistakably the same sun that comes up the next morning, the same moon that waxes and wanes, and in the background, except for the five planets that also have their appointed courses, there are, as it seems, the cycling but unchanging stars. We hear of some societies that "believe" that a new sun is created each day: anthropologists in particular are fond of reminding us that some societies will believe anything, including no doubt some societies of anthropologists. However, our assumed myth-maker is not believing anything yet: he is merely constructing. Milton, speaking of pagan mythology, uses the phrase "they fabled," instead of "they believed":[24] it sounds more tendentious, and Milton meant it to be so, but it is also more accurate, because fabling, unlike belief, is an activity that we can get some evidence for. For this version of creation mythology, the periodic return of the sun, moon, and stars sets the pattern for the cycle of the seasons, reflecting the work of an intelligent being who, like the God of the Old Testament, does not change, or, like the creating deity of Plato's *Timaeus*, imitates such a being.

The sky-begotten creation myth, then, would suggest the subordinating of becoming to being, of cyclical change to a power of stability that controls cyclical change and is not subject to it. Such a creation myth would not start with birth from sexual union but with some power assumed to be superior to both. It would be, in short, an artificial creation myth. The world must originally have been made, including the world of living things, however universal the process of birth and death may still be among living things. And just as the sexual creation myth most readily suggests an earth-mother, so the artificial myth would correspondingly suggest a sky-father. Sky, because of the predominance of the heavenly bodies in the materials of the myth, and father, because this creator goes about his own mysterious business without nursing his children.

An artificial creation myth suggests planning and intelligence, and planning and intelligence suggest a creator who could have originally produced only a perfect or model world, a world with no death or disease or decay in it at all. This model world is apparently the one described as being made in the first chapter of Genesis, where every aspect of creation calls for the comment "and God saw that it was very good," so good that he spent the seventh day of creation contemplating it. To account for the contrast between the model world that such a God must have made and the actual world that we find ourselves in now, a myth of a human "fall" must be added, an alienation myth which expresses the present human condition but does not attach it directly to the work of creation. Even in Plato's *Timaeus*, just mentioned, where the world is made by a demiurge, an artificer working in imitation of a model, whatever is wrong with our world is presumably part of the great failure of all imitations to reproduce their models accurately that, for Plato, recurs in human art.

The question "When did it all begin?" however inevitable it may seem, is a totally unanswerable question, because it is impossible to conceive a beginning of time. One may of course say that there was a creation which created time as well as everything else, or that our perception and experience of time are a result of our fallen state, but these are only verbal formulas concealing the fact that the beginning of time is an unthinkable thought. The sexual creation myth is no better off: to the problem of whether the chicken or the egg came first there is no answer. St. Augustine mentions someone who, irritated by questions about what God was doing "before" he made the world, said he was preparing a hell for those who ask such questions.[25] This is really another way of saying that the doctrine of divine creation is among other things a linguistic device for shutting off the question "what happened before anything else happened?" There is nevertheless an essential imaginative issue bound up with the word "beginning," which is the opening word of the Bible. We derive our notions of beginnings and ends from our own births and deaths, the two crucial events in which we first join a moving belt of phenomena and finally drop off it. The moving belt itself cannot really be thought of as beginning or ending, but, because *we* begin and end, we insist that beginning and ending must be somehow much more important than merely continuing.

Hence the artificial creation myth, where the world was made by an intelligent sky-father, the one that wins out in the Biblical tradition, is also a myth in which an absolute beginning is postulated, as something superior to all the continuity which follows. In the complete form of the myth an absolute beginning implies an absolute end. But such an end would have to be the end of death, not of life, a death of death in which life has become assimilated to the unending. Thus the Biblical creation myth takes us back to one of the most "primitive" of all views: that death, the most natural of all events, the one thing we know will always happen, is nevertheless somehow wrong and unnatural, not part of the original scheme of things. The author of the Book of Wisdom gazes serenely at the facts of his experience, every one of which confirms the law that there are no exceptions to dying, and remarks: "For God made not death . . . . the generations of the world were healthful; and there is no poison of destruction in them, nor the kingdom of death upon the earth" [1:13–14].

The sense of the importance of beginning and ending in traditional Christianity has in it a thick streak of what in the last chapter we called paranoia, and has produced some very bizarre situations. In the seventeenth century, the age of Galileo and Newton, Biblical scholars were still gravely explaining that the time of creation was probably the spring equinox of 4004 B.C., around two in the afternoon.[26] And during the past century there have been several assemblages of faithful gathered to await an "end of the world," often on the top of a mountain, the existence of which in itself indicates many millions of years of both age and of life expectancy for the earth.

For the artificial or sky-father myth, the metaphorical kernel for this conception of a total "beginning" would not be birth, but the experience of waking up from sleep. It is in the process of awakening to consciousness that we are most clearly aware of the sense of a beginning in a world both new and familiar, which we are quite sure is real, whatever the world "before" it was. The curious insistence in the Biblical account on a sequence of "days," and the recurring refrain "and the evening and the morning were the first day," etc., seem to be emphasizing the importance of this metaphor. In Milton's *Paradise Lost* and Michelangelo's Sistine Chapel the sense of the creation of Adam as an awakening of consciousness out of the sleep of matter is even stronger.

How there could be uncomplicated "days" of creation when the sun was created only on the fourth day is an old puzzle, and even St. Augustine felt that if God said "days" he must have had some mental reservation about the word.[27] Yet the institution of the Sabbath, and the importance given to the calendar week, seem still to be based on the connection of creation with the contrast of day and night, waking and sleeping. The fact that even in contemporary English the words "sunlight" and "daylight" are different words may suggest a remote period in which daylight was not causally associated with the sun, but it is doubtful if the original "light" of Genesis can be reduced to this kind of confusion.

It is natural to think that the earth-mother myth is the older of the two, being the myth more appropriate for an agricultural society, as its rival was for the more urban, tool-using, and patriarchal society that succeeded it. Certainly in Hesiod, one of the fountain-heads of Greek mythology, the sky-father Zeus is thought of as a relative latecomer, the third at least of a series of sky-gods, who establishes his supremacy by force over a much older earth-mother. The latter retires sullenly below with her defeated Titans, chthonic powers who, either as Titans or as giants, meet us many times in many mythological guises. In the first chapter of Genesis the artificial sky-father of the myth seems to have it all his own way. But there are two creation myths in Genesis, and the second or so-called Jahwist one, which begins in Genesis 2:4, is clearly much the older. In this account we start with the watering of a garden. The garden is a symbol of the female body in the Bible, recurring in the Song of Songs, where the body of the bride is described as "a garden enclosed, a fountain sealed." In the same account, too, Adam is formed from a feminine *adamah* or dust of the ground (Genesis 2:7). Not all the sexual myth has been excluded: enough has been vestigially left in to suggest that some still earlier creation myths are being incorporated.

However, both creation myths in the Bible seem at first sight intolerably patriarchal. Deity is associated exclusively with the male sex; man was created first and woman out of his body, in contrast to the later "fallen" cycle of birth from a mother; the fall was precipitated by the female, and as a result the male is to have dominance over her. There is no question that the story has got mixed up with patriarchal social ideology, and no question either that it has been constantly invoked and ruthlessly exploited to rationalize doctrines of male supremacy. But within the myth itself, there is an element in the symbolism of male and female which is distinguishable from the social relations of men and women. It would be useful if Western thought had developed something like the classical Chinese conceptions of yang and yin, which would express something of the imaginative and mythological relations of male and female without perverting them in this way. Aristotle, for example, remarked that sex was an analogue to his distinction of form and matter, without drawing morals about the social superiority of males (*Metaphysics*, 988a). But there is probably no such thing as an unperverted myth, nor is there likely to be for a long time.

The myth of a fall, being as we said an alienation myth, expresses the sense that the identity we are given at birth is, somehow or other, not our real or our whole identity. Such a sense is readily connected with the conception of God as a parent, because the parent stands for the whole of whatever has existed before us that has made our own existence possible. As that, the parent is the handiest symbol to express the feeling that we are born with an unknown identity which is both ourselves and yet something other and greater than ourselves. Of the two parental figures, the mother is the less convincing for this purpose, because the mother is the parent we must break from in order to get born. To come into life is to be delivered from a mother, but the deliverance is temporary, and the emphasis on the male in the Bible is connected with its resistance to the cyclical fatality of all religions founded on Mother Nature.

The Genesis account of the fall speaks of two trees, the tree of life and the tree of forbidden knowledge. The latter clearly has something to do with the beginning of sexual experience as we know it, and is symbolized by a limp serpent crawling away on the ground. Metaphorically, the two trees would be the same tree, which would imply a tree of life with a fully erect serpent of wisdom climbing up its branches, as in the version of Indian yoga known as Kundalini. The sexuality of the tree of life would in that case have something about it of what has been called the myth of the lost phallus,[28] a power of sexual experience where the relation of male to female has got free from the sado-masochistic cycle that dominates so much of our attitude to sex.

In the sexual creation myth with its earth-mother, the earth-mother is in the early stages a symbol of *natura naturans*, nature as a bursting forth of life and energy, its divine personalities the animating spirits of trees, mountains, rivers, and stones. This is the basis of what is called paganism, the instinctive faith of the *paganus* or peasant who is closest to the natural environment and furthest from the centre of the insulating envelope of culture. In the later stages of such "paganism," the preoccupation with cyclical movement climbs up into the sky and annexes the sense of *natura naturata*, nature as a structure or system which also manifests itself in cycles. Here the earth-mother expands into what Robert Graves calls the "Triple Will,"[29] the *diva triformis* or goddess of heaven, earth, and hell, Luna, Diana, and Hecate, who meets us in so many other female trinities, the Fates, the Norns, the three goddesses confronting Paris. The cosmological vision such a myth suggests is one of cyclical fatality, where, as in the riddle of Oedipus, the three phases of infancy, manhood, and old age succeed one another without change.

At this point it becomes clear that the myth of creation is a part of a larger mythological structure known as the social contract. In paganism the contract which binds together the gods, mankind, and nature in a common recognition of law appears, for instance, at the end of Aeschylus' *Oresteia*, where the gods ratify the order of nature and to some extent are bound by it themselves. As paganism develops, it becomes clear by imperial Roman times that, as the gods grew out of nature-spirits, they are really expendable in this contract, the only essential god being the divine Caesar. In the Biblical creation myth nature is not directly a party to the social contract, which is a "testament" between God and man, nature having no law of its own except what God bestows on it. Thus in New Testament times the two creation myths had expanded into two contract myths focused, one on Christ, whose divinity is an incarnation of God in man, the other on Caesar, who is Antichrist so far as he becomes a god by incarnating the link between moral and natural law.

As the longer and slower cycles complete themselves, there may be a sense of hope and renewal before the beginning of another cycle. At the time of Christ, when astrologers saw the sun moving into Pisces, many people talked about the dawn of a new and greater age, just as there are those who talk about an "age of Aquarius" now. The most famous expression of this was Virgil's *Fourth Eclogue*, which predicts the arrival of a new Golden or Saturnian Age when "the serpent shall die" [l. 24]. But although Christianity promptly seized on this poem as an unconscious prophecy of the birth of the Messiah, Christian writers also totally rejected all cyclical theories of history, whether hopeful or cynical in mood.

There are certain cultural disadvantages in an artificial creation myth, especially when presented as a deductive account of how the world and human life began. As what Plato in the *Timaeus* calls a probable narrative, or, as one translator has it, "a likely story,"[30] it reduces us to a passive role, inheriting the results of ancestral mistakes but unable to do anything about them. Thus the seventeenth-century New England poet Michael Wigglesworth represents the heathen at the Last Judgment objecting that it is hardly fair to send them to hell for Adam's sin, considering that they have never heard of Adam.[31] They are told that Adam was designed to be a "common root" of mankind, so that Adam's sin is their sin too, and they are compelled to agree, according to the poet, that the argument is irrefutable.

Then again, the conception of an artificer God, who starts everything off by making all things in more or less their present form, is not very encouraging for the human artist. If it is true that, as Sir Thomas Browne said, "Nature is the Art of God";[32] if the models of human creation, the city and the garden, were created by God before man existed, the human artist seems to be in a hopeless position of competing with God. This is particularly true of painters and sculptors, who have often been regarded with suspicion as potentially makers of idols, dead images set up in rivalry with the maker of living ones. In Islamic culture this prejudice has gone to the point of banning representational art altogether, and similar tendencies have appeared in both Jewish and Christian traditions. In an early Christian romance called the "Clementine Recognitions," where the apostle Peter is the hero, some frescoes on a public building are referred to, and it is noted with approval that Peter is impervious to their artistic merit.[33] There is no need to dwell on the iconoclastic movements that have swept over both East and West portions of the Christian world. As remarked in the first chapter, human creativity and divine creation often seem to be at loggerheads.

When painting and sculpture were tolerated, the religious prejudice against them carried on in some forms of critical theory, according to which artists in these areas were merely second-hand copyists of nature. Thus the Elizabethan critic George Puttenham, writing just before Shakespeare's time, says: "In another respect we say art is neither an aider nor a surmounter but only a bare imitator of nature's works, following and counterfeiting her actions and effects, as the marmoset doth many countenances and gestures of man; of which sort are the arts of painting and carving."[34] Painting and sculpture flourished because artists and their patrons had the sense to ignore this kind of criticism; but there are other hazards in the conception of a prefabricated created order.

One of these hazards derived from the slow but steady advance of science. Whatever man creates is essentially a machine, an extension of his personality but with no life or will of its own. The effect of physical science, from Copernicus to Newton, was gradually to depersonalize the cosmos, as the earth was displaced from the centre of the universe and the angels from the guardianship of the planets. By the eighteenth century there was a general tendency to think even of the divine creation in terms of an ingenious and complicated mechanism. At the end of the century a standard textbook on natural theology, Paley's *Evidences of Christianity*, used the analogy of a primitive man picking up a watch on a seashore left by some passing mariner. The primitive was supposed to infer that a watch meant a watchmaker, and similarly we should infer that if a complex world exists, somebody must have designed the complications. Samuel Butler pointed out that this assumed primitive would be much more likely to make a god of the watch, as the Lilliputians thought Gulliver did with his watch when he told them that he seldom did anything without consulting it.[35] But the analogy was regarded as a valid, even an unanswerable argument for a long time, and doubtless still is in some quarters.

The absurdities of the argument from design, more particularly of its illustrations, such as congratulating the Creator for his ingenuity in dividing the orange into sections for convenience in eating, had brought it into discredit even before Darwin's time. One cannot get very far with speculation on the mental level of a small child who assumes that a cat's tail is a specially designed handle for pulling it around. Yet the Darwinian revolution, transferring the designing power from God to a natural process, and showing that the argument from design was a projecting on God of the fact that man designs things, came as a profound shock to many intelligent people. Clearly the artificial myth of a creation had intellectual resources that we have so far not given it credit for.

The account of creation in Genesis is close to a group of sardonic folk tales, some of them much older than the Bible, that tell us how man had immortality nearly in his grasp, but was cheated out of it by malicious or frightened deities. It is hard to hear in its rather casual cadences what St. Paul heard in it, the iron clang of a gate shut forever on human hopes [Romans 5:12]. Neither is it easy to see in it the doctrine that man by his fall opened up a second and lower level of nature. The notion that nature fell with man is necessary to account for all imperfections in nature, ranging from human sin to thorns on the rosebush—an early Canadian Methodist circuit rider speaks of the clouds of mosquitoes he encountered in the New Brunswick forests as "mementoes of the fall."[36] But the fall of nature has to be read into the Genesis account, because it is not there: we are told only that God cursed the ground, a curse he removed after the flood.

In many creation myths the creation starts off with an event that comes much closer than Sophocles' *Oedipus Rex* does to illustrating what Freud means by an Oedipus complex. A sky-father and an earth-mother are locked in connubial sleep until their son separates them, and creates an intervening world of air and light. Similarly in Genesis, light and air (the "firmament") are created first: the firmament separates the waters above from the waters below, and according to the Book of Enoch the waters above are male and the waters below female.[37] In Christianity it is also a Son who does the creating, though no female principle is involved at this stage. The Son, however, is identified with the Word that calls things into being: the Word says *fiat lux*, and light appears. According to Hegel, creation is the symbol of absolute thought passing over into nature, nature being both the contrary and the dialectical complement of thought.[38] Being a philosopher, Hegel assumed that the Biblical Word and the philosopher's thought were essentially the same thing: poets, however, might see in the conception of a creating Word a more versatile power, capable of more things than dialectic. We seem to catch a glimpse, in fact, of a divine consciousness descending into experience. When man falls to a lower level of nature, the divine consciousness follows him there, until the process is completed by the Incarnation, the Word then becoming flesh, identical with human consciousness so far as it is human.

The assumption seems to be here that the term "Word," however metaphorical, has a very real connection with what in ordinary speech we mean by words, the elements of articulate consciousness. There are not many creation myths which give "Word" so central a creative function: one of those that do is the Mayan Central American myth preserved in what is called the Popol Vuh.[39] Here a primordial silence is broken by "the word" which begins the story of creation: of all creatures, man is placed in authority because he alone could use articulate language, in contrast to the grunts and squeals of the beasts. But as man continued to praise his gods, the gods grew restive, and began to wonder if all this articulateness did not threaten their privileged position. Hence, as in many Near Eastern myths, the gods plot to destroy man by a deluge for fear he will become too big for his breeches.

Naturally the Genesis account cannot explicitly present God as jealous or frightened of man, but there is a curious suggestion of it:

> And the Lord God said, Behold, the man is become as one of us, to know good and evil: and now, lest he put forth his hand, and take also of the tree of life, and eat, and live for ever: Therefore the Lord God sent him forth from the garden of Eden, to till the ground from whence he was taken. [Genesis 3:22–3]

Here God seems to be speaking to a council of other gods or angels, expressing a fear of some threat coming from mankind so great that he cannot even finish his sentence. It seems clear that man is in possession of something formidable connected with knowledge, whatever the knowledge of good and evil may imply. Even the Christian version of the myth implies that as soon as God speaks and becomes the Word of God, he has condemned himself to death; as soon as man falls with the power of speech, he becomes the potential murderer of God.

As further rationalized by Christian theology, this situation is explained as follows. Man is born into physical nature, the world of animals and plants, at least as they live at present, and this world is theologically "fallen." It was not the home originally destined for man, and man cannot adjust to it as the animals do. There is a higher order of nature which God intended man to live in, and everything that is good for man, such as law, morality, and religion, helps to raise him towards his own proper level of human nature. Many things are natural to man that are not natural to animals, such as consciousness, wearing clothes, being in a state of social discipline, and the like. In fact on this higher

level of human nature there is really no distinction between nature and
art. The complement of Sir Thomas Browne's principle that nature is the
art of God is the principle that Edmund Burke was still insisting on at
the end of the eighteenth century, that "art is man's nature."[40]

The agencies moving man upwards from his "fallen" state to something closer to his original one certainly include law, religion, morality,
and everything genuinely educational. Milton even defines education as
the process of repairing the fall of Adam by regaining the true knowledge of God.[41] Whether the arts belong among those educational agencies or not was much disputed. But a large body of opinion did see in
this situation a function for the arts, more particularly the verbal arts. In
Sidney's *Defence of Poetry*, for example, published around the time of
Shakespeare's earlier plays, we are told that nature, meaning the lower
or fallen physical order, presents us with a brazen world and the poets
with a golden one; also that art develops a "second nature," being natural to man but only to him.[42] Sidney's principle means that art, specifically poetry, can be tolerated in society only so long as, and so far as, its
function is essentially an idealizing one. The arts form a rhetorical echo
or chorus to the principles of morality and religion. They are there to
persuade the more primitive and emotional side of man of the truth of
what religion and morality teach, using concrete examples as a simpler
analogy to the abstract precepts which are addressed to more mature
minds.

Man, therefore, in the traditional Christian myth, is also born with a
goal ahead of him, the raising of his state to the human level which is
closer to what God intended for him. What is important about this for
our present argument is that this means moving closer to the original
vision of creation, so that creation here appears as the end of the human
journey rather than the beginning of it. The central image of this in our
literature is Dante's *Purgatorio*, where Dante adopts one of the oldest
and most widespread symbolic images in the world, the spiral ascent up
a mountain or tower to heaven, and makes it the journey of Dante himself as he climbs the mountain of purgatory, shedding one of the seven
original sins at each spiral turn. The garden of Eden is at the summit:
that is, Dante is moving backwards in time to his own original state, as
he would have been if there had been no fall of Adam.

What we have now is a vision of two opposing movements, related to
each other in what Yeats would call a double gyre.[43] One is that of a
divine consciousness being surrounded by experience as it descends

from creation to the final identity of incarnation. The other is that of a human consciousness surrounding experience, as it ascends from its "fallen" state towards what it was once designed to be. The ascending spiralling movement in Dante reminds us of Donne's image in his Third Satire:

> On a huge hill,
> Cragged, and steep, Truth stands, and he that will
> Reach her, about must, and about must go;
> And what the hill's suddenness resists, win so. [ll. 79–82]

This human vision of recreation is heavily stressed in modern poetry, as in Yeats's *Sailing to Byzantium*, where the sacred city is a human structure of art and yet preserves a vision of "sages standing in God's holy fire" [l. 17]. Here creation has finally become one with recreation, and the revelation at the end of human effort is also a recognition of something at the beginning.

In the previous chapter I spoke of the association of human creative powers with two visions: the vision of the tradition of art in the past, and the vision of an idealized society projected on the future. Both these visions, I suggested, arise from a partial release of repression, a qualified escape from the encumbrances of ordinary experience. Beyond the *Purgatorio* vision in Dante lies the vision of the *Paradiso*. In the last canto of the *Paradiso*, after casually mentioning the story of the Sibyl who wrote her oracles on scattered leaves, Dante suddenly sees, in the very presence of God, the whole universe "legato con amore in un volume," bound into a single Word with love.[44] As soon as Dante has this vision, it sinks to the lowest depths of repression: he forgot more of it, he says, than man has forgotten of his history since the Argonaut voyage (canto 33). The implication is that immediately following the last vision of paradise, time moves back again to the opening of the *Inferno*, with the poet lost again in a tangled wood, where all the voices of repression, or what Dante calls *letargo*, "lethargy," start clamouring that there can never be any way out. But we are expected to see a bit more and forget less, and in particular to see that at the summit of the human journey back to the creation Dante's great poem merges into the vision of a God who is Alpha and Omega, the beginning and end of all verbal possibilities.

Dante's journey is a journey back to the creation, the journey of a creature returning to his creator, and the initiative for the journey does not come from Dante himself. It is the energy and grace of the descending movement of the divine word, working through such intermediaries as Beatrice, which impel Dante and make what he does possible. Even in the revolutionary Milton, writing over three centuries later than Dante, man still has no real initiative: liberty, for example, in Milton is nothing that man naturally wants, but is something God is determined he shall have. But within another century or so we begin to move into the intellectual climate we still live in now. Here the central characteristic of traditional myth, the model or plan that existed before the beginning of time which repeats itself constantly in present human life, has totally disappeared. The majority of poets and thinkers today see no model or plan, no human essence or general human nature, established at the beginning of things, only various mutations imposed by cultural and social change. In the next chapter I should like to look at this situation and at some of its results and effects.

III

In the first two chapters I have tried to suggest that there are two ways of approaching the notion of creation. There is a traditional myth of creation in which God brings the world into being before man, who is himself a later part of creation. The models of human civilization are supplied by God, who plants a garden and places Adam in it, and who created an angelic city before there were any human cities. This creation was, we are told, perfect, or at least "very good," whatever the source of this value judgment. Man lost touch with the divine creation through his own sin and "fall," and now lives in an alienating nature in consequence. The other approach to creation starts with the vision that man has of a nature recreated in humanized form, the vision recorded in various forms of the arts, ranging from pastoral poetry to architecture. It culminates in a vision of recreation in which man himself participates, and which appears to be in fact the total aim and goal of human creative effort.

I discussed in the second chapter some of the impoverishing qualities of the myth of a special divine creation. In its more rigid form, at least, it assumes that the arts are only feeble and pointless imitations of what God has done infinitely better; it goes into bewildering verbal quibbles in efforts to "reconcile" God's goodness and the world's badness, and it becomes increasingly isolated from everything that the sciences have to tell us about human origins. The myth itself has a built-in explanation for its own sterility. It contains the implication that our minds have been too clouded over by the fall to respond directly to a vision of divine creation, and can only learn something about it on a level that we can fit into our existing mental categories. Thus W.H. Auden makes his Simeon say, in his "Christmas Oratorio" *For the Time Being*, that man's consciousness extends only to the limit of what is traditionally called original sin, of which "it is impossible for him to become conscious because it is itself what conditions his will to knowledge."[45] So, accepting the myth on its own terms, we can never get back to the vision of creation before the fall in our imaginations, however carefully we study the Genesis account. The myth speaks of an angel who guards the tree of life, whose flaming sword symbolizes the blinded mental conditions in which we approach it.

In the previous chapter I tried to show how in Dante the vision of the future goal of human recreation takes the form essentially of a return to God, a return which is also a response to God's initial effort to descend to man. The close of the *Paradiso* is the summing up of centuries of thought in which a view of creation derived from the Bible provided a conception of two levels of nature, an upper level which is man's original home, and is identical with the state of art, and a lower level which is the physical nature of plants and animals, and is not man's home but only his environment. Everything that raises man from his fallen level to his originally designed one involves some degree of returning to his original creation. It is recreation only in the sense that man is included in it: the actual process is God's redemption of man, man doing very little for himself that is of any real use. The whole process of human response, in Christian doctrine, is contained within the Holy Spirit, so that man's redemption is a drama within the persons of the Trinity in which man has a very limited actor's role. As the Holy Spirit guides the church, the doctrine of the Trinity, which is so central to Christian dogma in both Catholic and Protestant contexts, seems to have been, in its historical setting, a doctrine designed primarily to prevent man from slipping out of the grip of the church.

This view is part of an authoritarian structure, and a great deal of its power and influence collapsed under the hammering of the great capitalist revolutions of the eighteenth century. In the nineteenth century we see that the mythological picture which survived Dante for many centuries has finally and totally changed. There is no longer any functional place for a divine creation myth at the beginning of things: there is only human culture, and therefore at most only the sense of human recreation as a distant goal. But human culture and its goals are not guaranteed by anything like a universe of law rooted in the nature of God himself, much less by any will on the part of a God to redeem. On the contrary, they are guaranteed by nothing and are threatened by practically everything. Everywhere we turn in the nineteenth century, we find a construct reminding us of a Noah's ark bearing the whole surviving life of a world struggling to keep afloat in a universal storm. We have Schopenhauer's world of idea threatened by a world of will, Marx's ascendant-class culture threatened by a dispossessed proletariat, Freud's ego clinging to its precarious structure of sanity and threatened by the forces of the libido, Nietzsche's morality threatened by the will to power, Huxley's ethical values threatened by the evolutionary drive. These various thinkers take various attitudes of sympathy or hostility towards the threatening force, but the mythical construct is of much the same shape in every one.

Heidegger says that the first question of philosophy is "why are there things rather than nothing?"[46] but surely there is an even prior question: why objectify the world at all? or, more simply, why do we want to know? It sounds like a psychological question, but it is only partly that. The moment we ask it we are involved in the whole process of what I have called recreation, the constructing of human culture and civilization, and the question turns into something more like: "why is simple existence in the world not good enough for us?" Whatever the answer, the question itself seems to push us away from the Biblical story of a beginning creation, and towards the vision of recreation as a future goal in which our own efforts are involved.

This lands us in the antithesis of the traditional Christian view, a secular attitude in which man as at present constituted has to be regarded as himself the only creator in question. The end of human recreation, then, finds humanity looking at itself in a mirror. This is a somewhat daunting prospect: Narcissus at least had a beautiful face to look at, but the face of humanity that would look out of such a mirror is that of a psychotic ape. I discussed in the first chapter the fact that paranoia is a part of the secular attitude, and the two poles of paranoia are quite obviously present here, as they are in all the Noah's ark constructs just mentioned. If we select certain facts and attend only to them, we are the lords of creation and recreation alike, with an infinite destiny before us: if we select

others, we summon up a vision of hideous and total eclipse in a hydro-
gen bomb Armageddon. The Gospels represent Jesus as continually
casting devils out of the mentally ill: we may regard this as primitive
psychology, and feel that it is unreasonable to expect modern man, living in this advanced century of Hitler and Idi Amin and Mr. Jones of
Guyana,[47] to believe in evil spirits. But in other moods we may recognize that the mentally ill who know that they are possessed by devils are
in a sense the lucky ones, and that the rest of us are similarly possessed
but don't mind. The older construct wore out because it repressed the
sense of human autonomy, the awareness that there are more things in
man than any church or government can recognize or accommodate.
But a purely secular construct, whether humanist or Communist, may
be repressing complementary things.

The first person in the modern world who understood that the older
mythological construct had collapsed was William Blake. He also,
though without direct influence, set up the model for all the nineteenth-
century constructs just mentioned, where cultural values float on a perilous sea. In Blake we begin with the *Songs of Innocence*, which reflect a
child's view of the world, in which the world is controlled by a benevolent Providence, makes human sense and responds to the human need
for love and peace, and was probably made in the first place for the
child's own special benefit. As the child grows older, he enters the
world of "experience," and learns as an adult that the world is not in the
least like this. At that point his personality splits in two. His conscious
waking adult self, which Blake calls Urizen, struggles to adapt itself to
what for it is the real world; his childhood vision, which Blake calls Orc,
is driven underground into what we call the subconscious, where it
forms a boiling volcanic world of mainly sexual and largely frustrated
desire.

A typical song of innocence is the poem called *The Lamb*, where a
child asks a lamb the first question of the catechism, "Who made thee?"
He knows the answer: Jesus made both the lamb and the child himself,
and Jesus is also a lamb and a child, a creator whose creation is "very
good" because it is identifiable with his nature. The counterpart to *The
Lamb* in the *Songs of Experience* is *The Tyger*. Here, instead of one question
promptly and confidently answered, we have a long series of rhetorical
questions without any answers, culminating in the crucial question,
"Did he who made the lamb make thee?" This question also has no
answer, because in the world of the tiger, the world our adult minds

inhabit, the conception of a divine creator makes no sense. The tiger, as Blake sees him, is one of the forms of the angel guarding the tree of life, or what Blake calls the Covering Cherub. Perhaps we can eventually get past him to some vision of creation which will include his glowing and sinister splendour. But such a vision of creation would have to be at the end of a long journey to somewhere on the far side of the tiger. There can be no going back to square one and the child's vision of the lamb. This long-range vision of creation would also have to include and incorporate our own creative powers: we cannot go back either to a ready-made order supplied us by a pre-existing Providence.

But Blake, though he destroys a mythology derived from the Bible, is an intensely Biblical poet himself. He reads the Bible in what he calls its infernal or diabolical sense. According to him the creation of the world, the fall of man, and the deluge of Noah were all the same event, and the fall was a fall in the divine as well as the human nature. Hence what has traditionally been called the creation is actually a ruin, and there is no creation except human recreation, which is the same humanized form of nature that we find in the paradisal, pastoral, agricultural, and urban imagery of the Bible. Blake is far more interested than the Bible itself is, however, in seeing the relevance of the human arts to this transformation of nature. He speaks of poetry, painting, and music as the three forms of conversing with paradise which the flood did not sweep away.[48]

Blake's perspective on the theme of creation in the Bible begins with the Book of Exodus, with Israel in Egypt and a situation of injustice and exploitation already present. God intervenes in this situation, telling Moses from the burning bush that he is about to give himself a name and a highly partisan role in history, taking the side of the oppressed proletariat and holding out to them the goal of a "Promised Land" of their own, which they will have to work towards. Man has to depend at least partly on his own imagination and creative powers to lead him towards the goal symbolized in the Bible by its last book, the Book of Revelation, Blake's favourite Biblical book, where the form of the world that man should be living in is set out at the very end, following visions of appalling disasters before that end is reached. The vision of a created order is never an easily attained vision, but comes out of the depths of human anguish and effort. One very clear example in the Bible is the "Song of the Three Children" in the Apocrypha, meaning the three Jews in Babylon who were flung into Nebuchadnezzar's fiery furnace because they would not abjure their faith. It was from the midst of the fire that they sang their hymn of praise to God for his beautiful world, just as the hymns of praise in the Psalms and elsewhere come out of Israel's deliverance from the "furnace of iron" which is what Egypt is called by Solomon (1 Kings 8:51).

In Blake's illustrations to the Book of Job, made towards the end of his life, the same attitude to the structure and imagery of the Bible is equally clear. What the Book of Job seems to be saying, as we follow its argument through the deadlocks caused first by Job's three friends and then by Elihu, is that God himself intervenes in the discussion to convict Job of ignorance. He asks Job a series of rhetorical questions about whether he was present at the original creation or could do any of the things then done. Job wasn't and couldn't, and God seems to regard this as a triumphant argument in favour of the wisdom of his ways and the folly of Job's. For Blake, however, God is not indulging in crass bullying: he is telling Job that how he got in his situation is less important than how he is to get out of it again. Job is being pushed away from the creation and all efforts to find his way back to a first cause, and encouraged to look in the opposite direction, where he can see the alienating forms of nature, symbolized by the Behemoth and Leviathan who appear at the end, as the sources of the repressions, internal and external, which are preventing him from seeing his own original birthright.

Blake's reading of the Bible is so deeply rooted in the structure and imagery of the Bible that it is perhaps worth asking what principle his reading is based on. We cannot read far in the Bible, of course, without becoming aware of the importance of all the standard figures of speech, of which the most important is metaphor. In metaphor, we have two points of verbal reference existing together: "this is that." But there are also at least two figures of speech that exist in time. The more familiar of these is causality, which may be suggested by some things that go on in nature, but as a way of arranging words is a rhetorical figure of speech. The verbal progression in causal writing is normally forward from cause to effect: this becomes that, or, this results from that. But the mental operations preceding the writing out of the causal sequence move backwards. The causal thinker is confronted by a mass of phenomena which he can understand only by thinking of them as effects, after which he searches for their preceding causes. The movement backwards reminds us of, and may even be connected with, Plato's conception of knowledge as recollection [*Meno*, 81c–d]. Present things are understood by being related to past things in such a way that cognition becomes the same thing as re-cognition, awareness that a present effect is a past cause in another form. Causality is, of course, an essential basis of both scientific and metaphysical thinking, and its verbal expression is that of continuous prose, which seems to have been developed mainly for the purpose of putting causality into verbal structures.

The Bible is based mainly on another figure of speech which also moves in time, but in the opposite direction from causality. This is the figure traditionally called typology.[49] In the Christian view of the Bible, everything that happens in the Old Testament is a "type" or "figure" of which the New Testament provides the "antitype" or revealed meaning. Thus Paul (Romans 5:14) speaks of Adam as a *typos* of Christ, and 1 Peter 3:21 speaks of Christian baptism as the *antitypos* of the story of the flood. Such typology is not confined to the Christian perspective: the Old Testament, from a Jewish point of view, is quite as typological without the New Testament as with it, and its antitypes are still the restoration of Israel and the coming of the Messiah, though the context of these events is different from that of Christianity.

Typology is clearly not, like causality, anything that can be linked to a scientific or philosophical procedure. It belongs in the area indicated by such words as faith, hope, and vision. It has some affinities with allegory: the stories or myths of the Old Testament become types or parables of existential truths, and many parts of the Old Testament, such as the ceremonial law, have usually been read allegorically by Christians. But the normal structure of allegory, an imaginary narrative paralleled with the moral precepts which are its "real meaning," does not fit the Bible, where both Testaments are concerned with actual people and events. What typology really is is a vision of history, or more accurately of historical process. It insists that for all the chaos and waste in human effort, nevertheless historical events, or some of them, are going somewhere and meaning something. Our modern belief in historical process, whether it takes a democratic or a Marxist form, is an outgrowth of the cultural legacy of the Bible.

In the nineteenth century the conception of evolution suggested certain analogies in human life that gave us a new form of typological thinking. This was because evolution was interpreted purely from the human point of view. Evolution, as we see it, did the best it possibly could when it finally produced us, and whatever more it can do it can do only through us. Hence the kind of typology symbolized by science fiction and by all the forecasts of the future based on present technology: everything we can do now is a type of what we shall be able to do in the future. I spoke a moment ago of the manic-depressive insanity of these and similar attitudes as they shuttle wildly from dreams of unqualified progress to nightmares of unqualified disaster.

Kierkegaard wrote a small book on *Repetition* in which he proposed to adopt this term as a characteristic of Christian philosophy, one which is thrown forward to the future and is at once a contrast and a complement to the Platonic view of knowledge as recollection of the past. The Christian repetition, Kierkegaard says, finds its final formulation in the apocalyptic promise "Behold, I make all things new" [Revelation 21:5]. It seems to me that Kierkegaard's idea is derived from, as it is certainly connected with, the typological structure of the Bible. In any case the typology of the Bible links it to history in a way impossible for paganism, which remains based on the recurring cycles of nature. To use fairly familiar terms in a slightly different context, Biblical mythology is diachronic, pagan mythology synchronic. The diachronic dimension makes it possible for personality to emerge in Biblical mythology. Jesus and Adonis are both dying gods, with very similar cults and imagery attached to them, but Jesus is a person and Adonis is not, however many human figures may have represented him. Nietzsche drew from evolution a diachronic vision of human self-transcendence which he called the Superman.[50] But his preference for the synchronic Dionysus over the diachronic Christ forced him to enclose his Superman in a framework of identical recurrence which for me, and I should imagine for others too, totally destroys the dynamic of the conception.

At the same time typology cannot preserve its vitality indefinitely unless it keeps its antitypes in the future. By making the Old Testament a historical process fulfilled in the coming of Christ, Christianity was in danger of losing this vitality as that event receded into the past. A "Second Coming" or future transcendence of history had to grow up along with the doctrine of the Incarnation, and is very prominent in every part of the New Testament itself, but had to lead an increasingly furtive existence as the authority of the Church grew and history, like the Marxist state, continued to fail to wither away. What happened, in practice if not in theory, was that the entire Bible, including the New Testament, became a type or parable of which the antitype or revealed form was the structure of Christian doctrine as taught by the church. The role of the doctrine of the Trinity in this process has already been considered.

Some of the Protestant Reformers attempted to cut away this super-structure of doctrine in favour of a more direct dialogue with the Bible. The degree of their success does not concern us here, except for one major work of literature involved with it, Milton's *Paradise Lost*. We have suggested that an artificial creation myth, with its implication that everything man can do has already been done by God on an infinitely superior plane of reality, is a somewhat hampering one for the human creative impulse. Why, then, did the instinct of so very great a poet lead him in precisely the direction of retelling the story of creation in Genesis, and to retell it expressly for the purpose of rationalizing it, or, as he says, to justify the ways of God to men? It is an attempt to answer this question that takes up the rest of what I have to say, although the answer will take us a long way from Milton.

The basis of Milton's thinking is Paul's conception of the Gospel as the fulfilment, or what we are calling the antitype, the revealed form, of the Old Testament Law. The external acts prescribed for the specific nation of Israel become what Milton calls "shadowy types" of an individual's inner state of mind.[51] Again, the Law is the myth, the type, the parable; the Gospel is the existential reality that the Law symbolizes. Similarly, the story of creation functions as a type or model of that inner state of mind in which Adam, at the end of the poem, begins the long climb up towards his original home again. Eden as an external environment disappears, to reappear as the "paradise within thee, happier far" which is held out to Adam as a final hope.[52] Once more, the creation myth is a seed that comes to its own real fruition in a recreative effort in which Adam is involved. Adam is, of course, the representative human being, or, more precisely, the representative reader of the Bible. The Bible is in effect being read to him through the last two books of the poem.

It may sound fatuous to say that *Paradise Lost* was written for the sake of its readers, but Milton's more discerning critics have always recognized that there is something very distinctive about the role of the reader in that poem. Many critics have asked who the hero of *Paradise Lost* is, and have given various answers: Satan, Adam, Christ. But there is a lurking feeling that the question is somehow inappropriate. In Milton's theology the supreme authority is not the Bible but the reader of the Bible, the person who understands it and possesses what Milton calls the word of God in the heart.[53] From one point of view we can say that this is not the reader as human being, but the Holy Spirit within the reader, so that Milton is keeping the whole operation wrapped up inside God, as his orthodox contemporaries did. But there is enough vagueness and indecision in Milton's view of the Holy Spirit to make it clear that he is moving in the modern direction of regarding the reader, simply as human being, as the real focus of his poem and the final aim of all his "justifying" of the ways of God.

In my first chapter I quoted a passage from Oscar Wilde's essay "The Critic as Artist." This essay builds up an argument that seems to make an exaggerated and quite unrealistic importance out of the reader of literature, the critic being the representative reader. He is paralleled with the artist in a way that seems to give him an equal share at least in what the artist is doing. Here again Wilde is writing from the point of view of a later generation. For many centuries the centre of gravity in literature was the hero, the man whose deeds the poet celebrated. As society slowly changed its shape, the hero modulated to the "character," and in Wilde's day it was still the creation of character, as one sees it so impressively in Shakespeare, Dickens, and Browning, that was the primary mark of poetic power. At the same time the Romantic movement had brought with it a shift of interest from the hero to the poet himself, as not merely the creator of the hero but as the person whose inner life was the real, as distinct from the projected, subject of the poem. There resulted an extraordinary mystique of creativity, in which the artist became somehow a unique if not actually superior species of human being, with qualities of prophet, genius, wise man, and social leader. Wilde realized that in a short time the centre of gravity in literature and critical theory would shift again, this time from the poet to the reader. The dividing line in English literature is probably *Finnegans Wake,* where it is so obvious that the reader has a heroic role to play.

The literary critic of 1980 finds himself in the midst of a bewildering array of problems which seem to focus mainly on the reader of a text. What is a text, and what does a reader do to it when he reads it? Where is the text—in the book, in the reader's mind, or lost somewhere between? If a work of literature is read and appreciated centuries later than it was written, what is the social context of its meaning? Some of these questions may be peripheral, or resolved only by some kind of dead-end paradox, but the issue they relate to is still a central one. It seems to me that, once again, some such conception as that of "recreation" is needed to make sense of such problems. Every reader recreates what he reads: even if he is reading a letter from a personal friend he is still recreating it into his own personal orbit. Recreation of this sort always involves some kind of translation. To read is invariably to translate to some degree, however well one knows the language of what is read.

Let us take translation in its customary sense of changing a structure from one language to another, as a special case of recreation. The question of translation is peculiarly important in the Christian tradition, which has had a close connection with translation from the beginning. Moslem and Jewish scholarship are, inevitably, bound up with the linguistic features of the Arabic of the Koran and the Hebrew of the Old Testament respectively. But the New Testament was written in a *koine* Greek unlikely to have been the native language of its authors; and when those authors used the Old Testament, whatever their knowledge of Hebrew, they normally relied on the Septuagint Greek version. Then for over a thousand years the only Bible available in Western Europe was a Latin Bible, and modern movements from Luther to the missionary work of the nineteenth century brought with them a strong impulse to translate the Bible into every known tongue.

Everyone concerned with the study of literature knows how much of translation is a settling for the second best. This is most obvious in major poetry, where a translation has to be a miracle of tact without claiming to be a replacement for the original. The particular problem we are concerned with, however, is of a different kind. The cynical Italian proverb *traditore traduttore*, a translator is a traitor, has two points of reference. Granted sufficient scholarship, a translator does not necessarily betray his text: what he always does and must betray is his own cultural orbit, the socially conditioned limits within which he can operate. The English reader looking for translations of Homer can find an exuberant Elizabethan Homer in Chapman, a periwigged Homer in Pope, a Gothic-revival Homer in the Loeb Classics, a colloquial modern Homer in the Penguins. What he will never get in this world is simply Homer in English.

Similarly with the Bible. There may be something of Paul in the 1611 translation: "Charity suffereth long, and is kind; charity envieth not; charity vaunteth not itself, is not puffed up" [1 Corinthians 13:4]. But we also hear the anxieties of 1611, when the clouds of civil war were gathering and the British Empire was getting started with settlements in America and the founding of the East India Company, and where ambition and aggression seemed the most dangerous foes of charity. In fact Shakespeare's Wolsey, denouncing ambition at roughly the same time, employs a very similar figure to "is not puffed up" when he speaks of himself as having ventured beyond his depth like little boys swimming on bladders (*Henry VIII*, 3.2.359). There may be something of Paul too in the modern Phillips translation: "This love of which I speak is slow to lose patience—it looks for a way of being constructive. It is not possessive: it is neither anxious to impress nor does it cherish inflated ideas of its own importance."[54] But there are also the anxieties of middle-class democracy in these cadences, of a world where charity has a good deal to do with being a co-operative committee man.

At this point, translation merges into the wider question of recreation. What can be translated is loosely called "sense," the relation of many signifiers to a common signified. Each reader, translator or recreator, renders his text into a form determined largely by his own cultural context. To return to the terms of the first chapter, the arts form an extension of our own past, but find their meaning for us in our present situation. That present situation contains elements of vision which we project on the future, and those elements form the recreating aspect of our reading. Every work of literature that we continue to read and study meant something to its own time and something quite different to us. Both poles of understanding have to be kept in mind. If we disregard its original historical context, we are simply kidnapping it into the orbit of our own concerns; if we disregard its relevance to ourselves, we are leaving it unrevived in the morgue of the past. But if we keep the two together and in balance, we are stabilizing a tradition, and are engaged in a process which includes ourselves and yet is something bigger than ourselves. One end of this process is a creation, and the other end is a recreation.

There is another aspect of recreation, however, which expands into the whole history of language itself as a form of human communication and consciousness. We mentioned Homer, who is one of the purest poets we have, because his language comes from a time before abstract or conceptual thinking had developed. Homer's vocabulary, as Onians's monumental study of it, *Origins of European Thought*, shows us at length, is astonishingly concrete. Such conceptions as anger, cunning, thought, emotion, are all solidly anchored in parts of the physical body, such as the diaphragm and the lungs. This means that essentially Homer's vocabulary was not metaphorical to him, but must be to us. The metaphor is the figure of speech that expresses most clearly the sense of an identity between subjective and objective worlds, and Homer comes from a time when no very clear line was drawn between them. Since then, there have been several other developments in language, one of them the descriptive language of our own day, which is based on a clear separation between subject and object, between element of personality and element of nature. It is one of the functions of literature in our day, more particularly of poetry, to keep reviving the metaphorical habit of mind, the primitive sense of identity between subject and object which is most clearly expressed in the pagan "god," who is at once a personality and a natural image.

This means that the cultural affinities of poetry are with the primitive and archaic, a fact about poetry which has been recognized from early times. The metaphors of poetry take us back to a world of undifferentiated energy and continuous presence. Take these lines from a well known hymn:

> His chariots of wrath
> The deep thunderclouds form,
> And dark is His path
> On the wings of the storm.[55]

We may not be deeply moved by these lines—I am not presenting them as major poetry—but we could be by other lines as far removed from descriptive or objective meaning as they are. If we took them "literally," whatever that means, we should have an intolerably crude notion of the God they attempt to describe. But, of course, we do not take them in that way; we take them as poetic metaphor. Like other hymns, this one draws on the Bible, and in one of the Psalms it is said that God rode upon the back of a cherub, and did fly (Psalm 18:10; cf. 2 Samuel 22:11). But there the statement is still poetic metaphor. Some mythical rationalizers might want to carry the image back to a society so confused about nature that they would "believe" that thunder indicated a God riding around the sky in some sort of private airplane. But it is not necessary to assume that any such society ever existed: the statement is *radically* metaphorical. It is a way, perhaps the only type of way, that language has of conveying the sense of a numinous presence in nature, and that is where we stop. We notice incidentally that in these lines the Christian God is being represented by *a* god. In spite of the achievement of Dante and Milton, poets on the whole feel easier with pagan gods than with the Christian God, because pagan gods are ready-made metaphors, and go into poetry with the minimum of adjustment.

We think of the creation story in Genesis as essentially a poetic account. For Milton it was not a poetic account, yet he deliberately poeticizes it. By doing so he turned it into an intricate body of metaphors, conveying the sense of a spiritual force that includes man but does not originate from him. It is particularly in the account of creation itself, in book 7, that we realize how the poetic paraphrase renders our sense of creation, not in an ornamental or sophisticated form, but in a far more primitive form than the original does:

> Forth flourished thick the clust'ring vine, forth crept
> The smelling gourd, up stood the corny reed
> Embattelled in her field: add the humble shrub,
> And bush with frizzled hair implicit: last
> Rose, as in dance, the stately trees. [bk. 7, ll. 320–4]

The recreation of poetry and its metaphorical use of language leads to two principles, one specific, the other universal. First, it reveals the narrowness of our ordinary descriptive use of language. Nietzsche's statement "God is dead,"[56] which has been so widely accepted, even in theological circles, is primarily a linguistic statement, or, more precisely, a statement about the limitations of language. The word "God" is a noun, which within our present descriptive framework of language means that God has to belong to the category of things and objects. We may agree that God is dead as the subject or object of a human predicate. But perhaps using the word "God" as a noun in this way is merely a fallacy of the type that Whitehead calls misplaced concreteness.[57] We note that in the burning bush story in Exodus, God, though he also gives himself a name, defines himself as "I am that I am" [3:14], which scholars say would be better rendered as "I will be what I will be." Buckminster Fuller wrote a book called *I Seem to be a Verb*, and perhaps God is a verb too, not simply a verb of asserted existence but a verb expressing a process fulfilling itself. Such a use of language revives an archaic mode of language, and yet is oddly contemporary with, for example, the language of the nuclear physicists, who no longer think of their atoms and electrons as things but as something more like traces of processes.

Then again, the traditional doctrine of divine creation, we said, is creation with what we ordinarily mean by words. We have tried to show how the recreating of language attaches man to words in such a way that words become something much bigger than he is, hence we can well understand such thinkers as Heidegger and others when they suggest that language is not a machine or invention that man uses, but something that, in its full range, uses man, man being ultimately the servant rather than the master of language.[58] There is a further suggestion that there may be something linked to the human use of words which is a power of human self-transcendence, a step away from the narrow humanism that has to stop with the psychotic ape in the mirror.

There is also the term "spirit," which is so emphasized in the New Testament, with its insistence that the scriptures have to be "spiritually discerned" [1 Corinthians 2:14]. One of the things that "spiritually" must mean in this context is "metaphorically." Thus the Book of Revelation speaks of a "great city, which spiritually is called Sodom and Egypt" and is also identified with the earthly Jerusalem [11:8]. And one wonders, in studying Hegel's *Phenomenology of Spirit*, which has become a text used by Christians and Marxists alike, whether the antithesis of theist and atheist in our day may not be a quarrel of Tweedledee and Tweedledum over a word that neither really understands. For the atheist is still left with personality as the highest category in his cosmos after he has rejected the *theos*.

The terms "Word" and "Spirit," then, may be understood in their traditional context as divine persons able and willing to redeem mankind. They may be also understood as qualities of self-transcendence within man himself, capable of pulling him out of the psychosis that every news bulletin brings us so much evidence for. I am suggesting that these two modes of understanding are not contradictory or mutually exclusive, but dialectically identical. Certainly the goal of human recreation, whenever we try to visualize it, bears a curious resemblance to the traditional vision of divine creation at the source. As the fully awakened beings in Blake's *Four Zoas* say: "How is it that all things are changd, even as in ancient times?" [p. 138, l. 40].

To extend the meanings of "word" and "spirit" into areas beyond the human seems to make them into objects of belief. But it seems to me that there are two levels of belief. There is, first, professed belief, what we say we believe, think we believe, believe we believe. Professed belief is essentially a statement of loyalty or adherence to a specific community: what we say we believe defines us as Christians or Moslems or Marxists or whatever. But then there is another level in which our belief is what our actions show that we believe. With some highly integrated people the two levels are consistent. But professed belief, in our world, is pluralistic and competitive. It is characteristic of believing communities, anxious for their solidarity, to set up elaborate structures of faith that ask too much from their adherents in the way of professed belief, forgetting that any belief which cannot become an axiom of behaviour is not merely useless but dangerous. In some respects professed belief is a solid and satisfying basis for a community, yet in our world it seems that it is the worst possible basis for a *secular* community. Whether the community is nominally Catholic or Protestant or Jewish or Moslem or Hindu, every secular state guided by religious principles seems to turn them into a form of devil worship. The same thing is true of Marxism, which when it becomes socially established acquires a religious quality based on the doctrine of the infallibility of the Holy Communist Church. In the Soviet Union, as more recently in China, periodic "thaws," or pretences at democratic tolerance, take place for the purpose of discovering who the really dangerous people are, i.e., the people who do not subscribe to this doctrine of infallibility.

If there is a creative force in the world which is greater than the purely human one, we shall not find it on the level of professed belief, but only on a level of common action and social vision. At this level all beliefs become to some degree partial, not because they are untrue for those who hold them, but because the human mind is finite and the human will corrupt. To work within such a community no one needs to surrender or even compromise with a professed belief. But those whose professed belief is Christian, for example, would be recognizing the supremacy of charity over faith which is part of that faith itself, as well as the Gospel's insistence on "fruits" as the only valid proof of belief. This conception is close to what Blake, in a phrase taken from the Book of Revelation, calls the "Everlasting Gospel,"[59] a conception which implies that the human race already knows what it ought to be thinking and doing, though the voices of repression, made articulate by competing ideologies, keep shouting the knowledge down. They are all voices of Antichrist, whose first act recorded in the Bible was to build the Tower of Babel to the accompaniment of a confusion of tongues.

Every unit is a whole to which various parts are subordinate, and every unit is in turn a part of a larger whole. Religions, theistic or atheistic, are units which define themselves in such a way as to cut off the possibility of their being parts of larger wholes, even when they are compelled to act in that way by expediency. We are perhaps now in a period of history at which this looks more like pride and delusion than like faith. If we could transcend the level of professed belief, and reach the level of a worldwide community of action and charity, we should discover a new creative power in man altogether. Except that it would not be new, but the power of the genuine Word and Spirit, the power that has created all our works of culture and imagination, and is still ready to recreate both our society and ourselves.

5

The Double Mirror

8 April 1981

From Bulletin of the American Academy of Arts and Sciences, 35 (December 1981): 32–41. Two typescripts are in NFF, 1988, box 47, file 4. Originally
given as an address at the American Academy of Arts and Sciences, Boston.
Reprinted in MM, 229–37.

What I want mainly to talk about is my present preoccupation with the
Bible, which I am trying to study in relation to secular literature and criticism. This involves relating it to issues in critical theory, so far as I
understand them. I get a strong impression that many contemporary
critics are talking about the Bible even when they avoid mentioning it.
Many critical issues originated in the hermeneutic study of the Bible;
many critical theories are obscurely motivated by a God-is-dead syn-
drome that also arose from Biblical criticism; many of the principles
advanced by such theorists often seem to me more defensible when
applied to the Bible than they are when applied elsewhere.

The traditional view of the Bible, as we all know, has been that it must
be regarded as "literally" true. This view of "literal" meaning assumes
that the Bible is a transparent medium of words conveying a "true" picture of historical events and conceptual doctrines. It is a vehicle of "revelation," and revelation means that something objective, behind the
words, is being conveyed directly to the reader. It is also an "inspired"
book, and inspiration means that its authors were, so to speak, holy
tape-recorders, writing at the dictation of an external spiritual power.

This view is based on an assumption about verbal truth that needs
examining. Whenever we read anything our minds are moving in two
directions at once. One direction is centripetal, where we establish a

context out of the words read; the other is centrifugal, where we try to remember what the words mean in the world outside. Sometimes the external meanings take on a structure parallel to the verbal structure, and when this happens we call the verbal structure descriptive or non-literary. Here the question of "truth" arises: the structure is "true" if it is a satisfactory counterpart to the external structure it is parallel to. If there is no external counterpart, the structure is said to be literary or imaginative, existing for its own sake, and hence often considered a form of permissible lying. If the Bible is "true," tradition says, it must be a nonliterary counterpart of something outside it. It is, as Derrida would say, an absence invoking a presence,[1] the "word of God" as book pointing to the "word of God" as speaking presence in history. It is curious that although this view of Biblical meaning was intended to exalt the Bible as a uniquely sacrosanct book, it in fact turned it into a servomechanism, its words conveying truths or events that by definition were more important than the words were. The written Bible, this view is really saying, is a concession to time: as Socrates says of writing in the *Phaedrus*, it is intended only to call to mind something that has passed away from presence [274–5]. The real basis of the Bible, for all theologians down to Karl Barth at least, is the presence represented by the phrase "God speaks."

We have next to try to understand how this view arose. In a primitive society (whatever we mean by primitive), there is a largely undifferentiated body of verbal material, held together by the sense of its importance to that society. This material tells the society what the society needs to know about its history, religion, class structure, and law. As society becomes more complex, these elements become more distinct and autonomous. Legend and saga develop into history; stories, sacred or secular, develop into literature; a mixture of practical knowledge and magic develops into science. Society struggles to contain these elements within its overriding concerns, and tries to impose on them a structure of authority that will keep them unified, as Christianity did in medieval times. About two generations ago there was a fashion for crying up the Middle Ages as a golden age in which all aspects of culture were unified by common sentiments and beliefs. Similar developments, with a similar appeal, are taking place today in Marxist countries.

However, artists, historians, scientists, and theologians find increasingly that they make discoveries within the growing structure of their discipline, and that they owe a loyalty to that structure as well as to the concerns of society. Thus astronomers had to advance a heliocentric view of the solar system even when social anxieties demanded a geocentric one; historians of Britain had to reject the Arthurian story although popular feeling clung to it. Social authority gives ground in some areas more willingly than others. The presence pointed to by the Bible was, in practice, identified with a theological interpretation which was the right interpretation, to be understood before the Bible itself could be understood. These interpretations took different linguistic forms before and after the Reformation, but were always primarily structures of authority, intended to impose a unity on believers that was really uniformity, in public expression at least.

Such interpretations grew up partly because the verbal texture of the Bible is very different from that of descriptive writing, as a glance at it shows. A descriptive writer who aims at conveying some truth beyond his verbal structure avoids figures of speech, because all figuration emphasizes the centripetal aspect of words, and belongs either to the poetic or to the rhetorical categories. The Bible is full of explicit metaphors, hyperboles, popular etymologies, puns, in fact every figurative device possible, many of which are defined in dictionaries simply as errors of grammar or logic. But the vices of grammar and logic are often the virtues of poetry, and while no one would call the Bible a poetic structure, it has all the characteristics of poetry, which accounts for most of its very specific literary influence. Its narratives range from legend to partisan history, but historical fact as fact is nowhere marked off in it.

In short, the Bible is explicitly antireferential in structure, and deliberately blocks off any world of presence behind itself. In Christianity, everything in the Old Testament is a "type" of which the "antitype" or existential reality is in the New Testament. This turns the Bible into a double mirror reflecting only itself to itself. How do we know that the Gospel is true? Because it fulfils the prophecies of the Old Testament. But how do we know that the Old Testament prophecies are true? Because they are fulfilled by the Gospel. Is there any evidence for the existence of Jesus as a major historical figure outside the New Testament? None really, and the writers of the New Testament obviously preferred it that way. As long as we assume a historical presence behind the Bible to which it points, the phrase "word of God," as applied both to the Bible and the person of Christ, is only a dubious syllepsis. In proportion as the presence behind disappears, it becomes identified with the book, and the phrase begins to make sense. As we continue to study the significance of the fact that the Bible is a book, the sense of presence shifts from what is behind the book to what is in front of it.

As for "inspiration," if there is one thing that Biblical scholarship has established beyond reasonable doubt, it is that authorship, inspired or not, counts for very little in the Bible. The third Gospel is traditionally supposed to have Luke for its author, but the Gospel itself is an edited and composite document, with nothing, beyond perhaps the first four verses, of which Luke is likely to be in any real sense the author. Editing and compiling are highly self-conscious activities, and the word "inspiration" cannot add much to study of them. If the Bible is inspired in any sense, all the glossing and editing and splicing and conflating activities must be inspired too. There is no way of distinguishing the voice of God from the voice of the Deuteronomic redactor. This suggests a qualification of the view that Biblical language is poetic, however, as the poetic and the inspired are often popularly supposed to be related.

Poetic language is closely associated with rhetorical language, as both make extensive use of figures of speech. The Bible uses a language that is as poetic as it can be without actually becoming a poem. But it is not a poem; it is written in a mode of rhetoric, though it is rhetoric of a special kind, called by the theologian Bultmann, among others, *kerygma* or "proclamation." In a last effort to evoke the ghost of the referential, Bultmann says that to see this *kerygma* in the Gospels we must get rid of myth, which he regards as an obstacle to it.[2] To a critic, however, myth means primarily *mythos* or narrative, more particularly the kind of self-contained narrative which is meant by the English word "story" in contrast to history. Such myth is the only possible vehicle of *kerygma*, and as every syllable of the Gospels is written in the language of myth, efforts to "demythologize" the Gospels would soon end by obliterating them.

The literal meaning of the Bible, then, if we are right, must be a mythical and metaphorical meaning. It is only when we are reading as we read poetry that we can take the word "literal" seriously, accepting everything given us without question. There may be meanings beyond the literal, but that is where we start. In teaching the Bible I stress the unity and consistency of its narrative and imagery, and at some point a student will ask: "Why can't we have it both ways? Why not a body of narrative and imagery that is also a definitive replica of truths beyond itself?" The answer is that description is a subordinate function of words. Even one word is a sign and not a thing: two or three words begin to form grammatical fictions like those of subject and predicate.

What words do with greatest power and accuracy is hang together. Of course there are verbal structures that are based on description and reference, but the Bible is too deeply rooted in the nature of words to be one of them. At a certain point of intensity a choice must be made between figurative and descriptive language, and the Bible's choice of the figurative is written on every page of it.

Questions of Biblical criticism, we see, are models for many critical questions about secular literature. When I began the study of literature as a student, it was generally assumed that the critic's duty was to work out an "interpretation" of the poem before him, and that when all the really expert critics compared their interpretations a consensus would emerge that would be, more or less, the right way to look at the poem. The fact that no such consensus ever emerged was a problem to faith, but nothing more. I now feel that the word "interpretation" is a red herring: to be given a poem and look round for an interpretation of it is like being given the kernel of a nut and looking round for a shell, which seems to me as perverse an approach to poems as it is to nuts. What I do think is that the text before us is something other than ourselves, that we have to struggle with it as Jacob did with the angel [Genesis 32:24–32], but that there is nothing to come up from behind, like the Prussian army at Waterloo, to assist us. The otherness is the text itself. However, we are not quite as much on our own as Jacob was: there are other critics, and we do become increasingly aware that a text is the focus of a community.

This does not mean that all critics are going to agree any better than before, but that in their disagreements an element that we may call the egocentric can get gradually diminished. It was Oscar Wilde who defined, in two almost unreasonably brilliant essays, the situation of criticism today. One was called "The Decay of Lying," which attacked the view that literature gains dignity and validity from its reference to something beyond itself. The word "lying" calls attention to the fact that literature turns its back on all such reference. The other was called "The Critic as Artist," which promoted the reader to a co-creator with the poet, completing the operation that the poet is compelled to leave half done. By a "critic" Wilde meant, I think, a serious and representative reader, who knows that his response is socially and culturally conditioned, but is none the less capable of weeding out of that response an egocentric element, such as, "I don't like the way this poem ends because if I were writing it I wouldn't end it that way." I have always connected this egocentric element with the conception of the critic as judge or evaluator. It is a commonplace now that observation is affected by the observer, even in the most quantitative sciences, and the necessity for observing the observer is now fairly acute in literary criticism. What I think happens is a struggle for identity in the course of which the false subject or ego and the false object or the referential signified get thrown out together.

In ordinary experience we think of ourselves as subjective, and of everything else as objective. We also tend to think of the objective as the centre of reality and the subjective as the centre of illusion. But then we enter a theatre, and find that an illusion is presented to us on the stage objectively, as a sense datum. We could search the wings and dressing rooms forever without finding reality behind it: whatever is there that is not the play is in front of it, in the mood created in the audience. What reality there is seems to be emerging from the coinciding of two illusions. Thus in *The Tempest*, Prospero takes a group of people living in a reality so low as to be a form of illusion, soaks them in a different kind of illusion featuring hallucinations and elemental spirits, and sends them back home on a much higher level of reality.

We referred to Socrates' remark in the *Phaedrus* that the inventor of writing was told by his critics that his was not an art of memory (*mneme*) but of reminding (*hypomnomena*). What his critics did not realize was that the act of recalling is a far more vivid and intense experience than memory itself. When Elizabethan critics used Horace's phrase about poetry as a "speaking picture,"[3] they implied that poetry gives us, not the familiar remembered thing, but the glittering intensity of the summoned-up hallucination. On this basis we can perhaps understand the long-standing association between written books and the art of magic, another theme of *The Tempest*. Without his books, says Caliban, Prospero would be as much of a sot as I am [3.2.92–3]. Magic establishes a charmed circle where spirits can be invoked, held, and commanded by words, and in this unity of word and spirit we have perhaps the most genuine form of an altered state of consciousness.

It has often been noted that the question of human freedom cannot be worked out on the basis of the relation of man and nature alone. As our view of the world becomes more objective, the question arises of what is not objective. For everything we see in ourselves is objective also. What is left can only be, as I think, our participation in a community of language, whether the language is that of words, mathematics, or one of the other arts. This is all that can really be distinguished from the objective world. As Nietzsche said, nature has no laws, only necessities;[4] and just as we find our conception of necessity in the physical world, so we find in the languages of words and numbers and arts the charter of our freedom.

We notice that while the Bible ends with a vision of the end of time and of history as we have known it, it is a remarkably open ending. It ends with an invitation to "come" or approach, under the image of drinking the water of life. The implication is that its reality starts in the reader's mind as soon as he finishes reading. Milton speaks of the Word of God in the heart, the possession of the Word by the reader, as having an authority higher than that of the Bible itself.[5] Milton was not concerned about the chaos of "private judgment," the individual setting himself up as the measure of all things, because in his view the real reader was not the ego but the Holy Spirit, who would unite all readers without forcing them into uniformity.

Once again the Biblical principle is an analogy to procedures in secular criticism. If we say that authorship, inspiration, historical accuracy, and the like are not important in the Bible, what is important? One thing that seems to me to be so is the conception of canon, the idea of a collection of books unified, not by consistency of argument or doctrine—there are no true rational arguments in the Bible—but of vision and imagery. There are no definable boundaries between canonical and uncanonical, but there are different areas or contexts, where some things are closer to us than others.

Culture begins, we said, in a largely undifferentiated mixture of religious, historical, legal, and literary material which is important to the concerns of its society. It seems to be ending today in a vast chaos of *écriture* where there are no boundary lines between literature and anything else in words. Of course there are no boundary lines; but I think that when the present plague of darkness has lifted we shall start making discriminations again. We shall, I think, even re-establish the referential for the verbal structures that clearly require it, which would still exclude literature and the Bible. But our new discriminations will be contexts and not delimited areas. Such a word as "comedy" means something intelligible, and has conveyed an intelligible meaning for thousands of years. But there is no such "thing" as comedy: it cannot be defined as an essence which excludes other essences. We can express only its general range and ambience, and our feeling that sometimes we are inside it and at other times on its periphery or outside it.

Similarly, there is a canon in secular as in sacred literature, though there is no way of establishing such a canon on a basis of value judgments. In those passages in the New Testament where the Bible has become self-conscious enough to comment on itself, we are told that the word of God is a two-edged sword, dividing things and not reconciling things [Hebrews 4:12]. But this can hardly mean a dialectical instrument of the Hegelian kind, where every statement is a half-truth implying its own opposite. The real division is rather between the two worlds of spiritual life and spiritual death, and this division is made by a use of language that bypasses the argumentative and the aggressive. Much the same thing is true of secular literature. The word "classic" as applied to a work of literature means primarily a work that refuses to go away, that remains confronting us until we do something about it, which means also doing something about ourselves.

The main difference is one of initiative. The rhetoric of proclamation is a welcoming and approaching rhetoric, in contrast to rhetoric where the aim is victory in argument or drawing an audience together into a more exclusive unit. It speaks, according to Paul, the language of love, which he says is likely to last longer than most forms of communication [1 Corinthians 13:1, 8]. Wherever there is love there is sexual symbolism, and the rhetoric of the Bible, which seeks out its reader, is traditionally a male rhetoric, all its readers, whether men or women, being symbolically female. In secular literature, where the category is purely poetic, the sexual symbolism is reversed: there it is the poetic artefact that is symbolically female, the daughter of a Muse. These are metaphors, and of course any metaphor can be misleading or confusing. But metaphor was made for man and not man for metaphor; or, as my late and much beloved colleague Marshall McLuhan used to say, man's reach should exceed his grasp, or what's a metaphor?[6]

6

Repetitions of Jacob's Dream

13 October 1983

From the typescript in NFF, 1988, box 47, file 5. A typescript with holo-graph corrections is in NFF, 1991, box 39, file 4. First printed in EAC, *37–49. Originally given as an address at the National Gallery in Ottawa in connection with an exhibition entitled "Ladders to Heaven: Our Judeo-Christian Heritage." The exhibition, which ran from 19 August to 16 October, consisted of artefacts such as seals, ivories, mosaics, and ceramics from the Middle East and the Mediterranean region for the period 5000* B.C. *to ca.* A.D *500.*

What immediately attracted me about this impressive exhibition was its inspired choice of title, "Ladders to Heaven," and I thought that that would be an appropriate subject for me. As a literary critic, I have a particular interest in images and symbols that are found all over the world from ancient times to the present day, and the ladder, with its various relatives, is one of those images. The primary reference in this particular use of "ladders to heaven" is to Jacob's dream in the Book of Genesis [28:10–17]. This story tells us that Jacob came to a place called Luz, and lay down to sleep there, with his head resting on a stone. If we are to believe tradition, the stone still lies under the throne at West-minster. In his sleep he had a vision of a ladder, as it is called in the Authorized Version, stretching from earth to heaven, with angels ascending and descending on it. When he awoke in the morning he said, according to the same translation, "How dreadful is this place!" [28:17]. He meant, of course, how holy is this place, as the idea of the holy originates in a sense of awe or dread. Jacob called the place of his dream the house of God and the gate of heaven, and vowed to build an altar there. He also changed its name from Luz to Bethel, meaning house of God.

Several things about this story strike us at once. First, the antecedents of such a story would most naturally relate to a pre-Israelite sacred site, featuring either a sacred stone or a group of stones. In this earlier version the stone would probably have been much larger, perhaps part of a megalithic monument of a type still found in that part of the world as elsewhere. Second, the ladder that Jacob saw in his dream was a ladder *from* heaven rather than to it: it was not a human construction at all. Third, if angels were going both up and down on it, it was clearly more of a staircase than a ladder. Finally, although Jacob calls the place the house of God, he does not build a temple there, merely an altar. The ladder is the symbol of a connection between earth and heaven, but the story emphasizes that the real connection is made only by God, and the human response to it is a correspondingly modest one.

So the story, as it reaches us, is the acceptable version, as the Bible sees it, of an image found in all the ancient religions of the Near East. In Mesopotamian cities the temple to the god of the city would normally be in the centre and would be the highest building: it would therefore be, symbolically, the connecting link between the earth we live on and the world of the gods, which is almost invariably assumed to be "up there," metaphorically at least, in the sky. In Mesopotamia such temples took the form of what is known as a ziggurat, a building of several storeys, usually seven, with each storey recessed from the one below it. The different storeys were also connected by stairs, usually winding stairs, so that the ascent was in a spiral. There were winding stairs in Solomon's temple, even though it was only three storeys high. Herodotus tells us of more elaborate temples in Persia, where there were also seven storeys and seven flights of steps, coloured differently to symbolize the seven known planets, including the sun and moon.[1] At the top was the chamber in which the bride of the god was laid, awaiting his descent. The story of Danae, shut up in a tower but impregnated all the same by Zeus in the form of a shower of gold, seems connected with the same pattern.

In Egypt the step pyramids had a similar symbolic reference, and in the Pyramid Texts the ascent of a stairway was a crucial stage in the Pharaoh's journey after death to the realm of the gods. In mounting a ladder it is of course the last step which is the supremely important one, and we are reminded of this by the Greek word for ladder, *klimax*, which has become our word "climax." The judge of the dead in Egypt was the god Osiris, and one of the earliest epithets for him was "the god at the top of the staircase."[2] In these so-called "heathen" countries, we notice, the emphasis is on the human construct: man builds the temple, or tower, in the form of something that points to heaven and suggests a final entry into it. This is the emphasis that is ridiculed in another story in the Book of Genesis, the story of the Tower of Babel [11:1–9], whose builders thought to reach heaven but had to abandon their project when their speech was broken into different languages. The Book of Genesis derives the word Babel from *balal*, confusion, but Babel actually means what Jacob called the place of his vision, the gate of God.

Neither Babel nor the stairway seen at Bethel are explicitly said to be spiral, but that is how they appear in Brueghel's painting of Babel and Blake's of Jacob's dream. So here we have a cluster of images, ladders, towers, winding or spiral stairs, all with the general symbolic sense of reaching a higher state of existence from the ordinary one. The earth we live on has always been thought of mythologically as "middle earth," with a world above it and another below it. Sometimes the building or tower becomes a mountain, or the tower is intended to represent a mountain, and sometimes it is a tree, the world tree which is also the *axis mundi*, the vertical connection of the three worlds around which the universe revolves.

It seems obvious that the very widespread, almost universal, images of ladders and stairs and mountains and trees owe their existence to the fact that man cannot fly, and cannot think of any way to raise himself, physically or metaphorically, in space except by climbing. Some people tell us that the ancient Near East preserved a race memory of visitors from other planets who could blast off in rocket ships: if so, it seems rather a lame conclusion to come down to so homely an image as climbing a tree or ladder, or even a mountain. However, if Herodotus is right, and towers in Persia were equipped with winding stairs painted in different colours to represent the planets, then the planets themselves could be symbolically a stairway of heaven. This seems to have been an important element in the symbolism of Mithraism, the Persian sun cult that was a rival of early Christianity. In Mithraism there were seven degrees of ascent after death associated with the planets. This association, we are told, was so deeply rooted that Mithraism, if it had won out over Christianity, would have found it difficult to survive the Copernican revolution in astronomy. In Dante the same symbolic cluster is picked up again. Purgatory is a seven-storey mountain, and as the redeemed soul climbs it he finds one of the seven deadly sins disappearing at each turn round the mountain, until he stands at the top in the garden of Eden, where mankind should have been all along. There Dante meets a maiden called Matilda, and there Virgil ceases to be his guide and Beatrice takes over. The female elements in the imagery indicate the symbolic descent of the theme from the bride of the god at the top of the tower.

In Dante there follows a second climb through the planetary spheres in the *Paradiso*. In the last of these spheres, that of Saturn, we see Jacob's ladder again, symbolizing the remainder of Dante's journey from the manifest spheres of the redeemed into the heart of the eternal light. Dante's poem being Christian, Dante's ascent is not directed by his own will, but by the divine grace manifested in Beatrice. In Milton the emphasis on divine initiative is even stronger. In the third book of *Paradise Lost* we encounter the "paradise of fools" on the smooth surface of the primum mobile, or circumference of the universe, where those arrive who have tried to take the Kingdom of Heaven by force or fraud. A reference to the Tower of Babel precedes this description, and indicates its archetype. There follows a vision of stairs descending from heaven to earth, which, Milton tells us, were "such as whereon Jacob saw" the angels of his vision. These stairs are let down from heaven and drawn up again at the pleasure of God: Satan, on his journey to Eden, arrives at a "lower" stair, from which he descends to earth by way of the planets.

Dante and Milton are following the religious tradition that starts from Jacob's ladder, where there can be no connection between heaven and earth except through divine power. The cause of the divine action is love, in the sense of *agape*, God's love for man which is reflected in man's love for God and for his neighbour, and which the 1611 Bible calls charity (from the Latin *caritas* which translates *agape* in the Vulgate). The story of Babel, we said, was a parody of the human arrogance that tries to reverse the procedure by building a tower to reach heaven. This story is most unlikely to be a fair presentation of Mesopotamian or Egyptian religious attitudes, but there are widespread folk tales that also associate the attempt to build a ladder to heaven with futility. One such tale is current among British Columbia Indian tribes, where there is an original war between the Sky People and the Earth People, the latter being apparently animals. One animal or bird, generally the wren, shoots an arrow into the moon; another shoots a second arrow that hits the notch of its predecessor, and so on until there is a complete ladder of arrows from earth to sky. Then the animals climb up, until the grizzly bear breaks the ladder by his weight.

In other versions, however, the ladder remains in good shape: I am simply concerned to show that there are both ideal and ironic aspects of the theme. The Classical counterpart of the ironic version is the story of the revolt of the Titans, the sons of earth who piled mountains on top of each other to reach their enemy in the sky. One is reminded also of Blake's sequence of drawings called (in the later version) *The Gates of Paradise*. One of these drawings has the caption, "I want! I want!" and shows a young man starting to climb a ladder leaned against the moon. There is a young couple making a gesture toward him, but he ignores them, no doubt in the spirit of Longfellow's mountain-climbing hero, muttering "excelsior" when invited to sleep with an Alpine maiden. There is an ominous bend in the ladder, however, and we are not surprised to find that the next picture, with the caption "Help! Help!" shows him fallen into the sea, like his prototype Icarus.[3]

The starting point of a more secular conception of a ladder from earth to heaven that is at least partly the result of human effort is in Plato's *Symposium*, where we are told how the power of Eros, a human love and energy with its roots in the sexual instinct, raises the lover from the attractiveness of a beautiful body up, step by step, to identification with the Form or Idea of Beauty itself. From Plato there descended a mixed tradition. Some of it was mystical: mystics seem by temperament attracted to ladders and images of climbing by degrees, with or without benefit of Plato. Walter Hilton's *Ladder of Perfection* is a fifteenth-century English example. The revival of Platonic studies in the Renaissance renewed the emphasis on a secular ladder of love that was planted in human sexuality and took its way to a sublimated but still thoroughly secular goal. In Castiglione's sixteenth-century dialogue *The Courtier*, a panegyric of a ladder-climbing love of this kind is pronounced at the end, as a climax to its theme, the education of the ideal courtier, by Cardinal Bembo, to give him his later title.

The imagery seems to have lost nothing of its vitality even in the twentieth century. About fifty years ago the leading writers included T.S. Eliot, W.B. Yeats, Ezra Pound, and James Joyce. In Eliot's early poems there is a curiously urgent emphasis on the highest step of a staircase, where Prufrock and the narrator of *Portrait of a Lady* think of turning back, and where the girl in *La Figlia che Piange*, standing "on the highest pavement of the stair," haunts her deserting lover for the rest of his life. In *Ash-Wednesday* Eliot joins the Christian tradition of ladders, and follows Dante's *Purgatorio* in placing a winding stair at the centre of his poem. In the *Quartets* there is a great variety of such images, some derived from the Spanish mystic St. John of the Cross, whose *Ascent of Mount Carmel* is one of the best known mystical climbs.

At the time of *Ash-Wednesday*, around 1930, Yeats was publishing books of poetry with such titles as *The Tower* (1928) and *The Winding Stair* (1933), and searching for spirals and gyres in every aspect of experience. In contrast to Eliot, Yeats's imagery is Platonic rather than Christian, or at any rate for him, as he says, all ladders are planted in what he calls the foul rag-and-bone shop of the heart. Yeats even went to the length of buying a round tower with a spiral staircase in Ireland, though he did not spend much time living in it. Ezra Pound went directly back to Herodotus and his account of seven planetary staircases in Ecbatana and elsewhere, and adopted a similar imagery for his own ambitions in the *Cantos*. Even the *Pisan Cantos*, written out of the terrible experience of being confined in a cage after the war, begin with the still unshaken resolution "To build the city of Dioce whose terraces are the colour of stars" [*Canto 74*, l. 11]. In the fourth *Canto* he speaks of Danae, the bride of the sky-god placed on the top of the tower, and follows this immediately with a description of a medieval painting of the Virgin Mary, the "madonna in hortulo" who has a corresponding place in Christian imagery.

James Joyce built his last and most elaborate work on the Irish ballad of Finnegan, the hod-carrier who fell from the top of a ladder, an event Joyce associates with the fall of man on his first page. In the ballad he comes to life at his own wake, demanding a share of the whisky; in Joyce he is persuaded to go back to death by twelve mourners representing the cycle of the zodiac. His death then modulates into the sleep of his successor HCE, whose cyclical and repetitive dream is human history as we know it. In Joyce we become aware of another aspect of the imagery of ladders and their relatives: it is a vertical movement in direct contrast to images of the turning cycle of nature, where winter is followed by spring and then winter again, darkness by dawn and renewed night, life by death and reborn life.

The Latin word for ladder is *scala*, and that word extends the image of the ladder to the "scale," or measurement by degrees, which is so fundamental in scientific work and in some of the arts as well, notably music. The scale also forms the basis of one of the most persistent conceptions in the history of thought. It is expressed by no one more clearly than by Sir Thomas Browne in *Religio Medici* (1643):

> there is in this Universe a Stair, or manifest Scale of creatures, rising not dis-orderly, or in confusion, but with a comely method and proportion. Between creatures of meer existence, and things of life, there is a large dis-proportion of nature; between plants, and animals or creatures of sense, a wider difference; between them and Man, a far greater; and if the propor-tion hold on, between Man and Angels there should be yet a greater.[4]

This is the conception of the whole of creation as forming a great chain of being, stretching from God himself at the top to chaos at the bottom. The chain is polarized by the conceptions of form and matter: God is pure form without matter, and chaos, where the four principles of substance, hot, cold, moist, and dry, keep combining and recombin-ing by chance, is as close as we can get to pure matter without form. Above chaos is the mineral world, which has no life but none the less exhibits a hierarchy, with the "noble" metals, gold, silver, mercury, at the top and what we still call the "base metals," tin and lead, directly under them. Above this was the vegetative world, above it the animal world, and above the animals was man, who, being half formal and half material, was exactly in the middle of the chain, the microcosm or epit-ome of the whole of being. Between man and God was the spiritual world peopled by angels. That curious half-Christian, half-Platonic speculator called the pseudo-Dionysius (he took his name from a con-vert of Paul mentioned in the New Testament) gave us a table of nine orders of angels, apparently merely for the sake of setting up a hierar-chy of degrees in an unknown area of being.

This chain or scale or ladder of being was a structure of authority, in which all initiative came down from the top. Without the hierarchy imposed by the ladder, everything would dissolve in chaos. Hence it is necessary for human society to preserve the same kind of scale of degree, or it too will fall into anarchy and savagery. So at least we are solemnly assured in an eloquent speech by Ulysses in Shakespeare's play about the Trojan war, *Troilus and Cressida* [1.3.75–137], even though Ulysses' motives in making the speech are concerned with the best means of bringing anarchy and savagery to the city of Troy. The cosmic imagery is derived from a social structure. In medieval times the cosmos was reflected in the feudal principle of protection from above and obedience from below, and in Tudor times it was reflected in the authority of the ruler as it filtered down through the courts, legal and secular, to the common people. In the masques of Ben Jonson and others that were acted before King James, we usually move from a vision of a disorderly rabble in the antimasque up through various allegorical levels to the final compliments to the king or queen or whoever was the guest of honour in the audience and the representative of the climax of the ladder. For while ladders and staircases may not appear in the stage scenery of the masque, their invisible presence is everywhere.

Everything in the scale of being has its natural place, or what Chaucer calls its "kindly stead."[5] A heavy object held in the air and released will drop, because it is seeking its natural place in the sphere of earth. Bubbles of air rise in water because they are seeking their own sphere of air, which is above water. Man is an exception: because of the fall of Adam, he is born in a lower state of existence than he was intended to live in, and the order of nature around him, the world of animals and plants, is more alienated from him than it was in the garden of Eden. Man's primary duty is to regain as much as he can of his original state: the garden of Eden is gone as a place, but can be regained as a state of mind. Many things are natural for man that are not natural anywhere else in nature, such as wearing clothes: man belongs in a sphere of nature peculiar to himself, a sphere higher than physical nature. Law, morality, the sacraments of religion, everything that is genuinely educational, will help him to rise to his appropriate place in the scheme of things. This does not affect his place in human society: it is also natural to man to live in a structured social order, and he can only fulfil his true human destiny of reaching his cosmic natural place by staying in the social place he was born in. To rise above one's state is rebellion; to fall from it is delinquency.

This particular ladder is an expression of authority, as enforced by both church and state, and in many respects it is a most transparent rationalizing of such authority. Because it was an expression of authority, it lasted far longer than it should have done, but even so by the end of the eighteenth century, with American and French and Industrial Revolutions recent or imminent, it was beginning to look like a rather shaky means of ascent to a higher world. From Rousseau on, man is increasingly thought of as a child of nature rather than as a fallen child of God, and more and more emphasis comes to be put on human effort, human rights, human capacities. For Milton, a seventeenth-century revolutionary, liberty is good for man because God wants him to have it: left to himself, man not only cannot achieve liberty, he cannot even desire it. For Byron and Shelley the desire for liberty awakens in the human heart, is justified as a human need and a human right, and will probably involve conflict with the ghosts of old gods who are projections of human tyranny.

If we are looking for a literary work to represent the staircase of being and the human ascent to its proper place in the cosmic order, we shall find it in Dante's *Purgatorio*. The mountain of purgatory has its base on the surface of this earth, though on the other side of what Dante knew to be a sphere. At the top of this mountain is the garden of Eden, the original home of man, where the soul recovers its original freedom of will and becomes its own Pope and Emperor. This purgatorial ascent completes the essential pilgrimage of humanity, but even for a saint this pilgrimage needs an extension into an after-death world to be completed.

After the authoritarian construct of the chain of being had collapsed, we should expect another construct of a revolutionary shape, based on human powers and capacities: in short, a successfully completed Tower of Babel. I do not know of a work of literature that meets this formidable challenge, but there is one in philosophy, Hegel's *Phenomenology of Spirit*, which, however conservative in itself, has been the basis of revolutionary programmes of thought ever since. In this book we begin with ordinary sense experience, trying to connect subject with object, and find that a progressively larger series of structures begins to form, each implying its own negation, and expanding beyond its predecessor by swallowing its negation. After the Spirit has eaten all its negations, it becomes absolute knowledge, and enters the world of infinite spirit. What is remarkable about this book, from my point of view, is that while the language throughout is strictly philosophical, there is an unconscious (or at any rate unformulated) metaphor of a spiralling stairway that gives narrative shape to the entire argument.

So far we have been taking our ladders and staircases as spatial metaphors, leading to a world above which is thought of as "there," present as though in space. Descending stairways to a lower world are less frequent: Dante's hell is, like his purgatory, a cone that Dante traverses from base to apex, going down towards the centre of the earth, but this is an example of the way in which journeys to a lower world have become associated with the demonic. Usually a downward spiralling movement takes the form of the whirlpool, or maelstrom of death. In Shelley's *Prometheus Unbound*, as in other Romantic works, everything that makes for the greater glory of man comes from below, and the heroine Asia descends to the cave of Demogorgon in search of the Titan who eventually moves into the sky and pushes the tyrant sky-god Jupiter off his throne. But we are not told how she gets down there.

In any case, when it becomes too obvious that something does not exist, it begins to lose its appeal even in literature, where its existence ordinarily does not really matter. In the nineteenth century Rider Haggard and others wrote romances about lost cities and kingdoms in the heart of Africa or Asia. Contemporary romancers use the same themes, but in the age of the helicopter they have to put their lost kingdoms somewhere in outer space to make them rhetorically convincing. With a similar loss of credibility in worlds up or down "there," ladders and stairways have to shift from metaphorical space to metaphorical time.

During the centuries when the education of man was thought of as, in Milton's words, an attempt to repair the ruin of our first parents,[6] the ladder of improvement was connected with a paradise lost in the past. In Dante's *Purgatorio* Dante is, among other things, climbing back to his original state of childhood, not his individual childhood, but his generic childhood as a descendant of an unfallen Adam. His climb up the mountain is therefore in one sense a moving backward in time, as he loses one by one the sins which he has accumulated in its forward movement on the other side of the world. Similarly both the Renaissance and the Reformation were inspired by what is now called a pastoral myth, a belief that there was a state of things in the past which has been lost and must be climbed back to. With the Renaissance this was the Augustan age of first-rate Latin; with the Reformation it was the assumed purity of the early generations of Christianity; but the underlying figure was much the same.

The early twentieth century grew up with the figure implanted in its consciousness of a ladder of time projected into the future. This was suggested, of course, by the biological conception of evolution. Here we learn how the dinosaurs disappeared because they could not meet nature's preference of brains to brawn, after which there was a stairway of humanoids, those on the lower steps shambling and stumbling with their heads bent, those on the higher steps (us) walking erect and clear-eyed and holding their paunches in. The much-slandered Neanderthal man was supposed to be our immediate predecessor on this ascending scale of being. It is obvious that we are not dealing here with evolution or any other scientific conception: this is pure mythology, a product of human concern, where any evidence that does not fit must be squeezed until it does.

In history this mythical analogy of evolution took the form of a doctrine of progress, which has been a most versatile muddler of minds ever since. In my student days it was very generally accepted that socialism, whether of the type envisaged by Marx or by gradualists, represented a higher state of social evolution than capitalism, and that it was the duty of all right-thinking people to help in the general move to the next upward step. However, Communism established itself in largely preindustrial societies, and Communism and capitalism settled down to an adversary relationship. Each "system," as it is called, has improved itself slightly by borrowing from its rival, but of general evolutionary advance there is no sign. That staircase, like Jacob's, is an impressive dream structure, but will not bear any tangible weight.

One of the morals of this talk should have emerged by now: metaphors and diagrams and figures like the ladder underlie all our verbal constructs, those of philosophy and political theory no less than those of literature. And while many metaphorical pictures of reality can be very misleading, still the solid bedrock of metaphor will remain, as something we cannot do without. There *is* a "higher" form of existence, and there *are* ladders and staircases leading to it, however wrong our efforts to locate it in time or space may be. The difficulties begin with *projecting* the metaphor: the first step on the real ladder to a higher existence is the employing of metaphor itself.

In verbal metaphor we usually formulate a phrase of the "this is that" type, asserting that two quite different things are in fact identical. A Biblical example would be Jacob's prophecy of the twelve tribes in Genesis 49: "Joseph is a fruitful bough," "Naphtali is a hind let loose," "Issachar is a strong ass," and the like. If we ask what is the point of saying that A is B when A is so obviously not B, the answer is that metaphor is not a matter of asserting identities by overstrained analogies. It is rather an effort to extend our own being into the external world, to break down the wall between subject and object and start currents of verbal energy flowing between them. If we apply this principle of metaphor, which is verbal, to the pictorial arts, we can perhaps see what is involved more clearly. In Palaeolithic times the liveliest and most spirited paintings of animals were made in caves under incredibly difficult conditions of position and lighting. Doubtless there was some aesthetic motive at work, some desire to create a work of beauty, but this would be hopelessly inadequate to account for painting in such conditions. We can add such words as "religion" or "magic," but the fact remains that the complexity, urgency, and sheer titanic power of the motivation involved is something we cannot understand now, much less recapture.

The nearest we can come to putting such motivation into words, I think, is to say that the bisons and bears portrayed in those far-off times were a kind of extension of human consciousness and power into the objects of greatest energy and strength they could see in the world around them. This is the real function of what appears in words as metaphor: the assimilating of the energy, the beauty, the elusive glory, latent in nature to the observing mind. I speak of "the mind" as though it were the mind of a separated individual, but of course the community out of which the individual artist emerges guides his hand and controls his speech.

The purest form of metaphor is the god, who is an identity of some kind of personality or consciousness and some aspect of the natural world, as with a sea-god or sky-god or love-goddess. The descent of the god from the animal, recalling a time when man did not think of himself as the lord of creation, but saw in birds and animals powers and abilities he did not himself possess, is clear enough. All the Near Eastern cultures display gods in animal form, and in such myths as Zeus courting Europa in the form of a bull we can see that the same line of descent existed in Greece. Even without any explicit identification with a god, we can see the imaginative assimilating of the animal world in this exhibition, from a powerful early Mesopotamian bull to a delicate mosaic peacock of the Coptic period.

Then again, in the cave drawings we see animal forms with human eyes looking through them, and suspect that we are really seeing a sorcerer or shaman who has identified himself with the animal by putting on its skin. We also see "fish priests" and the like in this exhibition, and in some of the female fetishes, giving great prominence to the sexual organs but having no face, we can see how the primary aim is an identification with power or vitality or fertility rather than a sense of beauty. An aesthetic sense marks a more sophisticated development, because it tends to increase the distance between the object portrayed and the subject regarding it.

Archaeology is a science in which we dig underground, using steps and descending ladders as we go, to find what remains of civilizations that at one time towered high in the air. The theme of underground treasure is one of the most reliable formulas of romance, and in the early days of digging, say with Schliemann at Troy, there was still something of extracting buried treasure about the enterprise. There have been of course many dramatic discoveries, like Tutankhamen's tomb or the great man-bull sculptures at Nineveh now in the Louvre. But for archaeologists now the motive of treasure hunt is a very minor one, yet two levels of their work emerge clearly. So far as they clarify our historical knowledge of the ancient world, they show us competing empires that fought and killed, laid land waste, enslaved whole peoples, and recorded their hideous exploits in paranoid inscriptions. Among these exploits were vainglorious monuments of the type ridiculed in the Babel story, and, much nearer our own time, in Shelley's famous sonnet about Ozymandias, the "king of kings" whose works were the despair of his rivals, but cause no despair now except in those who are trying to find what is left of them. Knowledge of such enterprises extends, without much expanding, our general knowledge of human behaviour.

But archaeology also recovers, in the course of its work, objects of great beauty and power, and we realize that above ordinary history there has been a continuous level of craftsmanship, skill, and creative insight. The artefacts of a vanished civilization were produced in the normal climate of human cruelty and folly, but they themselves are in an unchanging state of innocence. They are what we still want to see, and we can take pleasure in them while abstracting their social context from them. Here is a real ladder to heaven, or at least to a paradisal world of beauty and keen intelligence, one that can be constructed only by the creative imagination, the one power that has been able to drive humanity beyond the needs of mere survival into a more abundant life.

Returning finally to Jacob's dream, we note that while its origin was in heaven, angels were ascending as well as descending on it. If we take angels to be instruments of communication between the divine and the human, perhaps the implication is that divine and human activities in creation are not so far apart after all, and that even in a contemporary high-rise city we could still see, with the late Victorian poet Francis Thompson, "the traffic of Jacob's ladder / Pitched betwixt Heaven and Charing Cross."[7]

7

The Bride from the Strange Land

25 May 1985

From Craft and Tradition: Essays in Honour of William Blissett, *ed. H.B. de Groot and A. Leggatt (Calgary: University of Calgary Press, 1990), 1–11. Previously published in Italian in* Mito Metafora Simbolo, *trans. Carla Pezzini Plevano and Francesca Valente Gorjup (Rome: Editori Riuniti, 1989), 119–31. Reprinted in* EAC, *50–61. Typescripts (one with corrections) are in NFF, 1988, box 49, file 3, and NFF, 1991, box 39, file 1. Originally given as an address at Holy Blossom Temple, Toronto. Unless indicated otherwise, the Biblical quotations in this essay are taken from the New English Bible (1970).*

I

The Book of Ruth is one of the five short books called "rolls" (*megilloth*) among the Writings which have acquired a specific liturgical importance. It is a rather striking fact that, of these five "rolls," three are narratives centred on female figures. The story of the book is familiar but needs to be summarized again for clarity.[1]

Naomi is the widow of a Bethlehemite named Elimelech, who had moved into Moab during a famine in Judaea, much as the family of Israel had moved into Egypt for a similar reason centuries earlier. He and the two sons Naomi had borne to him all died, leaving her with two Moabite daughters-in-law, both childless. In so patriarchal a society Naomi feels that she is under something of a curse, and she returns forlornly from Moab to Bethlehem to live out the rest of her blighted life. Her Moabite daughters-in-law, Ruth and Orpah, accompany her to the border of Moab, where she tries to persuade them to go back to their own land. She tells them that she is too old to produce more male chil-

dren herself, and that even if she did it would be twenty years before
they were marriageable, by which time their prospective brides would
be twenty years older also. Orpah finds this argument conclusive and
returns to Moab; Ruth, in the most famous scene of the book, states her
resolution to proceed with Naomi to Bethlehem. It has been well
observed that for a young foreign widow to identify her fortunes with
those of an older woman, also a widow with no prospects, in such a
society was an act of almost incredible courage and loyalty.

Back in the Bethlehem country, Ruth finds herself, by one of those
accidents which are clearly not quite accidents, gleaning in the field of
Boaz, a kinsman of her late father-in-law. It is the harvest season, when
the destitute were allowed to glean in the fields after the reapers had
passed through. Boaz's attention proves very easy to catch, and, following Naomi's advice, Ruth soon puts him in the position of wanting to
marry her. They are married, and a son is born to them named Obed,
who was the grandfather of King David.

Stories about women in the Bible fall into a very few well-marked categories, and there are, I think, three narrative themes that converge on
the story of Ruth and Naomi. The first of these themes is that of levirate
marriage, where a surviving brother-in-law or other near kinsman of a
childless widow is obliged to do his best to provide her with children,
preferably, of course, male children. Deuteronomy 25:5–6 says:

> When brothers live together and one of them dies without leaving a son, his
> widow shall not marry outside the family. Her husband's brother shall
> have intercourse with her; he shall take her in marriage and do his duty by
> her as her husband's brother. The first son she bears shall perpetuate the
> dead brother's name . . .

The best known story of this type in the Bible is the story of Tamar in
Genesis 38. Tamar was the wife of Judah's son Er, and therefore Judah's
daughter-in-law. Er was a bad man and the Lord took his life: Tamar
was, according to the levirate custom, transferred to his younger brother
Onan, who greatly resented and resisted the whole procedure. As God
approved of it, he lost his life also. There was a third brother, still a boy,
and Judah proposed that Tamar remain in the house until he had grown
up. But the third brother was not assigned to Tamar, so Tamar disguised
herself as a prostitute and put herself in the way of Judah, who got her
pregnant. Hearing that Tamar had been acting like a prostitute, Judah

said, with the casual ferocity of the age, "let her be burnt" [38:24, AV].
But Tamar produced the tokens he had given her, and he acknowledged
that she was right, because the third brother had been denied her. Of the
twin sons she had by Judah, one, Perez, was in the direct line of ancestry
to David.

Ruth is also a childless widow, but no brothers are involved, and any
claim on relatives of her late husband can hardly have been a legal
claim, in view of her Moabite nationality. But Boaz is too strongly
attracted to her for that to be an obstacle, and he is very willing to take
on the levirate obligation, except that he feels that as there is one still
nearer kinsman, the latter should have first choice. The other kinsman,
who is not named, resigns in favour of Boaz, and the way is cleared for
Ruth's marriage. Boaz's motive in approaching this kinsman was perhaps to establish Ruth's status as an Israelite widow instead of leaving
her simply a destitute foreigner to whom he had taken a fancy. The relevance of all this to the custom illustrated by the Tamar story is made
clear by the elders of Bethlehem, who say when the marriage is decided
on: "May your house be like the house of Perez, whom Tamar bore to
Judah" (4:12).

The second story-type is that of the son who is born to a woman past
the age of child-bearing, so that the birth is a direct manifestation of
divine favour. The best known story of this type is the birth of Isaac to
Sarah at an impossibly late age. Because Sarah laughed at the prospect
of bearing another child, the infant was given a name suggesting
"laughter" by a slightly miffed deity [Genesis 21:1–7]. There are several
other women who bear children after a long period of barrenness,
including Rachel and Hannah, the mother of Samuel. When Samuel is
born, Hannah sings a triumphant song in praise of a God who can bring
down the great people and raise up the small ones at pleasure [1 Samuel
2:1–10]. The same themes recur in the New Testament. John the Baptist
is born to his mother Elizabeth at a late age, his father Zechariah being
struck with a temporary dumbness because of his disbelief [Luke 1:20–
80]. The conception of Jesus by Mary is equally miraculous, though not
for the same reason, and Mary's song of triumph, known as the Magnificat, is modelled on the song of Hannah and makes the same point about
God's power to reverse ordinary social standards [Luke 1:46–55].

In the Book of Ruth this theme of late birth is associated, not with
Ruth, who is still a young woman, but with her mother-in-law Naomi.
After the birth of Obed, Naomi becomes the infant's nurse, and the

neighbours offer their congratulations in a very abrupt phrase: "Naomi has a son" (4:17). The identities of Ruth and Naomi are curiously confused in the final chapter, perhaps reflecting an earlier version of the story in which Ruth did not appear at all. In any case the story of Ruth is also a story about the filling, emptying, and refilling of the life of Naomi, for whom Ruth acts as a proxy.

The theme of late birth is connected with another frequent theme in the Bible: the passing over of the eldest son, who inherits by primogeniture but does something to forfeit his inheritance. A son born late would be either an only or a younger son. Thus Ishmael is passed over in favour of Isaac, Esau for Jacob, Reuben for Judah and Joseph, Manasseh for Ephraim, and, in a very slight extension of the theme, Saul, the first king of Israel, for David, who becomes Saul's son-in-law and also survives Saul's son and heir, Jonathan. The deliberate choice of a younger son symbolizes a divine intervention into the normal pattern of human affairs, and makes appropriate the theme of God creating revolutions in society, bringing down the great and raising the humble, which we find both in Hannah's song and the Magnificat. It was this aspect of the story of Ruth that impressed Josephus, who gives a rather arid summary of it, clearly regarding it as an interruption of his narrative, and then says, "I was therefore obliged to relate the history of Ruth, because I had a mind to demonstrate the power of God, who, without difficulty, can raise those that are of ordinary parentage to dignity and splendour, to which he advanced David, though he were born of such mean parents" (*The Antiquities of the Jews*, 5.9.4).[2]

We can also see a more tenuous resemblance between the story of Ruth and many folk tales and legends scattered over the world, of the type familiar in the story of Cinderella, in which a young woman who seems to have every kind of social handicap nevertheless attracts the attention of a man much higher in rank, and eventually marries him. Cinderella had a fairy godmother: Ruth has what is usually a more effective ally in this world, a co-operative mother-in-law. For thousands of years we have had stories of the type we frequently get in Shakespeare's comedies, where a clever and imaginative heroine, who knows what she wants but is not really unscrupulous about getting it, brings about a comic resolution that includes a successful marriage for herself. In the New Comedies of the Hellenistic period, some of which were adapted by Plautus and Terence, the heroine is a slave or prostitute, though really of more respectable parentage because stolen by pirates in infancy or the like. Ruth also begins operations on Boaz by saying, at least according to one reading, "treat me as one of your slave-girls" (2:13).

When Boaz lies down to sleep on the harvest field, somewhat drunk, and Ruth comes to him and asks him to spread his cloak over his "hand-maid," it is clear that with a very slight change of tone we should have a rather cynical seduction story in which Boaz is, as we say, being set up. Needless to say, that is not the tone of the Book of Ruth, nor what happens in it. But the type of story being told is first cousin to seduction and bed trick tales like that of Jacob's first night with Leah. Keats, whom we shall mention again later, remarks in one of his letters that it is always a pleasure to rediscover the fact that Cleopatra was a gipsy, Helen a rogue, and Ruth a "deep one."[3] A reference to Ruth in Joyce's *Finnegans Wake* makes the same point much more broadly and includes an oblique allusion to Shakespeare: "You're well held now, Missy Cheekspear, and your panto's off! Fie, for shame, Ruth Wheatacre, after all the booz said!"[4]

The third story-type to be linked with Ruth is the most controversial and complex one. This is the story of the bride from the strange land, which is illustrated perhaps most clearly in Psalm 45. This psalm seems to be a wedding song celebrating the marriage of a king of Israel and a bride who apparently comes from Tyre in Phoenicia. The bride is adjured to forget her religion and adopt that of her new home, but there is no suggestion that there is anything wrong with the marriage itself. In history, however, the most notable marriage between an Israelite king and a Canaanite princess was that of Ahab and Jezebel, which led to all kinds of disaster. Similarly, the Song of Songs seems to have connections with King Solomon and a Shulamite bride, and there are certainly affinities between Ruth and the black but comely bride who did not keep her own vineyard but went out to seek her beloved. But in the historical narrative we are told that Solomon's wives prompted him to build temples to foreign gods, including the god of Moab, on mountains facing the temple on Mount Moriah.

The return under Ezra and Nehemiah included stringent regulations preventing any Israelite from having any connection with "foreign" or "strange" women, however innocuous or nonexistent their religious views. What connections had already been made were to be immediately dissolved. It has often been suggested that the Book of Ruth, along with the Book of Jonah, supports a more flexible and less racist attitude toward foreign women, in making the point that the great King David had a great-grandmother who was a Moabite. Whether the Book of Ruth is specifically aimed against the policy of Ezra and Nehemiah or not would depend on the date we assigned to it, and there is not much of a consensus among scholars about this, though a majority seems to favour a postexilic date. But however early we may consider the book to be, it can hardly be earlier than the commandment in Deuteronomy 23:3: "No Ammonite or Moabite, even down to the tenth generation, shall become a member of the assembly of the Lord." Again, there is a variant of the levirate-marriage story which takes the form of parody in Genesis 19, where Lot's two daughters, finding a shortage of eligible men in the country in which they had taken refuge, make their father drunk and have intercourse with him. The two acts of incest produced the Moabites and the Ammonites.

As it is only from the Book of Ruth that we learn that David had a Moabite woman in his ancestry, it is difficult to avoid the conclusion that the book is making something of a political and religious point. Ruth has no interest whatever in Moabite religion: she does not even have any "teraphim," like Rachel. She is therefore welcomed by Boaz in the spirit of the law forbidding the oppression of strangers or widows (Exodus 22:21–2). Nothing could be more solidly Israelite than Leah and Rachel, yet they, as well as Tamar, are invoked by the witnesses of Ruth's marriage to Boaz: "May the Lord make this woman, who has come to your home, like Rachel and Leah, the two who built up the house of Israel" (4:11). Elsewhere we are told that David, when fleeing from Saul, took refuge in Moab and left his father and mother there (1 Samuel 22:4), and that the mother of Rehoboam, Solomon's son and successor, was an Ammonite. Solomon himself, of course, was the son of Bathsheba, originally the wife of Uriah the Hittite, and therefore no doubt a Hittite herself, whatever that may mean in the way of "foreignness." In any case there was ample precedent for marriage to "foreign" women, even if much of it is later than the period assigned to Ruth.

II

The Book of Ruth is practically ignored in the New Testament, but there is one curious puzzle in the latter which bears not only on the Book of Ruth but on this particular issue of foreign marriage. The New Testament begins with Matthew's genealogy of Jesus, starting with Abraham and going down through David, Solomon, Zerubbabel, and the rest. Luke has an even longer genealogy, though it differs from Matthew's, and he speaks only of fathers and sons. Matthew, however, seems to feel that women do somehow get involved with the genealogical process, and so includes five women in his list. The first is Tamar, whose relevance to the Ruth story we have mentioned. The third is Ruth herself, the only explicit reference to her or her book in the New Testament. The fourth is Bathsheba, mother of Solomon, and the fifth Mary, the mother of Jesus. It is the second name that is the puzzle: the mother of Boaz, whose name is given as Rahab.

The name of Boaz's mother does not occur anywhere else in the Bible, and where the compiler of Matthew got it remains a mystery. It is, of course, the same name as that of the celebrated harlot of Jericho, who is twice mentioned approvingly in the New Testament, as a pattern of faith in the Epistle to the Hebrews, and as a pattern of good works in the Epistle of James. That Matthew could ever have believed this Rahab to be Boaz's mother, as many commentators assume, seems most unlikely. If in fact they were the same, Boaz's somewhat adventurous approach to the married state may have been inherited. It is true that the names of women often appear in the Bible by accident: we know the names of David's sisters, for example, but not that of his mother. But it is just barely conceivable that the name "Rahab" in this context means simply "foreign woman," as the same name is also attached in the Bible to Egypt, with overtones of the hostile or chaotic world outside Israel (cf. Psalm 87:4). So many of the women who are mentioned in the Bible, whether by name or not, were "foreign" in one way or another that they may have some kind of symbolic significance, as representing either the permeation of the outside world by Judaism or the corruption of Judaism, depending on the women and depending also on whether one takes the view of the Book of Ruth or the Book of Nehemiah.

In Blake's *Jerusalem*, plate 62, there is a list of "foreign" women, including Ruth. In Blake's symbolism all human beings, men and women, are symbolically male, just as they are symbolically female in orthodox symbolism. What is female for Blake is Nature, and Nature has two aspects. As an order of existence controlled and regulated by the creative imagination, she is what Blake calls an "Emanation," Isaiah's "Beulah" or married land; as an objective otherness remaining aloof from humanity she is what Blake calls a "Female Will." As the latter, she is still a product of the human imagination, but in a perverted and projected form. The foreign women in Blake's list symbolize this "Female Will": the only allusion to Ruth I have found that distorts her story by exaggerating the purely symbolic and typological side of it. As a character in history or credible fiction, Blake would have the same affection for Ruth that nearly all her readers have, and shows that in the fine painting of Ruth, Naomi, and Orpah which he included in his one exhibition.

Other literary references to the Book of Ruth are rare and curiously barren, though for all I know there may be hidden riches in the Bulgarian and Latvian poems mentioned in reference books. A devotional treatise, called *Le livre de Ruth*, was written by a French abbé named Tardif de Moidrey in the nineteenth century, and was reprinted with a long (hundred-page) introduction by the poet Claudel in 1938. But neither the abbé nor Claudel really tells us much about the book. Dante places Ruth at the end of the *Paradiso* among women destined to be redeemed before the coming of Christ, along with Sarah, Rebecca, and others. But he does not mention her by name: he merely calls her the great-grandmother (*bissava*) of David—though David is not mentioned by name either, but is merely referred to as the author of the "Miserere" or fifty-first Psalm, the one that is understood to have been written by him after his sin in the matter of Uriah and Bathsheba. Milton adopts a different kind of typological reference, when he assures a "virtuous young lady," in a sonnet addressed to her, that

> The better part with Mary and with Ruth
> Chosen thou hast.[5]

In the house of Lazarus, where Martha was working in the household and her sister Mary was talking with Jesus, Mary was said by Jesus to have chosen "the better part": "one thing is needful: and Mary hath chosen that good part" (Luke 10:42). Later Christian typology identified these two "parts" with the active and the contemplative lives. The traditional Old Testament types of these were Leah and Rachel, who appear in this symbolic frame in Dante's *Purgatorio*. But of course, the more dramatic contrast in choice between Ruth and Orpah would also be available, and so Milton couples Mary with Ruth. I imagine however that Milton's real reason for referring to Ruth was that she provided a rhyme with "truth" and "youth." Again, Bunyan, in the second part of *The Pilgrim's Progress*, telling the story of Christian's wife leaving the City of

Destruction to journey to the New Jerusalem, mentions the parallel with Ruth, mainly, one feels, because he could hardly have avoided it.

Ruth is a common name, and many literary uses of it, such as Words-worth's *Ruth*, do not relate to the Biblical book. Neither does Mrs. Gaskell's Victorian novel *Ruth*, which is a straightforward honest story about what we should now call an unmarried mother, written by a cler-gyman's wife. Margaret Laurence, who is often quite specifically Bibli-cal in her allusions, has a Rachel and a Hagar who certainly reflect something of their Biblical namesakes.[6] But there seems to be no Ruth, nor do I think that the Naomi of Joy Kogawa's *Obasan* has Biblical con-nections. The situation is similar even with works of Biblical scholar-ship. The other day I picked up a volume of essays on literary aspects of the Bible, and found five references to Ruth in the index. Three of them, however, turned out to be the first names of contemporary women scholars—perhaps an example of the hazards involved in making an index by computer.

The finest literary treatment of the Ruth story I know is a poem by Victor Hugo called *Booz endormi*, one of the *Légendes des siècles*. In an ear-lier autobiographical poem in *Les contemplations*, [*Aux feuillantines*,] Hugo speaks of his affection for Biblical stories, and mentions Ruth, Joseph, and the parable of the Good Samaritan in particular. The juxta-posing of Ruth and the Good Samaritan parable is interesting, as both make the same point: that there may be good people even among hostile or hated nations. There is, I understand, a Haggadic tradition that Boaz was an old man of eighty when he met Ruth, and Hugo may have picked this up somewhere, as his Boaz is the same age. In Hugo, the dream of Boaz is a wistful, lonely reverie that culminates in a prophetic vision of what is more frequently called the tree of Jesse, the ancestral line stretching from David's father to Jesus, which is the basis of a superb stained-glass window design in Chartres Cathedral.

In English literature the best known allusion to Ruth is in Keats's *Ode to a Nightingale*, where the poet says that the nightingale's song may have pierced

> Through the sad heart of Ruth, when, sick for home,
> She stood in tears amid the alien corn. [stanza 7]

It is a beautiful but curious reference: as we saw, Keats certainly knew the Book of Ruth, but there is no hint in it that Ruth was ever homesick for Moab or that she regarded the corn fields around her as in any sense alien: after all, her late father-in-law still owned some of them. The tendency to sentimentalize the story recurs in a sonnet by Christina Rossetti, called *Autumn Violets*, which has as its last line "a grateful Ruth tho' gleaning scanty corn."[7] This is not, it is true, a direct reference to the Biblical book, but we may note that actually, thanks to Boaz's patronage, Ruth did fairly well out of her gleaning. I make these somewhat pedantic comments because I suspect that one reason for the comparative neglect of the Book of Ruth by later writers is the irrepressible cheerfulness of the story, which is all about completely normal people fully understanding one another, and leaves the literary imagination with very little to do. That said, we could justify the Keats allusion by observing that Ruth does not give the impression of being merely a mindless puppet of Providence, and may well have had darker and deeper feelings than the narrative presents.

III

The story of Ruth is so brief and unpretentious that many readers, following Goethe, simply mutter something about a "charming pastoral idyl" and pass on.[8] But if we look at it with any attention, its simplicity becomes very deceptive. Naomi is forced into exile by famine, brought to misery and sterility there, and finally makes her way back to her homeland and ends her life as a happy grandmother. Her lament, the only shadow on the general happiness of the story, where she remarks that her name should not be Naomi ("sweet") but Mara ("bitter"), recalls, on a small scale, some of the complaints of Job, and she uses also Job's favourite name for God, El Shaddai. The names of her deceased sons, Mahlon and Chilion ("weak" and "wasting"), seem clearly allegorical. The first chapter, again, emphasizes the changes on the word "return" (*shub*), which is one of the central thematic words of the whole Bible. Obviously Naomi is returning to her original home in Judaea; obviously Orpah is returning to her original home in Moab. What is Ruth doing? According to 1:22, "Ruth the Moabitess returned with her [Naomi] from the Moabite country." Ruth, then, has both a physical and a spiritual home, and she voluntarily chooses the latter. Hence, like the Israelites leaving Egypt for the Promised Land, she is returning to her appropriate place.

The sense of something providential taking charge of Ruth's life appears in Boaz's remark: "May the God of Israel, under whose wings you have come to take refuge, give you all you deserve" (2:12). Later, as we saw, when Boaz lies down to sleep on the harvest field, Ruth comes to him and asks him to spread the "skirts" of his cloak over his handmaid. The word translated to "wings" and "skirt" is the same (*kanaph*). There are also repeated references to a grace or kindness (*chen, chesed*) coming to Ruth from God through Boaz. Boaz also becomes the *go'el* of Ruth, a most versatile word rendered in the 1611 translation of Job 19:25 as "redeemer." Boaz is the *go'el* (2:20) of Ruth in the sense of being the most likely person to become her levirate husband, and the *go'el* of Naomi in a more general sense (4:14). Words closely related to *go'el*, and translated "redeem" in the Authorized Version, keep echoing all through the business arrangements with the nearer kinsman (4:2 ff.). It is difficult not to see in the story an epitome or microcosm, in small but concentrated compass, of the entire story of exile, return, and redemption that the Bible is telling, of how those that sowed their seed in bitterness may return in joy, bringing their sheaves with them (Psalm 126).

The book ends with a list of David's ancestors back to Perez, which tells us nothing new and is generally assumed to be an editorial addition. The real question is rather what, if the addition were removed, would be the last verse of the book: "Obed was the father of Jesse, the father of David" (4:17). Is this part of the original story or not? If it was, it is clearly the climax to which the whole book is leading up: it indicates a motivation on the part of the writer which is not literary. The statement is given as a historical fact, and it is hard to see how the Book of Ruth could ever have got into the Biblical canon if the statement had not been there or had not met with general acceptance. Many commentators are fond of saying that the book is purely literary, by which they generally mean that it is "merely" literary. But it is difficult to imagine the sort of cultural ambience out of which a "purely literary" story could arise in either pre- or postexilic Judaea. Certainly the literary merits of the book are remarkable, but the skill with which the writer has encapsulated the entire narrative movement of the Bible in four brief chapters is something else again.

A late colleague of mine, Professor W.E. Staples, wrote an article on the Book of Ruth back in 1937, in which he suggested that it was a Midrash on a fertility cult centred at Bethlehem.[9] Staples was a student of S.H. Hooke, who in turn was a disciple of Robertson Smith and Frazer. He interprets the names in the book as cultic names: Elimelech,

for example ("God is king"), becomes a Frazerian divine king. Naomi is
a fertility goddess, and Ruth is related to her as Proserpine is to Deme-
ter, another aspect of the same person. It is really Naomi who is
"redeemed" by Boaz and bears the son, whose original name would
have been something like "son of Naomi" and not Obed. In this suggestion Staples has been followed by others who also think that an earlier
story has been adapted to fit into the genealogy of David. Bethlehem
was an ancient cult centre, as its name ("house of bread") suggests, and
we remember that St. Jerome, the Latin or Vulgate translator of the Bible
in the fifth century, remarks that in Bethlehem there was a grove dedicated to Adonis even in his day.

Staples's argument is usually mentioned by later scholars only to be
dismissed, and it is of course true that such theses do not carry much
conviction now. The main reason is that there is so little evidence for
them beyond whatever suggestiveness may be inherent in some of the
proper names. But I think that this way of reading the story deserves
another look, even if we cannot buy the whole Frazer corn-spirit pack-
age. Writers of stories, however literary, do not invent their stories even
when they think they do: they inherit them. There are always and
invariably earlier versions of the general shape of their plots (*mythoi*),
and these earlier versions go back to the most ancient myths we have.
The Bible is comparatively a rather late product of Near Eastern culture,
and we can often see in it adaptations of earlier mythical themes. Some
stories, like those of Jacob's ladder-vision or Jephthah's daughter, give
us faint glints of pre-Biblical cults. With others, like the deluge story, we
can now compare Sumerian and other more ancient versions that clearly
belong on the same genealogical tree, even if they are not in the direct
line of ancestry. So I see no improbability of there being earlier versions
of the Ruth story, perhaps centred on Bethlehem, that take us back to
very primitive customs connected with harvesting and the myths
attached to those customs.

It was inevitable that the Book of Ruth should become associated with
the Feast of Weeks, because harvest symbolism and imagery saturate
the whole story, especially the two middle chapters. There is no reference to the book in the three volumes of Frazer's *Folklore in the Old Testament*, but *The Golden Bough* has an immense collection of harvest
customs from all over the world. Among these we find very frequently
ritual copulation on the harvest field, to ensure a productive harvest the
next year; the treatment of a passing stranger as an incarnation of the

spirit of the harvest; and a mythical relationship between an older and a younger goddess or female nature-spirit, representing the seed-corn of the previous year and the harvest of the present one. The author of Ruth has transformed these plot themes into credible and very warm human relationships: Boaz sleeps on the harvest field and Ruth asks him to shelter her; she returns from her gleaning operation carrying a bushel or so of wheat; the barren Naomi gains a son through Ruth. We may compare the way in which ancient fertility themes are transformed in the Song of Songs into a metaphorical identification of the bride of the marriage with the fertile land.

I think that when people speak of the Book of Ruth as "charming," they are really using a denatured synonym for something more like "serene." It is the unclouded serenity of the story that impresses the reader, a serenity that does for an agricultural and harvest setting what, let us say, the twenty-third Psalm does for a pastoral one. Like that Psalm, it expresses the feeling that if human beings give up their murderous and polluting ways, the physical environment will be seen as something identical with the human one, as something to live in rather than to dominate. At that point "serenity" becomes inadequate too, and moves into what is called *agape* in the Septuagint and New Testament and *ahabah* in Hebrew (compare the verbal form *aheb* in Ruth 4:15), and expresses the highest vision of human life within the context of the will of God that words can make.

8

The Mythical Approach to Creation

5 June 1985

From the typescript in NFF, 1988, box 49, file 2; another typescript is in NFF, 1991, box 39, file 4. First published in MM, 238–54. Given as an address to the Canadian Theological Society at the Learned Societies meeting in Montreal.

I

The title of this paper is slightly misleading. Creation is a myth, and there are no mythical "approaches" to it because there are no nonmythical ones. What I want to discuss is the progression of three phases in the social use of myth, the preliterary, the literary, and the postliterary, as illustrated by the creation myths in Genesis.

To summarize first of all my general view of myth: a myth to me is primarily a *mythos*, a story, narrative, or plot, with a specific social function. Every human society has a verbal culture, and in the preliterary phase, when abstract thought has not developed, the bulk of this culture consists of stories. Usually there then arises a distinction between stories which explain to their hearers something that those hearers need to know about the religion, history, law, or social system of their society, and less serious stories told primarily for amusement. The more serious group are the myths: they grow out of a specific society and transmit a cultural heritage of shared allusion. We may call the myth a verbal *temenos*, a circle drawn around a sacred or numinous area. The less serious group become folk tales, which travel freely over the world through all barriers of language. Myths travel too, but they tend to keep settling down: thus Sumerian myths eventually expanded into the Hittite area, and from there into archaic Greece.

Preliterary myth arises in a state of society in which there is not as yet a firm and consistent distinction between subject and object. A statement that a subjective A is an objective B is a metaphor, and at the centre of preliterary myths are the gods, who, being partly personalities and partly associated with some department of nature, are ready-made metaphors. It has been said that there are no metaphors in Homer, but in another sense Homer is all metaphor: what goes on inside the human heart, such as *thymos,* are events of the same entity as storms and the like in nature. The appearance of a god or goddess in the form of a well-known friend is unusual but quite in accord with the ways of gods. In Christianity a divine nature taking on a human form is a portentous miracle that can happen only once in history, but such a view is very remote from Homer. Again, the primary question about a preliterary myth is not, "Is it true?" because the linguistic problems in establishing verbal truth are not yet in the foreground. The primary question is something more like, "Do we have to know this?" and the affirmative answer characterizes the genuine preliterary myth.

As culture becomes more pluralistic and specialized, the conception of literature more or less as we know it comes into the foreground. The Homeric poems, for early Greek culture, were primarily writings that educated Greeks had to know, but for us they are safely within the category of literature. But as soon as that category is clearly recognized, the question arises that led Plato to attack not only Homer but all poets: What kind of verbal structure conveys truth?

In the popular mind there is only one way in which words can express truth, and that is the truth of correspondence, where a body of words describes a set of external facts or events or propositions, and is said to be true if we find the correspondence of the words and what they describe satisfactory. The basis of literature, of course, is hypothetical: we know, for example, that Jane Austen tells us a good deal of truth about Regency society, but the framework of her story is about people with no historical existence. The next step is the preposterous dilemma of an antithesis between truth of correspondence and all other uses of words. If truth of correspondence is the only form of verbal truth, then all literary or mythical structures are essentially untrue, and while non-literary structures may be true or false, all true structures must be non-literary.

This imaginary antithesis has been thrashed over so often, from Aristotle's *Poetics* on, that we may well feel that the question is obsolete. I wish it were. As it is, the religious bodies maintaining that revelation must be either literally true or else untrue are the ones that are most dramatically increasing their membership, appeal to the most devoted followers, and take in the most money, and we must either join or imitate them if we want that kind of success. A newspaper controversy can still be stirred up whenever a prominent churchman announces that he does not "literally believe in" the Virgin Birth or whatever, the statement being taken on all sides as heretical rather than as simply illiterate. The Bible is mythical rather than historical, because for its purposes myth is the only vehicle for what has traditionally been called revelation. But anyone who points this out is still likely to be called antihistorical.

It is generally accepted that the opening words of the Gospel of John, "In the beginning was the Word," were intended to form a Christian commentary on at least the first of the two creation myths of the Bible. The verse in Genesis, "And God said, Let there be light: and there was light" [1:3], implies for Christian commentary that the Word was the creative power that brought the thing it named into being. I have elsewhere called attention to the curious passage in Goethe's *Faust*, where Faust is confronted with the opening words of John, refuses to accept them, and eventually produces the mistranslation "In the beginning was the deed [or act]."[1] I should have added that this in fact has been the traditional Christian translation too, however much a reversal of what is being said. The assumption is still that in the beginning God did something, and the words are servomechanisms telling us what he did. There can be no "literal" belief in the creation, or in anything else, without the inference that what God did was prior in significance to whatever anyone, including God, said about it. In the cultural disputes of the early years of the Bolshevist revolution in Russia, Trotsky attacked the Formalists of his day by saying that they were bourgeois idealists who believed that in the beginning was the Word, whereas all good Marxists, being dialectical materialists, knew that in the beginning was the deed.[2] One can understand such a view in Marxism, but for Christianity to use words to decry the primacy of the Word seems very strange. If the Word is the beginning, it is the end too, the Omega as well as the Alpha, and what this principle indicates is that to receive the revelation of the Bible we must examine the total verbal structure of the Bible. This implies a deliberate and conscious renouncing of what is called "literal" belief, which always means subordinating the Word to what the Word is alleged to describe.

II

Myths, I have often said, stick together to form a mythology, unlike folk tales, which simply interchange themes and motifs so stereotyped that they can be counted and indexed. One reason why I have said it so often is that works of literature, which grow out of mythology, also stick together, but we have no word corresponding to "mythology" that expresses the unity that works of literature make up. However, a mythology nearly always begins with some form of creation myth, and all other myths unfold from it. A creation myth is in a sense the only myth we need, all other myths being implied in it. Some critics, notably Coleridge, also think that the only theory of literature we need is a theory of creativity, of how works of literature begin to be. Anyway, the Bible certainly begins with the theme of creation, and it is common knowledge that in the Book of Genesis there are two creation myths. The one in the first chapter, and the first three verses of the second, is usually called the Priestly account; the one that runs from Genesis 2:4 to the end of the second chapter is called the Jahwist account, from the name it uses for God. The Jahwist one is considerably earlier than the Priestly account, which is almost certainly postexilic, the textual order being the reverse of the chronological one.

The Priestly account, as we all know, is divided into seven stages, each being assigned a day of a week. First comes the creation of light, then of the "firmament" or sky separating upper and lower waters, then of vegetation, then of the sun, moon, and stars, then the creatures of water and air, then of the land animals, including human beings, and finally an archetypal Sabbath or day of rest. The Jahwist account may also be divided into seven stages. First, a "mist" or irrigating fountain is set up in the middle of a dry, parched earth. Second, the first human being is created, whom we may call "the being" or "the adam" with a lower-case "a." Third comes the creation of the garden; fourth the creation of the four rivers, fifth the creation of living creatures other than humans, sixth, the creation of the first woman out of the body of the "adam," and finally the statement, a human Sabbath corresponding to that of the other account, that the two human beings were in the state of innocence, naked and not ashamed.

In the Priestly narrative there is a strong emphasis on division and contrast: light is separated from darkness, land from sea, the "firmament" from chaos. The kinship of human beings to the land animals is clearly recognized, and men and women are created together. As in the Jahwist account, humanity forms the climactic work of creation, but in the Jahwist account human beings are in a totally different category from everything else that lives. The Priestly account is a vision of creation largely in terms of what was later to be called *natura naturata*, a cosmic structure or system reaching from chaos up through the human to the divine. The Jahwist account sees rather a *natura naturans*, a growing fertile nature with humanity at its centre.

Neither creation myth is a serious attempt to tell us the history of how the order of nature came into being. If either had ever been intended to do so, one would have expected the Priestly account, for example, to be just a little cleverer, and not had the world of vegetation created before the sun was. God's phrase when he creates the sun and moon, "let them be for signs," indicates that in the context of creation the sun and moon are elements of a calendar. But here we have something rather more than the fussiness of a pedantic deity making sure that his festivals are going to be celebrated at the right time. What is actually coming into being is the human consciousness, and what is being presented to that consciousness is the sense of order and design in the universe that has prompted every creative effort in human arts and sciences. Similarly, the day of rest at the end is not merely an explanation of the origin of the Sabbath: it means among other things that the creation has become objective to its Creator, which implies that it must become objective to human consciousness also. The Priestly cosmos is something to be contemplated and admired, and the door is left open for the later conception of nature as a second book or Word of God for man to read, as well as for all the feelings of wonder and awe and beauty that are central to the conscious human heritage.

Similarly, in the Jahwist account the vision of two human beings naked and unashamed is the culmination of a vision of creation as a home for conscious beings, a world where nature is not simply the human environment but an extension of humanity itself, with nothing of the alienation that it now has. The fact that human consciousness is the mirror of creation is symbolized by the bringing of land and air animals to the adam to be named, the bestowing of names being clearly regarded as a necessary completion of the creative process. This seemed so important to the God of Milton's *Paradise Lost* that he is constrained to add, somewhat apologetically, "Understand the same / Of Fish" [bk. 8, ll. 345–6]. Both creation myths are structures of human concern, but the ascribing of the creative process to God indicates that what is opened to humanity in the vision of the cosmos is infinite, and that we shall never find ourselves permanently in the position of Narcissus, gazing into a verbal and mathematical mirror of our own devising.

The fact that in the Jahwist account woman is created out of the body of the adam led to later speculation, in the Kabbala and elsewhere, that the original adam must have been androgynous, becoming male only after a female principle had been separated from it. The story of the fall is attached to the Jahwist narrative, and that story tells us that the woman took the initiative in breaking the divine prohibition regarding the tree of knowledge. This was of course a standard proof-text, for many centuries, rationalizing a patriarchal social system, and in fact the Jahwist account itself says that patriarchy would result from the fall. Commentary has been so anxious to make this point that it has overlooked the fact that the creation of woman is placed at the end of this creation account, as the climax of the whole procedure. Besides, the conception of fall is unintelligible without its complement of reconciliation. Humanity falls as woman, that is, as sexual being, and it is clear that the eating of forbidden fruit has a good deal to do with the loss of innocence and the developing of the sexual relation as we now know it, or what D.H. Lawrence calls sex in the head.[3] In the Jahwist account, as in so many forms of social psychology today, morality, the knowledge of good and evil, is founded on the repressing or sublimating of the sexual instinct. But if humanity falls as woman, humanity must be redeemed as woman. In Christian typology the souls of all human creatures, whether they are biologically men or women, are symbolically female, forming the body of the bride Jerusalem or the people of God. The Virgin Mary in Catholic thought is placed at the head of all created human beings, below only the Jesus who was begotten, and she is the second Eve in much the same sense that Jesus, in the Pauline phrase, is the second Adam.

There is no myth of fall attached to the Priestly account directly, but later legend and commentary filled up the blank with myths of a fall, not of human nature from a paradisal garden, but of demonic nature from a divine court. We have the story of Lilith, alleged to be the first wife of Adam, and the mother of all devils, and the story of the fall of Satan after a war in heaven. The two myths were of course combined later, when the serpent who initiated the fall of Adam and Eve, and who is nothing but a serpent in the Jahwist account, is assumed to be a mouthpiece for Satan. The fall of the rebel angels is referred to in the

New Testament, but is most elaborately recounted in the Book of Enoch.[4]

At this point I have to invoke a critical principle I have often mentioned before, a sequence of two acts in the critical operation. Once we "hear" a *mythos* or story being read, or read it ourselves in temporal sequence, we then make a *gestalt* or simultaneous apprehension of it which is usually described in a visual metaphor as an act of "seeing." Someone about to tell a joke may say, regrettably, "Have you heard this one?" After we have heard it, we then "see" the joke, grasp its simultaneous meaning, or what Aristotle would call its *dianoia*. But once we "see" the joke we do not want to hear it again. Similarly, we may read to the end of a detective story to "see" who the murderer is, but once we have discovered his identity we normally do not want to read the book again until we have forgotten it. Other *mythoi*, such as those used in religious rituals, show the same transition from hearing to metaphorical seeing. The reading of the Collect in the mass is followed by the elevation of the host; in the initiation rites at Eleusis, we are told, the initiates were shown a reaped ear of corn as the climax of the revelation involved; according to Zen Buddhism, after the Buddha had completed a sermon he held up a golden flower, the only listener who got the point being, of course, the founder of Zen. Every work of literature makes an appeal to us to grasp its total meaning in a single act of apprehension, and it is a common device for a novel, let us say, to bear the title of some visual emblem which symbolizes that total apprehension. Examples would include Henry James's *The Golden Bowl*, D.H. Lawrence's *The Rainbow*, and Virginia Woolf's *To the Lighthouse*.

It is because of the importance of this attempt at simultaneous understanding that the word *structure*, a spatial metaphor derived from architecture, has become so prominent in literary criticism. What we call a "classic" in literature is often a literary work so complex that understanding the "structure" becomes an indefinite and tentative sequence of responses. If we are presented with something like *King Lear*, we hear or read the play, and make an effort to understand what it means as a whole. We are soon oppressed by the inadequacy of this effort; we must hear or read it again and make a better attempt, and a process is started that could conceivably go on all through one's life, at least if one is professionally concerned with literature. In my book *The Great Code* I made a tentative effort to outline the "structure" of the Christian Bible when we attempt to "see" it as a totality, and found, not to my surprise, that the Book of Revelation at the end of the New Testament provided the best guide to that structure. Here I shall attempt to suggest a rough outline of the "structure" of the two creation myths, although, remembering that the two narratives were read as one for practically their whole history, we cannot separate them, beyond noting a few degrees of difference in emphasis.

The visual "emblem" of the structure of the creation narratives, corresponding to the examples given from secular literature, Henry James's golden bowl or Lawrence's rainbow, would obviously be some form of *axis mundi* image, something that suggests the linking of all aspects of the creation in a single concept. For the Priestly account the most natural form of *axis mundi* image would be the ladder, or staircase, of Jacob's great vision at Bethel, an image of which mountains and towers are predictable modulations. For the Jahwist account the readiest image would be the world tree, or tree of life, that stretches from earth to heaven in so many mythologies—so many, in fact, that it does not appear in the Bible except in parody form, though it is implied frequently enough.

One of the most important facts in the history of religion is that in later thought the cosmological ladder is assumed to represent a structure of hierarchy, order, rank, and degree. God is at the top of the cosmos; his court of angels, who are apparently being addressed in Genesis 3:22, would rank next. Then comes the paradisal home of man, taken from the Jahwist account, then the world of nature we see about us, also in ranks, with human beings at the top, then animals, plants, inorganic matter, and, at the bottom, the chaos or "face of the waters" mentioned at the beginning.

Two by-products of this ladder cosmos have been of particular importance in the history of thought: the great chain of being and the Ptolemaic universe. The first was a ladder of existence polarized by the conceptions of form and matter, and stretched from pure form without matter, or God, at the top to chaos at the bottom, chaos being as close as we can get to pure matter without form. Evil, the world of the devils, comes below this, but is not part of the order of nature. The Ptolemaic universe similarly stretched from a primum mobile, a circumference of a finite universe, down through the starry and planetary spheres to the "fallen" world of four elements. Every aspect of creation had its own stratified hierarchy. The metals, for example, were the aristocrats of the mineral world, and even they were subdivided into the noble metals, gold and silver, and the tin and lead that we still call the "base" metals.

A vision of the cosmos as essentially a structure of authority and degree naturally commended itself to all social establishments, and this view of creation lasted for so many centuries because it seemed to justify and rationalize a society similarly based. A society with a sovereign at the top, and aristocracy underneath, and stratified groups of commoners below that, was clearly the "natural" way for human beings to organize themselves, imitating as it did the originally created order. That is why the domain of evil, of the hell that Milton places below chaos, is not part of the order of nature: rebellion against God being totally unnatural, rebellion in human society is similarly unnatural. This hierarchical world consolidates into four main levels: the highest is that of heaven, in the sense of the presence of God, the next the paradisal home originally intended for man, the next the theologically "fallen" natural environment we live in now, and at the bottom is the demonic order. Man is born into the third of these worlds, and his essential quest is to try to raise himself, with the assistance of divine grace and such accredited human aids as institutional religion and social authority, as near as he can to the second level in the garden of Eden which is his proper home. The garden of Eden has disappeared as a place, but persists as an inner state of mind. However, the phrase I just used, "try to raise himself," is ungrammatical, because all initiative must come from above.

But whatever authority itself may say, none the less wherever there is authority there is also at least some conception of potential resistance to that authority, and, as we said, the later legends of the rebel angels tell us that there has even been resistance to the authority of God himself. We are told that close behind the Priestly account in Genesis lies a much older myth in which creation took the form of a victory over a dragon, out of whose body the cosmos was formed. Many Biblical writers, including those in Isaiah, Ezekiel, and the Psalms, are familiar with the dragon-killing myth as a poetic symbol for the creation, and for them the dragon-killing is associated not only with the original creation, but with the deliverance from Egypt and the final restoration of Israel. The Book of Job seems to have a particularly close relationship to the Priestly account, in the way that it sees the suffering of man as a battleground of divine and demonic cosmic forces. At the beginning we have a very puzzling dialogue between God and a Satan who is a tolerated guest in God's court; at the end we have a speaking God pointing out to Job the monstrous dragon from whom Job has apparently been delivered.

The Jahwist account, starting as it does with God as concerned with gardens, trees, and landscape rather than cosmic order, has bequeathed to later ages the sense of God as a benevolent designer who made all things for the convenience of man. It is largely this account that kept the criticism of the arts in so infantile a state for so many centuries, for here God himself is the supreme artist, and no human art can be more than the faintest of shadows of his workmanship. Man's primary destiny, we said, is to try to return to his original paradisal home in which nature and art are the same thing, nature being, as Sir Thomas Browne remarked, the art of God.[5] Another remark of Browne, referring to arguments from design and the doctrine that God made all things in nature primarily for human use, shows how far we have come from thinking in these terms: "How America abounded with Beasts of prey and noxious Animals, yet contained not in it that necessary Creature, a Horse, is very strange."[6]

More important even than the conception of divine design in the Jahwist narrative is the suggestion of a fall in sexual experience through eating of the tree of morality. Just as the Priestly narrative has a particularly close relation to the Book of Job, so the Jahwist one is symbolically close to the Song of Songs, that wonderful group of love poems in which a paradisal retreat, "a garden enclosed, a fountain sealed," is identified with the body of the bride. Here we meet another kind of ladder, the one that appeared in Plato's *Symposium* outside the Biblical tradition entirely, but was later forced on an unwilling Christian bureaucracy by the poets. In the Middle Ages a quest of love, so closely approximating the regeneration of the soul in orthodox Christianity as to amount to a parody of it, was established as a central theme of literature. Such a quest of love may be sublimated and devoid of explicit sexuality, as it is in Dante, or it may retain the theme of sexual union, as it does in *The Romaunt of the Rose*. But we are never far from the sense that the ultimate quest is not so much the sexual union of a man and a woman as the union of all human beings with the nature that forms their environment, a nature usually mythologized as a mother, in which the primitive metaphorical identity of the subjective and the objective has been reestablished.

Every central image in the Bible has its ideal or apocalyptic form, the one suggested by God to his people, and its demonic or parodied form, the one worshipped by the heathen kingdoms without. The world-tree image, we said, appears chiefly in the parody form, notably in Ezekiel and Daniel; the ladder image finds its parody in the story of the Tower of Babel. In Mesopotamian cities the temple or home of the god normally stood in the centre, and thus symbolically formed a link between heaven and earth. A common feature of such ziggurats, as they are called, was a spiral staircase, and according to Herodotus there were often seven of these staircases, each coloured differently to represent the seven known planets. At the top of the building, Herodotus says, was the chamber in which the body of the bride was laid to await the descent of the god [bk. 1, sec. 181]. Babel is not said to be spiral in shape, though portrayed as such in Brueghel's picture and elsewhere, but the figure of the spiral tower or mountain runs through Mithraic symbolism and reappears in a Christian setting in Dante's *Purgatorio*, where there are again seven complete turns, each one removing one of the seven deadly sins, and here again the original paradise of Eden, the enclosed garden and sealed fountain which is the body of redeemed humanity, the bride of God, appears at the top.

III

The cosmos of authority lingered until the eighteenth century, although of its two pillars, the chain of being and the Ptolemaic universe, the latter was in ruins by Isaac Newton's time. The chain of being was still in place for Pope early in the eighteenth century, but Voltaire was very doubtful about the *échelle de l'infini*, which he recognized to be a façade for the authority of the status quo.[7] And under the hammer blows of the American Revolution, the French Revolution, and the Industrial Revolution, the ladder as a spatial metaphor for the *axis mundi*, and as a cosmic vision guaranteeing the birthright of established authority, finally disappeared.

The effects of this in literature are what I am particularly concerned with, and they can be traced through the Romantic movement down to our own time. Let us look, as an example, at the imagery of four poets of the early part of this century, T.S. Eliot, W.B. Yeats, Ezra Pound, and James Joyce. In his early poetry Eliot seems fascinated by the staircase as an image of crisis: such a line as "Time to turn back and descend the stair" from *Prufrock* [l. 39] reminds us that our word "climax" comes from the Greek word for a ladder. In *Ash-Wednesday* we have a much more elaborate staircase, avowedly taken from Dante's *Purgatorio*, where the soul journeys from the seashore of experience and nostalgia to a garden at the top. Yeats, though he maintains that all ladders are planted in the human heart, is full of "tower" and "winding stair" images, where a "soul" ascends to the annihilating of its ego-centre and a "self" descends to a new life. He even bought one of the round towers with spiral staircases that still exist in Ireland as a personal symbol.

Ezra Pound begins his *Cantos* with an adaptation of the descent to the lower world in the *Odyssey*, where Odysseus first meets Elpenor, one of his crew who had fallen off a ladder and broken his neck, and then goes on to the central image of the spiral tower of Herodotus with its seven turnings, each coloured differently to represent the seven planets. Even the terrible experience of being locked in a cage during the Second World War did not prevent the *Pisan Cantos* from beginning defiantly with the resolve to "build the city of Dioce whose terraces are the colour of stars" [*Canto 74*, l. 11]. Joyce's *Finnegans Wake* is founded on a ballad about an Irish hod-carrier who, like Elpenor, fell off a ladder and broke his neck, later coming to life at his funeral wake to demand a share of the whisky. In Joyce the fall of Finnegan is associated with the fall of Adam and the flood of Noah on the first page: Finnegan himself, however, is dissuaded by the other members of the wake from waking up, so he continues to sleep and dream, his dream being the turning cycle of human history.

The use of this ancient ladder or staircase image by the four leading poets of their generation does not mean that any of them, even Eliot, have any interest in trying to set up the old cosmic image of social authority once again. What they are producing is a series of what it is now fashionable to call "deconstructions" of that image. Deconstruction, however, is in itself, I think, a birdshot critical technique: it aims at a variety of targets and bags whatever it happens to hit accidentally. I think the "deconstructions" going on in regard to this image have a more restricted aim, and are not simply a series of Darwinian mutations thrown out at random.

I said that the Priestly account of creation suggests a hierarchical ladder stretching from the divine to the demonic. One of the central themes of Romanticism, and one that crystallizes mainly around the figure of Byron, is the annexing of the demonic to the human. It is man who works evil and creates hell or, as the Romantic poet Beddoes remarked: "'Tis but one devil ever tempts a man, / And his name's *Self*."[8] The next stage is the separating of the real evil that man does from the activity that is merely assumed to be evil by those devoted to the status quo: the revolutionary acts, including most of the genuinely creative ones, that threaten authority. In English literature the most powerful treatment of this distinction is Blake's *Marriage of Heaven and Hell,* which lays down the programme that all Blake's later work follows. Humanity is ruled by inertia and terror: the expression of human energy threatens this; consequently human energy, which is rooted in the sexual instinct, is condemned as evil. There certainly is such a thing as real evil, but most of that comes from the defenders of established authority, who find cruelty essential to their ascendancy. This is a conception of human liberty that sees liberty as a birthright that man can and should lay claim to. It is a view of liberty similar to those of, say, Jefferson or Shelley, but very different from earlier theories. Even the revolutionary Milton did not think of liberty as anything that man wanted: man is terrified of the maturity and responsibility that liberty brings with it. Liberty is good for man because it is something that God wants man to have; but the initiative must come from the divine grace that is above man on the scale of being. After the Romantic movement, however, the ladder of being became a two-way staircase, with ascent as well as descent, just as Jacob originally saw it. For if the demonic is really an aspect of the human, the angelic is too: man has titanic powers for both construction and destruction that he has never consistently used, except in the service of the wrong kind of authority. The cosmic ladder reconstructed in this form is, mythologically, the liberation of Prometheus, and it is certainly no accident that Shelley's poetic masterpiece is called *Prometheus Unbound.*

The Jahwist myth of creation, where man falls out of the state of innocence into a state of sexual repression and alienation from nature, had always had its counter-movement in the cult of Eros, which, as I observed, had been forced on European culture in the Christian period by the poets. Naturally the cult of Eros continued and expanded in the Romantic period: we may notice two aspects of this expansion here. In the first place, the traditional ladder goes down into the demonic world; consequently, in spite of the prestige of Virgil, who in the sixth book of the *Aeneid* gave so memorable a vision of a descent to a lower world, there are very few such quests in Christian literature, apart from descents to hell like Dante's *Inferno.* But after the Romantic period descent themes become much more frequent, and, above all, the lower world comes to be associated with the world of dreams, which are soon recognized to be closely linked to the creative powers. In the second place, Romantic love poetry often touches on the theme of regeneration of nature. In the "Introduction" to the *Songs of Experience* in Blake, the "lapsed Soul," or what falls at the beginning of time, is not Adam or Eve but a female "Earth" (the *adamah* of Genesis 3:7) who contains humanity as well as its paradisal environment. Similarly, the poet proposes to his beloved in Shelley's *Epipsychidion* a union that includes much more than the merging of two human bodies:

> Let us become the overhanging day,
> The living soul of this Elysian isle,
> Conscious, inseparable, one. [538–40]

The influence of the two creation myths as I have sketched it illustrates most of the major features of the social function of myth. First, a myth has two aspects: it is part of a vision of the cosmos, constructed from human concern, and it is also very likely to be seized on by whatever establishment or pressure group is in power and expounded in their interest. Thus both myths, the Priestly one in particular, were interpreted as justifying various structures of social authority, but it was precisely this aspect of the myths that proved to be mortal. Similarly, the upward-moving Romantic myths were also turned into rationalizations of authority as soon as the theory of Darwinian evolution began to filter into popular mythology. This view saw the whole evolutionary process as leading up to humanity as its climax, and as able to continue only through humanity. Such a view was already implied, in fact asserted, in the Genesis accounts, where man is also said to be given the domination over the whole natural order. But various problems with ecology and the natural environment have begun to indicate to us that there is a limit to the domination of man over nature, and that if the domination becomes too great a tyranny nature may simply push him off the planet. It seems better not to turn visionary myths into authoritarian blueprints.

I have briefly glanced at the role of preliterary myth in human culture, and in discussing the Genesis creation myths I have been concerned with the second stage, where the mythical tends to be identified with the literary, and excluded from the conveying of genuine information. I have no space or time to outline a postliterary theory of myth, but I conclude with a suggestion or two about the factors involved.

We do not talk about verbal truth as confidently as we used to do, but I think there are three contexts in which what has traditionally been called or associated with truth can be brought into alignment with words. First is the context of the integrity of a verbal structure. We may, for instance, read an aphorism in the Book of Proverbs or elsewhere, and reflect how profoundly true it is, or we may read a work of literature and feel that it conveys, within a fictional or hypothetical framework, essential truths about either its own cultural context or about the human situation generally. We know, for instance, that Jane Austen tells us a good deal that is "true" about Regency society and that Wordsworth has a conception of nature that some of us find "true" to our own experience. Such structures integrate a great mass of incidental experiences, as a powerful magnet picks up piles of scrap iron. This is by far the most important association of words and truth, and is much the closest to the conception of faith in the New Testament as the *hypostasis* and *elenchos* of the unseen and hoped for. But it demands an active response to the structure of what is being presented, not a passive one to the content, and hence is often not realized to be a form of truth at all.

Second, there is the kind of sequential verbal truth of the type we call logic, but this is a highly specialized use of words, however important in itself, and in our ordinary verbal experience we seldom encounter it. What we encounter is usually rhetoric in a logical disguise. Third, there is the verbal truth of correspondence already discussed.

Truth of correspondence is of course essential, and we could hardly get through an ordinary day of experience without it. But it is also the most approximate and ambiguous form of the three, and though incessantly useful it is never definitive. Truth of correspondence is really a technique of measurement, where the standard or criterion of measurement is outside the verbal structure. And verbal structures have too many features peculiar to themselves for any external truth to pass through them undistorted. There is figurative language, for instance: most of the words we use contain a large and unacknowledged deposit of metaphor and analogy in them. And there are the syntactic relations, such as those of subject, predicate, and object, which we often assume to be built into the world around us, but are actually only built into the grammar of our language.

It is, I am convinced, through the criticism of mythology, which unravels the implications of a myth from within and studies its context with other myths outside it, that we arrive most closely to what we can learn through words, or the contact with words that has traditionally been called revelation. To examine the creation myth of the Bible, we said, we need to disentangle it from the various kidnappings by authority that distorted it into a justification of that authority. Doing this releases other myths, whose relation to it may be then clearly seen: I gave the example of the liberation of Prometheus and Eros myths. Marxism and Freudianism are two of the most powerful intellectual forces in the world today: I think it is quite intelligible to say that Marxism grew out of the myth of Prometheus, as Freudianism did out of the myth of Eros. As Emily Dickinson says, sardonically but with some affection as well, of the Christian God, "He will refund us finally / Our confiscated gods,"[9] and he does so as soon as his own mythology is detached from the wrong kind of authority.

The subject can never meet the object, the Other, as the Other, but can only encounter it in the intermediate realm of language, to which both subject and object are assimilated. My interest in myth and in metaphor is based on the fact that the language of myth and metaphor is self-contained, not dependent on reference to something else. And wherever I turn in pursuit of my verbal interests, I come up against the fact that our ordinary experience rests on unreal and fuzzy experiences of time and space, and that myth and metaphor are among other things techniques of meditation, designed to focus our minds on a more real view of both.

For example, metaphor says, grammatically and syntactically, that A is B: at the same time it suggests that nobody could be fool enough to believe that A really is B. The statement "A is B" is therefore neither logical nor antilogical: it is counterlogical. The word "is" is really there to destroy the sense of an intervening space between the personal element A and the natural element B, and leads us into a world where subject and object can interpenetrate with one another, as freely as they did in Homer's day. What the metaphor does to space the myth does to time. The myth asserts that something happened, and conveys also the sense that such a thing could not have happened in just that way. Myth does not, like history, present a past event as past: it presents it as present. But its present is not the unreal present of ordinary experience, chained to a dead past and an unborn future and never itself quite coming into existence at all. It is a present where, as Eliot says, past and future are gathered:[10] the present of Jesus' aphorism "Before Abraham was, I am" [John 8:58]. When we are at the point of taking in a vision of time and space of the kind that myth and metaphor offer us, we are ready to meet the conception of a mythical and metaphorical creation that was there from the beginning, but is there again, reborn as soon as we look at it with fresh eyes.

9

Crime and Sin in the Bible

15 April 1986

From Rough Justice, *ed. Martin L. Friedland (Toronto: University of Toronto Press, 1991), 3–18. First published in* MM, *255–69. Three typescripts, one with holograph corrections, are in NFF, 1991, box 38, file 5. Given as an address to the Faculty of Law, University of Toronto.*

The legally trained reader knows much better than I do how difficult it is to define a crime, a misdemeanour, or any form of antisocial behaviour, apart from a violation of a specific law already in existence. Some legislation may be empirical or pragmatic in its basis, like traffic regulations, but there seems to be a powerful deductive force in law that impels us to look for principles and premises from which we derive our laws. A country with a written constitution, like the United States, has at least that means of providing principles, though the amount of amending and reinterpreting needed to keep it functioning so often reminds us of the well known old knife with its new blade and new handle.

A written constitution is often the consequence of a successful revolution, and a country with a revolutionary tradition normally acquires a strongly deductive attitude to the social contract, or at least the more doctrinaire of its citizens do. Thus the American Revolution brought with it a popular involvement in the conception of what should be considered genuinely American behaviour and attitudes, a feature of American life that de Tocqueville discusses at length.[1] Similarly, Marxist revolutions may produce a climate of opinion in which undesirable behaviour can be characterized as remnants of bourgeois attitudes. Not all of these ethical trends are incorporated into actual law, but they can act as a powerful legal force none the less. The importance of this factor in law is that it seems to point further back than the major premises of a constitution, the rights of man, equality before the courts, and the like, to something more primitive embedded in human nature and destiny. Every constitution has to be thought of, in practice, as in some sense an inspired document. Defining the nature of its inspiration is another matter.

We may find it more relaxing to live in Canada, where nobody thinks about what a hundred per cent Canadian is, and where a committee on un-Canadian activities would be faced with a totally unintelligible agenda. But even a system of law based on precedent has problems with the pressures exerted by the majority on individuals and minorities. In Canada, before the Charter, our own "inspired" document, we had a series of *ad hoc* agreements and compromises like the Quebec Act,[2] which made some effort, in fact a rather remarkable one for the eighteenth century, to keep the civic rights of both English- and French-speaking Canadians in mind. But the indigenous peoples, the Japanese Canadians during the Second World War, and other such groups, would tell a different story.

The theory of precedent, of course, as formulated by Burke and by what is called the Whig interpretation of history, is that it operates in a liberal direction, toward increasing freedom and equality. The barons who compelled King John to sign Magna Carta were, on this view, ultimately acting for the benefit of the common man. But this conception of precedent has had to be modified a good deal, the reason that concerns us just now being that it does not go back far enough. If we pursue the ancestry of precedent, we eventually move into a prehistoric period in which laws are rationalized by a myth-telling society that they have been revealed by the gods. Once revealed, they are then enforced by an ascendant class, in whose interest the laws are interpreted. No conception of precedent can wholly shake off the influence of these mythical and prelegal origins. Let us listen to Blackstone, in the eighteenth century, commenting on the regulations about Sunday observance:

> Profanation of the Lord's Day, vulgarly (but improperly) called *sabbath-breaking*, is a ninth offence against God and religion, punished by the municipal law of England. For, besides the notorious indecency and scandal of permitting any secular business to be publicly transacted on that day, in a country professing Christianity, and the corruption of morals which usually follows its profanation, "the keeping one day in seven holy, as a

time of relaxation and refreshment as well as for public worship, is of admirable service to a state, considered merely as a civil institution. It humanizes by the help of conversation and society the manners of the lower classes, which would otherwise degenerate into a sordid ferocity and savage selfishness of spirit: it enables the industrious workman to pursue his occupation in the ensuing week, with health and cheerfulness; it imprints on the minds of the people that sense of their duty to God, so necessary to make them good citizens, but which yet would be worn out and defaced by an unremitted continuance of labour, without any stated times of recalling them to the worship of their Maker."[3]

The one secular principle involved here, that mandatory holidays create better working conditions, gets in by the back door. It is clear that the major premises from which Blackstone is deriving his argument are, first, the traditional rituals of Christianity, which go back to still earlier Jewish ones, and, second, the principle that the lower classes should be kept firmly in their lower place. Clearly, it would be profitable to look at some of the origins of these assumptions: in particular, the religious origin, which so often includes the myth already mentioned, that the original laws were handed down to a specific human society by divine beings.

The word "crime" is social and secular in context: murder and theft are crimes because they are disturbances of the social order. The word "sin" is religious in context, and has no meaning outside a religious framework. Sin is primarily man's effort to block or frustrate the will of God, and though, in a normal state of society, crimes are usually regarded also as sins, they are so only when and because God is assumed to disapprove of them. So any legal code that goes back to a divine revelation has the conception "sin" as its major premise from which the conception of "crime" is derived.

In primitive societies the conception of sin begins in such features as taboo, where, for example, certain things must not be touched, certain foods not eaten, certain ceremonies not witnessed by outsiders. There then develops the sense of certain ritual obligations owed to the gods, the neglect of which, even if unconscious, will bring disaster. In the Book of Exodus there is a list of prescriptions in chapter 34, described as "the ten commandments," which are concerned almost wholly with these ritual obligations, and consequently may be older than the better known Decalogue in Exodus 20 and Deuteronomy 5, which I shall return to in a moment. Central to these ritual obligations is the conception of sacrifice. At each of the three major festivals, sacrificial offerings are to be brought to God, "and none shall appear before me empty" (Exodus 34:20). Similarly, the period from Friday to Saturday sunsets is to be withdrawn from social and utilitarian pursuits, including the making of money. Every first-born male animal, including the first-born son of human beings, belongs to God as a sacrifice, though the son is to be redeemed by a lamb instead, or may be devoted to God in a more sublimated sense, like the infant Samuel.

The conception of sacrifice also enters warfare, and the most ferocious penalties are connected with disregarding the claims of God in war. If the Israelites are to conquer Canaan, all the loot they acquire belongs to God, which in practice means the priesthood. Joshua takes the city of Jericho, then meets with a sharp repulse at the city of Ai. He learns that an Israelite named Achan has kept some of the loot from Jericho for himself, so not only is Achan stoned to death, but his entire family is wiped out and all his possessions confiscated (Joshua 7:1–8:29). Similarly, prisoners captured in battle are to be killed as sacrifices to God. When King Saul captures the Amalekite king Agag he spares his life, as we should think, out of ordinary human decency, but the prophet Samuel, after denouncing Saul for having committed an utterly unforgivable sin against God, falls on Agag and hews him in pieces, and from then on King Saul never has any luck again (1 Samuel 15).

No doubt in pre-Biblical times these sacrifices were thought of as actually feeding the gods, as they still seem to be in Homer.[4] We can also see clearly enough a pre-Biblical cult of human sacrifice, which the Mosaic code is designed both to abolish and to re-establish on a more rational moral basis. But the prophets are emphatic that God has no need of the smoke of sacrifice and the like, and the rationale for these ritual obligations has to be looked for elsewhere.

The Hebrew word *torah* means the whole body of instruction necessary for the people of Israel, including the laws and such ritual obligations. The New Testament writers relied mainly on the Septuagint (Greek) translation of the Old Testament, and as the Septuagint rendered *torah* as *nomos*, the King James and other translations speak simply of the "Law." But if we look at the Book of Deuteronomy we see something far bigger than a legal code: it is a contract or treaty between God and Israel transmitted through Moses, and it gives us not merely a code but a theological and historical context for that code.

The details of this context are filled out in the other books of the Pentateuch. First comes the founding of the society of Israel on a revolutionary basis. Moses in Egypt is informed by the voice speaking from the burning bush that the God of Israel is about to give himself a name, enter history, and take a very partisan role in it, the role of delivering an enslaved people from the bondage of the Egyptian establishment (Exodus 2:23–4:17). The revolutionary origin gives, as remarked earlier, a strongly deductive cast to the structure of laws, and we are constantly being referred back to the original contract. For example, one of the most attractive features of the Deuteronomic code is its relatively humane attitude to slavery, and the Israelite community is frequently reminded of the central reason for adopting such an attitude: that they themselves were once slaves in Egypt.

Most of us, I assume, would share the assumptions about liberty and equality, which oppose slavery, as the basis of law that have been formulated at least since John Stuart Mill's time.[5] We take for granted the principle of the equality of all citizens before the law and the principle of the greatest amount of individual autonomy consistent with the well-being of others. To the extent that the laws are bent in the interests of a privileged or aggressive group; to the extent that citizens live under arbitrary regulations enforced by terror; to that extent we are living in an illegal society. If we regard our own society as at least workably legal, we also take largely for granted that the real basis for the effectiveness of law in such a society is an invisible morale. The law in itself is compelled to deal only with overt actions, so that from the law's point of view an honest man is any man not yet convicted of stealing. But no society could hold together with so loose a conception of morality: there has to be a sufficient number of self-respecting citizens who are honest because they like it better that way.

The Pentateuch in general, and the Book of Deuteronomy in particular, is an extraordinary tour de force of social thought in which certain obligations toward God are assumed to build up in each person this inner morale that, so to speak, insulates that person from becoming a disintegrating force in society. The *torah* is designed, among many other things, to provide a kind of vertical dimension to law. The relation of the individual Israelite to the God of Israel, built up by the habits of action and thought fostered by the laws of the Sabbath and the like, is the source of the inner moral energy that is needed to keep society together. Sin, thought of as primarily the neglect of ritual obligations, thus becomes the source of crime, so that one can never eradicate crime from society by secular legislation alone.

If we look at the familiar structure of the Decalogue, the ten commandments as we know them, we can see an illustration of this conception of secular crime being derived from ritual neglect (Exodus 20:1–17). The first four commandments are concerned with the obligations of religion: Israel must be faithful to its God, not make images of him or of other gods, take the name of God seriously, and rest on the Sabbath. The fifth commandment, to honour one's parents, makes a transition to the moral sphere, but is connected with the ritual group by the promise that observing it will be rewarded by God with long life. The four commandments following, the prohibitions against murder, adultery, theft, and slander, would, if they stood alone, be thought of as purely moral and secular. The final commandment against coveting brings us back to that inner state of mental integrity which is the real basis of all law.

This deductive construct, in which the commands of God, the neglect of which is sin, form the premises for social morality, or law in the context of "law and order," is not unmatched in the ancient world: the role of sacrifice and other ritual practices in Hinduism is very similar, and there are other religion-based legal codes, like that of Islam, that develop later partly under Biblical influence. Still it is a rare achievement: the legal code of Hammurabi in Babylon, for instance, impressive as it is, does not seem to have acquired anything like the same prestige among its people.[6] We note in passing that such codes enclose a specific society and mark it off from others. The Deuteronomic code implies that God is uniquely related to Israel, and that Israel's ritual obligations are not necessarily binding on other nations. But for most of its history Israel was not an independent nation, but a province subject to the authority of Egypt, Assyria, Babylonia, Persia, Greece, and Rome. These heathen nations were the source of the secular and moral law, not less so when they allowed the Israelites to keep their ritual obligations. So the question arises: what happens when sin and crime are violations of conflicting structures of authority?

We may take an example from perhaps the most haunting situation of the sort in human culture: the dilemma of Antigone in Sophocles.[7] Here Antigone is forbidden by Creon, the ruler of Thebes and the source of its secular law, to bury her brother's body, and yet not to bury it would be a sin against one of the most solemn of Greek ritual obligations. Antigone does not hesitate: it is the sin that it is important to avoid, not the crime. She suffers accordingly, but the disaster that befalls Creon vindicates her, in the eyes of the audience at least. Similar dilemmas rise to a climax in the persecution of the Jews under Antiochus of Syria, the persecution that provoked the Maccabean rebellion (1 Maccabees).

When the Christian religion began, a century or so after the Maccabees, this problem of a possible clash between religious and secular authority was very much in the foreground. Paul strongly advises submission to the secular authority of the Roman empire, but what he says sounds a trifle hollow in view of the persecutions that started almost immediately, affecting Christians and Jews alike. Apart from this, there was also the question: how far is the Old Testament code binding on Christians? In what sense are Christians to be regarded as a new Israel? In this controversy Paul emerged as the leader who proclaimed that Christianity was to be brought to the Gentiles outside Israel, and that the ritual obligations of Judaism, such as circumcision, were no longer binding on Christians. The effect of the Christian reformulation of law was to drive a much wider breach between the two conceptions of sin and crime, and the consequences of doing so are still with us. In the teaching of Jesus, especially in the Sermon on the Mount in Matthew (5:1–7:27), which includes commentaries on some of the ten commandments, the distinction between the inner integrity that resists sin and the overt action of a crime is pushed about as far as it will go. The overwhelming emphasis is on the inner state of mind. If A murders B, and C merely wishes with all his being that D were dead, A is legally a murderer and C is wholly innocent of murder. From the point of view of the Sermon on the Mount the chief difference between the A who murders and the C who feels murderous is that A has more guts. Again, Jesus interprets the prohibitions against murder and adultery and theft as positive enthusiasms for human life, for the respect and self-respect of women, for property. There is nothing here that cannot be paralleled in contemporary rabbinical teaching, perhaps, but some of the inferences drawn in the New Testament, more particularly by Paul, forecast another revolution.

Paul sees in the story of the fall of Adam in Genesis the existence in human life of what is called original sin. The beginning of sin for him is an inherent condition of the soul, which is there before any act is. Consequently ritual obligations, while they symbolize a desire to be rid of original sin, are still ineffective: it is the inner condition itself that has to be transformed. This transformation sets one free from the law, according to Galatians, which is perhaps the earliest of Paul's writings. But one is not set free from the law by breaking the law, only more tangled up with it than ever. Jesus said that he thought of his teaching as fulfilling the law, not abolishing it: that means that there is an aspect of the law, called by Paul the "spiritual" aspect, which is re-established, and another aspect that disappears.

This means that, for example, justice is the internal condition of the just man, and the external antagonist of the criminal. But the just man, to maintain his justice, has to be far stricter with himself than any law could provide penalties for. Justice as conceived by the Gospel cannot be legalized: if we tried to make the transformed inner state spoken of by Paul and Jesus into a new code of law, the most frightful and fantastic tyranny would result. One can have a law against rape, but Jesus' conception of adultery includes all the men who mentally rape every woman who catches their eye, and this kind of "adultery" cannot become a basis for legislation. If it did, we should have the situation of black farce in Gilbert's *Mikado*:

> The youth who winked a roving eye,
> Or breathed a non-connubial sigh
> Was thereupon condemned to die . . .[8]

This was the basis on which Milton argued for divorce in the seventeenth century.[9] Divorce is permitted in the Mosaic code, but is apparently prohibited by Jesus.[10] Milton claimed that Jesus was talking about marriage in the spiritual or Gospel sense, as a lifelong union that can be consummated, which means finished, only by the death of one of the partners. Its model is the relation of Adam and Eve before the fall, for each of whom there was, quite literally, no one else. But it is clearly nonsense, Milton says, to pretend that every sexual union in society is a spiritual marriage of this kind.

Of course the fact that Milton had to make such an argument, and was bitterly denounced for doing so, indicates that the original distinction between sin and crime was very largely ignored in practice. It was there in theory: in the Middle Ages the deadly sins were divided into seven groups, pride, wrath, sloth, envy, avarice, gluttony, and lechery. Preachers tended to leave lechery to the end as the most interesting. All crime is the result of one or more of these sins, but not one of them in itself necessarily results in crime. Still, the bulk of canon law was incorporated into secular law, and deviations from it were treated as crimes, whether the crime was eating meat in Lent or holding heretical doctrines. A new set of ritual obligations was set up, and it is clear that there is no change of principle when the day of rest is altered to Sunday from Saturday or the rite of circumcision replaced by the rite of baptism. Then, of course, there have always been the moralists, who want to turn as much sin, or what they consider sin, into crime as possible, and pass laws accordingly. In the seventeenth century there were also extreme Nonconformists who held that nothing was either sinful or criminal unless it was explicitly said to be so in the Bible. The Bible obligingly came through with denunciations of everything they disapproved of anyway except polygamy, which it nowhere condemns; that one had to be chalked up to the law of nature, a frantically muddled area of thought which I shall have to glance at in a moment. During the Prohibition era, the "drys," most of whom had strong Protestant commitments, ran into a similar difficulty with a Bible which, while it condemns drunkenness, never conceives of the possibility of a human life totally deprived of fermented beverages.

The original Christian distinction between sin and crime was a part of the revolutionary aspect of Christianity, and the progressive blurring of the distinction was the result of the revolutionary impulse being smothered under new forms of entrenched privilege. The significance of the revolution which appears at the beginning of so many legal codes, of Israel in Egypt, of the American, French, and Russian Revolutions of our times, is that a revolution repudiates an existing structure of law and authority. Christianity holds that Jesus was without sin, yet he was put to death as a criminal. This means that crime represents a social judgment, but society is never wholly capable of making such a judgment. It has no standards, in itself, for distinguishing what is below the law from what is above it: it cannot tell a prophet from a blasphemer, a saint from a witch, a philosopher from a teacher of subversive doctrines. Hence the martyred careers of Jesus, Joan of Arc, and Socrates.

This issue can hardly be called obsolete today, when Nazi Germany and similar dictatorships have made us familiar with the conception of a criminal society. Many liberal-minded Canadians, highly respected people who never come within sight of arrest or imprisonment, would, if they were living in South Africa, find their consciences nagging them because they were *not* in jail. Antisocial behaviour may result from motives that are considered good in other societies, or by the same society in a different phase of its history. Whether the relativity of crime could also apply to sin or not is a more difficult question. I think of a sardonic story by Marcel Aymé, in which a simple and saintly man in a French provincial town wakes up one morning to discover that he has acquired a halo, clearly visible except when he wears a hat. His wife is furious: nobody in *her* family ever had haloes, and how was she to explain this to the neighbours or to the concierge? As he could not wear his hat all the time, he would have to choose between her and the halo. So he conscientiously sets out to commit all the seven deadly sins, loses his reputation, his friends and his job, and finally ends up as a pimp in a brothel. But his motive in doing all this was so fundamentally innocent that the halo stayed firmly in place.[11]

The story, farcical as it is, indicates a genuine dilemma about the criteria for sin and crime. In a normally functioning society a crime is a breach of the legal code. But a society may pass laws so grotesquely unjust that obeying the laws of such a society may be the real crime. This at least, I assume, was the principle the Nuremberg trials after the Second World War attempted to establish. What criteria come into focus then? Many of the liberal-minded people I just spoke of, who would be dissidents in a racist or dictatorial country, have strong religious commitments, and for them a criminal society derives its criminal nature from sin, from being under the judgment of God. But the experience of our century indicates that any religious ideology, Christian or Jewish or Islamic or Hindu or whatever, is a most insecure basis for a modern state. In fact, as in South Africa or Iran, a religious ideology is often a major contributing factor to an intolerable legal code.

Conceptions derived from natural law or the law of nations as the basis for a "legal" society concern me here only insofar as they have been traditionally a part of the relation of crime to sin in the Bible. The notion of natural law is really not in the Bible: in the Bible the same God is in charge of both the moral and the natural orders, and nature is thought of as a fellow creature of man, who, like man, has an order imposed on it by divine will. In the Biblical view there cannot be such a thing, strictly speaking, as a miracle, because God does as he likes in both human and physical worlds. Natural law grew out of the sort of questions asked by the Presocratic philosophers. What is the world made of? Is there a primary substance? What really are the stars? Are there such things as atoms? These are questions that move in the direction of science, and from them came the observation that some things in nature behaved regularly enough to be predictable. It was a considerable set-back to science that this emerging view of natural law should have been associated, by a violent and foolish pun, with law in its human and social context. Natural laws are not "broken"; if we fall out of a tree we do not break the law of gravitation: we merely illustrate it. But the confusions engendered by the pun still persist, even when the conception of God is replaced by a mother-goddess figure of Nature. We have it still in Einstein's unwillingness to accept the element of chance in quantum mechanics, and in the frequent assertion that evolution did not arise by "blind chance," but chance operating within a framework of law. As long as law in nature means simply the human observation of the predictable element in it, this amounts to saying that things happened as they did because they happened as they did.

The law of nations, the *jus gentium* of Grotius[12] and others, which is often associated or identified with natural law, arose, according to Sir Henry Maine, in Roman efforts to define the legal status of non-Romans.[13] It is thus extra-Biblical in origin, but it became attached to the central myth of the Bible in a way that persisted down to at least the eighteenth century. According to this myth, which derives from Paul's emphasis on the fall of Adam and the original sin that resulted, there are two levels of nature. The upper or human level is the one God created with the garden of Eden and the original Adam and Eve. The lower or physical level is the one that Adam fell into, which all of us, being his descendants, are now born in. Man is not adjusted to this lower level of nature, as the animals and plants appear to be. Many things are "natural" to man, such as wearing clothes, being conscious, and using reason, which are natural to nothing else in the environment. Edmund Burke was insisting as late as the French Revolution that "art is man's nature,"[14] not something man has imposed on nature.

It follows that we cannot appeal to anything in physical nature to determine the answer to the question, "What is natural to man?" In Milton's *Comus* a chaste Lady is imprisoned by Comus, who tries to seduce her with arguments drawn from the animal world and its lack of self-consciousness about sexual intercourse. The Lady's answer is too virtuous to be altogether coherent, but the general line of her argument is that on the human level of nature it is her chastity that is natural, not promiscuity.[15] On the other hand, "nature" is often invoked as a standard against which socially disapproved behaviour, such as homosexuality or incest, may be measured. The hero of the late Greek romance

Daphnis and Chloe is tempted to a homosexual relationship, but refuses because, though a simple and untutored country boy, he has never seen such relationships among animals.[16] Being only the hero of a pastoral story, he does not do the research into animal behaviour that might have qualified his position. But we can already see what the general conclusion is. The humanly natural is what is natural on the human level of nature; that is, the form of human society sanctioned by custom and tradition and authority. What is natural to man, then, is a question with a completely circular answer: it is whatever constituted authority says is natural, and you will accept this or else.

Nothing in any of the traditional conceptions of natural law will help us to arrive at criteria by which to judge an unjust society. Let us go back to where we started, the Biblical view that crime is a by-product of sin, sin being rooted in one's obligations, ritual or moral, to God. These obligations, however universal the religion aims at being, are essentially tribal: they enclose the group of believers, even if they can be numbered in millions, and separate them from others with different obligations or with no traditions of any kind at all. Some of these excluding obligations are very potent: dietary laws, for instance, which separate different groups on the basis of what can become something like physical nausea. The nausea may work negatively also: a Moslem woman in Pakistan, for example, once remarked to me about Hindus, "I hate those people; they don't eat beef." An American senator of some years back similarly opposed any aid to the starving people of India on the ground that India had plenty of cows wandering around, which the Indians were too perverse to eat.

Those who know more law than I do will know better than I how such mutually exclusive bodies can be absorbed into a secular state. All I can contribute is the social vision I have picked up from the study of literature. The sense of obligations to God of course makes God objective to man, and his revelation of them equally so. It would not be difficult, however, to see behind every religion an expression of human concern, a word so broad that I hope it is self-explanatory. I think there are primary and secondary concerns. Primary concerns rest on platitudes so bald and obvious that one hesitates to list them: it is better to be fed than starving, better to be happy than miserable, better to be free than a slave, better to be healthy than sick. Secondary concerns arise through the consciousness of a social contract: loyalty to one's religion or country or community, commitment to faith, sacrifice of cherished elements in life for the sake of what is regarded as a higher cause. All through history primary concerns have had to give way to secondary ones. It is better to live than die; nevertheless we go to war. Freedom is better than bondage, but we accept an immense amount of exploitation, both of ourselves and of others. Perhaps, with our nuclear weapons and our pollution of air and water, we have reached the first stage in history in which primary concerns will have to become primary.

The reason why this interests me is that I think primary concern expresses itself in mythology, in the stories and rituals surrounding the food supply, the sexual relation, the work which is a socially creative act and not an alienated drudgery, the play which is the expression of energy and not a mere distraction. It is this mythology that develops into literature. Secondary concerns produce ideology, and the normal language of ideology is the dialectical language of argument and thesis, which is invariably aggressive, because every thesis contains its own opposite. I am not suggesting an original Golden Age of pure myth: every myth, in the most primitive society, also has an ideological social function. Every work of literature, therefore, which descends from mythology, is an ideological product, an expression of the culture of its age. But some literary works show the capacity to make contact with an audience far removed in space, time, and culture, and it is the task of the critic to reveal in such works the primary myth underlying the ideological surface. In an age of ideological deadlock like ours, with so many foolish and irresponsible people saying "Let's go to war to smash somebody else's ideology," I feel that this critical task has taken on a renewed social importance.

Not all mythology develops into literature. The Bible is a mythological sacred book, but not a work of literature, though it is full of literary qualities. What keeps it from being literature is the objective nature assumed about its God and his revelation. This objectivity restricts its appeal, or much of it, to the special response of belief, which includes belonging to one definite community and not another. But we may also think of the Bible as coming to us through the power of the creative human imagination, which it clearly does whatever we believe about its ultimate source. In that context, we can perform the same critical operation we perform with literary works, trying to isolate the original myth under all the accretions of ideology, which for the Bible extend over several millennia.

Central to that original and underlying myth within the Bible is the legal metaphor of the trial, with prosecutors, defendants, and, of course, a supreme judge. We find this most explicitly in the Book of Job, in some parables of Jesus, and in the Book of Revelation that concludes the New Testament, but it is there all through in some form. The role of accuser is typically that of the devil, the Satan or adversary of mankind; the role of the defendant is identified with that of Jesus in the New Testament, with that of the restorer of Israel in the Old. Accuser and defendant represent the aspects of our lives that relate to past and future: the accuser says, "This is what you have done"; the defendant says, "This is what you still may do." In history, a revolution, which so often results in a new legal code, may sweep away the accumulated crime and sin of the past and usher in a new social order looking to the future. As time goes on, the future vision fades out and the record of the past resumes its continuity. I think it is possible to see, in the central myth of the Bible, a vision that rises above the progression from past to future into a higher form of the present, a vision of human creative power continually making the new by reshaping the old. On this level we pass beyond the specific religious revelation into a more comprehensive view of human destiny. In such a view there would be included, I should think, an understanding of what has been called sin that does not have the arbitrary quality of the objectified revelation. This would include a fuller perspective of the crime that traditionally derives from sin, giving us a saner and less anxious vision of the origins of human evil and of the methods of encountering it.

10

The Bible and English Literature

14 July 1986

From Arts *(Journal of the Sydney University Arts Association), 13 (1987–88): 17–25. Transcript of a seminar given at the University of Sydney in Australia, edited by David Lawton.*

I thought it might interest you to hear some of the things I have been struggling with.

The successor to *The Great Code* has taken a long time to write, largely because I was thinking in terms of a sequel and of course no book of mine has ever been a sequel to anything. Every book you write has to be numbered "zero" and not "number one"; but I had been thinking about the literary patterns of the Bible and it struck me that in literature you have two processes in reading. You first read something which moves in time; you hear a poem being recited or a play being acted on the stage, or you're turning the pages from the upper left-hand corner of page one to the lower right-hand corner of page whatever it is, and in this movement in time, you're gathering in your impressions of what you're reading. And then after you're through, you make an effort to understand what you've been reading, and we describe this in terms of visual metaphors. You hear a joke and then you see the joke (if all goes well, that is); and you get an impression of the general shape of what you've been reading. Sometimes, with a long and complicated work like a novel, the novelist will give a title, like *The Golden Bowl* or *The Rainbow* or *To the Lighthouse*, which describes an image which somehow represents by synecdoche that whole simultaneous understanding.

The Bible is a narrative which starts where time starts and ends where time ends. It is long of reading, as you turn the pages from Genesis straight through to the end, but you notice that the last book of the Bible, a book which is explicitly called Revelation, is a book which presents you with the simultaneous understanding of the entire pattern of the Bible up to that point, in the form of an identity of all possible metaphors and images in the natural world with the body of the Messiah. If you take the analogy of the novelist again, like Henry James writing a long work of fiction: it may have taken rise from some anecdote he heard when he was at a dinner party, and that was a kind of seed, the enfolded form, of what the book unfolds. And in the structure of the Bible, you have that in the creation myth, and the creation myth, in a sense, gives you the enfolded structure of the entire Bible, just as the Book of Revelation gives you the unfolded structure.

Now, as you know, there are two creation myths in the Bible, and the one that comes first is chronologically the later one, the one that we call the "P," or Priestly, narrative, which takes in the first chapter of Genesis and the first three verses of the second chapter. The Bible divides the creative act into seven stages: the stage of light, the firmament, then the separation of land and sea, and the creation of trees, then the heavenly bodies—sun, moon, and stars, which are simply referred to as "lights"— then the creatures of water and air, then the land animals, including human beings, and then the seventh—the archetypal Sabbath—which is not an act but the rest of God.

Now one thing that is interesting about this account is the amount of discrimination and marking off of boundaries that you get. You have first the light, marking off the boundary between the cosmos of light and the chaos of darkness. Then you have the firmament separating the waters above (those very mysterious waters that only come through in the flood) and the waters below. And then the land and sea are separated, demarcated, in the same way. And the creatures of water and air precede the land mammals, and the link between human beings and the land mammals is very clearly recognized.

Now, if you take the other one, the "J" (for Jahwist) narrative, beginning Genesis 2:4, that consists of seven stages too, but they are not numbered, so nobody notices there are seven. First of all, you start with something which is called a "mist," which is sent up from a dry, parched earth, and that is followed by the creation of the adam: I say "the adam" with a small "a," because he's not Adam with a capital "A" yet.

Then there follows the creation of the garden of Eden—the planting of the garden with its trees, and the setting up of the four rivers of Eden. You notice that the fourth day concludes the theme of fertilizing moisture which begins with the mist of the first day, just as in this account the sun, moon, and stars are the lights which confirm the primordial light of the first day. And then there comes the creation of all living things, apart from human beings. And then there comes the creation of woman—of Eve—as the climactic act in this creation, and the creation of Eve, of course, is what turns the adam into a male being, Adam; up to that time there has been the same confusion between man and the male which has disturbed a lot of people ever since.

And then the seventh, again, is not a creative act; it is simply a statement about the world after it has been completed. That is the "state of innocence." They were both naked, the man and his wife, and were not ashamed. That bald statement, that they were naked and not ashamed, of course was too much for the later commentary stuffers; if you look at a book in one of the pseudepigrapha called *The History of the Rechabites*, you'll find there a story of a man who journeys to the earthly paradise and is cautiously informed that Adam and Eve before the fall were clothed in a spiritual garment and that everything was really quite decent.[1]

Now, the differences between these two accounts are quite obvious. For in "P" you have a sense of a cosmos emerging from chaos. And there is also a very strong sense of a relationship to human needs; that is, on the fourth day, what are created are the lights in the firmament of heaven, which are there primarily for the purpose of keeping a calendar, and this is the creation of fundamentally an objective world; and with the act of rest on the seventh day, where God surveys what he has done, the world becomes objective to God himself and consequently to human beings. Now in "J," of course, everything is fertilizing images—the garden, rivers—and the creation of humanity is very sharply distinguished from the rest of creation, whereas in "P" it is assimilated to it. Philosophers have always discriminated two aspects of nature: nature as a structure or system, *natura naturata*, and nature as a fertilizing force of life, *natura naturans*; and those are the two aspects of nature which you have in the two creation myths.

Now, to the earlier "J" account there is appended a story of a fall, for the simple reason that the world that God created must have been a perfect world, so you have to have the alienation myth of the fall to explain the difference between the world God made and the world that we're in now. The fall turned on two things: the discovery of sex, because they knew that they were naked as soon as they had eaten of the fruit; and the sense of morality, of good and evil; and so you get from them all the systems of morality which have as their driving force the repression or sublimation of sex. No fall story is really attached to the first account except insofar as the fall of Adam and Eve is attached to it, but later on in the Bible you begin to get references to titanic or demonic forces, that is, forces of chaos over against the shaping of the cosmos, and that comes to a culmination in the Book of Enoch, which tells about the story of the fall of the rebel angels.[2] Enoch never made the Bible, but it was very influential in the New Testament and elsewhere, and that whole demonology of titanic beings and the dragon of chaos who was concealed under this creation account, and so forth, belong to a kind of suppressed fall, which is a fall of the angelic into the demonic, rather than the fall of the original human into the later human.

The one thing that seems clear is that neither of these accounts is, or in my opinion was ever intended to be, a prescientific account of how the order of nature came into being. I think that if it had ever been intended to be that, it would have been a little bit cleverer, and would not have had the trees created before the sun was. I think that you will find that, as a general principle, a myth is not a proto-science: it is not talking about the objective world and the order of nature at all. It is talking about human wishes and anxieties and concerns and aggressions; and the "J" myth is there to try to account for the origin of such things as the repression or sublimation of sex and its relation to morality, and the "P" narrative is there to indicate rather the sense of something coming into being which is intelligible, that is, ideally, a conscious mind exists before the creation and the creation is really the sense of an intelligible order which is possible only to consciousness. And it's ascribed to God, partly to make it something more than simply the human mind gazing in the mirror of its own construction, and so you have a creator outside the human order, in order to guarantee, so to speak, that the implications of creation are inexhaustible and that man is not simply finding order in the world because he put it there.

Q: You connect Adam and Eve—the myth of Adam and Eve—with sublimation. . . . Could you also connect the sublimation with art, so that the fall is the beginning of art?

NF: Well, perhaps so. I think that it is really the fall story, of course, that brings in the self-conscious aspect of sex; they knew that they were naked, or what D.H. Lawrence calls "sex in the head,"[3] and in a sense that does connect with the artistic or creative impulse of man himself. I mean, you could look at these two creation accounts and say that a creation myth is simply a projection of the fact that man is creative and that he creates order in the scheme of things, and that that is why we assume that God must have done the original creating. The notion of a divine creation, of course, has had a rather unfortunate effect on the history of the arts, because it means that there are two strikes on man already as an artist; no matter what he tries to do as an artist, he's been outsmarted by God, who has created the supreme work of art, and that is one reason why Sir Thomas Browne says that if the world had stopped at the sixth day, without the day of rest, it would still be a chaos, because there would still not be the sense of an order constructed which is separate from its creator.[4] Notice in this account here that all the living beings are brought to Adam to be named (brought to the adam to be named), and in *Paradise Lost* Milton realized that there was something of a difficulty here, and so he has God saying to the adam rather apologetically, "Understand the same / Of Fish" [bk. 8, ll. 345–6].

But the verse in Genesis (and I think it's pretty accurately translated, because the translation's the same in whatever version I've consulted), "brought them unto Adam to see what he would call them" [2:19]—suggests to me that God was rather bored with all the attributes of omniscience that have been wished on him by theologians, and preferred to take the position of somebody who has created an unpredictable being with some kind of free will, and has the human, if not divine, impulse of curiosity to see what will become of his own creation.

I say that Adam, that the adam, only turns into Adam *after* the creation of the female body, because a male body makes no sense without a complementary female, so what the shape of the adam was before the creation of Eve, nobody knows, and consequently the libraries have been filled with speculation on the point.

Q: Why two accounts? Was "J" insufficient in some way?

NF: Yes, I think that "J" is certainly the older creation story. The Priestly myth is the one which emphasizes the sense of nature as an order. It is quite closely related to the very ancient Sumerian and Mesopotamian myths about the creation as the killing of the dragon; in the Babylonian creation, Marduk kills a dragon and splits her in two, and makes half of her heaven and half of her earth.[5] This Priestly account is perhaps more superficially philosophical than the other one, but what it does is to round out the two aspects of nature: nature as physical and nature as biological.

Q: Why let "J" stand after you have drafted "P"? Is it simply respect for tradition?

NF: Well, then you would not have the sense of nature as a pullulating force; also you'll not have the peculiarly human account of the fall into the lower aspect of nature. What you have here is a creation myth with a fall myth suppressed, which later comes into the Bible as the revolt of the demonic from the angelic order, and that is again not a complete creation story. To get a complete creation story with the kind of God you have in the Bible, you must have the "fall" story. There need to be other things in the order of nature that are thought of as well as human beings. Of course later on, the demonic forces, the rebel angels, Satan and the like, become incarnate in the heathen king so that the demonic world does enter the human world; and what interests me in the study of English literature is the way in which, from Romanticism on, this demonic fall of the rebel angels begins to become annexed to the human order. If you're thinking of the Greek equivalents for them, you would call this the creation and fall of Prometheus, and this the creation and fall of Eros.

Q: You mentioned before something concerning the translation of the Bible. What kind of latitude did some of the translators allow themselves?

NF: Well, there's a good deal of latitude in translations of the creation account. . . . But those variations, so far as I can see, don't affect the general meaning. There is a pun on the word "adam" which is a profoundly suggestive one. God, we're told, formed the adam from the dust of the ground, which is *adamah*, a feminine noun, and there is obviously a pun there, and a very far-reaching pun; so that in the *Introduction* to Blake's *Songs of Experience*, for example, what falls, the "lapsed soul," is neither Adam nor Eve, but a female being which is called "earth" and which represents the original unity of humanity with the nature around it. The fact that Eve takes the initiative in the fall is, of course, something which has been a source of comfort and consolation to patriarchal theologians; and in fact the Biblical account itself tells us that as a result of woman's initiative in the fall, human society is going to become patriarchal. The only thing is that if man falls as woman, that is to say, if man falls as sexual being, then man has to be redeemed as woman, and that is why in the later symbolism of the Bible the souls of all redeemed human beings, whether they are men or women, are symbolically all female. That redemptive process is carried on by the second Adam, the title that Paul gave to Christ, and the second Eve, the title that theology has always given to the Virgin Mary.

Q: What about Lilith?

NF: Well, Lilith is one of the attempts to make sense out of the two very different creation myths as they affect human beings. In the Priestly account, which is the one that students of the Bible would have read first, we are told that God formed animals from the ground and that he also created males and females, so that the story of Lilith comes as part of the attempt to flesh out and make more plausible the story of the revolt of the demonic from the angelic; that is, the original Lilith was supposed to have been the first sexual partner of Adam and the progenitor of all the demons; and that would bring the "P" narrative into line more sharply with the "J" narrative. But Lilith has always had a somewhat marginal existence. Her name comes from Isaiah [34:14], where she is a dragon of the night, but although she comes into some Jewish legends, she doesn't really get her literary innings until the time of the Romantics, when she comes into Goethe's *Faust*, and into George Macdonald's very remarkable nineteenth-century story of Lilith.

As I say, she's a somewhat marginal figure, and in *Paradise Lost*, which doesn't have Lilith of course, you have the story of how Adam fell because he would rather die with Eve than live without her. And if he had done the theologically right thing, he would have immediately repudiated Eve at that point, and gone crawling back to his Maker saying, "Look what that awful woman did; you've got to get rid of her." But dramatically and poetically our sympathies are entirely with Adam, because in his place we would have done the same thing that he did, and that's the main point of Milton's poem. But with Lilith, if we can look into so very hypothetical a case, apparently that would have been what Adam did; he would have repudiated her and saved himself at that point, even if he didn't later.

Q: Does knowledge of literature corrupt our reading of the Bible?

NF: Well, I don't know. I think one as a student of English literature dealing with a creation myth of Genesis is bound to be reminded of *Paradise Lost* because it's such a powerfully integrated poem, which relates the whole story of the fall of man to the whole sequence of human history, up to the theatre of the Civil War in the English seventeenth century. I don't know that that necessarily corrupts one's view of the Bible, if the critic is watching what he's doing. Bernard Shaw has the devil in Hell, and man as Superman is saying to this day every Englishman believes that the whole of Milton's silly story is in the Bible[6] and of course it isn't, and anybody who's dealing with the Biblical text has to be aware of the extent to which it is not. There is nothing about the invention of gunpowder by the devils in the Bible, for example.

Q: Just comparing the Biblical creation story with some of the other literature, there seem to be some *major* differences: for example, God is largely off-stage, and man and nature are centre-stage; do you think this may have had some particular influence on the character of the literature of Christian culture in the West?

NF: Well, it's very difficult to say, because the documentary evidence you can muster is so scrappy and so hypothetical; the Prose Edda for example has creation myth themes, which are also in creation myths older than the Bible, such as the creation of the world out of the body of a giant, who is dismembered; and that is a kind of aspect of a creation myth that would certainly attract any poet who came across it in English literature. So far as I know, nobody did come across it before the eighteenth century and there is always the question in a document like that, how far it has been influenced by Christianity in the first place, and it's just that the amount of evidence you can produce is very seldom clear; it dissolves into hypothesis. The most one can say is that all creation myths everywhere show certain family likenesses, and I think that those family likenesses are the result of similarities in design. Man is distinguished from the rest of the animals by his command of the word, by his mastery of language, and that being an idea that would be naturally in the forefront of almost anybody's mind who was thinking about original creation, you have the same principle, "in the beginning was the Word."

Q: We think we now know why there are two accounts of creation in Genesis; we've got the documentary explanation for it. What about the influence on early Christian exegesis of not knowing why there are two—I'm actually thinking of Origen, looking at the two stories, asking himself, "why should there be two—why should God have given us two creation stories which look inconsistent but can't be, because they are, after all, divinely inspired?" And his answer, very interestingly, because he too is actually thinking of St. John's Gospel, "in the beginning was the Word," is that the Word incarnate in the "J" account is ordinary, human, if you like Saussurean, language, and that God gives us not an alternative creation story but the creation of Platonic form before actual form. So that he gets the Platonic form, the idea of mankind, the idea of trees created in Genesis 1, and the actual earthly or if you like the sort of translation of what you might call divine word into human language in chapter 2, as it were in defiance of Saussurean linguistics. I wondered if you'd like to comment on that whole issue of language and Platonic form, which is clearly crucial to your view of the Bible?

NF: I think that you start out of course with the "P" narrative where there is a very heavy emphasis on the commanding word. There is "And God said" that there would be light "and there was light." In other words the real thing is created by the power of the saying of the word, and the characteristic of this creation myth is that whatever is created by the power of the word is fixed, is stabilized, whereas in "J" the word is rather that shifting power of intercommunication in which God says "now you can eat off all the trees except one," so Adam goes straight to that one and eats it. That's the way verbal messages operate in human society. And the one is a *natura naturata* type of world; the word becomes a kind of archetype, the creation being the result of the intelligibility of God's mind. In the other the creation is of a biological, a liquid flowing world of trees and water and a world in which the word passes down in the form of certain commands and is accepted or repudiated as the case may be. I think that this distinction that I've been drawing between the *naturata* and the *naturans* doesn't become fully formulated I suppose until the time of Spinoza but it's certainly linked in the Platonic and Neoplatonic speculations which came through the word.

Q: I'd like to raise a question about the Bible generally and not the creation myth. Obviously the Bible has been a great powerhouse of our literature and culture generally in the past and we have to know a lot about the Bible to be able to understand a lot about our literary heritage. How do you think it stands—what kind of powerhouse is it today?

NF: Well, I think that the Bible is potentially as much of a powerhouse as it ever was, and the current may not be turned on as strongly as it was a century ago. I'm interested in the way that the Bible has infiltrated English literature. I think the poets, if they repudiate the Bible or don't, or simply are not interested in it or are trying to work outside it, are going to come up with exactly the same forms as the poets who are steeped in it. I noticed for example in reading the fourth *Canto* of Ezra Pound, where he is talking about the creation of ziggurats in ancient Persia where there are seven turns of the spiral of the tower and on the top the bride is laid awaiting the descent of the god from the sky: this he sees as reflected in a Greek myth of Danae who was wooed by Zeus in the form of a shower of gold. Well, in Pound you simply have the reference to Danae followed instantly by a reference to a picture of the Virgin Mary carried in the procession in medieval Italy, so it's quite clear in Pound's mind the identification of the Virgin Mary with the legend of Danae. And when I first read that my mind went back to the poem *Assumpta Maria* by the Catholic poet Francis Thompson in which he gives the Virgin Mary a great number of names, one of them being Danae in the shower of gold. So it really doesn't matter what the poet thinks, it's what takes over the poet's mind and expresses itself that matters.

Q: May I take the opportunity to ask you, Professor Frye, whether the same would apply to you as a critic?

NF: I imagine so. I feel that I have been very lucky in having some idea of what actually has been chewing away at the top of my spine. I was brought up myself in a rather strict evangelical background and was all set to go all through the revolting patterns that would have been normal to one in one's adolescence from that kind of background. I came across Blake, and Blake made an imaginative sense of that background that I never dreamed possible and so when I tackled Blake I had certain advantages, a certain technical knowledge of the Bible. I'd had three years of theology by then and my work has been spiralling around Blake and Milton ever since and I think that it's been one of the major factors in my critical career that I've always been rushing up to my readers handing them a key and insisting that this is the key; at least it's the most central one I can think of in the whole Western tradition.

Q: What did the word "knowledge" mean in Biblical terms, when Adam was forbidden to eat from the tree of knowledge? It seems such a strange thing to be forbidden, when the whole directive is to gain knowledge.

NF: I usually answer that question by referring to Shakespeare's *Measure for Measure*. Claudio is betrothed to Juliet and has completed legal marriage except that he hasn't published the banns; therefore he is technically an adulterer and that is a capital offence in this extraordinary world that the Duke has walked out of. Angelo on the other hand has been engaged to marry Mariana but calls the marriage off because the financial arrangements fall through. Well, that in terms of the knowledge of good and evil, the knowledge of the law, makes Claudio a condemned criminal and it makes Angelo a pillar of the establishment. The thing is that no audience that ever listened to *Measure for Measure* is going to believe that and what that implies to me is that the knowledge of good and evil is forbidden to man because it is not a genuine knowledge of anything, certainly not a knowledge of what good and evil are. The knowledge of good and evil is something that results in a morality founded on sexual repression, but it is not a real knowledge.

DL: That's a marvellous note to end on. I would like to thank Professor Frye on your behalf for his customary generosity, his erudition, his intellectual passion, and above all for spending an hour of his seventy-fourth birthday with us today. Thank you.

11

On the Bible

17 April 1989

Address given in Venice. From the typescript in NFF, 1991, box 38, file 10. This lecture was given at the Ca'Foscari in Venice as part of a conference on "Venice and the Study of Foreign Language and Literature," which was organized by the language faculty at Ca'Foscari to coincide with Frye's presence in Italy to receive an honorary doctorate from the University of Bologna.

The Bible being a sacred book, the principles of Biblical criticism have to do with the question of what kind of language is appropriate for the approach to religion. We find in our own culture that the sacred events described in the Bible come to us entirely as verbal events. All statements of belief are verbal formulations; all ritual acts and observances are based on verbal explanations, and religious experience itself is unintelligible without its foundation in words. So the entire being of religion is expressed in the term "word," which is the word of God if the religion is theistic, or simply language if it is not. The principle in the New Testament "In the beginning was the Word" is not merely a theological but also a generic and critical principle. But although this statement is taken with great reverence, it is also as a rule denied in practice. The words are always regarded, in popular religion at any rate, as subservient to the events themselves. You remember the famous passage in Goethe's *Faust* in which Faust translates, or rather mistranslates, the first verse of John as "In the beginning was the act."[1] But before we dismiss Faust as merely stupid, we have to remember that he is simply following the traditional popular practice in the Jewish and Christian religions.

Traditionally, the arrangement of words that have to do with such criteria as truth and reality, are [*sic*], in the first place, descriptive language, and in the second place, conceptual, dialectical, or argumentative language.

Descriptive statements are those in which the words form a replica of certain phenomena being described in history or science. But while the descriptive predominates in short-run statements, continuous descriptive prose can hardly develop before certain technological and social inventions. We can hardly have proper history writing where the words of the historian coincide with a sequence of events until we have a proper historiography and the appropriate documents available. We can hardly have an accurately descriptive science without the technology necessary for its growth. So although descriptive writing has always been regarded as the literal basis of writing, and has always been taken to be the fundamental form of verbal meaning, it is in fact the latest historically to develop. And many descriptive-minded writers, such as Aristotle, were greatly hampered, Aristotle especially in his biological observations, by the absence of the proper techniques, and so he had to turn his attention to another form of verbal expression. That other form was of course the conceptual, the logical and compelling argument, founded on major premises which are supposed to be derived from experience though they seldom are. The deductive philosophies of the Middle Ages took the dogmas of faith as their major premises. The postulated myths of religious faith developed the conception of faith as superior to reason but explicable by reason.

This structure of descriptive and argumentative prose was reinforced by rhetorical and ideological forms of persuasion, such as we have with the sermon, the very high ranking of which is indicated by that curious idealization of the orator which runs through humanistic scholarship from Cicero to the eighteenth century. Rhetoric or persuasive language of this kind gives a certain emotional resonance to argument and suggests commitment rather than impersonal agreement. It also makes use of figurative speech because of the curiously hypnotic effect of metaphorical and metonymic language.

Now this threefold verbal system of the descriptive, the dialectical, and the rhetorical and ideological, gives us what the funeral service calls the comfort of a reasonable religion. It comes to terms with the split in ordinary experience between the subject and the object, the unconscious objectivity of nature being transferred to the personal objectivity of God. Again, this verbal system assumes a divine sanction for many human ways of manipulating words.

All three of these components are in origin words in relation to the external environment and are of Greek and polytheistic origins. On this basis all formulations of belief in religion are ideological, and they are essentially statements of adherence to a specific community as exclusive of others. But their inadequacy is based on the fact that the language of the Bible itself is not descriptive, as that would be a hopeless anachronism in view of the date of the Bible. It is not argumentative or dialectical, and it is not rhetorical in the narrow sense of persuasion. The language of the Bible throughout is mythical and metaphorical language. In other words, while the Bible is not a work of literature, it is literary in its linguistic idiom.

By myth here I mean *mythos*, story or continuous narrative. The continuous narrative of the Bible which runs from the creation to the Last Judgment is not a history, though it uses historical material, and it is not a doctrine, though it has doctrinal implications. And the recurrent images of the Bible form in the last book, the Book of Revelation, a single metaphorical structure united with the body of Christ. This mythical and metaphorical language of the Bible rightfully accommodates literary forms as we can see in the Book of Job, in the parables of Jesus, and in the units which are studied by the *Formgeschichte* critics in Biblical scholarship.

This means therefore that the literary critic of the Bible has a great deal to do, because he has to formulate the literary basis of Biblical language and consider the social implications of the Bible's use of that language. And for that he must develop a conception of Biblical and metaphorical speech which is not, as it has been in the past, simply a special-purpose form of rhetoric. That is very largely what is meant by the statement in the Bible that the Bible itself must be understood spiritually [1 Corinthians 2], which means many things but must among other things mean metaphorically, a form of comprehension which passes beyond the split between subject and object in normal experience. Thus in the Book of Revelation we are told that the earthly Jerusalem is "spiritually" called Sodom and Egypt [11:8], meaning (it can only mean) that the earthly Jerusalem is metaphorically to be identified with Sodom and Egypt.

For Paul, in the first letter to the Corinthians [2:14], the structure of descriptive, argumentative, and rhetorical language is the language of the *soma psychikon*, the soul–body, or mind–body unit which does not understand the Bible because it does not come to terms with the essential language in which the Bible has been written.

We might look for a moment at the definition of faith in the New Testament in the Epistle to the Hebrews [11:1]. Faith, the writer tells us, is the *hypostasis* of things hoped for, and the *elenchos*, the proof or evidence, of things which are unseen. One thing that is important here is that *hypostasis*, rendered in the Vulgate by *substantia*, cannot possibly mean a metaphysical substance, and *elenchos* can hardly mean a logical proof, or anything that a historian or a scientist would mean by evidence.

We notice that faith is described as the substance, the *hypostasis* of the hoped for, so two of Paul's three theological virtues, faith and hope, are very closely associated. Hope is, as Emily Dickinson reminds us, something which is entirely a literary virtue in the sense that its basis is fictional, or as Emily Dickinson says

> Could Hope inspect her Basis
> Her Craft were done
> Has a fictitious charter
> Or it has none.[2]

And even in ironic literature, the reader is expected to construct in his own mind a certain norm of a way things should be, of which the ironic texture of what he is reading is presenting the mirrored opposite.

So when the author of Hebrews says, in effect, that faith is the reality of hope, he is I think implying that the essential language of the Bible is literary language, but that there is a category beyond the literary which is the essential thing that the Bible has to say. As for the proof or evidence of things invisible, the things which are unseen in the New Testament are not, as they are in Neoplatonism, thought of as a separate order and a superior one to the visible world. Things unseen are thought of rather as a medium of visibility, and that is what the author of Hebrews goes on to say in another verse or two.

The air of ordinary experience is invisible because if it were not, nothing else would be visible. That is why air is the fundamental metaphor behind the conception of spirit. Air is the medium of the first birth, the event which separates the embryo from the baby, and spirit, which is metaphorically air, is the medium of the second birth. But as the function of air is to be invisible, in order to make the physical world visible, so the spiritual world is invisible in order to make spiritual experience possible and visible to the participant. So the second part of this definition of faith is telling us that faith is the reality, not only of hope, but of illusion.

There are two kinds of illusion, the negative illusion which merely fails to be a reality, and the illusion which exists as a potentiality or model in the mind, as a fiction which does not yet exist but may be brought into existence or realized by a creative mind. It is this realizing of illusion that is fundamental in the imaginative or poetic way of arranging words which proceeds in terms of myth and metaphor.

In a stage play, for example, the reality and the illusion are the same thing: the play is an illusion, but we shall not find any reality behind it if we explore the wings or the dressing room. *The Tempest* of Shakespeare is predominantly the play that expresses this interchange of reality and illusion in literature because there the play is essentially a play about constructing a play. The subjective illusion, such as the belief that the other characters are drowned, or the plot to murder the King of Naples, is a type of "reality" which turns into illusion, and the objective world, according to Prospero's speech after the wedding masque [4.1.148–58], turns into illusion also. All that remains is the created and constructed reality of the play itself. When we awake in the morning, we think that we are emerging from a world of illusion into a world of reality, but what we see around us, the furniture of our bedroom, is nearly all of human construction, and whatever human beings have made, human beings can remake.

The paradox of Tertullian, that I believe because it is impossible,[3] has at least the merit of not identifying the conception of belief or faith with the credible. The credible by hypothesis is what is believed already, and to believe only the credible means that there is no adventure of the mind: nothing is being made, nothing is being created or constructed. In literature the basis is that of hypothesis, where we proceed by assumption rather than by verified fact or logical argument or rhetorical persuasion. In literature alone anything can be true; one hypothesis is as good as another. The hypothesis of *War and Peace* and the hypothesis of *Alice in Wonderland* are equally literary.

The question which the Biblical definition of faith raises is the question of a faith which is a permanent and persistent myth to live by, a model to which one could adjust one's entire experience. This means then that faith as defined in the New Testament is a continuous creative act and reality is also a continuously creative act.

I wish in view of the locale of this conference that I had something Venetian to connect this with, but I'm afraid I only have the Neapolitan Vico's axiom of *verum factum*, what is true is what we have made.[4]

Biblical scholars and theologians have adopted the Greek word *kerygma*, meaning proclamation, to describe this myth to live by, though many of them attempt to deny the fact that this proclamation has its basis in the imaginative, poetic, mythical, and metaphorical approach to language. But this kind of proclamation which the theologians describe is something which superficially resembles rhetoric, but the language of prophecy is a rhetoric that goes far beyond the mere agreement between the speaker and his audience, which is what an oration aims at. It is also a transcending of myth which remains mythical in language and remains based on it. So the true proclamation of the Bible cannot go along with any form of "demythologizing" of the Bible, as some Biblical scholars insist,[5] but literary and mythical language must remain its basis. Actual literature, however, even on the highest level, does not suggest a myth to live by, or if it does it is essentially betraying its literary function.

To take an imaginative poetic literary approach to language as the basis of our approach to the Bible, therefore, means that any faith which one has in any religion has a basis in free choice and that makes possible an atmosphere of dialogue and tolerance and interchange of views.

We have been reading very much and hearing very much in newspapers and news media today about the bigotry of various religious movements, Christian, Moslem, Jewish, Sikh, Hindu, Buddhist. They seem to be almost totally undesirable as social phenomena, and the reason why they are, at least the reason that concerns me at the moment, is that they are based on a linguistic fallacy, on wrong ways of conceiving words and interpreting words.

I have spoken of creation as the basis of the experience described in the Bible as spiritual experience, and the Bible of course begins with an account of creation. This account of creation at the beginning of Genesis is not, and I think was never intended to be, a description of how the order of nature came into being at the beginning of time, there being no beginning of time at all. The account of creation there is rather an expression of the intelligible nature of the objective world, something that a conscious mind can contemplate and study endlessly and inexhaustibly. The condition for responding to the original form of creation, which we are told God saw to be good, was blacked out by the alienation myth of the fall of man, the fall of our first parents. According to the content of this story of the fall what man acquired when he fell by eating of the forbidden tree was a moral knowledge based on a sexual neurosis. This was forbidden because that is not a genuine knowledge of anything, even of good and evil.

To get back then to the original unspoiled creation which would seem to be good, one has to accept, according to the Bible, a divine guarantee not only of the reality of the world but of the reality of the verbal world and of the imaginative approach to it. At the other end of the Bible is the statement, "I make all things new" [Revelation 21:5], ascribed to God himself, the apocalyptic vision where the old creation is seen as the new creation, but one in which man now participates.

This overall vision of the Bible from beginning to end is summarized in the Book of Job, where Job originally lives in a state of happiness corresponding to the original earthly paradise. This is then turned into a state of misery through the malice of Satan. And when God finally enlightens Job he does so by dramatizing his own creation and pointing it out to Job, from his own presence at the top, to the monsters Behemoth and Leviathan at the bottom. Job sees the old creation as a new creation in which he now participates, and thereby gets it back: in fact he had never lost it.

The languages that I have spoken of, the descriptive, the argumentative, the rhetorical, all have some element of compulsion about them. An established fact cannot be argued about; a logical argument has compelling force which makes us accept it. The aim of rhetoric is to unite by an external force an agreed-on ideological principle. It follows that the response which the Bible itself insists on, the response of the spirit, is bound up with the conception of love, a word which perhaps means too many things in modern languages and may have rather a sentimental sound. But in the New Testament love is regarded not as one virtue among others but as the only virtue there is, and one which is possible only to God and to the spirit of man, a virtue which, in Paul's language, believes and hopes everything [1 Corinthians 13:7], and thereby includes all the other virtues because, outside the order of love, faith and hope are not necessarily virtues at all.

I have spoken of what the human subject is trying to do, but at a certain point we find ourselves entering a vaster operation where the human factors are still present, but where the human activity is no longer the only power or even the essentially active power. Here the initiative is seen to come not from some unreachable world, a world by itself, but from an infinitely active personality that both enters us and eludes us.

This is the theistic context which the Bible presents to us, but it has its analogies in what the poets tell us about the poetic process, the poetic approach to words being the only one in which the poet is not wholly dependent on his own will power or determination, but has to relax his will. Many major poets have told us that they do not think of themselves as making or creating their poems, but simply as being the places where those poems have occurred, and they also tell us that there is a kind of residual mystery independent of the conscious will in the creative process.

This may be what Dante was speaking of in the final canto of the *Paradiso*, where he is speaking I think not of his personal salvation, because he is still mortal and still has a second coming to go through, but rather of the salvation of the poetic and imaginative approach to language and its acceptance by the deity as a mode of approaching the furthest that can be approached by words. In any case, pursuing the dialectic of belief and vision until they merge is the first step on the ladder that Jacob saw in his vision [Genesis 28:10–17]: the first entrance into the *mysterium tremendum*, a mystery that is really a revelation, which is mysterious only because its revelation has no end.

12

The Double Vision:
Language and Meaning in Religion

May–July 1990

Toronto: United Church Publishing House, 1991. Reprinted by University of Toronto Press, 1991. Drafts of the work are in NFF, 1991, box 34, files 1–3. As the preface explains, the first three sections were given as lectures at Emmanuel College, Victoria University. The book's dedication reads "for Elizabeth."

> For double the vision my Eyes do see,
> And a double vision is always with me.
> With my inward Eye 'tis an old Man grey;
> With my outward, a Thistle across my way.
> William Blake[1]

Preface

The first three chapters of this book were delivered at the Emmanuel College alumni reunion on 14, 15, and 16 May 1990 at Emmanuel College. Although various lectures of mine that were addressed specifically to Victoria College are in print (e.g., *No Uncertain Sounds*, 1988), this is my first publication devoted specifically to Emmanuel College. I was very pleased that the lectures coincided with Douglas Jay's final year as principal, and consequently can be regarded as in part a tribute to him.

I say in part, because I had also hoped to make this small book something of a shorter and more accessible version of the longer books, *The Great Code* and *Words with Power*, that I have written on the relations of the Bible to secular culture. Many passages from the longer books are echoed here, in what I hope is a somewhat simpler context. After writing the lectures out in their final form, however, it seemed to me that the total argument implied by them was still incomplete, and I have there-fore, after considerable hesitation, added a fourth chapter.

The fact that these lectures were addressed by a member of the United Church of Canada to a largely United Church audience accounts for many of the allusions, for some of the directions in the argument, and for much of the tone. As is utterly obvious, they represent the opinions of one member of that church only. And even those opinions should not be read as proceeding from a judgment seat of final conviction, but from a rest stop on a pilgrimage, however near the pilgrimage may now be to its close.

N.F.
Victoria University
University of Toronto
July 1990

I The Double Vision of Language

The Whirligig of Time, 1925–90

I begin with a date. In 1990 the United Church of Canada, founded in 1925, reached an age often associated with superannuation.[2] Only a minority of its members now recall church union, and there are still fewer who acquired, as I did, their elementary religious training within the pre-union Methodist church. In Methodism, even of the episcopal variety to which my family belonged, there was an emphasis on reli-gious experience as distinct from doctrine and on very early exposure to the story element in the Bible. Such a conditioning may have helped to propel me in the direction of a literary criticism that has kept revolving around the Bible, not as a source of doctrine but as a source of story and vision. It may be of interest to explain what effect I think this has had on my general point of view on the world today, apart from the peculiar features of what I have written.

History moves in a cyclical rhythm which never forms a complete or closed cycle. A new movement begins, works itself out to exhaustion, and something of the original state then reappears, though in a quite new context presenting new conditions. I have lived through at least one major historical cycle of this kind: its main outlines are familiar to you, but the inferences I have drawn from it may be less so. When I arrived at Victoria College as a freshman in September 1929, North America was not only prosperous but in a nearly hysterical state of self-congratulation. It was widely predicted that the end of poverty and the levelling out of social inequalities were practically within reach. In the Soviet Union, on the other hand, the reports were mainly of misery and despair. The inference for general public opinion on this side of the Atlantic was clear: capitalism worked and Marxism didn't.

Next month came the stock market crash, and there was no more talk of a capitalist Utopia. By the mid-1930s the climate of opinion had totally reversed, at least in the student circles I was attached to. Then it was a generally accepted dogma that capitalism had had its day and was certain to evolve very soon, with or without a revolution, into socialism, socialism being assumed to be both a more efficient and a morally superior system. The persistence of this view helped to consolidate my own growing feeling that myths are the functional units of human society, even when they are absurd myths. The myth in this case was the ancient George and dragon one: Fascism was the dragon, democracy the maiden to be rescued, and despite the massacres, the deliberately organized famines, the mass uprooting of peoples, the grabbing of neighbouring territories, and the concentration camps, Stalin simply had to fit into the role of the rescuing knight. This was by no means a unanimous feeling—among Communists themselves there was a bitterly anti-Stalin Trotskyite group—but it extended over a good part of the left of centre.

That cycle has completed itself, and once again people in the West are saying, as they said sixty years ago, that it has been proved that capitalism works and that Marxism does not. With the decline of belief in Marxism, apart from an intellectual minority in the West that doesn't have to live with it, the original Marxist vision is often annexed by the opposite camp. Going back to the competitive economy that Marx denounced, we are often told, will mean a new life for the human race, perhaps even the ultimate goal that Marx himself promised: an end to exploitation and class struggle. Hope springs eternal: unfortunately it usually springs prematurely.

The failure of Communism, or what has been assumed to be Communism—it was more accurately a form of state capitalism—is apparently a genuine failure, but it would be silly to return to the 1929 naiveté. Marxist economies may be trying to survive by making extensive reforms in an open-market direction, but capitalism only survived the last half-century by abandoning the more nihilistic aspects of laissez-faire and making equally extensive reforms in a socialist and welfare-state direction. For all the see-sawing between nationalizing and privatizing, the permanent effects of the Roosevelt revolution in the United States, and parallel revolutions in Western Europe, make it impossible to put any confidence in back-to-square-one clichés.

In capitalism there is both a democratic and an oligarchic tendency, and the moral superiority of capitalism over Communism depends entirely on the ascendancy of the democratic element. Most citizens in North America, at least from about 1945 on, were only subliminally aware of living under a capitalist system: what mattered to them was political democracy, not the economic structure. Similarly, news analysts today put their main emphasis on the growing disillusionment with all forms of ideology in Eastern Europe, and the emerging feeling that systems do not matter: it is only freedom and dignity and the elementary amenities of civilization that matter. The view of Hegel that history was progressing through conflicts of ideas toward an ultimate goal of freedom was reversed by Marx into a view of history that identified the conflicting elements with materialistic forces, especially instruments of production and the class struggle over their ownership. Through a good deal of the twentieth century, it was generally assumed, even in the non-Marxist world, that Hegel's main contribution to philosophy was in getting his construct stood on its head by Marx. But now the original Hegelian conception is being revived, and the revolutions of our day are sometimes seen as manifestations of an impulse to freedom that may put an end to history as we have known it.

Freedom alone, however, is far too abstract a goal. As Heine said, freedom is a prison song: those who care about it are those who have been deprived of it. History tells us that, ever since Adam's six hours in paradise, man has never known what to do with freedom except throw it away. Involved in the Christian conception of original sin is the perception that no human society is likely to do anything sensible for longer than the time that it takes to break a New Year's resolution. Despite this, I think there is a real truth in the notion of an impulse to freedom, but it needs to be placed in a broader and more practical context.

Human beings are concerned beings, and it seems to me that there are two kinds of concern: primary and secondary. Primary concerns are such things as food, sex, property, and freedom of movement: concerns that we share with animals on a physical level. Secondary concerns include our political, religious, and other ideological loyalties. All through history ideological concerns have taken precedence over primary ones. We want to live and love, but we go to war; we want freedom, but depend on the exploiting of other peoples, of the natural environment, even of ourselves. In the twentieth century, with a pollution that threatens the supply of air to breathe and water to drink, it is obvious that we cannot afford the supremacy of ideological concerns any more. The need to eat, love, own property, and move about freely must come first, and such needs require peace, good will, and a caring and responsible attitude to nature. A continuing of ideological conflict, a reckless exploiting of the environment, a persistence in believing, with Mao Tse-Tung, that power comes out of the barrel of a gun,[3] would mean, quite simply, that the human race cannot be long for this world.

The Cold War gave us a Soviet Union upholding an allegedly materialistic ideology, at the price of chronic food shortages, sexual prudery, abolition of all property except the barest essentials of clothing and shelter, and a rigidly repressed freedom of movement. The United States offered vast quantities of food and drink, indiscriminate sexual activity, piling up of excessive wealth and privilege, and a restless nomadism—in other words, full satisfaction of primary concerns on a purely physical level. An evolution toward freedom, however, is conceivable if freedom is a primary concern, if it belongs in the context of enough to eat and drink, of normal sexual satisfaction, of enough clothing, shelter, and property.

The immediate concern of freedom is still a physical one: it is a matter of being able to move about without being challenged by policemen demanding passports and permits and identity cards, and of not being excluded from occupations and public places on the ground of sex or skin colour. I should explain also that when I speak of property I mean the external forms of what is "proper" to one's life as an individual, starting with clothing and shelter. These also include what may be called territorial space. A Hindu hermit meditating in a forest may need next to nothing of clothing and shelter, and no possessions at all, but he still needs space around him.

The United States, Japan, and Western Europe have been much more successful in achieving stage one of primary concern: as compared with the formerly Marxist countries, they are more attractive and more comfortable to live in. But the legacy of the Cold War is still with us, and not only does an adversarial situation impoverish both sides, but both sides catch the worst features of their opponents. We have seen this in the McCarthyism that imitated the Stalinist show trials, the McCarran act that imitated Soviet exclusion policies, and the interventions in Latin America that imitate the Stalinist attitude to the Warsaw Pact countries. Something, at the very least, is still missing.

Primitive and Mature Societies

When Jesus was tempted by the devil to improve the desert economy by turning stones into bread, he answered, quoting Deuteronomy, that man shall not live by bread alone, but by prophecies as well [Matthew 4:4]. That is, primary concerns, for conscious human beings, must have a spiritual as well as a physical dimension. Freedom of movement is not simply freedom to take a plane to Vancouver; it must include freedom of thought and criticism. Similarly, property should extend to scientific discovery and the production of poetry and music; sex should be a matter of love and companionship and not a frenetic rutting in rubber; food and drink should become a focus of the sharing of goods within a community. I pass over the violence, the drug addiction, and the general collapse of moral standards that accompany over-emphasis on the satisfying of physical wants, because one hardly needs to be told that they are the result of a lack of spiritual vision. The obvious question to raise next is, What is the difference between the spiritual aspect of primary concerns and the secondary or ideological concerns just mentioned?

I think the difference is expressed in two types of society, one primitive and the other mature. A primitive or embryonic society is one in which the individual is thought of as primarily a function of the social group. In all such societies a hierarchical structure of authority has to be set up to ensure that the individual does not get too far out of line. A mature society, in contrast, understands that its primary aim is to develop a genuine individuality in its members. In a fully mature society the structure of authority becomes a function of the individuals within it, all of them, without distinctions of sex, class, or race, living, loving, thinking, and producing with a sense of space around them. Throughout history practically all societies have been primitive ones in our present sense: a greater maturity and a genuine concern for the individual peeps out occasionally, but is normally smothered as society collapses back again into its primitive form.

The reason for this is that we all belong to something before we are anything, and the primitive structure has all the vast power of human inertia and passive social conditioning on its side. Fifty years ago, the great appeal of Marxism to intellectuals in the West was that it renewed the emphasis on primitive social values, providing a social gospel with the right answers in what purported to be not only a rational but a scientific system. Many conservatives of that time preferred a similar structure that some Roman Catholic intellectuals believed they had discovered in Thomist realism; people who simply hated human intelligence turned Fascist. In the United States only a minority wanted to buy any of these nostrums, but the Americans had their own primitive mattress to sleep on, the American way of life, with all its anti-intellectual cosiness.

What I am expounding may be called a bourgeois liberal view, which throughout my lifetime has never been regarded as an "advanced" view. But it may begin to look more central with the repudiation of Marxism in Marxist countries, the growing uneasiness with the anti-intellectualism in American life, and the steadily decreasing dividends of terrorism in Third World countries. The ascendant feeling in Eastern Europe now is that a collective ideology is no longer good enough for human dignity. What triggered the feeling, we said, was the failure of Communism to provide the physical basis of primary concern: food, possessions, and free movement. Even on the physical level, primary concerns are still individual: famine is a social problem, but it is the individual who eats or starves. But the spiritual form of these concerns is the sign of the real failure.

The spiritual form of primary concern, then, fulfils the physical need but incorporates it into the context of an individualized society. The ideological or secondary concern may be the same in theory, but its subordination of individual to social needs constantly frustrates, postpones, or circumvents the fulfilment of the primary ones. Where there is no awareness of such a distinction there are often arguments, in cultural circles particularly, contrasting socially engaged and activist art, where every book or film or picture is or should be a political statement, with introverted or ingrown creativity that concentrates on subjective feelings. The antithesis is false because it is an antithesis: in a mature culture it would disappear.

I said that an adversarial situation like that of the Cold War impoverishes both sides. The one adversarial situation that does not do so is the conflict between the demands of primary human welfare on the one hand, and a paranoid clinging to arbitrary power on the other. Naturally this black and white situation is often very hard to find in the complexities of revolutions and power struggles, but it is there, and nothing in any revolutionary situation is of any importance except preserving it. When we see it, we can realize that the difference between ideological and spiritual concern is, among other things, a difference in language. Before I can clarify this point I must turn to the confrontation of primitive and mature social impulses in the history of religion.

Religious organizations are much more bound than the better secular ones to what I have called the primitive form of society, the supremacy of social authority over the individual. It frequently appears to be practically an element of faith that the interests and reputation of the church as a social unit must take precedence over the welfare of the individuals within it, a faith rationalized by the claim that the two things are always identical. Church authorities appeal to a revelation from God, or a corresponding spiritual power, beyond the reach of revolutionary uprisings, of which they are the custodians and definitive interpreters. In many respects the twentieth-century Cold War repeated the later stages of the situation that arose with the Reformation in the sixteenth century. Then, a revolutionary movement, at first directed mainly toward a reform of abuses in the church, showed signs of expanding and breaking open a tightly closed structure of authority that claimed exclusive and infallible powers in both spiritual and temporal orders. What was centrally at issue was reformation itself, the conception of a church that could be reformed in principle and not merely through modifying the corruptions that had grown up within it. The Reformers thought of the church as subject to a higher criterion, namely the Word of God, and as obligated to carry on a continuous dialogue with the Word in a subordinate position to it.

Established authority reacted to this movement as established authority invariably does. The Council of Trent gives an impression of passing one reactionary resolution after another in a spirit of the blindest panic. Yet the Council of Trent succeeded in its main objective, which was to persuade Catholics that post-Tridentine Catholicism was not only the legitimate descendant of the pre-Reformation church, but was in fact identical with it. The logical inference was the claim of a power of veto over the Bible, a position set out in Newman's *Essay on the Development of Christian Doctrine,* where a historical dialectic takes supreme command in a way closely parallel to the constructs of Hegel and Marx.

There was also, of course, the argument that basing the church on justification by faith alone would lead to the chaos of private judgment and subjective relativism. What is important here is not the validity of such an argument but the fact that the main Reformed bodies tended to adopt it. When it came to establishing the Word of God as an authority, the Reformers themselves could only become the accredited spokesmen of that authority. And so the real reformation towards a more mature society of individualized Christians was betrayed by Protestants as well as opposed by Catholics. A historian might see the Lutheran and Anabaptist movements as primarily emphasizing different aspects of reformation, but Luther himself showed the same enthusiasm for killing off Anabaptists that, in the twentieth century, Communists showed for killing off Anarchists.

Many of the greatest spirits of Luther's time, such as Erasmus, looked for a movement toward a far greater spiritual maturity than either Reformation or Counter-Reformation achieved, and tried to hold to the standards of a liberalism that would transcend both the Roman Catholic status quo and its Lutheran and Calvinist antitheses. But for Erasmus, or for Rabelais, there was no attraction in a more hardened and sectarian version of what was already there.

So both sides took the broad way to destruction, with the bloody conflicts of civil wars in France and Germany, along with a war of Protestants fighting each other in Britain. In the course of centuries the adversarial situation gradually subsided into a cold war instead of actual war, which, however, did not eliminate, any more than its counterparts have eliminated in our day, endless persecution within individual nations. This cold war situation lasted roughly until our own time, when Vatican Two and ecumenical movements in Protestantism have begun to show how out of touch such antagonisms are with both the conditions of contemporary life and the spirit of Christianity. Religious parallels to the current political demands for greater individual autonomy sprang up in the more liberal Protestant circles in the nineteenth century and are now breaking into Catholicism on all sides, though still officially inadmissible to the upper hierarchy.

In the course of time the movement begun by the Reformation did achieve one major victory: the gradual spread throughout the Western world of the principle of separation of church and state. Something of the genuine secular benefits of democracy have rubbed off on the religious groups, to the immense benefit of humanity, and depriving religion of all secular or temporal power is one of the most genuinely emancipating movements of our time. It seems to be a general rule that the more "orthodox" or "fundamentalist" a religious attitude is, the more strongly it resents this separation and the more consistently it lobbies for legislation giving its formulas secular authority. Today, in Israel and in much of the Moslem and Hindu world, as well as in Northern Ireland and South Africa, we can clearly see that these religious attitudes are the worst possible basis for a secular society.

This principle applies equally to the dogmatic atheism and the antireligious campaigns that Lenin assumed to be essential to the Marxist revolution. I was in Kiev during the celebration of the thousandth anniversary of the introduction of Christianity to Ukraine, and it was clear that seventy years of antireligious propaganda had been as total and ignominious a failure there as anything in the economic or political sphere. In short, any religion, including atheism, which remains on the socially and psychologically primitive level, in the sense I have given to the word primitive, can do little more than illustrate Swift's gloomy axiom that men have only enough religion to hate each other but not enough for even a modicum of tolerance, let alone anything resembling charity.[4]

Michael explains to Adam, in the last book of Milton's *Paradise Lost*, that tyranny exists in human society because every individual in such a society is a tyrant within himself, or at least is if he conforms acceptably to his social surroundings. The well-adjusted individual in a primitive society is composed of what Paul calls the *soma psychikon*, or what the King James Bible translates as the "natural man" (1 Corinthians 2:14). He has, or thinks he has, a soul, or mind, or consciousness, sitting on top of certain impulses and desires that are traditionally called "bodily." "Body" is a very muddled metaphor in this context: we should be more inclined today to speak of repressed elements in the psyche. In any case the natural man sets up a hierarchy within himself and uses his waking consciousness to direct and control his operations. We call him the natural man partly because he is, first, a product of nature, and inherits along with his genetic code the total devotion to his own interests that one writer has called "the selfish gene."[5]

Second, he is a product of his social and ideological conditioning. He cannot distinguish what he believes from what he believes he believes, because his faith is simply an adherence to the statements of belief provided for him by social authority, whether spiritual or temporal. As with all hierarchies, the lower parts are less well adjusted than the upper ones, and "underneath" in the restless and squirming body, or whatever else we call it, is a rabble of doubts telling him that his intellectual set-up is largely fraudulent. He may shout down his doubts and trample them underfoot as temptations coming from a lower world, but he is still what Hegel calls an unhappy consciousness.[6]

For reassurance, he looks around him at the society which reflects his hierarchy in a larger order. A society composed of natural men is also a hierarchy in which there are superiors and inferiors, and if such a society has any stability, one draws a sense of security from one's social position, even if it is "inferior." Discontented inferiors, of course, are the social counterpart of doubts, and also have to be trampled underfoot. It is easy to see why the two most influential thinkers of the twentieth century are Marx and Freud: they were those who called attention, in the social and the individual spheres respectively, to the exploitation in society, to the latent hysteria in the individual, and to the alienation produced by both.

Inside one's natural and social origin, however, is the embryo of a genuine individual struggling to be born. But this unborn individual is so different from the natural man that Paul has to call it by a different name. The New Testament sees the genuine human being as emerging from an embryonic state within nature and society into the fully human world of the individual, which is symbolized as a rebirth or second birth, in the phrase that Jesus used to Nicodemus [John 3:3]. Naturally this rebirth cannot mean any separation from one's natural and social context, except insofar as a greater maturity includes some knowledge of the conditioning that was formerly accepted uncritically. The genuine human being thus born is the *soma pneumatikon*, the spiritual body (1 Corinthians 15:44). This phrase means that spiritual man is a body: the natural man or *soma psychikon* merely has one. The resurrection of the spiritual body is the completion of the kind of life the New Testament is talking about, and to the extent that any society contains spiritual people, to that extent it is a mature rather than a primitive society.

The Crisis in Language

What concerns me in this situation is a linguistic fallacy, the fallacy that relates to the phrase "literally true." Ordinarily, we mean by "literally true" what is descriptively accurate. We read many books for the purpose of acquiring information about the world outside the books we are reading, and we call what we read "true" if it seems to be a satisfactory verbal replica of the information we seek. This conception of literal meaning as descriptive works only on the basis of sense experience and the logic that connects its data. That is, it works in scientific and historical writing. But it took a long time before such descriptive meaning could be fully matured and developed, because it depends on technological aids. We cannot describe phenomena accurately in science before we have the apparatus to do so; there cannot be a progressive historical knowledge until we have a genuine historiography, with access to documents and, for the earlier periods at least, some help from archaeology. Literalism of this kind in the area of the spiritual instantly becomes what Paul calls the letter that kills [2 Corinthians 3:6]. It sets up an imitation of descriptive language, a pseudo-objectivity related to something that isn't there.

In the early Christian centuries it was widely assumed that the basis of Christian faith was the descriptive accuracy of the historical events recorded in the New Testament and the infallibility of the logical arguments that interconnected them. This pseudo-literalism was presented as assertion without the evidence of sense experience, and belief became a self-hypnotizing process designed to eke out the insufficiency of evidence. The rational arguments used were assumed to have a compulsive power: if we accept this, then that must follow, and so on. A compelling dialectic based on the excluding of opposites is a militant use of words; but where there is no genuine basis in sense experience, it is only verbally rational: it is really rhetoric, seeking not proof but conviction and conversion. It is seldom, however, that anyone is convinced by an argument unless there are psychological sympathies within that open the gates to it. So when words failed, as they usually did, recourse was had to anathematizing those who held divergent views, and from there it was an easy step to the psychosis of heresy-hunting, of regarding all deviation from approved doctrine as a malignant disease that had to be ruthlessly stamped out.

I am, of course, isolating only one element in Christianity, but cruelty, terror, intolerance, and hatred within any religion always mean that God has been replaced by the devil, and such things are always accompanied by a false kind of literalism. At present some other religions, notably Islam, are even less reassuring than our own. As Marxist and American imperialisms decline, the Moslem world is emerging as the chief threat to world peace, and the spark-plug of its intransigence, so to speak, is its fundamentalism or false literalism of belief. The same principle of demonic perversion applies here: when Khomeini gave the order to have Salman Rushdie murdered, he was turning the whole of the Koran into Satanic verses. In our own culture, Margaret Atwood's *The Handmaid's Tale* depicts a future New England in which a reactionary religious movement has brought back the hysteria, bigotry, and sexual sadism of seventeenth-century Puritanism. Such a development may seem unlikely just now, but the potential is all there.

For the last fifty years I have been studying literature, where the organizing principles are myth, that is, story or narrative, and metaphor, that is, figured language. Here we are in a completely liberal world, the world of the free movement of the spirit. If we read a story there is no pressure to believe in it or act upon it; if we encounter metaphors in poetry, we need not worry about their factual absurdity. Literature incorporates our ideological concerns, but it devotes itself mainly to the primary ones, in both physical and spiritual forms: its fictions show human beings in the primary throes of surviving, loving, prospering, and fighting with the frustrations that block these things. It is at once a world of relaxation, where even the most terrible tragedies are still called plays, and a world of far greater intensity than ordinary life affords. It does, in short, everything that can be done for people except transform them. It creates a world that the spirit can live in, but it does not make us spiritual beings.

It would be absurd to see the New Testament as only a work of literature: it is all the more important, therefore, to realize that it is written in the language of literature, the language of myth and metaphor. The Gospels give us the life of Jesus in the form of myth: what they say is, "This is what happens when the Messiah comes to the world." One thing that happens when the Messiah comes to the world is that he is despised and rejected, and searching in the nooks and crannies of the Gospel text for a credibly historical Jesus is merely one more excuse for despising and rejecting him. Myth is neither historical nor antihistorical: it is counterhistorical. Jesus is not presented as a historical figure, but as a figure who drops into history from another dimension of reality, and thereby shows what the limitations of the historical perspective are.

The Gospel confronts us with all kinds of marvels and mysteries, so that one's initial reaction may very well be that what we are reading is fantastic and incredible. Biblical scholars have a distinction here ready to hand, the distinction between world history and sacred history, *Weltgeschichte* and *Heilsgeschichte*. Unfortunately, there is as yet almost no understanding of what sacred history is, so the usual procedure is to try to squeeze everything possible into ordinary history, the bulges of the incredible that still stick out being smoothed away by a process called demythologizing. However, the Gospels are all myth and all bulge, and the operation does not work.

As the New Testament begins with the myth of the Messiah, so it ends, in the Book of Revelation, with the metaphor of the Messiah, the vision of all things in their infinite variety united in the body of Christ. And just as myth is not antihistorical but counterhistorical, so the metaphor, the statement or implication that two things are identical though different, is neither logical nor illogical, but counterlogical. It presents the continuous paradox of experience, in which whatever one meets both is and is not oneself. "I am a part of all that I have met," says Tennyson's Ulysses; "I am what is around me," says Wallace Stevens.[7] Metaphors are paradoxical, and again we suspect that perhaps only in paradox are words doing the best they can for us. The genuine Christianity that has survived its appalling historical record was founded on charity, and charity is invariably linked to an imaginative conception of language, whether consciously or unconsciously. Paul makes it clear that the language of charity is spiritual language, and that spiritual language is metaphorical, founded on the metaphorical paradox that we live in Christ and that Christ lives in us.

I am not trying to deny or belittle the validity of a credal, even a dogmatic, approach to Christianity: I am saying that the literal basis of faith in Christianity is a mythical and metaphorical basis, not one founded on historical facts or logical propositions. Once we accept an imaginative literalism, everything else falls into place: without that, creeds and dogmas quickly turn malignant. The literary language of the New Testament is not intended, like literature itself, simply to suspend judgment, but to convey a vision of spiritual life that continues to transform and expand our own. That is, its myths become, as purely literary myths cannot, myths to live by; its metaphors become, as purely literary metaphors cannot, metaphors to live in. This transforming power is sometimes called kerygma or proclamation. Kerygma in this sense is again a rhetoric, but a rhetoric coming the other way and coming from the other side of mythical and metaphorical language.

In the Book of Job we have the rhetorical speech of Elihu, defending and justifying the ways of God; then we have the proclamation of God himself, couched in very similar language, but reversed in direction. The proclamation of the Gospel is closely associated with the myths that we call parables, because teaching by myth and metaphor is the only way of educating a free person in spiritual concerns. If we try to eliminate the literal basis of kerygma in myth and metaphor, everything goes wrong again, and we are back where we started, in the rhetoric of an all-too-human effort to demonstrate the essence of revelation. The reason for basing kerygma on mythical and metaphorical language is that such a language is the only one with the power to detach us from the world of facts and demonstrations and reasonings, which are excellent things as tools, but are merely idols as objects of trust and reverence.

Demonic literalism seeks conquest by paralysing argument; imaginative literalism seeks what might be called interpenetration, the free flowing of spiritual life into and out of one another that communicates but never violates. As Coleridge said (unless Schelling said it first), "The medium by which spirits understand each other is not the surrounding air, but the *freedom* which they possess in common."[8] As the myths and metaphors of Scripture gradually become, for us, myths and metaphors that we can live by and in, that not only work for us but constantly expand our horizons, we may enter the world of proclamation and pass on to others what we have found to be true for ourselves. When we encounter a quite different vision in, say, a Buddhist, a Jew, a Confucian, an atheist, or whatever, there can still be what is called dialogue, and mutual understanding, based on a sense that there is plenty of room in the mind of God for us both. All faith is founded on good faith, and where there is good faith on both sides there is also the presence of God.

The same thing is true of variations of belief among Christians. Some prominent cleric may announce, after much heart-searching and self-harrowing, that he can no longer "believe in" the Virgin Birth. What he thinks he is saying is that he can no longer honestly accept the historicity of the Nativity stories in Matthew and Luke. But those stories do not belong to ordinary history at all: they form part of *Heilsgeschichte*, a mythical narrative containing many features that cannot be assimilated to the historian's history. What he is really saying is that some elements in the Gospel myth have less transforming power for him than others.

His version of Christianity could never have built a cathedral to Notre Dame de Chartres or written the hymn to the Virgin at the end of Dante's *Paradiso*, but his version is his, and that is his business only. However, if he had been a better educated cleric he would not have raised the point in the wrong context and created false issues.

The Epistle to the Hebrews says that faith is the *hypostasis* of the hoped for and the *elenchos* or proof of the unseen [11:1]. That is, faith is the reality of hope and of illusion. In this sense faith starts with a vision of reality that is something other than history or logic, which accepts the world as it is, and on the basis of that vision it can begin to remake the world. A nineteenth-century disciple of Kant, Hans Vaihinger, founded a philosophy on the phrase "as if," and the literal basis of faith from which we should start, the imaginative and poetic basis, is a fiction we enter into "as if" it were true. There is no certainty in faith to begin with: we are free to deny the reality of the spiritual challenge of the New Testament, and if we accept it we accept it tentatively, taking a risk. The certainty comes later, and very gradually, with the growing sense in our own experience that the vision really does have the power that it claims to have.

I use the word "risk" advisedly: I am not minimizing the difficulties and dangers of an imaginative literalism. All through history there has run a distrust and contempt for imaginative language, and the words for story or literary narrative—myth, fable, and fiction—have all acquired a secondary sense of falsehood or something made up out of nothing. Overcoming this perversion of language takes time and thought, and besides, there are as many evil myths and vicious metaphors as there are evil doctrines and vicious arguments. But the author of Hebrews goes on to talk, in the examples he gives after his definition of faith, about the risks taken by vision, and he suggests that such risks are guided by more effective powers than merely subjective ones. Besides, we are not alone: we live not only in God's world but in a community with a tradition behind it. Preserving the inner vitality of that community and that tradition is what the churches are for.

I have been trying to suggest a basis for the openness of belief that is characteristic of the United Church. Many of you will still recall an article in a Canadian journal that emphasized this openness, and drew the conclusion that the United Church was now an "agnostic" church.[9] I think the writer was trying to be fair-minded, but his conclusion was nonsense: the United Church is agnostic only in the sense that it does not pretend to know what nobody actually "knows" anyway. The article quoted a church member as asking, If a passage in Scripture fails to transform me, is it still true? The question was a central one, but it reminded me of a story told me by a late colleague who many years ago was lecturing on Milton's view of the Trinity. He explained the difference between Athanasian and Arian positions, and how Milton, failing to find enough scriptural evidence for the Athanasian position, adopted a qualified or semi-Arian one. He was interrupted by a student who said impatiently, "But I want to know the truth about the Trinity." One may sympathize with the student, but trying to satisfy him is futile. What "the" truth is is not available to human beings in spiritual matters: the goal of our spiritual life is God, who is a spiritual Other, not a spiritual object, much less a conceptual object. That is why the Gospels keep reminding us how many listen and how few hear: truths of the Gospel kind cannot be demonstrated except through personal example. As the seventeenth-century Quaker Isaac Penington said, every truth is substantial in its own place, but all truths are shadows except the last. The language that lifts us clear of the merely plausible and the merely credible is the language of the spirit; the language of the spirit is, Paul tells us, the language of love, and the language of love is the only language that we can be sure is spoken and understood by God.

II The Double Vision of Nature

Natural and Human Societies

I have taken my running title "The Double Vision" from a phrase in a poem of Blake incorporated in a letter to Thomas Butts (22 November 1802):

> For double the vision my Eyes do see,
> And a double vision is always with me.
> With my inward Eye 'tis an old Man grey;
> With my outward, a Thistle across the way.

The surface meaning of this appears to be that Blake is adding a subjective hallucination to the sense perception of an object, and that adding this hallucination is what makes him the visionary poet and painter that he is. If this is what Blake is saying, he is talking nonsense, and Blake very seldom talks nonsense. The general idea, however, seems to be that simple sense perception is not enough. We may be reminded of a well known bit of doggerel from Wordsworth:

> A primrose by a river's brim
> A yellow primrose was to him,
> And it was nothing more.[10]

Well, what more should it be? If I were a primrose by a river's brim, I should feel insulted.

Clearly a good deal depends on what is meant by "more." If it means something in addition to the perception of the primrose, we seem to be headed for some kind of deliberate programme of disorganizing sense experience of a type later proposed by Rimbaud, who said that the poet wishing to be a visionary must go through a long and systematic unsettling (*dérèglement*) of sense experience.[11] But there seems to be something unreliable about this programme, if it had anything to do with the fact that one of the greatest of French poets stopped writing when he was barely out of his teens. If, on the other hand, Wordsworth is simply speaking of seeing the primrose itself with a greater intensity, that may be part of a "more" stable and continuous process.

We have to give the context of what Blake says at this point, as we shall be referring to it later. He has acquired, he tells us, a double-double or fourfold vision, although it is still essentially twofold, in contrast to what he prays to be delivered from:

> 'Tis fourfold in my supreme delight
> And threefold in soft Beulah's night
> And twofold Always. May God us keep
> From Single vision & Newton's sleep!

However paradoxical his language, Blake is not recommending that one should try to awaken from the sleep of single vision by seeing two objects instead of one, especially when one of the two is not there. I think he means rather that the conscious subject is not really perceiving until it recognizes itself as part of what it perceives. The whole world is humanized when such a perception takes place. There must be something human about the object, alien as it may at first seem, which the perceiver is relating to. The "old man grey" is clearly an aspect of Blake himself, and stands for the fact that whatever we perceive is a part of us and forms an identity with us.

First, there is the world of the thistle, the world of nature presented directly to us. This is obviously the world within which our physical bodies have evolved, but from which consciousness feels oddly separated. Nature got along for untold ages without us: it could get along very well without us now and it may again get along without us in the future. The systematic study of nature, which is the main business of science, reflects this sense of separation. It is impersonal, avoids value judgments and commitments to emotion or imagination, and confines itself to explanations that are largely in terms of mechanism. This is the view that Blake associates with the outlook of Isaac Newton, and although Newton was a religious man who saw many religious implications in his own science, there is a sense in which Blake was right. There is no God in the scientific vision as such: if we bring God into science, we turn him into a mechanical engineer, like the demiurge of Plato's *Timaeus* or the designing watchmaker God of the various Christian and deistic attempts at natural theology.

True, science has abandoned *narrowly* mechanistic explanations in one field after another since Blake spoke of Newton's sleep. It is sixty years since Sir James Jeans, in *The Mysterious Universe*, gave God a degree in mathematics rather than mechanical engineering, mathematics being a field that admits of paradox, even of irrationalities. It is an equally long time since Whitehead criticized the conception of "simple location"[12] that underlies Blake's polemic against single vision. But scientific explanations are still mainly nonteleological, confining themselves to the *how* of things, though there are signs that science may be coming to the end of this self-denying ordinance.

The first aspect of the double vision that we have to become aware of is the distinction between the natural and the human environment. There is the natural environment which is simply there, and is, in mythological language, our mother. And there is the human environment, the world we are trying to build out of the natural one. We think of the two worlds as equally real, though we spend practically our whole time in the human one. We wake up in the morning in our bedrooms, and feel that we have abolished an unreal world, the world of the dream, and are now in the world of waking reality. But everything surrounding us in that bedroom is a human artefact.

If science is more impersonal than literature or religion, that is the result of certain conventions imposed on science by its specific subject matter. It studies the natural environment, but as part of the human constructed world. It discovers counterparts of the human sense of order and predictability in nature, and the scientist as human being would not differ psychologically from the artist in the way he approaches his work. The axiom of the eighteenth-century Italian philosopher Giambattista Vico was *verum factum*: we understand nothing except what we have made.[13] Again, it is only the human environment that can be personal, and if God belongs in this distinction at all, he must, being a person, be sought for in the human world.

As the natural ancestry of human beings is not in dispute, it was inevitable that at some point the question should be raised of how far a "natural society" is possible, and whether man could simply live in a state of harmony with nature, instead of withdrawing his consciousness from nature and devoting his energies to a separable order of existence. Such speculations arose mainly in the eighteenth century, in the age of Rousseau. They have not stood up very well to what anthropology has since gleaned from the study of primitive societies. There seems to be no human society that does not live within an envelope of law, ritual, custom, and myth that seals it off from nature, however closely its feeding and mating and hunting habits may approximate those of animals.

When our remote ancestors were tree opossums or whatever, avoiding the carnivorous dinosaurs, they were animals totally preoccupied, as other animals still are for the most part, with the primary concerns of food, sex, territory, and free movement on a purely physical level. With the dawn of consciousness humanity feels separated from nature and looks at it as something objective to itself. This is the starting point of Blake's single vision, where we no longer feel part of nature but are helplessly staring at it.

Thomas Pynchon's remarkable novel *Gravity's Rainbow* is a book that seems to me to have grasped a central principle of this situation. The human being, this novel tells us, is instinctively paranoid: we are first of all convinced that the world was expressly made for us and designed in detail for our benefit and appreciation. As soon as we are afflicted by doubts about this, we plunge into the other aspect of paranoia, feel that our environment is absurd and alienating, and that we are uniquely accursed in being aware, unlike any other organism in nature, of our own approaching mortality. Pynchon makes it clear that this paranoia can be and is transformed into creative energy and becomes the starting point of everything that humanity has done in the arts and sciences. But before it is thus transformed, it is the state that the Bible condemns as idolatry, in which we project numinous beings or forces into nature and scan nature anxiously for signs of its benevolence or wrath directed toward us.

The Bible is emphatic that nothing numinous exists in nature, that there may be devils there but no gods, and that nature is to be thought of as a fellow creature of man. However, the paranoid attitude to nature that Pynchon describes survives in the manic-depressive psychosis of the twentieth century. In the manic phase, we are told that the age of Aquarius is coming, and that soon the world will be turned back to the state of innocence. In the depressive phase, news analysts explain that pollution has come to a point at which any sensible nature would simply wipe us out and start experimenting with a new species. In interviews I am almost invariably asked at some point whether I feel optimistic or pessimistic about some contemporary situation. The answer is that these imbecile words are euphemisms for manic-depressive highs and lows, and that anyone who struggles for sanity avoids both.

We do emerge, however, to some degree, from the illusions of staring at nature into building a human world of culture and civilization, and from that perspective we can see the natural environment as the "material" world in the sense of providing the materials for our unique form of existence. Practically all of our made world represents a huge waste of effort: it includes the world of war, of cutthroat competition, of stagnating bureaucracies, of the lying and hypocrisy of what is called public relations. Above all, it has not achieved any genuine rapprochement with nature itself, but simply regards nature as an area of exploitation. Where God may belong in this duality we have yet to try to see, but as he is not hidden in nature, he can only be connected with that tiny percentage of human activity that has not been hopelessly botched.

The reason for this is that we have separated from nature but are still regarding it as a mirror of ourselves, from within the prison of Narcissus. In the state of nature there may well be a good deal of what the anarchist Kropotkin called, on the basis of the studies that he made of the subject, "mutual aid."[14] But what are more obvious and picturesque in nature are the patterns of tyranny and anarchy that are constantly appealed to by rationalizers of bad social systems. The communities formed by animals are full of hierarchies and pecking orders, of females forcibly seized by stronger males, of fights over territorial disputes, and the like, even if they fall short of the total obliterating of the individual that we see in communities of social insects. There are patterns of laissez-faire anarchy, too, in the hunting of predators like the great jungle cats: calling the lion the "king of beasts" helps to reassure us that a society in which the predators are the aristocracy is the right one for us as well.

But humanity's primary duty is not to be natural but to be human. The reason why idolatry is dangerous is that it suggests the attractiveness and the easiness with which we may collapse into the preconscious state from which we have been trying to emerge. As long as idolatry persists, and humanity is seeing in nature a mirror of itself, it forms primitive societies (in the sense used earlier) as an imitation of nature. Nearly all human history shows one society after another sinking back into the order of nature as thus conceived, setting up regimes of tyranny and anarchy in which mere survival is all that is left of human life for the great majority. Human beings get along as best they can in such a world, but the human spirit knows that it is living in hell.

While humanity is continually sliding back into a state of nature to which it is totally unadapted, there is still a steady process of work that transforms the natural environment into a human one. In the Bible the images of this transformation, the flocks and herds of the animal world, the harvests and vintages, farms and gardens of the vegetable world, the buildings and highways made from the inorganic world, symbolize the fulfilling of what I call human primary concerns. This process is a social and communal enterprise, and if tyranny and exploitation are relaxed for a moment, the genuinely social virtues of co-operation and neighbourliness soon emerge. But the energy of social work, though certainly intelligent and conscious, tends also to be uncritical and instinctive.

Criticism and Civilization

In the nineteenth-century work that transformed Ontario from a forested environment into an agricultural one, there were many largely unexamined assumptions: the immense destruction of trees and slaughter of forest animals were necessary to "clear" the land, and nothing else needed to be said about it. In the twentieth century a largely farming and small-town population was transformed into an urban one, a process again largely uncritical. But eventually certain crises, especially pollution and such questions as what to do with our garbage and sewage, force us into a criticism of what such work is doing. Here we have moved into a higher power of consciousness and a new dimension of concern.

In the construction of the human world we recognize two elements. One is the element of work, which is energy expended for a further end in view. The other is play, or energy expended for its own sake. In the animal world play seems to be important mainly to young animals, and to have the function there of a kind of rehearsal for more mature activities. In the human world play is more complex: it opens up a world of freedom and leisure out of which the typically human form of consciousness comes, and it produces the creative arts. In communities preoccupied with physical labour, the members of such communities are usually regarded as either manual workers or slackers, and the creative arts are often thought of as socially expendable, or even irresponsible. But just as the play of puppies indicates something of what they will be as grown dogs, so the creative arts set up models of what I have been calling primary concerns. Fiction and drama in literature, I have said, depict people making love, gaining property, wandering off on adventures, struggling to survive. Some aspects of literature, such as the comic and the romantic, lean in the direction of wish-fulfilment; the tragic and the ironic emphasize frustration and maladjustment. This latter especially means that in the verbal arts at least a creative and a critical element are inseparable. In fact Matthew Arnold even spoke of poetry as a criticism of life.[15]

Every human society is mired in all the miseries of original sin, but we never fail to find something in its culture that is attractive, and not only attractive but communicable, speaking directly to us across the widest abysses of time or space or language. With simpler societies we find most of this sense of a kindred human spirit in what are called useful arts: pottery, textiles, basketwork, and the like, which are preserved in museums for their potential cultural contact. It used to be that the fine arts were ranked above the useful arts, which are obviously closer to the world of work, on the analogy of the old social ranking of a leisure class above a working class, but this tiresome nonsense is now abandoned. We no longer think of leisure and work as associated with different classes, but as alternating activities within all classes, so far as we still have classes. What is relevant is that the useful arts may be well designed or badly designed, and may include or exclude ornament. Design and ornament both imply some transcendence of the world of work.

The connection with work, however, makes it clear that creative and critical energies come from human society as a whole. They give the individual a far greater importance in the work of society, but they cannot be simply "subjective" if by subjective we mean something confined to the individual psyche. Psychology has much to say about the creative process, and psychology, though it is increasingly concerned with group therapies, still takes the individual as its main base of operations. Freud was the first to link the dream within the individual, which expresses the primary concerns of the individual, with the myths that are the main verbal culture of primitive societies and go on to form the shaping narratives of literature. But literature, even in its most mythological phases, communicates, and the dreamer cannot, without special training, understand his own dreams. Jung went a step further in identifying a collective unconscious, where we find images representing rudimentary designs of the human cosmos. But the collective unconscious is by definition still unconscious. The arts, said Plato, are dreams for awakened minds:[16] only a collective consciousness can perform their communicating tasks.

I spoke of the sense of individual integrity as the sign of a mature society, but the isolated individual, even when equipped with a conscience and a private judgment, is essentially a sleeping animal: he can pursue his primary concerns on a physical level, but his creative and critical powers cannot extend beyond dreams. Luther did not say at Worms, "Here I stand, because my conscience and private judgment tell me to." He said, "Here I stand, until I can be convinced otherwise by arguments drawn from the Word of God." His individuality was rooted in his social and religious conditioning, growing out of them as a tree grows out of its roots; but it was not a simple expression of conditioning, or we should never have heard of him again.

The creative impulse, however central to all that is best in human life, has still much in it of what a more old-fashioned way of speaking calls "instinctive." It certainly employs intellectual and rational powers, but often circumvents them, working by an intuitive skill or flair that avoids explicit formulation. For many creative people consciousness would be only a self-consciousness that would block and frustrate them. Let us turn to the critical faculty. The Book of Genesis tells us that God made the world in six days and rested on the seventh, devoting six days to work and one day to the contemplation of what he had done. It adds that as this forms part of God's activity, it is a model for man to imitate. Man's consciousness[17] of being in nature though not wholly of it is potentially a sabbatical vision, and one which includes a more leisurely and detached vision of what he is doing and why he has done it. This kind of leisurely freedom of consciousness is part of what is expressed by the word "liberal" as applied to education.

New categories of consciousness, such as those expressed in such words as "beauty" or "ugliness" begin to arise here. To paraphrase Matthew Arnold again, many things are not seen in their full reality until they are seen, not necessarily as beautiful, but as existing within the context of beauty.[18] Arnold was followed by Ruskin and Morris, who insisted that the reality of Victorian civilization was bound up with the sense of how much ugliness was included in it. For us too, no one who drives through the Ontario countryside can miss the reality of beauty in the woods and crop lands and running streams, or the reality of ugliness in the outskirts of towns and cities. It follows from all we have said about the priority of social to individual consciousness that such helplessly subjective formulas as "beauty is in the eye of the beholder" will not do, however flexible such judgments may be. If there is not a consensus of some kind, we are not working with very useful conceptions.

The word "beauty" went out of fashion for a long time because it was subject to heavy ideological pressures of the wrong kind. Whether applied to Mozart's music or Monet's painting, to a nubile young woman in a bikini, or to the trees, flowers, butterflies, and sunsets that we see in nature, it tended to be associated with a sense of what was comfortable and reassuring. Entering the young woman with the bikini in a "beauty" contest seems to imply that only young, healthy, and, very often, white, bodies can be beautiful. We may come to understand that our sense of the reality of beauty grows in proportion as we abandon this exclusive rubbish and discover beauty in more and more varieties of experience. But something of the static and established convention clings to the word. William Morris urged us to have nothing in our homes that we do not either know to be useful or believe to be beautiful.[19] The shift in the verb is significant: as we saw earlier, belief, like beauty, often seeks the goal of reassurance rather than discovery.

I think we can use our conception of primary concern to come to a more satisfactory criterion of beauty and ugliness. These concerns, food, sex, property, and mobility, obviously have to be central in all the work we do to build a human environment out of the natural one. When the work energy relaxes to the point at which leisure, contemplation, and critical evaluation begin to supplement it, we start thinking in terms of what in the environment is genuinely human and what is, as we say, "dehumanizing." What we accept as beautiful or attractive or in accord with the way we want things to be has some connection, however indirect, with the satisfying of these concerns, and what we call ugly or dehumanized—air choked with pollution, land turned into waste land by speculators, infernos created by technological idiocies from Chernobyl to Exxon Valdez—with the frustration of them. For a long time the established powers in society looked at their civilization and said, "Probably much of it is very ugly, but that doesn't matter as long as we make profits out of it, and certainly nothing is going to be done about it." When it becomes clear that ugly is beginning to mean dangerous as well, however, the point of view may slowly change.

The greatest of all philosophers who took criticism as his base of operations, Kant, examined three aspects of the critical faculty. First was pure reason, which contemplates the objective world within the framework of its own categories, and hence sees the objective counterpart of itself, the world as it may really be eluding the categories. Second was practical reason, where a conscious being is assumed to be a conscious will, and which penetrates farther into the kind of reality we call existential, even into experience relating to God. Third was the aesthetic faculty dealing with the environment within the categories of beauty, a critical operation involving, for Kant, questions of the kind we have just called teleological, relating to purpose and ultimate design.

For Kant, however, the formula of beauty in the natural world at least was "purposiveness without purpose."[20] The crystallizing of snowflakes is beautiful because it suggests design and intention and yet eludes these things. To suggest that the design of a snowflake has been produced by a designer, whether Nature or God, suggests also that somebody or something has worked to produce it: such a suggestion limits its beauty by cutting off the sense of a spontaneous bursting into symmetry. "Fire delights in its form," says Blake, and Wallace Stevens adds that we trust the world only when we have no sense of a concealed creator.[21]

The argument of Kant's *Critique of Judgment* thus turns on the close connection between aesthetic and suspended teleological judgments.

This is connected with the fact mentioned earlier, that scientific explanations tend to the mechanistic and avoid the teleological. Science is concerned with parts of a whole: teleological explanations reason from the whole to the parts, and science cannot adopt this perspective unless the scientist is prepared to say that he understands the mind of God or the hidden designs of nature. What teleology we do have is surrounded by a very limited human perspective. Isaiah may imagine a state in which the lion lies down with the lamb [cf. 11:6], but we live in a state in which the lion could not exist without eating lambs, or something dietetically equivalent. If the lion had a teleology, he would say that lambs exist for the purpose of being eaten by lions; if the lamb had one, its view would be that lambs exist for the sake of being lambs, and that lions are an unwarranted and evil intrusion into their world. So naturally, when we come to the human view, we tend to assume that nature was created for man to exploit, man being the predator set in authority over all other predators.

It is clear that within the last two or three decades we have come to something of a crisis in our views both of the relations of human beings to one another and of the relation of the human to the natural environment. The questions of teleology, of the purposes and final causes of our existence, cannot be ignored much longer, even if we cannot as yet consider such questions outside the human perspective. All around us we hear demands for a society where the concerns of everybody should be recognized, where there is enough peace and freedom to enable human beings to live with full human dignity and self-respect. The Gospels suggest that the ultimate reason for wanting to live in such a world is that only in it can there be any real love. In the civilized state of humanity we love those who are close to us: for those farther away we feel the tolerance and good will which express love at a distance. In the pure state of nature we feel only possessive about those close to us, and hostile and mistrustful of those further away. The latter do all sorts of vaguely irritating things, like speaking different languages, eating different foods, and holding different beliefs.

However, the immense increase in the speed of communication today has also increased our sense of involvement with people at a distance, and even people who actually are totally alien to ourselves in their mental processes. It is difficult not to feel some involvement even with the fantasies of a psychotic murdering women who want to be engineers. One hopes that underlying the drive toward peace and freedom in our time is an impulse toward love growing out of a new immediacy of contact. The word "love" may still sound somewhat hazy and sentimental, but it does express some sort of crisis: "We must love one another or die," as W.H. Auden says.[22]

Such love readily extends from the human to the natural world, and the feeling that nature should be cherished and fostered rather than simply exploited is one of the few welcome developments of the last generation or so. Here, again, love at a distance expresses itself as tolerance: if we can't exactly love sharks or piranhas we can still be curious about them, study their habits, and leave them alone to fulfil their function in maintaining the balance of nature. The balance of nature, as these examples show, is amoral but not immoral: standards of morality are relevant only to the human world. What is immoral is humanity's inept interference with the balance of nature that has encouraged pathological developments like the Dutch elm blight or the presence of lampreys and zebra mussels in the Great Lakes.

The Redemption of Nature

To recapitulate, with the coming of consciousness humanity is sufficiently detached from nature to see it as an objective order. Apart from the efforts at survival, we are impressed with nature's size and strength and our own littleness and insignificance. This is the stage in which we find the numinous in nature, the stage that the Bible calls idolatry and that Blake regards as continuing in the mechanistic scientific outlook that he symbolizes by the name of Newton. In the next stage we realize that human values are to be found only in the human world, and that God, as distinct from the gods created by man out of nature, is to be sought for through human and social means. With words like "beauty" we begin to get some glimpse of Blake's "threefold [vision] in soft Beulah's night." Beulah for Blake is the earthly paradise, the state of innocence, the peaceable kingdom and married land of Isaiah 11:6 and 62:4. Beulah in Blake is much the same as the holiday world of the imagination that I identified earlier with literature and the other arts, where there is entertainment without argument. Blake describes it elsewhere as a place "where no dispute can come."[23] What he meant by a fourfold vision is beyond our present scope.

There is always something of the kindergarten about garden paradises: in Isaiah's peaceable kingdom the predatory animals converted to a new way of life are led by a child, and Adam and Eve, living in a garden planted by a benevolent parental figure, are also clearly children whose curiosity and lack of experience get them into trouble. We normally think of an earthly paradise as a world of beauty, and the word "beauty," as we saw, has inherited some of these immature and overprotective associations. It was for this reason that the eighteenth century added the conception of "sublime" to the conception of beauty. The sublime conveys the sense of the majestic and awful in the natural environment: that is, it preserves something of the alienation that we also feel there, but an alienation that we can find exhilarating rather than humiliating. With the present feeling for the importance of "wet lands" and the like, we begin to understand what the poet Gerard Manley Hopkins meant by his line "Long live the weeds and the wilderness yet"[24] and take one more step toward envisaging a human order that has come to terms with nature on something more like nature's own terms.

We see, then, human beings continually trying to struggle out of the atavisms of tyranny and anarchy, knowing that they are better than these conditions, repeatedly forced back into them by all the perversities of their own will, yet never quite losing hope or the vision of an ideal. Such an ideal has to be present and realizable, as opposed to the dream of restoring a paradise lost in the past, or in what is symbolized by the past.

From what has been said already it is clear that this realizable ideal is the spiritual kingdom revealed by Jesus in the Gospels, which is something that only Paul's *soma pneumatikon* can even understand, much less enter. The programme of spiritual awareness laid down in that tremendous philosophical masterpiece, Hegel's *Phenomenology of Spirit*, turns on two principles that are relevant here. First is Hegel's introductory principle, "The true substance is subject." That is, the gap between a conscious perceiving subject and a largely unconscious objective world confronts us at the beginning of experience. All progress in knowledge, in fact in consciousness itself, consists in bridging the gap and abolishing both the separated subject and the separated object.

At a certain point, for Hegel, we move from the soul–body unit, Paul's natural man, into the realm of Spirit (*Geist*: the first translation of Hegel's book into English mistranslated Geist as "mind," which confuses, among other things, the whole religious dimension of Hegel's argument). Spirit, says Hegel, enters the picture as soon as "We" and "I" begin to merge, when the individual speaks as a discriminating and independent unit within his society. In his "substance is subject" principle Hegel continues a philosophical tradition going back to the Latin church fathers, brooding on the relation of person and substance in the Trinity and translating *hypostasis* not as *substantia* but as *persona*. The problem is to define what is at once spiritual and substantial, the spirit which is also a body. The mirror, where a subject sees an object which is both itself and not itself, is a central metaphor of knowledge, and such words as "speculation" and "reflection" point to its importance. Hegel is in search of a self-awareness that culminates, for him, in "absolute knowledge," where we finally break out of the mirror, the prison of Narcissus.[25]

A celebrated ceramic known as the Grecian urn, which some scholars believe to have been a piece of Wedgwood pottery, informs us, in the context of an ode of Keats, that

> Beauty is truth, truth beauty: that is all
> Ye know on earth, and all ye need to know.[26]

We have seen that a knowledge of ugliness, in both human and natural worlds, is just as essential. Again, gaining knowledge of the physical environment in the natural sciences is a pursuit of truth, even though we accept the fact that there are no permanent or final truths in science or any other human discipline. But truth always has a "whether we like it or not" element about it, and it is difficult to separate liking or repulsion from the beauty–ugliness category. Keats saw things with an intensity that only the highest genius combined with tuberculosis can give, but here he must be speaking from a different and more idealized context.

I think Keats means that truth and beauty are both fictions, both something created by humanity out of the natural environment. One is concerned with the ordering of what is there, the other with the vision of what ideally should be there. In actual experience these two things are always different, but that is because actual experience is largely unreal. The world in which the real and the ideal become the same thing is by definition real, even if we never live in it. Truth is beauty only if the spiritual is substantial.

This understood, it is clear that the pursuit of truth in science, or anywhere else, opens up an infinite number of roads to beauty. Similarly, there may be, first, a great beauty in a literary structure which is detached but not turned away from the social and natural worlds, regardless of the content, which, because it may reflect any aspect of life, could be squalid, terrible, obscene, or insane. Second, imaginative structures contain a vast amount of truth about the human condition that it is not possible to obtain in any other way.

So Matthew Arnold's definition of literature as a criticism of life is a great deal more than a paradox. Creation includes criticism as a part of itself. For Kant, as we saw, aesthetic questions were bound up with the critical faculty of judgment. Critics have been deluded into thinking that their function was to judge works of art, but their judicial role does not go in this direction at all. They do not judge the writer, except incidentally: they work with the writer in judging the human condition. The writer may let them down: there is as much falsehood in literature as there is in any area of human utterance. To give a random example, the adoption of a "socialist realism" programme in Stalinist Russia meant that every Soviet novel had to lie from beginning to end, or its author would find himself in a concentration camp in Siberia. In other societies authors may struggle to tell the truth as they see it, but they are limited beings in a limited society, and what they say will reveal both kinds of limitation. That is why we have to have a tradition of criticism that keeps studying and commenting on the literature of the past, recognizing its relation both to its own time and to the critic's time. Out of this may come, eventually, a consensus that will broaden and deepen our understanding of our imaginative heritage.

The previous chapter drew a distinction between primary and secondary concerns, in which the secondary ones were ideological and the primary ones physical, though the physical concerns needed a spiritual dimension. This immediately raised the question of the difference between secondary concerns and spiritual primary ones. I answered this tentatively by saying that secondary concerns referred to "primitive" societies that absorbed the individual into the group, and that the spiritual primary ones existed only in "mature" societies that existed for the sake of individuals. We can perhaps see now that what we have been calling criticism in the larger sense as a process that takes over from the critics is the key to the distinction.

We have to have this critical approach in all the arts, and in fact in every aspect of life, so that the word "criticism" expands until it is practically synonymous with education itself. It covers all we know on earth and most of what we can know, if not quite, perhaps, all we need to

know. In religion, too, we must keep a critical attitude that never uncon-
ditionally accepts any socially established form of revelation. Otherwise, we are back to idolatry again, this time a self-idolatry rather than
an idolatry of nature, where devotion to God is replaced by the deifying
of our own present understanding of God. Paul tells us that we are
God's temples [1 Corinthians 3:16]: if so, we should be able to see the
folly of what was proposed by the emperor Caligula for the Jerusalem
temple, of putting a statue of ourselves in its holy place.[27]

Criticism in the human world, however, is inseparably bound up with
creation. We also think of God as above everything else a creator, as the
opening sentence of the Bible tells us he is. I said earlier that we have
abandoned the snobbish social analogy in the distinction between fine
and useful (or "minor") arts, but another distinction of some importance
is involved here, in a different context. We normally say that people
"make" baskets and pots and textiles, but "create" symphonies and dra-
mas and frescos.[28] Traditionally, however, we ignore this distinction
when we speak of God as having "made" the world. To call God a maker implies that divine creation is a metaphor projected from something
that man does, although the Hebrew word for "created" (bara) is never
used in a human context. There is something denigrating to God in
regarding him as a maker, as preoccupied with ingenious designs, to be
complimented, as he was by natural theologians in the eighteenth century, on his cleverness in dividing up the orange into sections for convenience in (human, of course) eating. It was this consideration that led
Kant to his "purposiveness without purpose" formula for beauty. God
did not make a humanly useful world; his creation relates to a world, or
rather to a condition of being, that exists for its own sake, and for his.
For a designing craftsman-God, a super-Hephaestus, there would have
been no point in a sabbatical vision to become the model for an expanding human consciousness: only a creating God would provide a Sabbath, and with it the escape for man from natural into spiritual vision.

III The Double Vision of Time

Space and Time

In the first chapter I tried to distinguish spiritual language, founded on
the principle that literal meaning in religion is metaphorical and mythi-

cal meaning, from natural language, which is founded on the principle that the literal is the descriptive. In the second I tried to distinguish spiritual and natural visions of the spatial world. The natural vision of space is founded on the subject–object split, and whatever is objectified in ordinary experience is "there," even if it is in the middle of our own backbones. At the centre of space is "here," but "here" is never a point, it is always a circumference. We draw a circle around ourselves and say that "here" is inside it. What is, in the common phrase, neither here nor there does not exist, at least in space.

As natural perception develops, the "here" circle keeps enlarging: the very word "nature," the sense of the objective as an order, shows how far we have gone in overcoming the subject–object split. In proportion as spiritual perception begins to enter the scene, we are released from the bondage of being "subjected" to a looming and threatening objective world, whether natural or social. In the spiritual world everywhere is here, and both a centre and a circumference. The first book of philosophy that I read purely on my own and purely for pleasure was Whitehead's *Science and the Modern World*, and I can still remember the exhilaration I felt when I came to the passage: "In a certain sense, everything is everywhere at all times. For every location involves an aspect of itself in every other location. Thus every spatio-temporal standpoint mirrors the world" (114). This was my initiation into what Christianity means by spiritual vision.

We saw that we have two stages to pass through, the natural and the social, before the spiritual vision of space is fully emancipated. I now want to distinguish the spiritual vision of time from the natural one, and here again we have a distinction between time in the physical world and time in the social or human world, the latter being what we call history. Philosophers have been extremely profound about time: I do not have enough philosophy to be profound, so I shall have to settle for simplicity, which in a technical subject always means being simplistic.

In our ordinary experience of time we have to grapple with three dimensions, all of them unreal: a past that is no longer, a future that is not yet, and a present that is never quite. We are dragged backwards along a continuum of experience, facing the past with the future behind us. The centre of time is "now," just as the centre of space is "here," but "now," like "here," is never a point. The first thing that the present moment does is vanish and reappear in the immediate past, where it connects with our expectation of its outcome in the future. Every present experience is therefore split between our knowledge of having had it and our future-directed fears or hopes about it. The word "now" refers to the spread of time in between.

We know nothing of the future except by analogy with the past, and analogy tells us that we are mortal. It even seems probable that the basis of consciousness, Paul's *soma psychikon*, is the awareness that the uneasy pact between soul and body will dissolve sooner or later, whether the soul is confident that it will survive the separation or not. Meanwhile there is, coming from the bodily side, a will to survive of which the motor force is usually called desire. The continuum of desire consists largely of avoiding the consciousness of death, and acting on the assumption that we are not going to die at once. This means that our life in time is a conflict of desire and consciousness producing a state of more or less subdued anxiety, and all the higher religions begin by trying to do something about that anxiety. Buddhism tells us to extinguish desire and cut off the anxiety rooted in the past; the Gospels tell us to take no thought for the morrow and cut off the anxiety rooted in the future.

We may talk about a beginning and an end to time, but we cannot realize such things in our imaginations. Whether we speak of a creation by God which began time (that is, our experience of time) or of a big bang many billions of years ago, the human mind cannot help thinking that there must have been time "before" that. St. Augustine was bothered by this question, which he raises several times, notably in a famous passage in the *Confessions*, where in effect he answers the question, "What was God doing before creation?" by saying, "Preparing a hell for those who ask such a question."[29] If we were to guess at the repressed elements in the saint's mind when he wrote this, they might well have run something like this: If you ask God what happened before time, you embarrass God, who probably doesn't know either, and as God hates to be embarrassed, you are risking a good deal by asking.

Life in time represents the revolt of the finite against the indefinite. Time never begins or ends; life always does. Our experience of the present moment, or now, where "now" is the spread of time between a second or two of past and future, repeats in miniature the whole sequence of our lives. Life in its turn is founded on the alternating movements in time, the cyclical patterns that give us light and darkness, summer and winter, and any number of other cyclical rhythms not yet wholly understood. The relation of life and time to language follows similar patterns. For animals, what corresponds to speech seems to have its roots in the rituals that are punctuation marks in the flow of time, and crucial points in its cycles. Thus we have mating rituals, territorial rituals, rituals of hostility to an invader, or of solidarity within a group, usually connected with communication by sound, as in the songs of birds. The same associations of speech with erotic or hostile or socially binding rituals reappear in human life. But in human rituals we have a more complex factor.

In some societies rituals may be observed on a more or less unconscious basis. If asked why such rituals, which may be very elaborate and apparently significant, are performed, such a society may have little to say to a visiting anthropologist except "we have always done this." But it is more usual to have some explanation of ritual at hand and to recite it as an essential part of the ritual itself. Such an explanation regularly takes the form of a myth, or story (*mythos*), recounting some event in the past of which the ritual is a commemoration or repetition, in the same way that Christmas commemorates and repeats the birth of Christ, even though we do not know the day when Christ was born. A myth in its turn is part of a mythology, or interconnected group of myths, many of them growing out of the rituals of a society's liturgical year. And, of course, the myth springs out of life, not time: it performs the same revolutionary and arbitrary act of beginning and ending.

In the Athens of the fifth century B.C., a momentous step in human consciousness occurred when the rituals associated with Dionysus developed into drama, and the great evolution of what we now call literature out of mythology took a decisive turn. The specific literary genre produced on that occasion was tragedy, and tragedy, as analysed by Aristotle, exhibits the same shape, a parabola in which "now" is spread between a past and a future, that we have been looking at, though of course on a larger scale. Oedipus, for example, is a humane and conscientious king of Thebes, whose kingdom is ravaged by a drought. The gods are angry, and it is his responsibility to find out why. He consults an oracle, the prophet Tiresias, and is told that he himself killed his father long ago and is now living in incest with his mother. Oedipus had no knowledge of this, but ignorance of the law is no excuse. So he tears out his eyes in a revulsion of horror. The knowledge that Oedipus gets from Tiresias about his own earlier life constitutes for him the moment of what Aristotle calls *anagnorisis* [*Poetics*, 10.4–8], which may be translated either "discovery" or "recognition," depending on whether one remembers it or not. As a structural principle in tragedy, *anagnorisis* is a point of awareness near the end that links with the beginning, and shows us that what we have been following up to that point is not a simple continuum but something in the shape of a parabola, a story that begins, rises, turns, moves downward, and ends in catastrophe. This last word preserves the downward-turning metaphor.

This parabola shape occurs at every instant of our lives. Every experience is a recognition of having had it an instant earlier. It follows that the past is the sole source of knowledge, even though it extends up to the previous moment. The same parabola shape encompasses our entire lives. As we grow older, we find our childhood experiences becoming increasingly vivid, and the speech of old men is full of reminiscences of early life. One reason why such reminiscence is apt to be tedious is that these memories are mainly screen memories, memories not of what happened but of what they have reconstructed in their minds since. However, if they recalled what actually happened it might well be even more tedious.

The great achievement of Oedipus' life came when he encountered the sphinx and was asked the riddle, What animal crawls on four legs, then walks on two, then staggers about on three? The answer, of course, is man, who in the tragic perspective of human life is thrown blindly into the world, rises from the ground to an erect posture, then sinks slowly back toward the ground again. Some years ago an anthropologist visiting one of the South Sea islands (Malekula) found an interesting myth there.[30] When a man dies, he meets a ferocious monster who draws half of an elaborate pattern in the sand: if the departed spirit has not been taught the other half of the pattern, and cannot complete it, the monster devours him. Similarly, what the sphinx gave Oedipus was only half of the tragic riddle of man: it was Tiresias who enabled Oedipus to complete it. Completing the pattern did not save him; it destroyed him, but Oedipus was living in this world, where completed patterns are normally tragic. Since Freud's work a century ago, we have come to understand that everyone's life repeats the Oedipal situation, and, more generally, that our character and behaviour are based on patterns formed before we can remember forming them.

Aristotle explains that a tragic action is usually set off by an overweening or aggressive act on the part of the hero, which disturbs the balance of nature, angers the gods, or provokes retaliation from other men [*Poetics*, 13.5–7]. The aggressive act is called hubris, and the restoring of order after such aggression, which takes the form of a tragic catas-

trophe, is called nemesis. But long before Aristotle, the philosopher
Anaximander had suggested that merely getting born is an aggressive
act, a rebellion of life against time, and that death is the nemesis or
restored balance that inevitably follows.[31] Tragedy is thus a special
application of life as a whole, though more striking, because the tragic
hero is usually larger than life size, and his death proportionately more
remarkable. Time itself seems to have no purpose except to continue
indefinitely, and we are often told that it will eventually pull all life
down into a heat-death in which no form of life will be able to come to
birth at all. This law of entropy applies only to closed systems, and there
is no certainty that the entire universe is a closed system or even that
there is a universe, but the law sounds so pointlessly lugubrious that it
instantly carries conviction to many people.

In the metaphorical diagrams that we always use in discussing such
subjects, time inevitably has the shape of a horizontal line, the "ever-
rolling stream" that carries us along with its current. Life with its beginning and ending forms a series of parabolas, of rises and falls, along this
line, following the cyclical rhythm that nature also exhibits. So far as our
experience goes, the manifestations of life are always new: the eggs and
rabbits of this Easter are not those of last Easter. For religions that accept
the myth of reincarnation the same life may appear over and over: this
doctrine does not seem to be functional in the Biblical religions, though
the Bible has parallel conceptions based on metaphorical identities. In
Revelation 11:8, for example, Sodom, Egypt, and Jerusalem at the time
of the Crucifixion are all "spiritually" (metaphorically) the same place.

In any case, if time is metaphorically a horizontal line or something
that moves that way, is there a vertical dimension to life that a conscious
mind can grasp? Most religions, certainly the Biblical ones, revolve
around a God who is metaphorically "up there," associated with the sky
or upper air. In Christianity Christ comes down from an upper region
(*descendit de coelis*, as the creed says) to the surface of this earth, then disappears below it, returns to the surface in the Resurrection, then, with
the Ascension, goes back into the sky again. Thus the total Christian
vision of God and his relation to human life takes the metaphorical
shape of a gigantic cross.

Time and History

Let us turn now from the natural context of life in time to the social and human context that we call history. Here we have, first of all, the unceasing flow of time to which society adapts in the form of what Edmund Burke calls the continuum of the dead, the living, and the unborn.[32] It is this social continuum out of which we grow, and it is clear that an impulse toward social coherence and stability is as deeply rooted in the human consciousness as anything can be. I cannot think of any society in history that has disintegrated simply through a lack of will to survive. Consequently I do not believe what I so often hear from the news media today, that Canada is about to blunder and bungle its way out of history into oblivion, leaving only a faint echo of ridicule behind it.

Burke felt that this continuum of society was the true basis of what is called the social contract, and that to discover what a society's contract is we should look at its present structure.[33] Much earlier, Thomas Hobbes had come up with the myth of an *original* contract in the past, one which began history as we know it.[34] According to this, human individuals, finding life unbearable in isolation, got together to surrender authority to a leader. Of course Hobbes's individuals could never have existed except as members of previous societies, but his version of the contract has its own mythical integrity. In a state of nature man faces what is still largely unknown, and whenever man is faced with the unknown he starts projecting his fears and anxieties into it. He projects, in this case, a whole cosmos of mysterious external authority, beginning with the gods and including the laws that are usually thought of as coming to a society from an external or objective will lost in the mists of time. The next step is to see a concrete manifestation of this external authority in his own society. At the beginning of recorded history societies are dominated by rulers with gods supporting them, a fusion of spiritual and temporal authority most complete in Egypt, where the Pharaoh was an incarnation of God. The West Semitic peoples preferred to think of earthly rulers as adopted (or "begotten," as in Psalm 2) sons of God, but both forms of authority were present and each reinforced the other.

The vertical dimension of a God above man was thus, from the beginning, bound up with the conception of authority and a hierarchical society. In Christian metaphor God has always been a king, a sovereign, a ruler, a lord; and earthly rulers, whether spiritual or temporal, were only too ready to claim that they were the representatives of God on earth. In the course of time other conceptions proliferated: of a chain of being stretching from God at the top to chaos at the bottom, of a universe stretching from the presence of God beyond the stars to the centre of the earth, and various others. In the later eighteenth century, with the American, French, and Industrial Revolutions, the assumption of the divine right of rulers and of an ascendant class to be perpetually on top of society began to be questioned. But questioning the visible aspect of external authority soon led to questioning its invisible aspect as well.

In the later nineteenth century, with the rise of Marxism and Nietzsche's proclamation of the death of God,[35] the vertical dimension of the cosmos disappeared for many people, and only the horizontal, or historical, dimension remained. The metaphor of William James contrasting tough-minded and tender-minded people is very central to most of us:[36] we all want to be tough-minded, capable of grappling with things as they are and not taking refuge in consoling but outworn formulas. And for many the religious dimension of existence was by definition a tender-minded attitude. But although it was common, and still is, to hear people say, "I believe only in history," it is not easy to see what there is in history by itself to believe in. The record of humanity from the beginning is so psychotic that it is difficult not to feel, with Joyce's Stephen Dedalus, that history is rather a nightmare from which we are trying to awake.[37]

Marxists, for example, though always vigilant to pounce on anyone who suggests the reality of a vertical dimension of being as totally lacking in "historicity," are really looking for the redemption of man within history, the "historical process" of Marxism being assumed to lead to the end of history as we have known it. Michel Foucault, in his book *The Order of Things*, studies the shift from "classifying" systems of thought which arranged things along hierarchical and vertical patterns of authority, and which dominated culture down to the eighteenth century, to the "causal" or historical systems that succeeded them in the nineteenth. He remarks, "The great dream of an end to History is the utopia of causal systems of thought, just as the dream of the world's beginnings was the utopia of the classifying systems of thought."[38] But the Marxist historical process appears to have betrayed the millions of people who have tried to live by it, and perhaps it is time to re-examine our visions of history and time.

Let us go back to our first principle. Just as when we pull a plant up by the roots the surrounding soil will cling to it, so when we examine our experience of the present moment we find it surrounded by the immediate past and future. The Bible sees the relation of God to time as an infinite extension of the same principle. The metaphors of creation and apocalypse, at the beginning and end of the Bible, mean that in the presence of God the past is still here and the future already here. The coming of Christ from a human perspective is split between a first coming in the past and a Second Coming in the future. The existence of the New Testament, by making this historical-prophetic event a verbal event, transfers not only the pastness of the first coming into our own present, but the futureness (there *has* to be such a word) of the second one. The vision of the future as already here is not a fatalistic vision: it means simply that we do not have to wait or die to experience it. We speak of the eternal presence of God as timeless, but once again the language fails us: we need some such word as "timeful" to express what the King James Bible calls the fullness of time.

The movement of the Biblical narrative from creation to apocalypse, though it takes place entirely within the present, is not a closed cyclical movement: it moves from a creation to a new creation. The new one is also the old one restored: it is new only to mankind, and represents not only a new but an enlarged human experience. Similarly in the Book of Job, God intervenes in the dialogue to describe to Job the past creation that Job never saw. But, once brought into Job's present experience, it becomes a new creation in which Job is no longer a mere spectator but a participant. The restoration of Job takes place in the immediate future, but it is already incorporated in the vision. Yet the future promise is an essential part of the vision, because, as Eliot says, only through time is time conquered.[39]

Again, Ezekiel's vision of the valley of dry bones (37) was probably, in its original context, a vision of the restoration of Israel from captivity, a future event to Ezekiel. Christianity regards it as a prophecy of the resurrection begun by the Resurrection of Christ, again a future event. But there is another dimension even to the Christian view, the dimension that the Book of Revelation (14:6) calls the everlasting gospel. For Paul, the Messiah was the concealed hero of the Old Testament as well as the revealed hero of the New. The prophecy includes the future but is not fixated on the future. What Ezekiel was really seeing, then, was actual resurrection, a vertical movement from a dying present into the living presence of the spiritual body. And although Jesus often speaks of his spiritual kingdom in metaphors of the future, he makes it quite clear, in the parable of the talents and elsewhere, that it is not a good idea to throw away our lives on the assumption that an "after" life will be a better or easier one.

History is the social memory of human experience, and in writing about it we look for beginnings and ends, even though these beginnings and ends are at least partly a technical verbal device. We also impose narrative patterns, like Gibbon's "decline and fall" for the Roman Empire or Motley's "rise" for the Dutch Republic, to give shape to our understanding. There is thus a combination of continuity and repetition in history writing, and the repeated or sequential themes are a mixture of fact and organizing fiction, or myth. From Virgil to Nietzsche there have been occasional visions of history as totally cyclical, an unending movement of time in which the same events recur indefinitely. There seems to be better evidence, however, that time is irreversible, and general cyclical views of history are not convincing. That there are cyclical elements in history, that is, recurring patterns that exist in events themselves and are not simply fictions in the mind of the historian, seems inescapable.

A very frequent primitive view of history is that it consists of a series of re-enactments in time of certain archetypal myths that happened before human life as we know it began.[40] In some societies this dominance of repetition over history is so powerful that in a sense nothing ever happens. In the Egyptian Old Kingdom a Pharaoh may set up a stele recording his defeat of his enemies, with the enemies, even their leaders, carefully named. It seems like a genuine historical record—until scholars discover that it has been copied verbatim from another monument two centuries older.[41] What is important is not that the Pharaoh won, but that he continues to say that he won, in a ritual pseudo-history where no defeat ever can occur. This obliterating of history is much the same as the incessant rewriting of history in totalitarian states, which turns history into a continuous record of the infallibility of the ruling party.

Sometimes this sense of repetition develops a movement to create a new kind of history by reincarnating a myth out of the past. The patron saint of all such efforts is Don Quixote, who tried to force the society around him to conform to a lost age of chivalry. We note in passing that no previous age thus invoked ever existed: quixotic versions of history are secular parodies of the Christian view of the fall, and, as Proust says, the only paradises are those we have lost.[42] The Nazi movement in Germany purported to be a recreation of a mythical heroic Germany, though it soon became clear that what the Nazis were interested in re-creating were infantile sadistic fantasies. The reason is obvious: infantile fantasy is all that really presents itself to the quixotic mind. Even the garden of Eden, as we saw, was really a place of immortal childhood.

Karl Marx had something similar in view when he spoke of events occurring first as tragedy and secondly as farce.[43] He was thinking, among other things, of the French Second Empire, where Napoleon III became emperor simply because his name was Napoleon. It is true that the end of the Third Reich was not worthy of the name of tragedy, and was more accurately a hideous farce, though a farce that only the devil would find amusing. Other attempts to live in a myth abstracted from history, such as the nineteenth-century Utopian communities in America and the Quebec separatism inspired by the motto *je me souviens*, are closer to the skewed pathos of Quixote himself.

There is a corresponding fixation on the future. In Christianity this usually takes the form of a fearful expectation of a Second Coming or simply a postponing of spiritual life, of the "some day we'll understand" type, the assumption that death automatically brings enlightenment. Secular parodies of this take the form of beliefs in revolution or progress, and in their demonic form employ the tactic of sacrificing the present to the future. Such visions can be quite as horrible in results as their Fascist counterparts. It seemed logical in Stalin's Russia that if hundreds of thousands of kulaks were murdered or sent to concentration camps right away, Russia might have a more efficient system of collectivized agriculture within the next century. But such means adopted for theoretically reasonable ends never serve such ends: they merely replace them, and the original ends disappear. All that the murdering and persecuting of kulaks accomplished, in short, was the murdering and persecuting of kulaks. The operation was not simply evil, it was unutterably futile, for in far less than a century the Soviet Union realized that it needed kulaks again. There is no reason to feel complacent about Stalin's Russia, however: many Canadians defend the destruction of their country by such phrases as "you can't stop progress," unaware that "progress" in such contexts is an idol on the same level as the legendary Hindu Juggernaut or the Old Testament Moloch.

Time and Education

Hitler and Stalin between them are sufficient commentary on an attitude to time and history that becomes obsessed by its relation either to the past or to the future. We saw also that there is an element of repetition in time, in life, and in history. Let us look at this element of repetition in human experience. There are two kinds of repetition: one is inorganic, a matter of merely doing the same thing over and over; the other is habit or practice repetition that leads to the acquiring of a skill, like practising a sport or a musical instrument. Inorganic repetition is precisely what the word "superstition" means: binding oneself to a continuing process that is mere compulsiveness, often accompanied by a vague fear that something terrible will happen if we stop. The acquiring of a skill transforms mere repetition into something that develops and progresses. If we ask what it develops into or progresses toward, we may provisionally say something like an enlargement of freedom: we practise the piano to set ourselves free to play it. In any case, this kind of directed repetition is constantly turning into larger and more complex forms of itself: it seems even to be reduplicating the process of life, where embryo turns into infant and infant into adult.

Acquiring a skill in human life is possible, so far as we can see, only for the individual. But the social basis of individual life may provide, in its institutions, a continuity, a sense of stable and relatively predictable movement in time, on which the individual can build his directed repetition. The church, with its sacramental system and its constant proclaiming of its Gospel, exhibits a continuity of this type: so does law, with its dialectic of precedents, and so does education, so far as education presents the repeating elements of knowledge from the alphabet and multiplication table onward. It may seem strange to speak of living a religious life in terms of acquiring a skill by practice, but there is a parallel: the New Testament writers constantly use such phrases as "without ceasing" when exhorting us to continue the practice of prayer or charity.

When the Preacher said that there was nothing new under the sun [Ecclesiastes 1:9], he was speaking of knowledge, which exists only in the past, and where nothing is unique. The passing of experience into knowledge is closely related to the tragic vision of life. It is part of a reality in which at every instant the still possible turns into the fixed and unalterable past. We feel partly released from this tragic vision when we are acquiring skills, getting an education, or advancing in a religious life: there we are exploiting our memory of the past to give direction along the present. Consequently the Preacher also said, "To every thing there is a season" [3:1]. Here he was speaking of experience, where everything is unique and everything is diversified. What he means by wisdom is a double movement: it starts with present experience disappearing into past knowledge, but then reverses itself and becomes past knowledge permeating and irradiating present experience. What sounds at first like pessimistic melancholy turns into something very different as he goes on and begins to say things like "Go thy way, eat thy bread with joy, and drink thy wine with a merry heart" [9:7]. Wisdom for him is a force moving against the normal flow of time, going from the "vanity" or emptiness of the past into the fullness of the present, and the process is a constant liberation of energy.

Thus the tragic aspect of time in which every moment brings us toward death, and in which we know only what has been, and never what is or is going to be, is counteracted by the directed and progressive attack on time that underlies all genuine achievement in everything that matters, in religion, in education, in culture most obviously. This building up of habit through incessant practice creates a new vertical dimension in experience, though it grows from the bottom upward and through the individual, however much the individual may depend on a social consensus in church or university. This vertical dimension is once again a hierarchy and a structure of authority, but these words no longer relate to temporal authority or to the supporting social structure. No human being or human institution is fit to be trusted with any temporal authority that is not subject to cancellation by some other authority. Spiritual authority, which is alone real, inheres in such things as the classic in literature, the repeatable experiment in science, or the example of the dedicated spiritual life; it is an authority that expands and does not limit the dignity of those who accept it. All personal authority in the spiritual world is self-liquidating: it is the authority of the teachers who want their students to become their scholarly equals, of the preachers who, like Moses (Numbers 11:29), wish that all God's people were prophets.

The hierarchy I spoke of begins with the bottom layer of the human psyche, or what is called the unconscious, a chaos of energy quieted and ordered by the repetition of practice. A pianist may come through practice to play thousands of notes in a few moments without consciously attending to each one. But there is of course a consciousness attending all the same, the faculty I have linked to criticism, which does not stop simply with self-criticism, but goes on to a conscious awareness of the historical context of what one is doing. The functionaries of churches and schools and courts, when they become entrenched bureaucracies, may at any time retreat into superstition, simply handing on what has been handed to them. Criticism is one of the forces that can strike a new energy out of a dormant one: it approaches the past in a way that relates it to contemporary life and concerns. Works of literature, music, and the other arts do not, apparently, improve or progress with time, but the understanding of their meaning, their importance, and their function in history can and to some extent does improve. In Christianity, while we do not think of revelation itself as progressing, the human response to it clearly can progress. In the sciences criticism is even more deeply rooted. In science every new discovery attaches itself to the total body of what is already known, so that with every major advance the whole of knowledge is created anew.

When one is a beginner, this attempt at reversing the flow of time by progressive achievement is attracted toward a future goal, the goal of mastery of the skill. But at a certain point the future is already here, the sense of endless plugging and slugging is less oppressive, and the goal is now an enlarged sense of the present moment. One has glimpses of the immense foreshortening of time that can take place in the world of the spirit; we may speak of "inspiration," a word that can hardly mean anything except the coming or breaking through of the spirit from a world beyond time. One may, as I have done myself, spend the better part of seventy-eight years writing out the implications of insights that have taken up considerably less than an hour of all those years. Here the shadow that falls between the present moment and the knowledge that one has lived through the present moment has disappeared, and experience and the awareness of experience have become, for an instant at least, the same thing. When this happens in a Christian context, we may say that the human spirit has found its identity with the spirit of God, and ought to know now, even from the split second of insight it has had, what is meant by resurrection and deliverance from death and hell.

For about two decades in this century a vogue for Oriental techniques of meditation, Indian yoga, Chinese Tao, Japanese Zen, swept over North America. The genuine teachers of these techniques stressed the arduous practice that was essential to them, and pointed out the futility of trying to avoid the work involved by taking lysergic acid and the like. The goal was enlightenment, the uniting of experience and consciousness just mentioned. There was some gullibility and groupie mentality in these cults, especially among those who were ready to believe any-thing that was Oriental and nothing that was Western. For them such words as *samadhi* and *satori*, as they had not read the New Testament, did not connect with such conceptions as "born of the spirit," "fullness of time," or the sudden critical widening of the present moment expressed by the word *kairos*. But some analogies may have come through by osmosis.

For example, the Oriental scriptures tell us that very advanced stages of enlightenment bring miraculous powers of various kinds, including healing, but that these powers should never be regarded as more than incidental by-products, and may even distract one from the real goal of liberation. If so, the miraculous element in the Gospels, which describe a life lived on a plane of intensity that none of us have much conception of, should cause no surprise, and there are clear indications that the Gospel writers were more impressed by Jesus' miracles than Jesus him-self was. Jesus performs his miracles with reluctance, almost with irrita-tion; he imposes secrecy on those he cures; he tells his disciples that they can do as well as that themselves. But the Oriental analogues may begin to give us some faint notion of what *Heilsgeschichte* or sacred history really talks about.

I mention these cults because they seem to me to be an aspect, even if a minor one, of a general weariness with history, with being bullied and badgered by all the panhistorical fantasies of the nineteenth century, of Hegel and Marx and Newman and Comte, who keep insisting that by history alone can we be saved, or rather by putting some kind of con-struct on history that will give it a specious direction or meaning. Even the arts may sometimes give an impression of wearing out their histori-cal possibilities. The most profoundly original artist still forms part of a larger process of cultural aging: the music of Beethoven could only have come later than Haydn and Mozart and earlier than Wagner and Ber-lioz. And while we are not likely to tire of Beethoven, the cultural tradi-tion he belongs to may reach a point of exhaustion where it becomes oppressive to carry it on without a major change.

I sometimes feel that we may be in such a period of doldrums now, with so many artists in all fields circling around overexplored conven-tions of literary irony or pictorial abstraction or architectural con-ventions that have produced the loveless and unloved erections contemplated by Prince Charles. However grateful we may be for the many writers and painters and builders we have who are so much better than that, I sense a longing for some kind of immense creative renovation, which, I should imagine, would have to be the product of a large-scale social movement. Earlier in the century a proposal for such an awakening would automatically have been responded to by the word "revolution," a donkey's carrot still held before the student rebels of the 1960s. Revolutions, however, are culturally sterile: they weaken the traditions of the past but put nothing in their place except second-rate versions of the same thing. I think the real longing is not for a mass movement sweeping up individual concerns, but for an individualized movement reaching out to social concerns. Primary concerns, that is: food, shelter, the greening of the earth, and their spiritual aspects of freedom and equal rights.

The provision in the Mosaic code for a jubilee year showed a profound insight into the psychology of human beings living in time. I said earlier that cyclical visions of history lack convincingness, but that cyclical elements in history clearly do exist. One of these is the one so heavily featured in the Bible, the cycle of bondage and release, the cyclical oppression and restoration of Israel. We celebrate the Resurrection every Easter, but Easter by itself does not suggest resurrection; it suggests only the renewing of the cycle of time, the euphoria with which we greet the end of winter and the coming of spring. There is a similar euphoria in society when a tyranny comes crashing down and proclamations of freedom and equality are voiced on all sides. We heard this euphoria a few years ago in Haiti and in the Philippines; we are hearing it now in Eastern Europe. But we cannot trust its permanence; far less can we trust the effect produced by it on us. There are people trying to get rid of an unworkable economy with its unworking bureaucracy and there are neo-Nazi skinheads; there are crowds demonstrating for freedom and crowds demonstrating against minorities; there are revivals of free discussion and revivals of anti-Semitism. One hopes for a society that can remember on Tuesday what it thought it wanted so desperately on Monday, but on the human plane even the pressure of primary concerns, food and shelter and freedom to move and talk, cannot always be relied on to preserve such a memory. As Coleridge said, "I could weep for the criminal Patience of Humanity!"[44] Perhaps the most effective help may come from the mammon of unrighteousness: from greed and self-interest and xenophobia and the conflicts they bring with them, when harnessed against their will to better causes.

I have not spoken of the providence of God, because it seems to me that the providence of God operates only in its own sphere, not in the sphere of human folly and frivolousness. I think immense changes could be brought about by a Christianity that was no longer a ghost with the chains of a foul historical record of cruelty clanking behind it, that was no longer crippled by notions of heresy, infallibility, or exclusiveness of a kind that should be totally renounced and not rationalized to the slightest degree. Such a Christianity might represent the age of the Spirit that the thirteenth-century Franciscan Joachim of Fiore saw as superseding the Old Testament age of the Father and the New Testament age of the Logos.[45] Such a Christianity would be neither an inglorious rearguard action nor a revolutionary movement creating suffering and death instead of life more abundantly. It would be a Christianity of a Father who is not a metaphor of male supremacy but the intelligible source of our being; of a Son who is not a teacher of platitudes but a Word who has overcome the world; and of a Spirit who speaks with all the tongues of men and angels and still speaks with charity. The Spirit of creation who brought life out of chaos brought death out of it too, for death is all that makes sense of life in time. The Spirit that broods on the chaos of our psyches brings to birth a body that is in time and history but not enclosed by them, and is in death only because it is in the midst of life as well.

IV The Double Vision of God

Gods and God

In the three previous chapters I have been trying to suggest something of the contrast between the natural or physical and the spiritual vision in regard to language, space, and time. We can now try to see where this takes us in our efforts to distinguish the natural from the spiritual vision of God. We are told in the New Testament that God is spirit, that Jesus has no kingdom except a spiritual one, and that only the spirit can understand what the New Testament is saying. On the other hand, no God or numinous presence can be found within nature, the attempt to find him there being the great error that the Bible calls idolatry. The metaphorical vision may see the reflection of God from his works in nature, but it is only through the distinctively human elements in the world that we can come to the spiritual God.

Let us begin by looking at some features of the development of "pagan" or "heathen" religion in countries outside the Bible but contemporary with it. For human societies organized in small tribal units, dependent on nature rather than masters of it, the gods take shape as projections of human hopes and anxieties into the more mysterious aspects of nature. Local deities of rivers, trees, mountains, along with the sun and moon, are among the most primitive of divinities and develop into the nymphs and fauns and satyrs of later mythology. The cult of animals that we find in Egypt and elsewhere also reflects a sense of something numinous in modes of being quite different from the human consciousness. Such a cult is not a "worship of animals," but a recognition that humanity is only one presence among others in its world. The sense of the numinous in nature is the bedrock of the pagan or heathen religion, which is based first on tribal and local societies, then on rural and nonurbanized parts of civilization. A pagan is etymologically a peasant (*paganus*), and a heathen a heath-dweller.

Although there is unlikely to be any clear-cut sequence, as societies form bigger units and become more elaborately class-structured, the gods take on the features of a human aristocracy. The more important gods often dwell on mountain-tops like the Greek Olympus, and dispense a rough justice like a human aristocracy, sometimes benevolent, sometimes tyrannical, but above all concerned with preserving their privileges and inflicting vicious punishments on anyone who challenges their authority, even by a boast. By that time there are many gods of primarily political and social reference, gods of war, of wisdom, and of justice, but they still reflect the arbitrary and whimsical elements in both human and physical nature.

As nations expand into empires, and their rulers begin to think of themselves as kings of the world, a supreme god appears, and religion approaches the great divide between the gods of nature who are human creations and a God who is supreme over both human and physical nature. An imperial monotheism, in which the ruler of a world-empire is the incarnation or adopted son of God, as mentioned previously, is a very different thing from the revolutionary and still largely tribal monotheism of the Bible; but still it is monotheism, and it marks an immense advance in the human comprehension of the environment. First, such monotheism is relatively tolerant: it may even encourage local cults, on a general assumption that smaller gods are emanations or reflections of the supreme one. When the Mesopotamian empires that held their conquests only by force were superseded by the better organized Persian Empire under Cyrus, the benefits for the Jews held captive in Babylonia were immediately marked. The Roman Empire, too, was tolerant of a plurality of cults to a remarkable degree.

The physical image that suggests monotheism is usually the sky, the superior world that is above us everywhere. Some students of mythology think that most primitive communities have some potential monotheism in which a supreme God is there, but has abdicated and left the rule of the world to lesser spirits. Such a conception reflects a human society confined to small competitive groups, unable to unite even by force. Of the objects in the sky, the sun alone seems to have an obvious and immediate relevance to human concerns, and hence the ruler-figure in imperial monotheism is often associated with the sun. This association has persisted from ancient Egypt to contemporary Japan, and enters Christendom with the "sun king" Louis XIV of France.

Then again, monotheism of any kind indicates an increase in the human mastery of nature, both intellectual and physical. The sense of the unity of God forms part of a growing sense of nature as an order: in fact this sense goes so far as to reverse our initial statement about nature as the source of idolatry. There is a strong philosophical tradition, stretching from the Stoics to Spinoza and beyond, of identifying God and nature, though this "nature" is no longer a world of mysterious presences but is conceived as an order obeying certain laws. Such a nature is less alien to humanity and more of a reflection of human consciousness. Of course in an originally polytheistic religion the gods do not give up at once: they are still there, if increasingly vestigial, in pagan Rome up to Julian the Apostate. Yet as early as the *Iliad* we have in the foreground a group of quarrelling gods, some lobbying for Greeks and some for Trojans, and in the background a hint that, as the fifth line of the poem tells us, a single divine purpose (Zeus) is working its will. Even that will appears sometimes to be overruled by a fate which is impersonal, and which even the greatest of personal gods must obey.

The sense of a natural order grows along with the sense of a moral order. From Plato onward there is an increasing feeling that whimsical, arbitrary, capricious gods are too human to be really divine. Our notions of the best human behaviour ought surely to be the place where our conceptions of divine behaviour should start, or, as Plutarch says, gods of whom indecent stories can be told cannot be real gods [*Moralia*, 417e–f]. He is thinking of such stories as the one in the *Odyssey* of the

lovers Ares and Aphrodite caught in a net constructed by Hephaestus
(who at the time was Aphrodite's husband), to the great amusement of
the other gods.

Such developments are obviously important for religion: they also
accompany the gradual transformation of mythology into literature. The
theory called euhemerism, where gods are thought to be deified human
heroes, is an inadequate theory for mythology, because such deification
appears to be the exception rather than the rule. But the reverse process
is a very real one: gods modulate into human heroes of saga and
romance, and so initiate the development of secular literature, or the
original myths may be thought of and retold as essentially literary stories, as they are in Ovid's *Metamorphoses*. After the coming of Christianity, Jupiter and Venus become purely literary figures, but are much
more genuinely real as gods than they were when temples and sacrifices
were connected with them. The true gods thus become more like what
the Greeks called Muses, symbols of the creative powers of humanity,
like the Eros who appears to Dante in the *Vita Nuova*, and says to him
"ego dominus tuus": I am thy Lord [pt. 3, l. 36]. False gods, in the Christian period, are those regarded as objective existences independent of
human imagination: as no such gods exist, they can only be illusions
thrown up by the demonic powers. We notice a cosmos of three levels
here, a point we shall return to: the genuinely divine, the demonic parody, and the human world in between that is turned by grace from a
demonic direction toward a divine one.

We have not forgotten that monotheism of the kind discussed here is
imperial, and that the human being at the top of the social structure is its
personal focus, becoming increasingly so as the other elements of religion become more impersonal. In Egypt the Pharaoh was an incarnation
of two gods, of Horus during his life and of Osiris after his death. Obviously the deifying of a human ruler is a powerful political instrument,
and one that was adopted in the Roman Empire in a ritual following the
emperor's death. This device was effective enough for Augustus, but
something of a strain when the emperor was one of the contemptible
creatures who followed Augustus. The philosopher Seneca wrote a satire in which he described the deifying of the emperor Claudius as an
"apocolocyntosis," the apotheosis of a pumpkin. Still, the need for a personal focus kept the absurd custom going, and the resistance of Jews
and Christians to participating in it turned them into political criminals.

Later centuries were fascinated by the contrast between the temporal ruler of the world, Augustus Caesar, and its spiritual ruler Jesus, who was born during Augustus' reign. Contemporary with Jesus we have the whole mythological side of Classical culture summed up in two great masterworks, Virgil's *Aeneid* and Ovid's *Metamorphoses*. Ovid provides a kind of encyclopedia of mythology in which the central theme is metamorphosis, the incessant dissolving and reshaping of forms of life. Toward the end of his long poem, he brings in the philosopher Pythagoras to expound a gloomy philosophy based on the same theme. The *Metamorphoses* starts with creation and deluge myths, and Pythagoras sees at the end of time a running down of the world into a kind of entropy, or chaos come again. But there are also eulogies of the Caesars, particularly Julius, as the only symbols of what can transcend metamorphosis. In Virgil, similarly, the myth that Rome was founded by Trojan refugees expands into a vision of history in which the Roman Empire represents a kind of goal or *telos* of the historical process.

There is a certain amount of Stoicism behind Virgil, and Stoicism was a philosophy, or religion, that originally put its main emphasis on equality and the brotherhood of man, and had no place for a dictatorial ruler. But the logic of a revolutionary situation, which elevated the emperor to the top of the social pyramid, compelled Stoicism to adapt itself to becoming an intellectual support for the empire. Stoic and emperor, of course, merged in the figure of Marcus Aurelius. There are some odd parallels with the Marxist developments in our day: first the vision of equality in Marx himself, where the state eventually withers away, then the adulation of Lenin as the power-figure who consolidated the revolution with himself as leader, then a series of tyrants.

There are thus two foci of non-Biblical religion, the ruler vested with supreme authority and the sense of nature as an impersonal structure of law and order. The ruler manifests this order in human society, and is therefore symbolically divine. Similarly, there may be a supreme personal God in Zeus for the Stoic poets, but Zeus owes his personal dignity to his impersonal aspect as a manifestation of law. The principle involved here is that religion tends to outgrow the notion of a personal God in order to reach its loftiest ideals. Or, to put it another way, we can build a higher tower of Babel with a God so transcendent that he transcends first personality and then himself, eventually disappearing beyond the bounds of human categories of thought. Even in Plotinus, who retains a personal God, that God is so remote that language cannot say what he is except "one." Then we come down through an immense ladder of Word, Spirit, ideas, demons, and the like to something approaching the (ugh) physical world we live in. Such constructs reflect the pyramid of authority, nevertheless, in that very world.

The temporal ruler is the chief executive officer of nature, history, and God. There are two kinds of such rulers, the *tyrannos*, whose power springs from his natural abilities as a leader, and the *basileus*, who rules by hereditary right. (*Basileus* does not invariably mean a hereditary ruler, but I need some word.) Cromwell, Napoleon, Lenin were forces of nature; hereditary monarchs are attached to a social contract. The latter stand for continuity as the *tyrannos* does for revolutionary upheaval.

We think of God as the author of our being, and hence use the metaphor of "Father" for him. If we think of the authors of our being in a natural context, we think of our parents, then of our direct ancestors. The association of divinity and nature underlies the tendency in society to produce an aristocracy, a class considered entitled to special privileges because their direct ancestors possessed them. At their head is the king, who is king because his father was a king. Such continuity is a conservative social force: once it is broken by a revolution, the *tyrannos* or natural force appears again. As Marvell says of Cromwell's ousting of Charles I:

> Nature that hateth emptiness
> Allows of penetration less,
>   And therefore must make room
>   When greater spirits come.[46]

Hebraic and Hellenic Traditions

Christianity is founded on the New Testament, and the New Testament is founded on the Old Testament only. The New Testament is unintelligible until it is understood that its writers regarded their message as primarily an interpretation of the true meaning of the Old Testament, the spiritual fulfilment of its laws and prophecies. Nevertheless there were many in the early Christian period who thought that the break between Judaism and Christianity did not go far enough. Many of the Gnostics regarded the Jehovah of the Old Testament as an evil demiurge, and the work of Jesus as an effort to deliver humanity from his tyranny. This position was close to that of the Manicheans, who, like the Second Coming sects of the previous century, were anxious to hasten the apocalypse, to jump out of matter into spirit by abstaining from sexual intercourse and the like. For the central tradition of Christianity, spirit and nature could not be instantly divorced in this way, and the Incarnation implied that the same God presides over both spiritual and natural worlds.

So Christianity retained the conception of the integrity of the Bible and of the positive relevance of the Old Testament to the New. When Augustine denounces the errors of the Manicheans, their negative attitude to the Old Testament is frequently cited. At the same time there was increasingly a search for philosophical principles to serve as an infrastructure for the Biblical revelation, and to form the necessary link between the two orders. As all our philosophical traditions in the West are Hellenic in origin, this meant constructs derived ultimately from Plato or Aristotle.

There were several intellectual traditions in the Middle Ages that were Neoplatonic in their main inspiration: one of them was introduced by Dionysius the Areopagite, although he would probably have got nowhere if he had not given himself a fraudulent name out of the New Testament. It was a more concrete Aristotelian tradition, with its greater reliance on form and language, that finally prevailed with the great Summas of St. Thomas Aquinas. One difficulty here is that every philosophical construct is bound to be a differentiation from every other such construct, and this cannot be fully recognized in societies preoccupied with a uniform ideology. As in all repressive cultures, most of the more penetrating thinkers of the Middle Ages were dissidents accused or at least suspected of heresy: they included Siger of Brabant, Scotus Erigena, Peter Abelard, John Wyclif, Roger Bacon, Nicholas of Autrecourt, Meister Eckhart, William of Occam, and Joachim of Fiore. Dante got one or two of these into Paradise, and his own *De Monarchia* on the Index. With the Lutheran and Calvinist movements there came a renewed emphasis on the Old Testament as the sole basis for Christian doctrine, and something close to an abandoning of all attempts at an integrated philosophical infrastructure. In the Middle Ages, St. Thomas was the greatest Catholic theologian, and therefore its greatest philosopher. In the sixteenth century, Luther and Calvin were the greatest Reformed theologians, and were therefore not philosophers at all.

The funeral service speaks of Christianity as providing the comfort of a reasonable religion. It is not always understood that the reasonable and the rational are opposed attitudes, and that the comfort of a reasonable religion can hardly coexist with the prickly discomfort of a rational one. The reasonable person proceeds by compromise, halfway measures, illogical agreements, and similar signs of mature human intelligence. Rationalism is a militant use of language designed to demonstrate the exclusive truth of what it works on and with. Inferior grades of rationalism usually amount to a simple defence of intolerance and obscurantism by a trumpery show of pseudo-logic, an abuse of language that succeeds only in articulating original sin. For the Reformation it would have been reasonable to have developed an interest in Judaism as the *fons et origo* of Christianity, and in the way that Jews read their own Bible. There were marginal improvements in the attitude to Jews: a progress in the study of Hebrew through the sixteenth century and later, which depended on Jewish teachers; a slightly greater degree of social tolerance in seventeenth-century Holland (Rembrandt is sometimes thought to have been Jewish), and, after Cromwell, in England; there was even a Christian form of Kabbalism, which turned mainly on putting the letter *shin* in the middle of the Hebrew YHWH and thereby changing Yahweh to Yeshua. But it was centuries before there was any serious Christian interest in Jewish culture. Matthew Arnold's dialectic of Hellenic and Hebraic influences on the culture of nineteenth-century Britain, in *Culture and Anarchy*, is vitiated by the fact that the Hebraic was not really an influence from a different culture, but a narcissistic kidnapping of an originally Hebrew book into the reader's own cultural orbit.

There was, however, a genuine clarification of the Christian revelation involved in the renewed emphasis on the Bible, and I have often reverted to a passage in Milton's *Paradise Regained* (bk. 4, ll. 285 ff.) that illustrates what it is. In that poem, which deals with the temptation in the wilderness, Satan first tries to persuade Christ to join the Parthians and become a kind of Genghis Khan, then to become emperor of Rome and achieve temporal power over the world. Failing in these, he goes on to suggest that Jesus attach himself to the Hellenic philosophical tradition. Jesus denies that there is any relevance to his own Messianic function in the Greek tradition, and refuses to have anything to do with any culture outside the Old Testament. The passage is often regarded as evidence of a tired, irritable, even sick reaction on Milton's part; but in its context what Jesus says makes complete sense. The world, including the wisdom of Plato and Aristotle, is in Satan's possession: Jesus must reject every atom of it before he can enter on his ministry. After he has done that, he can redeem everything in that world that is not inseparably attached to the demonic, including Hellenic culture. It is only because

Christ rejects Plato and Aristotle that Milton himself can study them.

The conception of redemption is a centrally Christian element in contrast to, for example, the more simplistic Manicheanism, where there are only the divine and demonic worlds, and those elected for salvation are not so much redeemed as rescued. A man rescued from a shipwreck is simply pulled out of the water, and wants to have nothing more to do with water; but redemption means fulfilling what one formerly was, as well as separating it from the demonic or parody world of evil. A redeemed slave has his bondage annihilated, but his essential human life fulfilled; similarly with the Old Testament law as the New Testament conceives of it, which is fulfilled in one aspect and abolished in another.

Thus the immense benefits of Hellenic culture for the Western tradition, including Christianity, are not in question here: the question is the emphasis on Hellenic philosophical conceptions rather than the Old Testament as the basis of Christian teachings. The growth of democratic ideology increasingly compelled Christianity to be reasonable, to soft-pedal its claims to being the exclusive means of human redemption, and not simply to tolerate but to enter into dialogue with other religions or anti-religions. But in all centuries there is a perpetually renewed hankering for a rational infrastructure that will demonstrate the unique validity of the Christian revelation once and for all. In the twentieth century this tendency produced, two generations ago, a revived Thomism in Catholic thought, set up to be a comprehensive intellectual system in opposition to Marxism. In Protestant circles, Harnack audibly wished that Christianity had been based on Classical rather than Hebraic sources. Matthew Arnold, with many qualifications, would probably have agreed. Such revisionism would doubtless not have translated the "Logos" in the Gospel of John as "Word," but would rather have tried to assimilate it to the philosophical Logos in Greek thought from Heraclitus onward, where it is more like a principle of order in the mind that recognizes a corresponding order in the physical world. Most Protestantism, however, turned to history rather than metaphysics as an infrastructure for revelation. We have already glanced at the method resulting: we first distinguish secular from sacred history, then ignore the mythical structure of sacred history in favour of extracting a credible historical Jesus of secular history from the wrong context.

Paul could explain to the legalistic Romans that Christ was the fulfilment of the law, and to the erotic Corinthians that Christ was the fulfilment of love. Perhaps if he had succeeded in founding a church at Athens he would have written an Epistle to the Athenians that would have clarified something of the Hebraic–Hellenic relationship. He shows a token interest in Hellenistic culture, at least, in quoting Menander and the Stoic poet Aratus of Solis (1 Corinthians 15:33; Acts 17:28). In default of such an epistle, the only reasonable thing to do is to return to our principle that the language of both testaments is the language of myth and metaphor.

Metaphorical Literalism

The general position we start from is, once again, that the true literal sense of the Bible is metaphorical. This conception of a metaphorical literal sense is not new, or even modern. Dante said that his *Commedia* was, like Scripture itself, "polysemous," having many meanings, though in his exposition the literal-descriptive is the basis of all meaning.[47] He passes over the immense difficulties involved in explaining how a poem could have this kind of literal meaning, and one of his first commentators, his son Pietro, remarks that there are in fact different kinds of literal meaning, of which the metaphorical-literal is one.[48] But this insight remained undeveloped in Biblical criticism because of official anxieties about dispensing with the simplistic-literal.

In Matthew and Luke, genealogies of Jesus are given to show that he was legitimately descended from David as the Messiah was supposed to be by prophecy. It is hard to see just what these genealogies establish: apart from the fact that the two lists are quite different for the postexilic period, they both trace the descent through Joseph, who according to the Virgin Birth story was not Jesus' father at all. Besides, while Jesus was a Jew, descended from Abraham like all Jews, we are told (Matthew 3:9) that the Jews need not pride themselves on that descent, as God could raise up more descendants of Abraham from stones (an image curiously similar to the story of Deucalion and Pyrrha in Ovid's flood myth) [*Metamorphoses*, bk. 1, ll. 318–415]. As for the Virgin Birth, it looks like an importing of the common Mediterranean myth of the hero with a divine father and a human mother, complete with the need for concealing the miraculous birth from the person threatened by it, in this case Herod. The most likely reason for importing it appears to be the Septuagint rendering of *halma*, young woman, as virgin, *parthenos*, in Isaiah 7:14.

This kind of disintegration is as far as we can get with what Blake calls single vision. But the real literal question is not, "Did this happen just like that?" but, "Is this an essential part of the revelation of the Messiah?" If we look back at what we said about *basileus* and *tyrannos* authority-figures in secular life, we can see that the story of the Messiah must include the *basileus* theme of Davidic descent, but that in the double vision which includes the spiritual one, it is equally necessary that the hereditary succession should be interrupted by a divine intervention. Otherwise we should be ascribing divine right to the natural father or direct ancestor, as human monarchies do. The line of David itself was established by divine intervention, though Saul remained the Lord's anointed after his rejection. The Virgin Birth, where God raises up a son of David, not out of a stone but certainly without a natural father, is essential to understanding what the real or spiritual significance of Jesus is.

Jesus is a spiritual *basileus*, a legitimate king, totally unrecognized as such in a historical context, except in mockery, but invariably addressed as "Lord" by his followers. He is also a spiritual *tyrannos*, owing his unique abilities as leader not to nature or fate or the historical process, but directly to the will of God. In contrast, Augustus, the temporal ruler of the world when Jesus was born, is a potential Antichrist figure, that is, a human ruler who claims divine honours, and he became an actual Antichrist, as mentioned earlier, when deified by the Roman cult.

We note that the principle of metaphorical literalism takes its chances with the possibility that the Gospels are cleverly concocted pious frauds. If the Gospel writers had simply made up what they say out of their own imaginations or even out of their convictions, what they produced would still have been superb works of literature, though they would not have been the Gospels. A superb work of literature is a very precious thing in a literary context, and to the extent that this context is involved, the Gospels are authentic literary treasures. Approaching the Gospels as one would approach works of literature, however, though a correct approach on the literal level, is confined to that level. The Bible is still polysemous, and has many other dimensions of meaning beyond the suspended judgment of the imaginative. Some of them would recapture everything that the single-vision literalist is trying to gain, but an exclusive single-vision literalism will not work.

In *Twelfth Night,* when Viola and Sebastian appear together, the Duke says, "A natural perspective, that is and is not!" [5.1.217]. The phrase "natural perspective" refers to the fact that in ordinary experience it is impossible that even twins could be so much alike, but this is a play, and in a play we may have visual confirmation of what otherwise would be only the metaphor of "identical" twins. In Mark 1:6, John the Baptist is described as wearing camel-hair clothes and a leather girdle. Ah, says the single-vision reader, at last a realistic detail. There are no realistic details in the Gospels: this detail is there to identify John with the Elijah of 2 Kings 1:8. That is, John the Baptist is Elijah reborn, as Malachi 4:5 says Elijah had to be in the day of the Messiah, and as Jesus confirms (Matthew 11:14). When John the Baptist himself is asked if he is Elijah, he says he is not (John 1:21), and if he were the fact would contradict the whole negative attitude to literal-descriptive reincarnation in Christianity. Great difficulties here for the single vision: none whatever for a metaphorical language in which the paradox of "is and is not" is functional.

The question often arises, Why can't we have it both ways? Why can't there be a definitive literal-descriptive dimension along with a spiritual vision of it? The reason, apart from the contradictions and inconsistencies involved, is that the former is a passive response and the latter an active one, and if they were both there the passive one would take over and eliminate the active one. The human mind, like the human body, has a strong pull toward inertia built into it. Most religions teach a doctrine of immortality that by definition implies a release of a new source of unfettered energy at death, but the great majority of petitions for the after-death state ask for peace, repose, untroubled sleep in the bosom of God. "After the first death, there is no other," says Dylan Thomas,[49] saying something that those who accept immortality and those who do not can agree on.

Similarly, faith involves risk and adventure: it cannot rest in assured certainties, because there are no certain propositions that are not tautologies. Two and two certainly make four, but only because four is another way of saying two and two. The practical certainties of sense experience, or the self-assurance that one would have had them at the time specified, neutralize the genuine energy of faith. Hence Sir Thomas Browne's remark in *Religio Medici*: "I bless my self and am thankful . . . that I never saw Christ nor His Disciples."[50] A Chinese philosopher is said to have remarked that in practice unicorns do not exist, because if anyone saw a unicorn he would instantly tell himself that he had not seen it and forget the memory. The spirit of this remark is in the Gospels too, where so frequently people do not hear what they hear, and do not see what they see. The "both ways" we have, therefore, are only the alternatives of the choice between using the Gospels as spiritual batteries, so to speak, for charging one's spiritual energies, and looking at them objectively as aesthetic productions.

In pagan religion two factors stand out: the personal focus, associated with the temporal ruler, and the sense of nature as a manifestation of law, which accompanied the decline of belief in the earlier capricious gods. I will look at the personal focus first. One who voluntarily assumes responsibility and devotes himself to decision and action enters a situation of guilt, however admirable his motives in doing so may be. Lying, half-truths, the threat of violence, pressures of self-interest, surround him on all sides, and it takes exceptional integrity, astuteness, and a certain amount of luck to avoid being infected by them. Even the idealized description of the magnanimous man in Aristotle's *Nicomachean Ethics* [4.3.1–34] gives the impression of a kind of moral ballet dancer, whose skill in avoiding error attracts more admiration than his actual virtue. To acquire power, on the other hand, is to be led into temptation, from which the Lord's Prayer asks deliverance, and the temporal ruler, for all the adulation he may receive in his lifetime, seldom lasts long as a role model.

The spiritual personality of Jesus as set out in the Gospels, however, remains unchanged as a role model, or rather as *the* role model, for Christians. He remains aloof from decision and action, apart from those decisions that affect his own life, but is totally concerned with the world, even though he has a high regard for privacy. What he does is renounce temporal power, as the episode of his arrest shows in particular. Anyone with his abilities of concentration might have been able to eliminate much of the physical pain of the Crucifixion, but it seems clear that he was called upon to renounce that too. It is only after his resurrection that he says, "All power is given unto me" [Matthew 28:18]. Yet there is nothing ghostly about him, and nothing of the sense of antagonism between soul and body. In fact he is ridiculed as one who "comes eating and drinking" (Luke 7:34) instead of being, like Plotinus, an ascetic ashamed of being in a body, as holy men are often conventionally supposed to be.[51]

The ideal portrayed here has parallels in other religions: one is the hero of the *Tao Te Ching* in China who seeks the humble "way of the valley" and the kind of non-action out of which all effective action ultimately comes [sec. 28]. But this remains on the level of precept only, and even so the supreme sacrifice of dying for the people does not appear to be anything that would appeal to a Taoist. The dilemma faced by pagans in trying to get their gods to behave decently, and thereby including them in a growing sense of order and coherence in both society and nature, is much more complex. For the Epicureans, including Lucretius, the gods can preserve their integrity only by not soiling their hands with human affairs. Stoics and Neoplatonists took less easy ways out; but here Christianity itself had a crucial problem. We said that the sole basis of the revelation of the Messiah in the New Testament is the Old Testament; but what does the Old Testament provide us with?

The Humanized God

The Jehovah of the Old Testament develops into a monotheistic God out of the stage known as henotheism, where he is specifically the God of Israel, without the reality of heathen and hostile gods being denied. Syrian invaders explain to each other (1 Kings 20:23) that Jehovah is the god of a hilly country, skilful therefore at hill-fighting, so that the Israelites have to be enticed to lower ground in order to make him ineffective. We are here on the Homeric level of gods fighting each other, when Trojan gods are defeated along with the Trojans. Of course this is only a heathen army getting it wrong, but we also read of "contests" with Dagon of Philistia [1 Samuel 5:17] and Baal of Phoenicia [1 Kings 18]. And while many aspects of Jehovah rank with the highest possible conceptions of God, such as the Shepherd of the Twenty-Third Psalm and the Suffering Servant of the second Isaiah, the God of the Old Testament is on the whole not presented as a theologian's model or perfect being, but as an intensely humanized figure, as violent and unpredictable as King Lear.

What, for example, are we to do with a God who drowns the world in a fit of anger and repeoples it in a fit of remorse, promising never to do it again (Genesis 9:11); a God who curses the ground Adam is forced to cultivate after his fall, but removes the curse after Noah makes a tremendous holocaust of animals, the smell of their burning flesh being grateful to his nose (Genesis 8:21); a God who rejects Saul as king after he spares his enemy Agag out of human decency (because he should have been offered to God as a sacrifice) and inspires Samuel to hew Agag in pieces and tell Saul that he has committed an unforgivable sin (1 Samuel 15); a God who observes children mocking the prophet Elisha and sends bears out to eat up the children (2 Kings 2:24), and so on? All mythologies have a trickster God, and Jehovah's treatment of the Exodus Pharaoh (hardening his heart), of Abraham, perhaps even of Job, shows clear trickster affinities. Some of the most horrendous of his capers, such as the sacrifice of Isaac, are tests or trials of faith, implying a lack of knowledge of what is already in Abraham's mind and will. We spoke of the pagan gods who reflected the whimsical and capricious elements in a still unknown and mysterious nature; but is there any real superiority to that stage here?

We notice first the stark simplicity of the Biblical scenario, in contrast to the complexities both of polytheism and of later theologies. There are only God and Israel, though Israel may be in different contexts an individual, a society, or a metonymy for the human race. Jesus himself is a spiritual Israel in individual form. Again, Jehovah has nothing of the "Olympian" about him, nothing of the god who is removed from the human situation unless something exceptional attracts his attention: his preoccupation with his people is continuous, insistent to the verge of fussiness.

When we look at the Bible from the point of view of later Christianity, we often get a vision of a God sitting up in a metaphorical sky, presiding over moral and natural law, omnipotent, omniscient, loving, compassionate, merciful—all the right words—but leaving the outcries of pain and misery from the world below largely unheeded. To his devotees he is the source of grace, a quality or power almost always associated with metaphors of descending from a remote height. To others he seems a picture of impotence, an empty hypothesis.

This is not intended to be anything but a caricature: what I am describing is the disparity between this metaphorical structure and the intensely limited and concrete relation of God and man to which the Bible mainly confines itself. This is especially true of the Mosaic books, which set out God's intimate, even cosy, relations with Adam, Noah, Abraham, Jacob, and Moses. To the writing prophets God is still close, but mainly as an invisible voice. Yet even in the wisdom literature, while terms of infinite transcendence are certainly applied to God, there is little interest in God's traditional metaphysical attributes. With Jesus' relation to his Father in the Gospels, the original intimacy is not only restored but increased to the point of identity ("I and my Father are one"). Nowhere does the Bible seem to be afraid of the word "anthropomorphic."

We often meet with miraculous events in the Bible, such as the triumphant vindication of Elijah on Mount Carmel before the priests of Baal (1 Kings 18), where a voice within us keeps insisting that God does not act in this way, that he does not interrupt the course of nature arbitrarily, and that a contemporary of ours who attempted Elijah's feat would encounter the same silence that the priests of Baal did. To cling to the authenticity of the event sooner or later suggests the question, If God could do it then, why can't he do it now? This is the attitude of looking for a "sign" that Jesus condemns (Matthew 12:39). In any case the historical event, whatever it was, is out of our range: it is only the verbal event that concerns us, and the verbal event may be the starting point of an adventure in understanding. This story in particular illustrates the curious intimacy of God and man which seems uniquely Biblical. Magicians and miracle-workers are worldwide, but only in the Bible would God and his prophet co-operate in putting on a show for a public. And however "incredible" we may find the story, its haunting power has some connection with all the occasions where the wrong kind of help has let us down and only the authentic kind breaks through.

At this point we are still on the metaphorical-literal level where stories are simply stories, considered with the suspended judgment of the imagination without relation to the area we vaguely describe as "truth." Beyond that lie the "polysemous" levels in which the Biblical stories form a myth to live by, transformed from the kind of story we can construct ourselves to a spiritual story of what has created and continues to recreate us. According to Milton, the Bible should be read by the "rule of charity."[52] That is, the Bible is the charter of human freedom, and any approach to it that rationalizes the enslaving of man has something wrong with it. For example, when chloroform was discovered and doctors began to use anaesthetics to lessen the pain of childbirth, some clergymen objected that this violated the commandment in Genesis 3:16, "In pain you shall bring forth children." One can read any book as a mirror of oneself, and here, perhaps, we think of the comment of the eighteenth-century writer Lichtenberg that if a monkey looks into a mirror, an angel will not look out.[53] But we should not dismiss such objections as mere perversity, but consider them as examples of the fallacy of a kind of legalism inherent in the literal-descriptive view, according to which every event or prophecy or commandment in the Bible establishes an identical precedent for the present day. One hears this doctrine of precedent often enough from pulpits still, but the application of it in detail would often lead to such absurdities as the example just given.

The next step up from the metaphorical-literal in reading the Bible is traditionally the allegorical, where the story "really means" something expressible in discursive language. Non-Biblical religions allegorized their myths extensively in the effort to give them profounder meanings, and Plato ridicules this procedure (technically called *hyponoia*), as his aim was to supplant mythology with dialectic [*Republic*, 378d]. The Biblical religions had to go in the direction of *hyponoia*, however, as they had only their stories. But the discursive element in allegory keeps something of the divisive "I must be right and you must be wrong" quality in it.

Paul, for example, refers to the story in Genesis of Abraham's two wives, in which one wife became jealous of the other and succeeded in getting her rival sent into the desert. Paul says that this story is an "allegory" (Galatians 4:24) in which the excluded wife represents the bondage of the Jewish Law and the accepted one the freedom of the Christian Gospel. A Jewish reader of Paul's interpretation, seeing that the Jews are identified with the Ishmaelites and the Christians with the Jews, might well say that this view of the story was about the most preposterous that it was possible to hold, and that a method of this kind could say anything about anything. A further advance in meaning is clearly needed, something that goes in a more catholic direction, such as, "Freedom is within the orbit of God's will and bondage is outside it." Not that Paul would rule out further advances of this sort by any means.

Above the allegorical level, in the medieval system, is the moral or tropological level, the reading of the Bible that takes us past the story into the reordering and redirecting of one's life. The clearest examples of this kind of meaning are probably the parables of Jesus, explicitly fictions, but fictions that end with "Go, and do thou likewise." The divisiveness we noted at the allegorical level remains to some degree in all religions, in the form of "This makes sense to me if not to you," but it is difficult to argue against the human compassion in such stories as those of the Good Samaritan and the Prodigal Son. We may note that the former story ascribes a genuine charity to someone outside both the Jewish and the embryonic Christian communions. With such parables we begin to suspect that there may be two readers within us, and that one is beginning to form a larger vision that the other has only to attach itself to. That is, we are moving from a single or natural vision to a double or spiritual one.

This movement is a purgatorial journey in which God and man are visualized as working within the same human units, whether individual or social. A glance at the human situation around us reveals war, famine, arbitrary acts of injustice and exploitation, violence, crime, collapse of moral standards, and so on almost indefinitely. Even in prosperous countries a spiritual barrenness produces innumerable acts of ferocity and despair. How does human life of this kind differ from life in hell? Hell is often supposed to be an after-death state created by God in which people are eternally tortured for finite offences. But this doctrine is merely one more example of the depravity of the human mind that thought it up. Man alone is responsible for hell, and much as he would like to pursue his cruelties beyond the grave, he is blocked from doing so. God's interest in this hell is confined to "harrowing" or redeeming those who are in it. At the same time there are honesty, love, neighbourliness, generosity, and the creative powers in the arts and sciences. Human life appears to be a mingling of two ultimate realities, which we call heaven and hell. Hell is the world created by man, and heaven, or at least the way to it, is the world created through man by God.

Hence the stories of the Bible may exhibit all three of the levels we spoke of in connection with Milton's *Paradise Regained*: demonic parody, redemptive power, and apocalyptic vision. The name Israel, which is traditionally supposed to mean "one who strives with God," was given to Jacob after the extraordinary episode in Genesis 32 usually called "wrestling with the angel." There are some very archaic elements in this story: the "angel" is, like the demons of darkness, including Hamlet's father, a being who is compelled to disappear at daybreak. He seems also to be a local demon, like the river-god whom Achilles fights with in *Iliad* 21, and who would have destroyed the great hero if the latter had not been given an abundance of supernatural help. The river in Genesis has shrunk to a brook (Jabbok), but traces of a guardian spirit in nature are still there. The Homeric god, though he has a name, is usually referred to by Homer simply as "river" (*potamos*). Similarly when Jacob asks for the name of his antagonist, he gets no response: he would acquire too much power over his opponent if he knew his name. Another very primitive element is the use of a myth as an explanation of a dietary taboo (verse 32).

However anxious the angel is to get away, Jacob clings to him demanding a blessing, though what he eventually gets is a touch in the thigh that lames him for life. The antagonist himself is called a "man" in verse 24, but he is clearly no man, and by verse 30 we have a very strong hint that in some way and some sense Jacob has been striving with God himself, though surely one can strive with God only by striving with or through oneself to obtain a spiritual vision of God. So we have, first, a demon of darkness who attacks and mutilates those who encounter him, then a redemptive context in which Jacob demands a blessing from an angel, and a final outcome in which Jacob is transformed by divine power into Israel, the individual centre and starting point of God's people.

The story of the sacrifice of Isaac also has a demonic basis: the sacrifice of human children which was practised around Israel but forbidden to the Israelites themselves. This story also sets up a demonic situation and then moves in a redemptive direction, where Abraham becomes aware of the uncompromising priority of God's right to human devotion against the closest of earthly ties. We may compare Jesus' remark in the Gospels that he had come to bring not peace but a sword, and cause division even among families. The redemptive vision of Abraham is eloquently expounded in Kierkegaard's *Fear and Trembling*, where Kierkegaard's personal sacrifice of his love Regina is part of the situation. There is also a poem by Emily Dickinson where that poet's troubled but utterly honest vision sees the story as a contemptible act of arbitrary tyranny on God's part.[54] Textually speaking, both perspectives are "true," but the Dickinson poem remains on the metaphorical-literal level of the story and Kierkegaard explores the redemptive dimension in it.

Sometimes the journey of understanding leads, in Hegelian fashion, to the opposite of what the physical event suggests. Let us imagine a speaker in Flanders or Leningrad or anywhere where there is a war cemetery memorializing hundreds of thousands of dead soldiers, explaining to an audience that aggressiveness is essential to humanity because of its survival value. A kernel of truth in a bushel of vicious nonsense; but in contemplating the nonsense our understanding begins to turn inside out. The conventions of secular literature, as they descend from Homer to medieval romance, keep the aggressive hero in the foreground as a central poetic theme. These conventions are also reflected in the Old Testament period between Joshua and David. Other elements in the Bible eventually push us in the opposite direction of seeing that endurance under adversity is the real form of courage. Here the genuine survival values become the spiritual ones given by faith and hope, even when we are not quite sure what our faith is in or what our hope is for; even when their goal is certain death.

Faith and hope, however, seem to get implicated in the question of the postponed promise. If God promises prosperity to Israel, why so long a period of exile, servitude, even massacres to a point at which only a "saving remnant" survives? More bluntly, why is God portrayed as incessantly promising better things, when history records so little in the way of performance? Taking Israel to be typical of the human situation as a whole, the question expands into the stock question of what is called theodicy, or why a good God permits evil and suffering.

The virtues of faith and hope are purgatorial virtues, and culminate in the paradisal vision of love. Love in the New Testament is *agape* or *caritas*, God's love for humanity reflected in the human love for God and for one's neighbour. The sexual basis of love is subordinated, because the primary emphasis is on the individual and the community, but erotic love is clearly a part of the total vision. Such love, it seems to me, has to begin with the human recognition that it is only human beings who have put evil and suffering into human life, and that no other entity than ourselves, certainly not God, is responsible for its persistence. I have expressed this elsewhere by suggesting that love or charity begins by asking the question, "Why do *we* permit so much evil and suffering?"[55] The story of the Exodus shows God in the role of guide to a Promised Land out of Egypt, the symbolic "furnace of iron" or hell-world of bondage. He is unalterably opposed to any turning back to this "Egypt," and those who try to do so have to face his "wrath." But if our general thesis is right, this wrath has nothing of the human egocentric feelings of anger or desire for revenge or love of punishment, however much the rhetoric of the prophets may suggest such things. Wrath is, so to speak, honest criticism, and points out consequences: it does not interfere with free will.

There is certainly a demonic state of being, but it appears to be really an intensification of the human one. Conceivably the divine state is too, or, at least, progress in human love might be thought to bring us to the point of identity with God. Traditional Christianity tends rather to follow the view, which goes back to Augustine at least, that the advance of the spirit, wherever it ends, certainly makes us more authentically human. This is usually taken to refer only to the individual human, but the question arises whether there could be social spiritual advance as well. If so, we are involved again in some conception of progress, though of a very different kind from those mentioned earlier.

Every one of us is defined by our social conditioning, but while our conditioning defines us, it also limits, even imprisons, us, and awareness of the limitations built into being who and what we are is one of the central elements in education, particularly religious education. One of the most encouraging signs of social change in the last half-century is the growing momentum of such awareness, a momentum that has increased to the point of being a social movement. Earlier in the century we realized how much we owed to Marxism for illuminating the "bourgeois" conditioning of which most of that class had up till then been unconscious. Similar is the Freudian illumination of unconscious conflict in our minds and the way we rationalize it. Both these movements, however, especially Marxism, tended to polarize every situation dialectically, and we are beginning to find this incessant polarizing less and less convincing.

The news media now devote a great deal, perhaps even most, of their attention to the way that our conditioned attitudes block our own freedom, ranging from the cruder stereotypes of racism and sexism to the subtler arrogance in regard to the natural environment. Such a growing awareness also prevents us from a facile idealizing of the past. Bernard of Clairvaux was one of the greatest saints of his time, but by the standards of contemporary awareness anyone who put so much time and energy into preaching a crusade would not be a saint at all, however intense his spiritual life and however numerous his miracles. There may be just wars, but no holy wars, because the "good" side is never holy and the "bad" side is still human. The question that concerns us at present is, Can a growing insight into our own conditioned limits also be connected with a process of, so to speak, cleaning up the human picture of God?

Such a phrase as "consciousness-raising" may often refer to niggling pedantries of no real importance; but behind it is something that could be of revolutionary religious significance. The single vision of God sees in him the reflection of human panic and rage, its love of cruelty and domination, and, when it accepts such a God, calls on him to justify the maintaining of these things in human life. The double vision sees this as taking the face of God in vain, as it were, and tries to separate the human mirror from God's reality. The point is that his reality comes far closer to human life when purified of the reflection of human evil: that is why the Bible presents so anthropomorphic a picture of him, even in the centuries before the Incarnation.

We must now very briefly sum up the relation of our "double vision" in language, space, and time to our double vision of God.

One of the benefits of the coming of the kingdom of the spirit, the prophets tell us, is the restoring of a "pure speech" (Zephaniah 3:9). Such purity can hardly be the abstract purity of logic or descriptive accuracy, much less the isolation of one existing language from others. It is rather the purity of simple speech, the parable or aphorism that begins to speak only after we have heard it and feel that we have exhausted its explicit meaning. From that explicit meaning it begins to ripple out into the remotest mysteries of what it expresses and clarifies but does not "say." Not all pure speech is in the Bible: T.S. Eliot and Mallarmé tell us that purifying the speech of the "tribe" or society around us is what gives a social function to the poet.[56] Such purity of speech is not simply a creative element in the mind, but a power that recreates the mind, or perhaps has actually created the mind in the first place, as though it were an autonomous force deriving from an authentic creation; as though there really were a Logos uniting mind and nature that really does mean "Word."

We also spoke of Blake's double vision, which seems at first to be reverting from the conscious awareness of an objective order to the old superstitious notion of presences haunting it. But we also suggested that Blake is really talking about a third stage of development, one in which the vision of gods comes back in the form of a sense of identity with nature, where nature is not merely to be studied and lived in but loved and cherished, where place becomes home. A new covenant with nature, Hosea tells us (2:18), will come after war has been swept from the face of the earth. The growth of nature from a manifestation of order and intellectual coherence into an object of love would bring about the harmony of spirit and nature that has been a central theme of this work. Some recent writers have been deeply impressed by the conception in Chinese culture of a harmony between two similar worlds, usually translated as "heaven" and "earth," which is the goal of all genuinely human aspiration. We should perhaps not overlook the fact that what seems like the same kind of harmony is prominently featured in the Lord's Prayer.

Our physical bodies are part of a world usually described as material, but if matter is simply energy cooled down to the point at which our physical bodies can live with it, perhaps spirit can enter a world of higher energies where the separate things spread around objective heres and theres are no longer things to keep bumping into. In such a spiritual nature, a nature of "implicate order," as it has been called,[57] or interpenetrating energies, and no longer the nature of congealed objects, we should be gods or numinous presences ourselves. If the spirit of man and the spirit of God inhabit the same world, that fact is more important than the theological relation between them.

Reverting to our remark about the God of promises, all our conditioning is rooted in our temporal existence and in the anxiety that appears in the present as the passing of time and in the future as death. If death is the last enemy to be destroyed, as Paul tells us [1 Corinthians 15:26], the last metaphor to be transcended is that of the future tense, or God in the form of Beckett's Godot, who never comes but will maybe come tomorrow. The omnipresence of time gives some strange distortions to our double vision. We are born on a certain date, live a continuous identity until death on another date; then we move into an "after"-life or "next" world where something like an ego survives indefinitely in something like a time and place. But we are not continuous identities; we have had many identities, as babies, as boys and girls, and so on through life, and when we pass through or "outgrow" these identities they return to their source. Assuming, that is, some law of conservation in the spiritual as well as the physical world exists. There is nothing so unique about death as such, where we may be too distracted by illness or sunk in senility to have much identity at all. In the double vision of a spiritual and a physical world simultaneously present, every moment we have lived through we have also died out of into another order. Our life in the resurrection, then, is already here, and waiting to be recognized.

On Special Occasions

13

The Freshman and His Religion

October 1933

From Canadian Student *(magazine of the Student Christian Movement, or SCM), 16, no. 1 (October 1933): 6–9. Frye had graduated in June 1933.*

Obviously, if we are to convey anything intelligible by this title, we must define our terms at the start. The freshman class is a more or less homogeneous group, but individual frosh may believe in anything from determinism to the evil eye. Any general statement about freshmen must, therefore, be taken for what it is worth, simply as a generalization, and we must be willing to concede a broad and tolerant basis for our definition of religion. Let us understand by religion the relationship of the individual soul to God, and through him to other men. Our civilization is so far committed to Christianity for the expression of its religious impulses that we have no hesitation in regarding "Christianity" and "religion" as interchangeable terms.

The freshman class, composed of individuals who vary widely from one another, is, in an incredibly short space of time, welded to a unity and absorbed into a higher organization. Such a phenomenon would be impossible without a bond of mutual understanding in which is contained the epitome of the freshman's relation to his fellow men. The source of this bond is the common search for training, which, being a search for guidance, light, maturity, and understanding, may be taken as a corresponding epitome of the freshman's relation toward God. The freshman's religion, then, is his existence as a freshman.

We shall never grasp this fundamental principle if we shrink from the immense implications of a university training in the life of a Christian. It is however a well known fact that, when anyone receives training in any subject, he sums up at the outset everything he already knows about that subject, part of which will be integrated, the rest merely unlearned. College being, in the catch-phrase, a training for life, it follows that the typical freshman should sum up his entire adolescence during his first year at college. Sensitive natures are often metamorphosed in this way. The freshman is a neophyte, an initiate into the art of living, a seeker after self-coordination. Religion representing the principle of coordination in the world, a more purely religious activity than college life would be hard to find. This fact is usually lost sight of, of course, owing to the immense secularizing pressure exerted by the contemporary world. It is also possible that many organizations which are concerned with adolescent training give rise to more confusion of thought than they intend. For the majority stress a fourfold development in which religion is merely a factor coequal with physical exercise, study, and social recreation. Such a scheme is based on a complete misunderstanding of the true size and power of religion, which is nothing if it is not the causal and integrating central force of the personality. This confusion is carried over into college life. Most impartially minded people concerned with education are ready to admit that physical and social activities are necessary to adequate college training. They may stress one side, saying that work after all comes first, or that what one studies at the university is less important than the social contacts one makes. But if all three are admitted essential, there cannot logically be any arguments over precedence. Study, exercise, and social intercourse are essential, but essential to what? When this question is pressed, most people take refuge in generalizations, such as a "proper outlook on life" or "a really balanced education." But anyone who understands the reality of religion can see that every element of university training converges on religious development. The practice of religion is a struggle for coherence, and means, in the last analysis, education. It is by no idle metaphor that the SCM regards all students as members of it *ipso facto*.

When a student fails to get from college what he feels he is entitled to receive in the way of adequate comprehension of problems and stability of outlook, he fails through not realizing this principle, either consciously or subconsciously. But he can be excused for not doing so when we consider how alone in the world he is. The college organization is purely secular, the course in religious knowledge very seldom, and then accidentally, having any unifying relationship to his course as a whole. There is no religious organization among students which realizes that its underlying problem is to show the connection of academic training and religion. We have said that the freshman sums up his adolescence at college. Now in religion, the difference between a childlike and an adult approach is the difference between a literal, superficial acceptance of the dogmas and parables in which it is embodied, and a symbolic view which takes in more of their larger significance. The freshman, then, is just ready to outgrow the uncritical passivity of his earlier instruction, and start actively relating his religion to reality; that is, taking the great conceptions of the Christian church as the mainsprings of a world outlook. To take a concrete instance: as a child he accepts the doctrine of the Trinity, perhaps not in the form of a shamrock but certainly not in any more developed sense. He is now ready to exchange this for the Trinity which is the embodiment of the tremendous vision of a tripartite world of which our greatest mystics and philosophers can afford only a partial and one-sided view. Failing entirely, in most cases, to get this, it is natural that he should fall to exclaiming, as he frequently does, against the orthodox who regard God as a three-headed monster. Or, if he meets with those diplomatic Christians who pass by on the other side of creed and rest their case on platitude and sententiousness, he tends to associate religion with a vague emotional spasm which, so far from having any vital connection with the work he is doing, necessarily disturbs it.

It will be obvious from what has been said that the problems which worry the freshman are the most elementary known to religion. Organized discussion groups inhibit most of the participants, partly because of their innate artificiality, but mainly because of the crudity and banality of the ideas held. As a freshman I have attended some of these meetings, but I spent my first year in a predominantly frosh residence in which impromptu discussions occurred quite frequently, and I consider the former, deliberate type afforded very few valid inferences concerning the real thoughts of the freshman about religion which were immediately disclosed in the more spontaneous. For one thing, in the former, half the audience is usually lacking—the unsympathetic, destructively critical half. The questions here raised are the eternal problems: Why does a good God permit suffering? What has a merciful God to do with hell? How can a devil exist against an infinite good? To what extent is the Bible inspired? How much of the miraculous and supernatural in religion can a modern man be reasonably expected to believe? These, and others like these, are the questions the freshman asks himself, and occasionally other freshmen. But it is only among his own kind that the left-wing freshman will say: "Well, I've decided that, as far as I'm concerned, Christianity is the bunk." Only among his fellows that the right-wing supporter will grumble: "Never knew there was such a buncha atheists in the house." The leader of the average discussion group, where of fifteen polite but highly self-conscious members, eleven are silent and the other four shuffle uneasily around such words as "experience," "belief," "conviction," "agnostic," "inspiration," does not always realize that these same fifteen might on another night be sprawled over beds or slouched in arm chairs, and all yelling at once about the Immaculate Conception. Religion, no matter in what aspect, is a matter of vital and painful interest to the freshman. It could hardly be religion otherwise.

Religion is the interpretation of the personality, and with a student it should represent the concretion of academic study; that is, bringing scholastic pursuits from isolated and cloudy abstractions into the living pulses of the learner. It would appear, then, that the natural unit of activity of students' religion is the course. Modern History and Political Science students should be led to look toward Christianity for the immutable principles underlying the establishment of social institutions. Science students should understand that all our science is a rationalized commentary on the great concepts of the Christian mystics and poets. Modern Language students should comprehend something of the force of Christian passion that moulded our literatures. All study is wasted time unless a point of view is attained. That can only be completely achieved by absorbing it, not into the brain but into the blood where religion centres. Canada will never produce a great mathematician—using the word "great" advisedly—until she produces one with a soul that can feel enough affinity with Descartes, Newton, Leibnitz, Pascal, to understand in some measure what Christianity meant to these men. We will never have a really great musician until someone catches a glimpse of the power that lay behind Bach and Haydn. The principle holds good in small as well as large fields. The religion of the freshman is his work. Religion is always that when it is alive. No matter what course of study he pursues, he should be forced to realize constantly, until he graduates at least, that all cultural activity is the expression of a religious impulse, which is in our case Christianity. This alone will give him an intellectual bond of sympathy with other students to round out his social friendships, for that religion is the sole source of enthusiasm is confirmed even by etymology. And this alone will give him a coherent starting point from which to get something out of his course, and to be able in consequence to present his Master with twice the number of talents he was given. If the problem of accepting Our Lord Jesus Christ were presented, not vaguely or sentimentally, not with a shamefaced attempt at geniality or good fellowship, not as a delectable and soothing anodyne, but in all the terrible naked strength of its iron logic, it would command more of the respect and prestige it deserves.

14

Merry Christmas (I)

December 1946

From Canadian Forum, *26 (December 1946): 195. Reprinted in* RW, *378–9.*

Christmas is far, far older than Christianity, as even the pre-Christian Yule and Saturnalia were late developments of it, and it was never completely assimilated to the Christian faith. Our very complaints about the hypocritical commercializing of the Christmas spirit prove that, for they show how vigorously Christmas can flourish without the smallest admixture of anything that could reasonably be called Christian. Christmas is the tribute man pays to the winter solstice, and perhaps to something in himself of which the winter solstice reminds him. We turn on all our lights, and stuff ourselves, and exchange presents, because our ancestors in the forest, watching the sun grow fainter until it was a cold weak light unable to bring any more life from the earth, chose the shortest day of the year to defy an almost triumphant darkness and declare their loyalty to an almost beaten sun. We have learned that we do not need to worry about the sun, and that there is no monster big enough to swallow it. We have yet to learn that no atomic bomb will ever destroy the human race, that no Dark Age will (as it never has done) totally overspread the earth, that no matter how often man is knocked down, he will always pick himself up, punch drunk and sick and morbidly aware of his open guard, spit out some more teeth, and start slugging again. At that point there is a division between those for whom Christmas is a religious festival, and for whom the new light coming into the world must be divine as well as human if the struggle is ever to be won, and those for whom the festival is human and natural and points to an ultimate human triumph. With this difference in outlook the *Canadian Forum* has nothing to do, but to all of its readers who recognize the primary meaning of Christmas, and who realize that generosity and hospitality and the sharing of goods make a better world than misery and persecution and the cutting of throats, it wishes a merry Christmas.

15

So Many Lost Weekends

March 1947

From Canadian Forum, *26 (March 1947): 269. Reprinted in* RW, *379–80.*

The latest gathering of the Ontario Temperance Federation, which coincided with the lifting of the liquor ration, included an abortive proposal to form a temperance party. It is with genuine concern that one sees the public utterances of Protestant churches increasingly identified with those of a group of full-time temperance agitators, who give the public the impression that their churches regard the "liquor traffic" as of far greater importance than any theological doctrine, any other social question, or any other moral weakness. We say weakness, for the refusal to make any moral distinction between drinking and drunkenness is part of the whole temperance position. No one can deny that drunkenness constitutes a grave social problem; but unfortunately the effect of losing all sense of proportion about it is to make it seem almost trivial. And it can hardly be denied either that many clergymen have completely lost their sense of proportion about drinking, and have transformed a real issue into a superstitious taboo which is injurious to religion (it has, for example, alienated a large number from the churches whose support could have been had for the asking), which has no intelligible relationship to politics, and which is steadily losing all connection with doing good.

Many temperance advocates are only church politicians, but many are men with long and honourable careers in the support of liberal and socialist causes—a fact which is reflected in a certain realism with which they associate the drinking problem with profits and private enterprise. One is all the more surprised, therefore, to find them falling into the common reformers' error of mistaking an effect for a cause. People take to drink because of psychological maladjustments or economic insecurity. The former any serious religion would regard as falling within the province of the "cure of souls"; the latter is an evil which nothing but an intelligently planned socialist movement can really cure. Socialists ask for the support of the Christian churches on the ground that the present system of monopoly capitalism is immoral as well as inefficient; and to divert all one's reforming energies from the central problem of insecurity to one of its by-products is, as drunkenness is, like pulling a leaf from a tree and expecting the tree to wither away.

16

Merry Christmas?

December 1947

From Canadian Forum, *27 (December 1947): 195. Reprinted in* RW, *380–1.*

A passage in the *Christmas Carol* describes how Scrooge saw the air filled with fettered spirits, whose punishment it was to see the misery of others and to be unable to help.[1] One hardly needs to be a ghost to be in their position, and as we light the fires for our Christmas they throw into the cold and darkness outside the wavering shadows of ourselves, unable to break the deadlock of the UN, unable to stop the slaughter in China or India or the terror in Palestine,[2] unable to release the victims of tyrannies still undestroyed, unable to deflect the hysterical panic urging us to war again, unable to do anything for the vast numbers who will starve and freeze this winter, and above all unable to break the spell of malignant fear that holds the world in its grip. Yet Dickens's ghosts were punished for having denied Christmas, and we can offset our helplessness by affirming Christmas, by returning once more to the symbol of what human life should be, a society raised by kindliness into a community of continuous joy.

Because the winter solstice festival is not confined to Christianity, it represents something that Christians and non-Christians can affirm in common. Christmas reminds us, whether we put the symbol into religious terms or secular ones, that there is now in the world a power of life which is both the perfect form of human effort and all we know of God, and which it is our privilege to work with as it spreads from race to race, from nation to nation, from class to class, until there is no one shut out from the great invisible communion of the Christmas feast. Then the wish of a merry Christmas, which we now extend to all our readers, will become, like the wish of a fairy tale, a worker of miracles.

17

Merry Christmas (II)

December 1948

From Canadian Forum, *28 (December 1948): 193–4. Reprinted in* RW, *386–7.*

The world clings to Christmas with a kind of desperation: it is the only traditional festival, apart from a flurry of new hats at Easter, that retains any real hold on ordinary life. The reason for its persistent vitality is not easy to see. It is not primarily the influence of Christianity, for in the Christian church Christmas is only one event in a long calendar. The unique popular Christmas outside the church is hardly a Christian festival at all. Its presiding deity, so far as it has any, is the carnival figure of Santa Claus. The cynical answer is that commercial advertising keeps Christmas going, but that is nonsense. The public is quite capable of resisting pressure of this sort if it has no answering response to its appeal. No: people want Christmas, though they hardly know why they go through all that bother every year.

Perhaps the answer is that people go through the bother of Christmas because Christmas helps them to understand why they go through the bother of living out their lives the rest of the year. For one brief instant, we see human society as it should and could be, a world in which business has become the exchanging of presents and in which nothing is important except the happiness and well-being of the ultimate consumer. It is only a symbol, and humanity can hardly stand more than about twelve hours of really civilized behaviour, but still it is there, and our Christmas shopping may be inspired by an obscure feeling that man is done for if he loses entirely the vision of life that Christmas represents.

Potentially, therefore, there is a tremendous revolutionary power in the idea of Christmas. When Christ was born there was already a Christmas in Rome, a late December festival called the Saturnalia held in memory of a Golden Age when men were free and equal. The distinctive feature of that festival was the licence given to slaves, who were allowed to answer their masters back, sit down at table with them, and even be waited on by them. It was a dumb, helpless ritual which said symbolically that the structure of Roman society was all wrong. It did not save the Roman Empire, any more than a futile pretence of making things easier for the underprivileged at Christmas will save us. A helpless Christmas is an intolerable hypocrisy, especially when associated with Christianity. It is unlikely that the evangelists who told the Nativity stories would have thought that a cosy, cuddly, sentimental good time was an appropriate way of celebrating Christ's birth. Christianity speaks of making the earth resemble the kingdom of heaven, and teaches that the kingdom of heaven is within man. This is something very like the conquest of the whole year by the spirit of Christmas, and is the kind of thing we mean when we wish a merry Christmas to all our readers.

18

Merry Christmas (III)

December 1949

From Canadian Forum, *29 (December 1949): 193–4. Reprinted in* RW, *398–9.*

The original Christmas was born of primitive fear. The fear of the growing darkness and the shortening days produced the rite of kindled fires, and the fear of winter the cult of the evergreen tree. Since then, Christmas has been wrapped up in one layer after another of an advancing civilization. Christianity came with its lovely serene story of a divine child and a virgin mother: the Middle Ages brought the carols, and then came the presents, the roast fowls, the mince pies, and the plum puddings. Our present form of Christmas, with its Santa Claus, its Christmas tree, and its exchange of cards, is a nineteenth-century invention, largely of German origin, the product of the age of Dickens and Albert the Good, of the British Empire and voluntary charities.

Yet even in this cosy urban middle-class Christmas something of the old panic recurs. There is unmistakable panic in the advertisers' desperate appeals of "only so many shopping days left," with its lurking threat that only if enough people spend enough money will this dollar civilization be able to stagger once more around the calendar. There is, if not panic, at any rate compulsion, in the popular response to this appeal, in the set faces of the women checking items off a list and in the apathy of their husbands trudging behind them, envying the bears.

What is the thoughtful observer to make of all this? Apart from the children, is it not the frivolous who enjoy Christmas, or pretend to enjoy it? Who else would find any real release in an orgy of synthetic gaiety as this dreadful century lurches to its halfway mark? Surely one is not a sour-faced Puritan if one feels, after listening to the radio reports of the cheering crowds in Times Square: "There is nothing here that reminds me of the birth of Christ; there is much that reminds me of Belshazzar of Babylon, who feasted while his city was in flames, and who could not read the writing on the wall" [Daniel 5].

One may find it instructive to compare the two Christmas stories in Matthew and in Luke. The Christmas story that we know and love is almost entirely from Luke. Matthew tells a terrible and gloomy tale of a jealous tyrant who filled the land with dead children and wailing mothers, while the wise men escaped from the country in one direction and the Holy Family in another. It is a tale in which all the characters except the tyrant and his minions are either murdered or refugees. Today we know as never before that this, too, is part of the Christmas story. But the story of Luke, with the shepherds and the manger and the angels singing hymns of peace and good will to men, does not cease to be true because the story of Matthew is also true. The story of Christmas, from its primitive beginnings to the present, is in part a story of how men, by cowering together in a common fear of menace, discovered a new fellowship, in fellowship a new hope, and in hope a new vision of society.

As Dickens shows us, the ghost of Christmas past brings us only regret for the past, and the ghost of Christmas future brings us only the terror of the future. But he also shows us that one of the surest ways of making the possible nightmare in the future come true is to fail to know and appreciate better the spirit of Christmas present. And so, without hypocrisy and as far as possible without frivolousness, we wish our readers once more a merry Christmas and a happy New Year.

19

The Church: Its Relation to Society

1949

From The Living Church: A Book in Memory of the Life and Work of Rev. Richard Davidson M.A., Ph.D., D.D., Principal of Emmanuel College Toronto, *ed. Harold W. Vaughan (Toronto: United Church Publishing House, 1949), 152–72. Reprinted in RW, 203–19. The book was a collection of essays by former pupils of Davidson, who had been principal, 1932–43, and died in 1944. This text incorporates changes made by Frye in the Emmanuel College Library copy.*

I

The study of social ideologies begins with the *Republic* of Plato, in which Socrates sets out with a group of disciples to find the meaning of justice. Abandoning all efforts to define a mere abstract noun, Socrates decides that one can realize what justice is only by seeing, with the eye of the soul, the form or idea of society.

In this situation there are three societies involved. One is that of fourth-century Greece, in which the defeat of the cultured Athenians who lacked discipline by the ignorant and brutal Spartans who possessed it may have provided an inspiration for Plato's conception of a communized military aristocracy. Another is the ideal form of the state as the dialectic of Socrates evolves it: a philosopher-ruler supported by a military caste of guards ruling over the artisans or producers. The third society is the symposium itself, the free discussion group in which Socrates' vision is achieved.

The state described by Socrates can, perhaps, be called "ideal" in Plato's sense: it expresses very accurately the underlying form of society, in which a priestly and a military aristocracy hold the workers and producers in subjection to their ideology and privileges. The ideal relationship in Plato of the soldier, the philosopher, and the worker is very similar to their historical relationship in the caste system of India, as well as in the feudal system of the Middle Ages and in a host of other societies from ancient Egypt to our own time. But is it desirable, and will it meet Plato's ethical standard of "the Form of the Good"? Surely most people today would see, in its rigorous autocracy, its unscrupulous use of lies for propaganda, its ruthlessly censored art, and its subordination of all the creative and productive life of the state to a fanatical military caste, all the evils that we now call "totalitarian." Plato admits that dictatorial tyranny is very like his state-pattern entrusted to the wrong men. But in practice would the two differ much, unless we can believe in the perfectibility of philosophers?

Plato sees the order of the state as a social projection of order in the individual. The philosopher-ruler, the military clique, and the artisans correspond to the reason, will, and appetite as they are related in the disciplined mind. He also remarks that whether the form of the state can ever be substantiated on earth or not, the true philosopher will always behave in society as far as possible as though it did exist [592b]. The individual is free only when he is perfectly disciplined as an individual. The free man is free because his chaotic and lustful desires are hunted down and exterminated, or else compelled to express themselves in ways prescribed by the dictatorship of his reason. He is free because a powerful will is ready to spring to action to aid that reason to do whatever it sees fit, acting as a kind of "thought police" suppressing every impulse not directly related to its immediate interests. But what frees the individual seems to enslave society: at any rate, something goes all wrong with human freedom when we take an analogy between individual and social order literally. Our experience of society is that it must be far more relaxed if the individual is to achieve his freedom to discipline himself at all. The three essentials of civilized life, leisure, privacy, and freedom of movement, all involve a certain slackness and illogicality in the functioning of the social machine. This residual anarchism in human life is a source of great irritation to totalitarian minds, but any attempt to eliminate it from the social order wreaks havoc in the individual.

We need a fragment of the Christian revelation to make complete sense of Plato's argument. The basis of the analogy between the individual and the social order is the fact that the real form of human society is the single body of one man, which is inconceivable unless that man is also God. The wise man, for Christianity, lives in society as though the real social body were the real presence of an incarnate God. Such wisdom is not philosophy, but charity. Apart from this revelation, all human societies are molecular aggregates of human egos, and have to be held together by the molecular tension of physical power, not by a single informing spirit, like the living body. The *Republic* is one of the profoundest books in the world if read as an allegory of the inner life of man, as an allegory of the City of God, or as an analysis of the essential structure of society. But it must be read with Christianity's absolute separation of the kingdom of God from the kingdom of fallen men kept clearly in mind. If we read it as the perfect state for fallen man to live in, it becomes a vision of human life dedicated to war and power, the poets expelled, science at a standstill, religion perverted into military propaganda, leisure, privacy, and freedom of movement all wiped out—in short, a vision of hell on earth.

The Christian does not see any ideal form of human society as such: he sees that the two eternal forms of human existence are heaven and hell, both of which are constantly active principles in human life. God wills the establishment of the kingdom of heaven on earth; the passions of man will the lusts of Babylon and the armies of Gog. Of the three societies in the *Republic*, therefore, the fact that Christianity transforms its conception of ideal society into the City of God gives it a special dialectic in dealing with actual society. Actual society follows much the same rhythms now that it followed in Plato's time. In 1940 the cultured French who lacked discipline were defeated by the ignorant and brutal Nazis who possessed it, and the defeated nation developed the philosophy of existentialism, which says once more that the wise man, whatever society is like, should behave as though he were free. Yet at every moment of history the Christian sees the possible and imminent realization either of heaven on earth or of hell on earth. Society is a mixture of love and power, of the spiritual authority of God and the temporal authority of Caesar. We can never get rid of the hope of reaching a society of perfect love, and we can never get rid of the fear of reaching a society of pure power.

The society of power is always a close and searching parody of the society of love. So close and searching, in fact, that without revelation it is hardly possible for man to separate the latent heaven from the latent hell in his own society or in his social thinking. In the kingdom of God there is no place for Caesar as Caesar, for there is no respect of persons there; in the kingdom of Caesar there is nothing but respect of persons, and hence no place for God as God. In such a society Caesar has to become God. There is no alternative to Christ except Antichrist, and the form of Antichrist is the form of the society of power incarnate in a divine king, an inspired dictator, or an infallible counsellor. Tyranny is primarily the perverted misapplication of Christianity's unquestioning obedience to an omnipotent will to the society of fallen man. Such a society is verbally just like heaven, and actually just like hell.

We enter society paying our dues both to Caesar and to God, because society is a mixture of good and evil which can only be separated by an apocalypse. But the due that Caesar has always been most interested in, from the Pharaoh of Egypt to the Sol Invictus of Rome and the Führer of Germany, is divine worship. The Christian has constantly to resist the pull of the Caesarian tendency, which of course is also the tendency of the natural man, toward a deified military, hierarchical, and dictatorial state, and has to follow the revolutionary ideals of liberty, equality, and fraternity, because Christ brings freedom to man and those who love one another are necessarily brothers and equals. (These revolutionary ideals were formulated as secular ideals, but can never remain so, as we shall see.) The society of power always tends to resemble the pyramid or tower of Babel: the society of love tends to resemble the communion table. To paraphrase a punning argument of Milton's, "ruling" in the spiritual sense is not physical compulsion but the application of the "rule" or measuring reed of the temple of God to human society.[1] Christianity thus works toward social equality by trying to wither up the natural root of the desire for power, a desire which must always remain on the level of lust.

To use Toynbee's language for a different purpose, society is best off when there is a "creative minority" of those who work within society without too much regard to their hierarchical status in it.[2] It is worst off when those who possess ability without charity form a "dominant minority." The personal dictator is essentially an army commander: his prestige depends on maintaining an emergency war-time situation. The dictatorship of a class is more solidly established, but equally destructive to creative life. The aristocracy of the Middle Ages and Renaissance patronized their culture because they benefited spectacularly from it, but they produced very little of it themselves, and in our day the reserves of creative energy in the proletariat assumed by Marx have not yet made their appearance. Creative life apparently has to come mainly out of the middle of society: in practice this has meant the middle class, but only because it is in the middle: a bourgeois dictatorship is equally sterile.

The Christian's only social criteria are the visions of the two eternal forms of human life: he struggles against tyranny, inequality, and enmity, because he sees, behind the pragmatic evils that they bring, the eternal prison of torture and despair out of which they have emerged. The best place to look for visions of an imminent heaven is, naturally, in the eschatological part of the New Testament: the best place to look for visions of an imminent hell is in contemporary literature. Koestler, Kafka, Malraux, Farrell, Wright, Sartre, Orwell, are only a few of those who seem to write at their best when seeing in modern society the form of a modern *Inferno*. Such titles as *No Exit* and *Darkness at Noon* speak for themselves. Since the Christian dialectic entered the world, the one form of existence for man which has become entirely impossible is a purely human existence running along on an even keel without reference either to the hope of heaven or to the fear of hell. A primitive society may go on doing the same thing over and over for centuries, but revelation condemns the world to an apocalyptic neurosis.

The third society involved in the *Republic* is the free discussion group or symposium in which the vision of the form of justice is contained. The word "free" is essential: we may perhaps see a reflection of the philosophical despotism of the *Republic* in the fact that Socrates does all the talking, but Socrates would say that the principle of freedom in discussion lies in the argument itself. One must free the dialectic, let the argument take its own form. The idea of the symposium appears in modern society, under Christian influence, as the "idea of the university," as Newman calls it. All art and science is a single idea or form by virtue of the fact that it derives from the unity of God, or is contained in the Logos or Word which is the revealed form of God. The content of the university is what Matthew Arnold calls "culture," but Newman's conception of "university" expresses better than "culture" the fact of a total form of education and creative life. While such education is "liberal," or designed for the free man, its liberality consists in its own integrity as a part of the truth that makes free, not associating special privileges with those who learn it, whether of thought, wealth, or activity.

I do not of course confine the word "university" to the aggregate of business enterprises which employ cultural experts in a mass production of social techniques. But such enterprises help to maintain the vast free discussion group in society ranged around the arts and sciences which is the real university, and which embraces the school, the press, the theatre, and the public meeting as well as the degree-granting institution. The relation of the university in this expanded sense to society as a whole is a neglected but essential aspect of social theory. John Stuart Mill saw that democratic freedom must rest on some kind of paradoxical combination of majority rule and minority right.[3] If the minority rules, it is Toynbee's "dominant minority," and will bring tyranny; if it is impotent, majority rule will bring another kind of tyranny. But what gives a minority a right? Criminals are a minority, but have no right to be criminals. Mill eventually decided that society derives its freedom from its maintenance of a free discussion group, and that what gives a minority a right is the actual or potential possession of a contribution to this discussion. The autonomy which a free society must grant to the expression of thought and to its cultural institutions implies, of course, only independence, not secret power. As the scholar in memory of whom these essays are written made his significant impact on society within the university, the social and religious importance of the university should be clearly recognized here.

II

The first fact about the relation of the individual to society is society. Society precedes the individual, who is born involuntarily into it, and is forced to accept the heritage of a mental and bodily conditioning which he can alter only within strictly prescribed limits. He begins as a new baby, and in his novelty is his chance for freedom, but he will always resemble his parents in appearance and his immediate contemporaries in thinking. He will be, in short, his own society appearing once again in a sort of monad of consciousness.

There is such a thing as a theory of social contract, not as a fable about something that happened in a past too remote for any evidence to disturb the fabler's assertions, but as an explanation of the existing social structure. The social contract according to Rousseau assumes that individual life is prior to social life, even if not prior in time. Here freedom consists in recreating one's essential solitariness. But a gospel of liberty that divides one man from another belongs to the society of power, and soon passes into its opposite. A prior individuality which is humiliated, or at least lowered in intensity, by joining the herd looks on social life as at best a necessary compromise. As this compromise should not involve the essential inner life, it should be a pure and if possible unconscious ritual. The development of German Romanticism down to the Nazis affords many examples of the connection between introversion and automatism.

It would make a little more sense to think of the individual as having developed his freedom out of society. Society has no freedom except when the individual articulates or focuses freedom for it by fulfilling the bondage of its law in his own self-discipline. Individual freedom is a social product, and is therefore always socially responsible, otherwise it is mere parasitism. In pagan societies such freedom is only for the enlightened, Plato's philosophers, who form a self-contained university or natural aristocracy. The forming of a pagan society of love thus depends on the perilous link between intelligence and virtue. The liberty of the Gospel is another matter, and dissolves all natural aristocracies.

What is true of actual society is true of the other societies. The idea of the university implies that a new discovery in science is not essentially new, but articulates what was already present in the order of nature. This is simple enough, but in the arts the notion of a poet sitting down with some blank paper and producing a poem in an act of creation *ex nihilo* is still common. Nothing of the sort, of course, happens. The poet manifests what is already latent in the order of words, and every work of art is the focus of a community, again an antecedent community formed by the traditions and conventions of culture. Similarly the student at the university has, by the act of calling himself a student, accepted the priority of the university over his individuality, and every man with a "calling" makes at least a gesture of renouncing the self. Wherever a man is or goes, the society already there defines the form in which his individuality must fulfil itself, until he completes the fulfilment by discovering, beyond his destiny, his predestination.

In the Gospels, we may see that the Christian university was born when Jesus, as a young student, left his home to dispute with the doctors, "hearing them, and asking them questions" [Luke 2:46]. The phrasing is significant, as it implies the autonomy of the university. The Christian dialectic which resolves the world into a heaven and a hell was established during the temptation, when Jesus saw the form of "this world" offered him by Satan as hell, and thereby broke it off eternally from his own kingdom. The church itself of course was born in the moment when the first man recognized him as the Son of God. All three belong to "revelation," a word which replaces the idea of novelty with the idea of a manifestation of what is present but veiled.

The Christian church, so far as it is a social institution, is distinct from the university, the world, and the city of God, though it is present in all three, and has their unification as its chief function. The difference between the Catholic and the Reformed conceptions of the church naturally complicates the issue. For Newman, the idea of the university is a Catholic idea, one which grew up during the vast synthesis of creative and temporal life achieved by the church in the Middle Ages. In a Catholic university theology, the study of the revelation of one God, forms the objective centre of human knowledge, and the student possesses a corresponding subjective centre in his own mind. In the world, the student is at once faced with the Christian dialectic. Either he must remain attached to the objective centre in the Catholic church, or be left with a self-centred culture, which, as it cannot avoid being a work of pride, must insensibly drift toward the society of power. Newman's example of demonic culture, the correct one, is Julian the Apostate, the divine Caesar and the prototype of Antichrist.

I do not know that anyone has attempted to outline the idea of a Protestant university, but the Protestant subordination of the church to the Word of God makes the university, both as an institution and as the totality of education and culture, much less a function of the church. As long as the church listens to a Word of God distinct from itself, culture will always have a potentially prophetic office, and the Word may emerge from a destructive critic of the church as easily as from Balaam's ass. The classical statement of the principle of toleration which this implies for Protestantism is Milton's *Areopagitica*. As the Word of God is infinite and man's understanding of it finite, any kind of metamorphosis may be involved in human mental processes. That is why there are so many enigmas in Scripture: as Paul says, we now see in a riddle [1 Corinthians 13:12]. The questions of Job are not directly answered, for an answer to a question consolidates the mental level on which it is asked, and revelation tries rather to raise the asker's mind to a level at which he can see that his question was unmeaning.

Newman staked his Catholicism on the principle of an evolutionary unfolding of revelation to man which excludes the possibility of a revolutionary transformation of the church.[4] For him theology is a science, and all sciences develop legally like Whig liberalism, broadening down from precedent to precedent. But actually sciences leap from one mental world to another, and no student of physics can go from Newton to Planck without a metamorphosis or reformation of the mind. The Reformation proper implies the same principle in theology: a principle which is essentially distinct from its historical projection as a movement from the old to the new, and has nothing to do with a temporal progress of revelation.

Newman reflects the synthetic pattern of Catholic and especially medieval thinking, which takes the truths of revelation as major premises and moves deductively toward a broadening intellectual vision of the orders of grace and nature. The Protestant approach has much in common with the inductive and empiric techniques of modern science, in which the scientist subjects himself directly to the impact of nature, as the church subjects itself directly to the impact of Scripture. Induction is not a pure logic, and its hypotheses and axioms are always capable of restatement: their truth is not thereby negated, but reformed. Every rational synthesis, whether it involves revelation or not, must decline when the virtue goes out of the "all too human" connective tissue of the reasoning. Descartes' "I think, therefore I am"[5] will unite thinking and being only so long as the mind responds to the cogency of the word "therefore" in that context.

The same emphasis on deductive progress in the Catholic church appears in its relation to the world. By making the papal supremacy a point of doctrine, it comes very close to Plato's argument that the society which is according to the pattern laid up in heaven is the ideal or spiritual form of the society of power. The Catholic church is, of course, far better equipped than Plato was to distinguish this spiritual form from the society of power itself. Yet it was never more socially effective than when Western Europe had developed a pyramidal structure closely parallel to its own over which it could claim authority. The Holy Roman Empire is the only intelligible form of what some confused people today call "Christian civilization." Catholic action is revolutionary but not empirically so: the essential revolutionary act having happened once for all, its social strategy, like its conception of reason, is directed toward the realizing of a fixed pattern of revealed vision.

A revolutionary attempt to establish once for all the kingdom of *man* on earth, without reference to God, would have to take the form of an atheistic parody of the Catholic church. This principle explains most of the phenomena of modern Communism, though the theoretical statement of it is clearer in Comte and Proudhon, who were brought up Catholics, than in Marx. Postponing its original apostolic hope of a Parousia, Communism has built up a pyramidal structure of authority which uses the writings of Marx, Engels, and Lenin as a canon of revelation. The central authority alone is entrusted with the evolution of doctrine and with the direction of social strategy, the theory and practice of Marxism, as of Christian theology, being inseparable. As the example of Jugoslavia shows, the refusal to acknowledge the supremacy of Moscow is schismatic and heretical. A deductive approach to knowledge has also made its appearance. In a party-line speech on the recent genetics controversy, for instance, I find a curious neo-scholastic method of arguing: the speaker first proves the correct attitude to genetics out of Marx and Engels, and then asserts that this attitude will be found to fit the facts when the facts are examined.[6] In the controversy with Trotsky Communism has in effect declared the doctrine of an anarchist classless society superseding the proletarian dictatorship to be a heresy, as Catholicism (though with less inconsistency) condemned the corresponding doctrine in Joachim of Fiore.

Just as the Protestant church subordinates itself to the impact of Scripture, so in temporal matters it subordinates itself to the "higher powers," without claiming temporal authority. This renunciation extrudes the society of power from the church itself, which thereupon builds itself up on the pattern of Christian liberty, forming an apostolic community in which members are made free and equal by their faith. Temporal authority must then come to terms with this free and equal community in its midst. The divine right of kings and the inscrutable inspiration of dictators clearly show up, in contrast to such a community, as Caesarian attempts to seize the things that are God's. Eventually it becomes clear that all autonomous temporal authority must be irresponsible, for if it were responsible to the community it would be delegated, and if it were responsible to God it would be spiritual authority. The liberal axiom, "all power corrupts, and absolute power corrupts absolutely," means that every holder of autonomous power is an Achan, keeping for his own use something that ought first to be surrendered to the community, then given by the community to God [Joshua 7:18–21]. The axiom was formulated by a Catholic:[7] in Protestantism it is clarified by the renunciation of the principle and claim of temporal authority from the church itself. The social dialectic of the Reformed church thus, when logically carried out, tends to make the "higher powers" wither away and society as a whole to fall in with its own pattern of a free and equal society. To sum up this part of our argument, the relationship of Protestantism, liberal democracy, and inductive science rests, like the relationship of Catholicism, the Holy Roman Empire, and Aristotelian logic, on something much more solid than mere analogy.

With the word "liberal" we reach an area in which the opponents of Protestantism move with much more assurance than its defenders. Is it not precisely an alliance with liberalism that has infected Protestantism with all the distempers and peccant humours of modern thought? Surely to see Protestantism as liberal is to admit the force of the "butter-slide" argument, that Catholicism and atheism are the only logical positions, and that the Protestant can only slither down the intervening stages of Reformed theology, the Broad church, emotional pietism, Deism, and ethical rationalism, and try to decide which one he will stop at. Even so, he will be troubled by the lesser dialectic between a liberalism which is afraid of theology, and so is merely secular, and a theology which is afraid of liberalism, and so is merely obscurantist. If this is really the Protestant's dilemma, then Protestantism has been left far behind by the march of history, like the empty jar that Alice put on a shelf while she was falling from one world to another.[8]

There are many answers to this, of course: we are concerned with the social one. It should be realized that Protestantism, like Catholicism, has had to struggle with a sacrilegious parody of itself, a struggle far harder to get one's bearings in than the other. This parody is best described as laissez-faire, the industrial anarchism which represents the doctrine of individual liberty transferred from the society of love to the society of power.

After benefiting greatly from capitalism as long as it was dissolving the concretions of feudal authority, Protestantism was considerably baffled when it turned demonic with the Industrial Revolution. The uninhibited grabbing of corruptible possessions, conceived not as a perennial fact of human nature but as a programme of human action, is the first open defiance of law and Gospel in modern history, for even the revolutionary Deism which preceded it made moral ideals out of Christian conceptions. As Ruskin points out in his trenchant polemic *Unto This Last*, the merchant under laissez-faire, unlike professional men, has no "calling," no antecedent social reason for his existence.[9] Hence he cannot make any sacrifice of his natural will. From this fact two great fallacies designed to rationalize laissez-faire have originated. One, which goes back to Rousseau, is the conception of the "rights of man" as identical with the natural will of man. The other is the conception of history as the working out of the will of the natural society. The latter is sometimes called social Darwinism, because it misapplies Darwin's biological theory to history, and presents us with a vision of historical progress through the survival of the fit, the fit being those who fit the progress of laissez-faire by the possession of an unusually strong lust for power and profits. These two major fallacies have spawned a fruitful brood of minor ones, which we should take care, in talking about "liberalism," to distinguish from those which are essential to a coherent Christian outlook.

The defences of laissez-faire offered today usually assume that the political form of it is democracy. This is nonsense: its political form is an oligarchic dictatorship. Every amelioration of labour conditions, every limitation of the power of monopolies, every effort to make the oligarchy responsible to the community as a whole, has been forced out of laissez-faire by democracy, which has played a consistently revolutionary role against it. The Russians today interpret laissez-faire precisely as we do Communism, as a unified conspiracy to conquer the world emanating from a single nation, America having disposed of or absorbed all its rivals. We may feel that this is considerably oversimplified for propaganda purposes, that democracy in America has the oligarchy too well in hand to permit a repetition of the bid for power that produced Hitler. We may even feel that the Marxist ideal of the withering away of the state is closer to realization in America, for all the forces working against it, than it will ever be under Communism in Russia. Nevertheless, the Russian case contains part of the truth, even if it is the part that we prefer not to look at. The fear of the Russian people for America is a real fear with a real basis. It may however not be honestly shared by their rulers. It is good Marxist doctrine that despots are often inspired by the fear of their own subjects to make common cause with tyranny in other countries, and two anti-Russian Marxists may be cited as having raised this point. The essential identity of interest between the tendency to dictatorship in America and the achievement of it in Russia has been stated, though with some distortion of emphasis, in James Burnham's well known book, *The Managerial Revolution*. How such a revolution could make its power absolute and permanent by a not-too-lethal form of permanent war is shown with great clarity in George Orwell's terrible satire *1984*, perhaps the definitive contemporary vision of hell.

The mutual infiltration of laissez-faire and democracy has not only confused the church, but caused democracy to turn for much of its inspiration to the secularism of its opponent. In this situation, all that the church can immediately do is to keep on insisting that there is no liberty except Christian liberty, and that a secular belief in human freedom is a contradiction in terms. Secularism cannot distinguish the natural from the regenerate will, and the natural man cannot desire freedom: he can only desire mastery. Failing mastery, he will sink into a narcotic isolation of the natural self, and will give the name of freedom to a querulous plea to have his natural desires left alone. Failing that, he will achieve mastery vicariously, by a glad and eager acceptance of slavery. These three natural distortions of freedom produce respectively the dictatorial, bourgeois, and proletarian versions of the City of God. It is an error to assume that slavery implies drabness: the true slave of the state is inspired by a total will, and in wars, parades, public trials, and everything which gives a militant interpretation to life he sees the splendour and glamour of that total will made manifest. Here is the kingdom of heat without light, with a pleasant sense of dramatic torment continually going on. It is all to end very soon, of course—but it can never end, for the coming of real peace would putrefy and decompose it. There is in the world however a powerful will toward genuine freedom, which is ready to accept the responsibility and co-operation involved in freedom, and which would welcome permanent peace as a release of spiritual energy. Such genuine freedom comes chiefly from the Christianity that is still seeping through our educational and cultural traditions by a kind of osmosis.

This last statement will seem a frantic paradox to those who are accustomed to think of Christian spokesmen as a brake on social progress, continually squealing that the pace is too fast. Of course the real dynamic of democracy is not progressive but experimental, but the belief in progress owes much to anti-clericalism. The world has been so often denounced by the church on obviously interested or superstitious grounds that it has come to feel, like a restless adolescent, that whatever its spiritual fathers object to most loudly is probably the "advanced" thing to do. This is regrettable, but the church has done a good deal to earn its reputation for "cultural lag." It has wasted its energies in an inglorious rearguard action against the incidental vices of bourgeois life in which it shows a chronic inability to distinguish cause from effect in moral evil. It has alienated many who are longing to sink their instinct for human decency into the Christian vision of love which produced it, but who find the shallow pruderies of the church a profitless exchange for the shallow bigotries of the world. It is a curious paradox in Christianity that the more worldly the church becomes, the more quickly it loses its urbanity. Far too much of the social influence of Christianity today is due to God's ability to use other instruments when those which should be nearest him are blunt and rusty.

The third great religion of the Bible has also thrown a demonic shadow into the society of power. Judaism is based on the conception of an elect people of God united with him in a covenant of blood. Take God away from this covenant, and the result is Nazism, which is why, though of course it persecuted Christians, Nazism found in the Jew the chief symbol of its mania. We are now witnessing Communism's bid for power, which, though of course it persecutes Protestants, finds its central foe in the Catholic church. A human covenant of blood leads to a war of blood, but Communism, unlike Nazism, does not regard war as an end in itself, and the current struggle takes the form of a "cold war." It may of course become a war of blood, but such a war would be, not a hideous necessity like the war against Hitler, but a hideous accident. How hideous, it is unnecessary to say: the facts seem to be impressive even to the awful frivolity of man.

The Nazi attempt to exterminate the Jews met the same fate as the earlier attempt recorded in the Book of Exodus: plagues, the destruction of armies, and the independence of Palestine. The present struggle can hardly fail to strengthen the prestige of the Catholic (not necessarily only the Roman Catholic) idea throughout the world, and in fact has already done so. But Catholicism apparently still follows the strategy of consolidating the temporal order into a subordinate structure of authority, and such action must always work toward a revived Holy Roman Empire, a future autocracy of which the various clerically-supported Fascist movements of recent years are a portent. So the possibility of a third struggle between managerial dictatorship and democracy, with Protestantism supplying the vision for the blind good will of the latter, looms up already in the background. Such a conflict, however ferocious, could hardly be either a genocidal war or a war of excommunications, but would have to be primarily evangelical and prophetic.

Forecasts of the future are beyond our scope: the above is not offered as prophecy but as an indication of the scale on which the Reformed churches today might well be conceiving their social mission. The church has been tempted by the world to present its faith as an obstinate reiteration of traditional myths, insisting in the teeth of all natural law that they are facts, and defying the advance of science as a dog howls at the rising moon. It must learn again to present its faith as the emancipation and the fulfilment of reason. It has been tempted by the world to condemn human liberty as an illicit encroachment on the divine prerogative. It must learn to explain once more how it is God's will that man should be free. But it may well be that the church is nearing the end of its period of temptation: if so, it can enter upon its ministry anew, coming among men eating and drinking, making friends with publicans and sinners, insisting that thieves get out of its temple, ridiculing hypocrites and helping the blind to see, befriending Lazarus and warning Dives [cf. Luke 16:19–31], going about doing good and turning the world upside down.

20

Man and the Sabbath

February 1950

From Canadian Forum, *29 (February 1950): 241, 245.*

A plebiscite on the legalizing of Sunday sports was the most controversial and highly publicized issue in the recent municipal elections in
Toronto, and the results have a significance not confined to that city.
The Protestant churches seemed to take the issue as a test case of their
social influence, and brought all the pressure they could to persuade
their flocks to vote "no." Cardinal McGuigan also came out on the "no"
side. Two Toronto papers which seemed inclined to support the question promptly went "no" too (the third one, the *Star*, remained firm in
its conviction that the Toronto Sunday should never be profaned by
anything more secular than the *Toronto Star Weekly*). Hardly a single
candidate for office, except one controller who had more or less stuck
his neck out on the subject, dared to say that he was anything but unalterably opposed to Sunday sport. In addition, the wording of the
proposal was so loaded as to make it, if not impossible, at least illogical,
for many voters to vote for it and in accordance with their consciences
as well. Nothing remained but to roll up a thumping "no" majority.
The vote went the other way. The "yes" majority was not large, but
considering the circumstances it amounted to a decisive rejection of
clerical advice on the part of the electorate.

This result tends to confirm the general correctness of Professor
Hart's thesis[1] in relation to Windsor, where the Sunday sport question
went "yes" by a two-to-one vote. A modern industrial town tends to
become increasingly secularized and to find its social and moral sanc-
tions in, say, the labour hall rather than in the churches. But this is not

the whole story. Toronto municipal voters are largely a middle-class tax-paying group, and it is extremely unlikely that all or even the great majority of "yes" voters were entirely outside all Christian communions. If the vote means anything, it surely means something like this: people are increasingly unable to believe in the disinterestedness of the churches, or in their ability to distinguish a moral issue from one that merely appears to threaten their social and economic position. That the churches are spending far too much of their energies in an inglorious rearguard action against the incidental vices of society; that they cannot distinguish cause from effect in social evil; that they have not only tended to retreat into the propertied middle class, but are no longer coming to grips with the real needs even of that class. This is clearly the attitude, or something like the attitude, implied in the Toronto vote. It may be utterly wrong; but an institution committed to humility and self-examination cannot afford to underestimate or disregard the good faith of its critics.

21

The Analogy of Democracy

February 1952

From Bias *(Student Christian Movement of Canada), 1, no. 2 (February 1952):*
2–6. Reprinted in RW, *219–28.*

One difficulty about defining the word "democracy" is that it is not the
name of a specific form of government, like republic or monarchy. It
represents, rather, an informing idea, a process which, because it has
developed out of the past, is traditional, and, because it is moving
toward a future goal, revolutionary. It is to Dean Acheson that we owe
one of the decisive statements about our own time: that democracy is
the central revolutionary force now transforming the world, and that
the tactics of Communism represent (to use a Communist term) a deviation from the real revolution.[1] Thus democracy is to be judged, not by
what it does, but by what it aims at in spite of what it does. The supremacy of civil over military power, the full publication of all acts of government, the toleration of unpopular opinion, are all recognized to be
unchangeable principles of democracy even when they are flouted as
often as exemplified. Further, any feature of democracy which is nothing more than a safeguard designed to prevent the democratic process
from congealing at a certain stage in its development may disappear
when democracy passes that stage. We may find that even such apparently essential things as a two-party system of parliamentary government may so disappear. On the other hand, the fact that democracy is
not in itself a form of government makes it possible for it to adapt itself
to a wide variety of such forms. If the United States decided to adopt a
soviet system or, as in Bernard Shaw's *The Apple-Cart*, to recognize

George VI as their king, the move might be inadvisable, but it would not be in itself a threat to democracy.

Once democracy is recognized to be a process and not a form of government, its relation to human history can be more clearly seen. It is basically an attempt to realize the form of community appropriate to man at the stage at which he has discovered and explored his entire planet and has, with the Industrial Revolution, developed a technique of increasing or modifying his productivity at will. This form of community supersedes the older idea of the "state," which was founded on two principles: a sharp division between a ruling and a ruled class, and an equally sharp definition of the boundaries of the former's rule. Democracy is anarchistic in the sense that it is an attempt to destroy the state by replacing it with an expanding federation of communities, a federation which reaches its limit only in a worldwide federation. Thus while economic laissez-faire, the vast empires it built up, and the world wars it caused were certainly antidemocratic in themselves, they seem to have been part of the growth of democracy in its aspect of a devourer of states.

It is permissible to say that democracy represents the present stage in the evolution of human society. But we should not give to the word "evolution" any Darwinian overtones of a process throwing out experiments at random until it finally achieves the appropriate mutation of species. The form of human community envisaged by democracy is not new: it is the real form of human community which has been with us since the beginning of history, obscured by human weakness, ignorance, passion, and greed. It is, in short, natural society, and it has always been an axiom in human thought that the natural is the reasonable, the simplicity that the mind seeks in the complexities of experience. Democracy has for long been influenced by Rousseau's theory of a natural society buried under history, but we have moved a long way from Rousseau's primitivism and its assumption that man's lost birthright is his own nature. Man's nature, as we can see now, is expressed in his institutions; it is not his nature but his destiny that may be good. And democracy also offers the hope that Marxism offered and appears now to be betraying: the hope of putting an end to history as we know it, the record of the oppression of the ruled interrupted by the lethal quarrelling of the rulers. When Stephen Dedalus, in Joyce's *Ulysses*, speaks of history as a nightmare from which he is trying to awake,[2] he speaks for all modern men.

When the reason attempts to articulate the structure of the natural society, it produces law. And democracy is so bound to law that we can practically say that the fulfilment of democracy would be a kind of epiphany of law. We do not think of law now as an automatically self-articulating force that makes freedom in Tennyson's poem broaden slowly from precedent to precedent.[3] We tend to think of it more existentially, as a dialectic that, in each crisis of social conflict, defines the legal relations of both contenders. Thus democracy attempts to contain its class conflicts in a system of legal machinery. It tries to contain its conflict of political opinion in a parliament, in contrast to the state which expresses the will of the ruler and defines everything else as conspiracy or treason. It tries to contain its labour disputes in legal settlement, in contrast to the Communist conception of the labour dispute as an episode in a class war. It tries to embody social service in legislation, in contrast to the impulsive giving of alms to the poor by the rich out of their abundance. It is now struggling to break up the conception of law as confined to the state, which we have had ever since the days of Grotius, and to arrive at an international conception of law which will make a war between France and Germany as impossible as a war between Nebraska and Iowa would be now.

In saying this we are not expressing any "belief in law," which would be a semantic absurdity. Law is not a force by itself, and certainly not a creative or a regenerating force. It merely says what the relationships within a society are, and, in relation to democracy, it defines the progress democracy has made in realizing itself. It has, it is true, a stabilizing effect on the behaviour of society in time: we legislate, as Burke said, for the dead, the living, and the unborn,[4] and hence law helps to make revolutions accord with tradition and to make tradition itself a revolutionary force. But in itself it merely shows man what his present social strength is, and he derives that strength from other sources. At the same time the ability to express that strength in law confers an enormous prestige: if we get through our present situation without a third world war, it will be partly because man is more afraid of being illegal than of being wicked. The present theory of democracy owes much to the radicals of the previous century who insisted on the illegal structure of the state: who pointed out that hereditary privilege was usurpation, that the making of profits from labour was theft, that war was murder, and that what was called "charity" was about as close to St. Paul's *agape* [1 Corinthians 13] as paying for the protection of a racketeer. Democracy seems in fact to have benefited much more from such radicalism than the Communism which claims to be its more direct descendant.

This slowly consolidating body of law tends to define the responsibilities of each member of society. The dialectic of democracy works against the position of general leadership. We have not yet come to the stage at which we can dispense with the pyramidal structure of society which we have inherited from the state. We still feel the need of a titular top position, whether king, president, or premier, to make society look unified, and there is still a great clamour for "leadership," both in politics and in the theory of education. The clamour reflects the present embattled state of the democracies and of their consequent assimilation to a military hierarchy. The latter is the essential form of the state, and is therefore always pyramidal. The absence of strong leaders is one of the signs of a healthily functioning democracy, and indicates that society is attaining a more mature form of mutual responsibility.

We may note in passing that the view of human nature implied by democracy is a secular form of the conception of original sin. It assumes that man, whether good or bad by nature, is in no case to be entrusted with secret or autonomous power, because the possession of such power is certain to corrupt both the holder of it and his society. The conception of power is in fact one which the dialectic of democracy tends to eliminate from social relationships, including the power of the people or the community as a whole. A government controlled by the will of the people alone is as great a tyranny as any other social order founded on unconditioned will. The doctrine of majority rule was, it is true, essential to democracy while it was shaking off the better organized despotism of minority rule. But with the rise of the social sciences and a growing permanent civil service, it is possible that we may be developing a self-controlling administrative structure which will be able to dispense with much of the cumbersome and badly run apparatus of appeals to majority power. Voting for grossly oversimplified issues, and electing representatives who are controlled by a party machine and not by their electors, are safeguards which in time to come may be as outmoded as the dinosaur or the dictator. The gloomy axiom that the price of liberty is eternal vigilance is no doubt a sound one, but it should not imply that there is no solid progressive achievement of liberties, of a kind that makes certain kinds of vigilance unnecessary.

When we look at democracy as a social process, taking into account what it has done, is doing, and appears to aim at, we can see that many popular ideas about its nature need re-examining. The belief, still held by many Americans, that laissez-faire is the economic basis of democracy is clearly nonsense. Laissez-faire, the negative answer to the question of Cain,[5] is a conception of society which regards it as an amorphous aggregate of individuals. Its ideas of welfare are subjective, charity-denying ideas, and the dialectic of its development is towards managerial dictatorship. Militant democracy in the last century has worked mainly through labour movements, and at present all democratic political parties are largely agreed that democracy is moving away from pure laissez-faire: they differ only in their estimates of how far and how fast the movement should be. Again, the notion that democracy implies an optimistic view of human nature, or assumes that man is capable of self-perfection, can hardly be proved from a theory of politics which gives a primary place to continuous opposition, criticism, and reform. The dynamic of democracy, and the basis of its hope, is not that man is good, but that neither men nor their institutions are ever as good as they could and should be.

The more one thinks of what democracy aspires to, the more one feels that it is based, not so much on the assumption that man is entitled to life, liberty, and the pursuit of happiness, as on a far profounder vision, one that may be expressed as "let's see what happens when we start organizing society on the assumption that we are all members of one body." The vision itself is so deeply charitable that we have long passed the stage at which we can simply say that a religion is not to be judged by the quality of its political influence. People attached to churches often speak of political issues as though the church were withdrawn from the world, waiting for the world to offer it various theories of government and then inspecting them in order to decide whether they are compatible with Christianity or not. No such remoteness exists. Members of the church are in the world from the start: their secular passions and prejudices inform and shape their conceptions of religion at every point: to be persistently wrong about the contemporary world is a theological error. We have reached the stage in democratic development at which we can roundly say that if any twentieth-century Christian sincerely repudiates what democracy stands for, there is something radically the matter with his Christianity.

I suggest, then, that the ultimate aim of democracy is to reach what is not only natural society, but a secular analogy of Christianity. The church is a community whose members are made free and equal by their faith. It is ordered by its Master to take society as it finds it, to render to Caesar what is Caesar's [Matthew 22:21]. This of course excludes the worship of Caesar as a divine being, which is one of the things that the Caesars of this world are most interested in, and Caesar finds other difficulties in trying to digest this free and equal community in his pyramidal state. To the extent that it obeys the command not to resist evil, the church's social dialectic works towards compelling the whole social order to fall into a pattern analogous to its own. This triumph of the church in manifesting its Master's victory over the world is the real meaning of the democratic revolution of today.

Many members of the church do not want this kind of victory: they want to see society reflect, not the shape of the church, but the particular social and moral rituals which they attach to their life in the church. Hence they are dismayed when they find that the present dynamic of democracy seems to be so largely a secular one. It looks, however, as though the secular basis of a Christian society has to be established by secular power, and the willingness to grant some measure of moral autonomy to that power is the contemporary form of rendering to Caesar what is Caesar's. The church can mediate between the Gospel and the law only after they have been clearly separated. Failure to separate them is Pharisaism, the legalized bastard gospel. When we look at the way the church uses its social energy and influence, in crusades against liquor, divorce, birth control, church absenteeism, and the like, we can hardly be reassured about the courage, wisdom, or effectiveness of the church's approach to society. The secular approach to such problems often seems very much wiser. This is not preferring the world to the church: it is preferring the self-criticism of the publican to the frivolous certainties of the Pharisee. In the first thousand years of the church's existence as a social power, church and world both discovered a good deal about the evils resulting from the temporal power of the church. In the last few centuries they have discovered a good deal about the evils resulting from the spiritual power of the state. They would do well not to forget either fact. Yet it is clear that without some measure of temporal authority in the church, medieval civilization would have been a pretty ramshackle edifice. And it is hardly reasonable to deny that without the influence of secular ideals, the modern world would be far worse off than it is. I have read the writings of many prominent intellectuals who have gone through well publicized conversions to religious authority, and I have been amused to notice how their apologetics so often take the form of justifying the church by the quality of its worldliness.

There is a crucial difficulty here. Law is the expression of temporal authority; justice is law informed by the vision of freedom and equality; the vision of freedom and equality is a steady vision only within the Christian church. Outside the church it is only a vague hope or a fitful glimpse afforded by the lucky chance of a good ruler. Nobody with the slightest understanding of Christianity denies the central and primary place of charity, of letting the light of the Christian vision shine before men. Then why is so much of the social influence of the church today Pharisaic rather than Christian? Why does it seem to have more appeal to those who are looking for a masochistic surrender to an external authority than to those who are looking for something to fulfil and emancipate the secular vision?

I think that the answer, if there is an answer, is to be found in the democratic conception of culture, which is also its conception of individual freedom. The classical statement of this is in Mill's essay *On Liberty*. A mature society, Mill says, has outgrown the kind of fetishism that is obsessed by social rituals. Hence it is willing to tolerate a large amount of eccentricity, which may be defined as individuality expressing itself in harmless, though as far as we can see socially unproductive, behaviour. Such toleration is of more importance to society than it sounds, for it enables the individual, who qua individual is always eccentric, to live in society without a sense of claustrophobia. But on higher levels individual freedom is primarily the possession of culture. Mill distinguishes freedom of thought from freedom of action: the former should be limited only by the individual's desire to find truth rather than falsehood; the latter may be limited more sharply by the need of society to preserve its balance. The point is that to permit freedom of thought is to curtail freedom of action, as it tends to eliminate spasmodic, impulsive, unthought-out action.

The area of free discussion in society is, though Mill does not say so, the real "idea of the university" in the modern democratic world. Toleration is essential to it, not because one guess at the truth is as good as another, but because the whole truth about anything is far beyond the limits of the comprehension either of an individual or of an institution. Every synthesis of human thought, however catholic, is a tentative synthesis; its facts and postulates may be sound, but the cohering force of the synthesis is always a fiction. "I think, therefore I am"[6]—where does

Descartes get his "therefore"? He gets it from an intense desire to derive existence from consciousness, and the sources of that desire lie deep in the social structure of his age. As long as the desire is effective, the logic of the "therefore" will be cogent, but no longer.

Hence in every aspect of human thought we find, not a continuously aggregating body of facts continuously increasing the same kind of comprehension, but revolutions in human comprehension itself. Many incautious utterances could be collected in the history of scholarship, boasting of a nearly complete knowledge of some subject that a few years later was transformed out of recognition by a complete mental reorganization. This has happened to physics several times; astronomers construct and blow up new universes as children do balloons. For a time theology tried to scramble along after them, producing from the horse of science and the jackass of natural theology that curious sterile mule of modern rationalism, an apology for Christianity founded on conceptions of entropy and laws of thermodynamics. But it has given up, and a new approach is clearly in order.

The basis of Christian faith is revelation and the acceptance of the Word of God as that revelation. To identify the Word of God with the person of Christ is faith; to accommodate revelation to the operations of the human reason is a part of charity; to deify the logical structures erected by the human mind in making that accommodation is only idolatry. The reception of an infinite revelation by a finite mind is surely one that ought to create intellectual humility in the latter. When revelation is the basis of reason, the basis is sound; but the connective tissue of the reasoning is as mortal as the thinker. That is why the church has to separate itself from the Word of God, listen to it and not to its present understanding of it, relax its prejudices, fears, preconceptions, jealousies, and habitual axioms, and catch again the still small voice [cf. 1 Kings 19:12]. The church has the power to save the world when it is itself saved, and the saving power will work largely outside it until it is.

22

At a Memorial Service for Deceased Students

January 1963

From the typescript in NFF, 1992, box 3, file 1. As Frye indicated in his year-end report in Victoria Reports, *13 (May 1963), four undergraduate students died suddenly and unexpectedly during the term: Gene Packman, Brian Bower, Kurt Nitchke, and Edith Okany.*

At the approach of death we turn to thee, the Holy Spirit of the living God. The inheritance of fear stirs in our minds: at the death of the young we feel shock and outrage; at the cutting off of lives full of promise we ask angry questions; at violent separation we are bewildered. We feel that there has been an unjust choice, even though we know that there is no choice: that all must enter the dark at a decreed time. But thou art the giver of life, and thy gifts are not given in vain. For many generations the young have mocked at danger and death, and however thoughtlessly, they have borne witness as they did so to the victory of thy Resurrection. Through all the cruelty of nature and the malice of man, we hear the exultant song of the life that knows no death: the hymns of thy angels sound in the ruins of our cities: thy eternal purpose shapes to thy will all the destruction that our folly can invent or our fury unloose.

Thou hast blessed those who mourn, and we mourn only for ourselves, and for our loss. We do not ask about those who are gone before us into thy city of light, and thy apostle has instructed us that we are fools when we ask, for our questions are born of the uncomprehending darkness. We know only that it is well with them; that if our lives are the poorer, thy kingdom is the richer. Thy kingdom is our birthright also, and with the loss of those we love, we think less of our own lives, for we move a step nearer to our own inheritance. Without such loss, without the deeper knowledge brought by suffering, we should feel that our broad highway to death was the only path. But in the valley of the shadow we know that thou art with us.

Among those who go before us there is no difference of faith, for their faith is now a vision. Their hope is now a certainty, and there is no shadow of wistfulness upon it. Their love for others they now see to be thy love for them. We neither can nor would recall them to this world of death: neither do we ourselves long for death: we long for thy presence, and in thy presence there is no death. May the light of thy kingdom shine through us as we commit our comrades to thy care and turn again to the tasks that are thy will for us.

23

Baccalaureate Sermon

19 March 1967

From Victoria Reports, *17 (April 1967): 3–10. Originally given as a sermon to the graduating classes of 1967 of Victoria and Emmanuel Colleges, in the Victoria College Chapel. Reprinted in* RW, *243–50.*

> Take therefore no thought for the morrow; for the morrow shall take thought for the things of itself. [Matthew 6:34]

The baccalaureate sermon is traditionally the one occasion when a church-related college speaks to its students in the name of the church. The assumption underlying it is that every important crisis of your life is at bottom a religious crisis. It is only what the Spinks Report calls a "sectarian college"[1] that can tell you that; you cannot learn it from a purely secular institution. The advantages of being an agnostic are obvious: one does not have to pretend that one knows things that in fact one does not know. But the advantage of speaking from the pulpit of a "sectarian college" is that I do not have to pretend, out of politeness, to be ignorant of a number of things that I know perfectly well. I do not know, nor in this context do I much care, whether or not you believe in the saving or losing of the soul, in the indwelling of a divine presence in man, in heaven and hell, or whether you realize that the human situation is a debased form of the human inheritance. But I do know that you will experience the truth of these things, in fact have already experienced it. Perhaps that is what the New Testament means by faith: knowing what it really is that one is experiencing.

The usual cliché of graduation oratory used to be that you have now completed your preparatory studies and are going out to deal with the world. I always resented this line when I was a student, and it seems even more incompetent to me today. In the first place, you are now fully participating in society, not preparing for something else more important. Nothing is going to happen to you which is more important than what has happened. In the second place, you are not going anywhere else: you are merely re-entering the world of education. Still, this is a time when you are thinking very deeply about the future and about the rest of your life, so why should I choose so perverse a text as "take no thought for the morrow"? Does this mean that you should never look forward to anything, never take out insurance, never plan your future career? I don't think it means any of these things, but if you have ever read, or seen on the stage, Beckett's play *Waiting for Godot*, you should have a clue to what it does mean. What you are being warned against is emptying your present life of all real meaning by throwing everything on the future. The characters in that play are not living; they are merely putting in time waiting for a certain Godot to arrive. He never comes, and the audience realizes that he never can or will come, at least not in that form, and that they are wasting their lives for nothing.

To take a deliberately crude example: consider the man who thinks he will lead a gay and carefree life filled with wine, women, and song, if he can only make enough money to retire. Thirty years later he has made the money, but has also acquired a heart condition and high blood pressure and other impediments to the gay and carefree life, and perhaps he would have done better to have filled his life as he went along with less expensive pleasures. Or again, consider the man who sacrifices his life so that his children will have all the things that he has not had. He assumes that his children will want these things as he wants them to have them, but perhaps the children will grow up to repudiate his values; or they may accept them and feel that their lives have been warped and stunted in consequence. There even used to be a version, or perversion, of Christianity which asserted that real life began after death. This is not much in fashion now, but in its day it doubtless encouraged some people to die without ever having come alive. Again, whenever we are at war, a donkey's carrot is always held out to us: as soon as we have won the war, we shall make the world safe for democracy, abolish poverty, and do all sorts of wonderful things. The war stops, but there is still just one temporary and regrettable necessity to be got over first before we enjoy our millennium; and our political leaders trust that our short memories and distracted attentions will not notice that the series of temporary and regrettable necessities never comes to an end.

The text is not saying that you should have no ambitions, but it does imply that you should be very careful what they are. The things you now most deeply desire you will in all probability get, and they will look very different once got. Jesus is recommending, as you see, a considerable amount of disillusionment. I can never understand why people should think of disillusionment as something that makes one sad and doleful: surely living in an illusion is the greatest of torments, and becoming disillusioned ought to feel like being let out of jail. This is true even of pleasant futures: I have so far said nothing about futures that we contemplate with anxiety and dread, and which empty the present moment far more completely. The most terrible revenge that society can take on anyone is to sentence him to be hanged six months after the date of sentence. The terror is not so much in being hanged as in having to spend six months in hell. Today is Palm Sunday, and the story of Palm Sunday [John 12:12–36] tells how Jesus rode in triumph into Jerusalem among the plaudits of a crowd he knew would be shrieking for his death before the week was out. A man with any pride would have been ashamed to accept the homage of so fickle a crowd: but Jesus accepted the homage because it was right at that moment, however wrong the people who offered it were going to be in a few days. That was not taking thought for the morrow, on a level of detachment that you and I would hardly be capable of; perhaps if we were capable of it we could save the world.

It is, however, more subtle and insidious forms of taking thought for the morrow that I want to call particularly to your attention. You can already see how wrong it would be for me to tell you merely that this is a time of rapid change, that the world you are in would have been inconceivable a hundred years ago, and that it will change still more drastically in the next century. If I were merely to try to inspire you with a queasy dread of an unknown future, I should only be telling you to wait for Godot. It is more important to realize that we live our lives on different levels, and that whatever changes rapidly is relatively trivial. Moral principles do change, it is true, but they change very slowly, and the moral principles you have now will undoubtedly do you for the rest of your lives. But above moral principles, on a much more superficial level, are all the conventions, vogues, and fashions where there is no standard except general usage. In matters of convention, such as the use of narcotics or cosmetics or the wearing of clothes, what everybody is doing is what is right. If we were to take conventions seriously, we'd say that Victoria College today cannot be the same place as the small Methodist college of fifty years ago, where the conventions were so different. But it is, and the alumni of Victoria who were graduated fifty years ago are living quite contentedly in the world of the 1960s. People with frivolous minds are always trying to blow up matters of convention, like drinking or using "four-letter words" in print, into moral principles, prophesying blue ruin and the end of the world whenever these conventions change. Those who are not capable of faith have to settle for anxieties instead. It is the same kind of people who today are engaged in earnestly discussing those unutterably tedious topics, LSD and the contraceptive pill. Here again we are discovering that a good deal of what some people assume to be moral is really conventional, and, spiritually considered, is not worth a damn, which is a seventeenth-century Dutch coin worth about half a farthing.

The trouble with the frivolous attitude is that it not only tries to make conventions into moral principles, but that it also assumes that moral principles are really conventions. That is, it assumes that murder is wrong only because relatively few people are engaged in committing murders. As soon as society goes to war and murder becomes mass murder, it becomes all right, because everybody is doing it. The youth carrying a sandwich board to protest against the war in Vietnam may have longer hair and looser "morals," or conventions, than President Johnson, but—who knows?—he may hold a higher rank in the Kingdom of Heaven for all that.

Most of us find our balance fairly quickly, and get to be able to distinguish the superficial from the profound. But there is so much in our lives that is superficial that we can't square the past with the present. The continuous and traditional social institutions, like the church and the university, are often urged to get with it, to speak to the modern world in a language that the modern world can understand, or, more frequently, to adapt themselves to the modern world. The trouble is that the modern world has no standards as such: nothing is permanent or lasting in it; it is only a flux, the river of Heraclitus into which nobody steps twice.[2] Perhaps church and university, like moral principles, should change slowly, should keep something archaic about them, something of a voice from another world. A woman of sixty who tries to look like a girl of eighteen not only fails to look like a girl of eighteen, but robs herself of the dignity that ought to belong to her sixty years; and jazz masses and experimental colleges, as soon as they have got established, may begin to look more out of date than the Academy of Plato or the prophecies of Isaiah.

All these are aspects of a problem that is now, for you, beginning to take on a new insistence and prominence. This is the problem of living continuously in society. Children, and adolescents in a different way, relieve the strain of their social lives by retreating periodically into a private and inaccessible world. But as you mature an inseparable social personality begins to form, and you are now entering that part of your lives where you will constantly be under social inspection. Some of you will discover what a classroom or pulpit feels like from the other side, where you are looked at instead of looking. Others of you will be dealing, much more intensively than before, with colleagues and associates, and most of you in any event will be exposed to the steadfast and most relentless gaze of all, the gaze of your own growing children. The strain of "keeping up a front," as we say, is reflected in the amount of emotional disturbance it causes among people who want to return to the private worlds of childhood and youth, sometimes by taking to the bottle for a second time. Most sensible people set up a mechanism for dealing with social life, a mechanism founded mainly on habit and reflex. The fact that it is a mechanism indicates the limits of its importance, and the danger of getting too involved with it.

Our social lives are a contribution to society; consequently, their value or worth is judged by society. In this context, what others think we are is what we are. But you can easily see why wearing a social personality is a strain. Granted a reasonable amount of good will and lack of envy in our society, other people take a more charitable view of us than we can afford to take of ourselves, if we have any honesty about ourselves at all. A man may write a shelf of books and get a reputation as a formidably erudite scholar, but he will know what he knows, and it won't be much. Further, he will not finish his books with any sense of achievement, but only with a feeling that he has once more come 'round to the point at which he can begin again. I often think of the remark of Isaac Newton, made toward the end of his life, which is commemorated on one of these chapel windows: "I do not know how I may appear to the world, but to myself I seem to have been a child playing with stones on a beach, while the great ocean of truth lay all undiscovered before me."[3] That is the kind of detachment that a wise and good man can attain from his own life. Without some measure of such a detachment, we shall make our-selves very miserable, if we try to judge our own lives as a body of things achieved, accomplished, or done. Society is a better judge of what we have done, partly because it knows less. If there is a final or last judgment to be made on our lives, it cannot be made by ourselves, or by our friends, or even by those who love us, who come much closer to it than anyone else. It could only be made by an omniscient but infinitely compassionate being.

What I am saying is that if you look forward to the future, with the expectation of identifying your lives with a definite body of work achieved, you are doomed to the bitterest disappointment. The future is too slippery to rely on: other things over which you have no control frustrate your intentions and twist everything you do into unrecogniz-able shapes. The morrow takes thought for the things of itself. If you go into business, your achievement may be only to adulterate goods and raise prices; if you go into politics, your achievement may be only to compromise your principles and raise taxes. It is much better to detach oneself from the whole notion of achieving anything, leaving that dimension of one's life to others if they are interested.

So if you give up the notion of achieving anything, what else can you do? Well, that's what your education has been about. We have tried to teach you only what can be directly taught, specific knowledge in spe-cific disciplines. But we quite realize that you will remember very little of this specific information three months after you write your examina-tions, unless you have some definite occasion to use it later. What you get from your college education, ultimately, is something that cannot be directly taught. It is really a vision of society, a vision derived from the record of the best that humanity has done: the concepts of philosophy, the imagination of the arts, the accuracy and the discoveries of the sci-ences. This vision is not itself knowledge but a practical wisdom, which you take with you into society, which you apply as a criterion to society, and which is the source of your own expertise and special abilities. This means that what is important about your life is not that you should achieve something, but that you should manifest something. For exam-ple, a social worker does her work with a vision, in her mind, of a more just and equitable, a more adequately privileged, a cleaner and less neu-rotic Toronto than the Toronto she is working in. She does not feed her-self on the delusion that her efforts will bring this better Toronto into existence in the future. But the light of that vision shines through what she does, and it is that light, not the consequences of what she does, that makes her work effective.

In taking this vision of practical wisdom with you, as an educated person, into your social life, you may also have a few glints, a few hints and suggestions, of a greater wisdom still. You can live without this greater wisdom, and perhaps some of you would prefer to do so. But if you want it you can certainly train yourself to recognize it. If I am to speak here for Christianity as well as for a liberal arts college, I have to take one more step.

It is very hard to give up the childish habit of projecting our parents into the universe, and creating there some omnipotent Santa Claus, floating free in space, who will fill our plate with goodies if we only believe in him. Later on, we may start calling this figure by flossier names, like the historical process or the technological revolution or the great society, all aliases of the great Godot who will come without fail tomorrow. But whatever we call him he is still the same dead, stuffed, grinning Santa Claus. A more mature view is to think that if there is any power or intelligence in this absurd world that makes more sense than we do, or than nature does, it can only be a power or intelligence that has entered human life, that works with human instruments under the limitations of the human condition, that suffers with man's humiliation as well as sharing his rare genuine triumphs. And perhaps, as we struggle to apply our education and practical wisdom to society, we may occasionally feel a sense of a Presence which is ourselves yet infinitely bigger than ourselves, which lives with us but will not disappear into death when we do. Such feelings do not come very often, and when they do come there is no guarantee of their validity except in our own subjective and hidden lives. They may come in moments when we feel we have made a difficult and painful but nevertheless right decision, a decision that may even land us in jail or an internment camp—I have had students who have found the meaning of their lives there. Or they may come in moments when we lose someone greatly loved, and feel that nothing so precious can really be totally and forever lost. Whenever they occur, it is in such moments that, as Jesus says, wisdom is justified of her children [Matthew 11:19].

24

Symbols

10 October 1968

From Acta Victoriana, *93 (November 1968): 32–4. A clean typescript is in NFF, 1988, box 2, file pp. Originally given as a brief sermon at a dedicatory service in the Victoria College Chapel.*

I suppose the most primitive sense that we have is the sense of the contrast between light and darkness. There is a visible world of the eye, the world of appearance in the light, and there is a dark world of the ear, where we can see very little, and have to listen intently for sounds, sounds of reassurance or of warning. The Bible begins by telling us that at first everything was dark, and that out of the darkness a word spoke, calling for light. At that point the world in all its visible variety began to burst into being. And so, whenever we look at the visible things in the world, we should remember that their daylight appearance is not their whole reality. Ultimately, they are not things but creatures; that is, they are really symbols, symbols of the creative power that spoke in the dark, before anything appeared.

Perhaps, however, we should start our creation story with man. That means, of course, starting it with alienation and anxiety, man's sense of loneliness in nature. The voice of anxiety, whether in a crying child or in a protesting student, is apt to bring the response, What is it that you want? What does man want? We have no clue except in what it is that he does. He creates societies, builds cities, plants gardens, transports goods, produces works of art: this must be the kind of thing he wants. All the objects and processes of human civilization, then, are really symbols, symbols of human creativity and of the human desire to live in a world that makes some kind of human sense.

The New Testament begins by echoing the Old Testament. First of all there is a creative Word, and this Word produces light, a light shining in uncomprehending darkness. The Word is identified with Jesus, and Jesus tells us how the same process repeats itself in each man. In each one of us there is an inner dark world of our own privacy, a world in a closet behind a closed door. That is the world where we can see nothing, but where we can talk and listen to ourselves, or whatever else is there. For a religious man it would be a world of prayer, or dialogue with God; for most people it is a world of self-dialogue, the world of wish and dream and ambition and hope, where our resolves are made and our purposes formed. Out of this dark world of inner sounds there proceed the things that we do, and those things, Jesus says, ought to be full of light, clearly visible to others, not hidden under extinguishers. So all the things that we do are symbols of their own uncreated forms: that is, what we do is a symbol or representation of what we have determined to do or wanted to do. The New Testament also calls this world of inner dialogue the world of faith. What we believe is not what we say we believe, think we believe, or believe we believe; what we believe is what our actions show that we believe. Our actions, then, are symbols of our beliefs. What we do is of no enduring importance in itself; human life is too chancy. It is our faith that justifies us, whether for good or for ill, faith being the reality that our actions symbolize.

If we look more deeply into that dark world of inner dialogue, we find that the most central belief in it is the belief in death. The fact that we are going to die is primary in our consciousness, which means that all the works of our hands, all the achievements of our civilization, are expressions of an awareness of death. Our works are mortal because they are symbols of the death in the power that created them. The wisest among us are the prophets, men who can read the signs of the times, who can see the events going on around them as symbols of the forces that have produced them. Prophets are unlikely to be optimists; they are also unlikely to be strong or successful men. As most tragedy reminds us, strength and success bring illusion rather than reality. The peculiar prophetic mission entrusted to Israel was not one that brought strength or success; what it brought was suffering and endurance. The reason was that Israel saw the power and the glory of the empires around them as symbols only of a hidden power and glory which it had reached in the darkness of the holy of holies. To commit one's final loyalties to an empire in the world is to be guilty of what Israel summed up in the word "idolatry." And so Israel became hated, and in the century of Hitler and Stalin is still hated, as the accursed nation that cannot accept any temporal power as having the kind of reality that it associates with God.

The teaching of Jesus follows the pattern of that of Israel. He insists that the reality behind everything we do, the dark world of inner words, is a kingdom in its own right, and the only kingdom to which we really owe loyalty. Christianity says that we can know God only as a man, not a strong or successful man, but a man who is hated by both Pilate and Caiaphas, both secular and spiritual power, who is continually being humiliated but continually refuses to be silenced, who is continually dying but will not die, who forbids us to believe that anything in the world is a reality beyond symbol, a reality to commit oneself to. We are even told that our knowledge of death is not as certain as we have thought it to be, and that when we reach our own death, we shall be drawn out of the daylight world of appearance into a world where beliefs are the only realities, where there are no longer any symbols, and where real existence is to be inseparably part of a God who is also this rejected man. Such a belief is what is symbolized by the rite of communion, the act of eating and drinking a body which is the uncreated form of God, man, and nature. The rite points toward a state of existence in which our ordinary associations with light and darkness go into reverse, when we discover that it is this sunlit world that is really the uncomprehending darkness, and the darkness where we can only listen to the Word really a blaze of light, a golden city.

But while nothing in the eternal world is symbolic, everything in this world is. That is why, in speaking of his inner kingdom, Jesus does not use philosophical language; he uses the language of symbol, example, and parable that religion speaks in common with poetry, a language of bridegrooms and weddings, of pearls of great price, of runaway sons and of people beaten up on highways, of fair-minded and swindling petty officials. It is good to make our beliefs reasonable, but of course all doctrinal statements contain their own opposites. If we say, "I believe in God," we have already implied the possibility of not believing in him. The language of reason is implicitly aggressive. It is only the language of symbol that can express a faith which is pure vision, and has no wish to attack or improve on anyone else's faith. In short, the language of symbols is the language of love, and that, as Paul reminds us, will last longer than any other form of human communication [1 Corinthians 13:8].

25

Funeral Service for Virginia Knight

8 July 1969

From the typescript in NFF, 1988, box 3, file cc. Virginia Knight was the mother of David Knight, professor in the English department of Victoria College. A handwritten note on the typescript (which begins with page 6) says that pages 1–5 included readings from the Book of the Wisdom of Solomon 1–3, 2 Esdras 2, Psalm 176, Jeremiah 30–1, Zechariah 8, and Revelation 21.

The purpose of a memorial service of this kind is not to mourn for a death, but to celebrate a life. The impulse to speak nothing but good of the dead is not superstition: it is one of the deepest and most accurate feelings about life that we have. The passages from Scripture that I read you speak of the lame and the blind, the oppressed and the mournful, flocking into the city of light, where all these handicaps and sufferings cease to exist. As long as we live, all of us are more or less blind and crippled, although we do not pay much attention to the fact. But when someone close to us dies, we get an intense impression of all the positive and permanent things that that person was and stood for. All those of us who are gathered here to honour the memory of Virginia Knight have vividly in our minds the remembrance of her brilliance, her graciousness, and her charm. This is what our religion calls the Last Judgment, the deliverance or release of the real person from the flux of time. In ordinary life we see everything we have done slipping away into the past, where it seems to have vanished forever. Some of the things we do we are not sorry to have destroyed in this way. But among the feelings that perhaps only death can bring us, there is a distrust in our ordinary experience of things. There is something in having lived that is real, and therefore something in death that is unreal. Nothing that is real can be wholly destroyed, and at every death that touches us we are touched also by the sense of a world of light that is all around us, even though we live in a darkness that cannot comprehend it. From the experience of the death of others we can learn to understand that while we shall die ourselves, whatever we do that is really ourselves is not destined for death. In the magnificent Ninetieth Psalm which I am just about to read, the world's greatest death-song, the poet speaks of the shortness and uncertainty of life, but ends with a vision of what we do and are as established in a world beyond the reach of time.

Lord, thou hast been our dwelling place in all generations.

Before the mountains were brought forth, or ever thou hadst formed the earth and the world, even from everlasting to everlasting, thou art God.

Thou turnest man to destruction; and sayest, Return, ye children of men.

For a thousand years in thy sight are but as yesterday when it is past, and as a watch in the night.

Thou carriest them away as with a flood; they are as a sleep: in the morning they are like grass which groweth up.

In the morning it flourisheth, and groweth up; in the evening it is cut down, and withereth. . . .

The days of our years are threescore years and ten; and if by reason of strength they be fourscore years, yet is their strength labour and sorrow; for it is soon cut off, and we fly away. . . .

So teach us to number our days, that we may apply our hearts unto wisdom. . . .

O satisfy us early with thy mercy; that we may rejoice and be glad all our days.

Make us glad according to the days wherein thou hast afflicted us, and the years wherein we have seen evil.

Let thy work appear unto thy servants, and thy glory unto their children.

And let the beauty of the Lord our God be upon us: and establish thou the work of our hands upon us; yea, the work of our hands establish thou it. (Psalm 90)

Our Saviour and Redeemer, thou hast shared the loneliness of thy creatures; thou hast known our sufferings and our bondage; thou hast followed us into the solitude of death. Thou hast destroyed our prison of darkness; thou hast risen from death in the full power of thy glorious body which can subdue all things in itself. Therefore we cannot sorrow at the death of thy servant, as though we had no hope, but bid her farewell in the tranquillity of mind that thy word creates anew within us.

Blessing, and honour, and glory, and power, be unto him that sitteth upon the throne, and unto the Lamb for ever and ever. [Revelation 5:13]

Amen.

26

Sermon in Merton College Chapel

7 June 1970

From the typescript in NFF, 1988, box 3, file cf. Published as "All Things Made Anew" in RW, *254–6.*

The Old Testament lesson is a collection of proverbs, there being something about the proverb, in all ages, that seems to stir the collector's instinct. Proverbs are an expression of *popular* wisdom: they are usually addressed to people without great advantages of birth or wealth, and they are much concerned with prudence and moderation, with knowing one's place, with getting through life with the minimum of trouble. They are deeply conservative and traditional: they say a good deal about wisdom and folly, but by wisdom they mean the tried and tested way, the way of the elders, and the fool is the one who takes an old fallacy to be a new truth. The anxiety of continuity, of preserving the way that things are done, echoes throughout all these admonitions beginning, "Give ear, O my son," and it is still echoing through Polonius' advice to Laertes in *Hamlet* [1.3.59–80] and through the letters of Lord Chesterfield to his bumpkin heir. In the morality of proverbs, the most important virtue is humility. Humility is partly a negative virtue, a way of avoiding self-exposure and disarming criticism. But it can be a positive virtue too: a sense of one's own limitations is the basis of all security, even of sanity. Humility may be only hypocrisy, as with Uriah Heep;[1] it may be only a form of masochism, and in a religious context it may be only a form of superstition. We read in Ovid and elsewhere how much the gods dislike to hear men boasting of their merits [*Metamorphoses*, bk. 6, ll. 1–312]: they react as a human aristocracy would do, with resentment and fear for their privileges. Superstition warns us to walk

humbly with our gods, because if we don't they will play vicious practical jokes on us. Secular humility is more realistic: it advises us to be
modest, even diffident, about our achievements, because there is still so
much we don't know and can't do. Genuinely religious humility, as we
get it in the New Testament lesson from the Sermon on the Mount [Mat-
thew 5:3], takes this attitude to its logical conclusion. It thinks of life, not
as a series of things done or accomplished, but as a series of new beginnings. If we accomplish something in life, such as publishing a book, the
importance for us is not in the accomplishment itself or its value, and it
is only neurotic to remain attached to it. Posterity will judge of its value:
posterity is a lazy, ungrateful, and partisan judge, and even when it is
right it judges in its own terms and not ours, but it is the only judge we
have. Writing a book or creating something in the arts is only one obvious case of the general principle that every act we perform acquires a
life of its own: it separates from us like a child from a mother, and we no
longer possess it. The importance of the accomplishment *for us* is that
we have got rid of it and have come around to the point at which we can
begin again. We think of Sisyphus, pushing his stone up the hill, and of
Camus's remark that real life begins only when we have realized that
Sisyphus is a happy man.[2]

To attach ourselves to what we do is to expect profit or reward, that is,
recognition of our merits on our terms. If we expect this we shall be disillusioned, and conclude that the world is absurd and that God is a monster of injustice because he makes his sun shine not only on us, but on
the people we dislike. We think of disillusionment as misery, but it is
being shut up in illusion that is the real misery, and disillusionment
ought to feel like a release from prison.

It is at this point of creative and exhilarating disillusionment that the
Sermon on the Mount begins. Jesus assumes that we have outgrown the
religion of Job's comforters, expecting rewards for good actions, and
that we are ready to take the view of Socrates that the wise man, wherever he lives, will live by the laws of a just republic which he cannot see
around him [*Republic*, 592b]. The Sermon on the Mount is a commentary
on the law which turns the negative command into a positive vision. We
are not told simply that murder is wrong: we are urged to work for a
more abundant life, both for ourselves and for others. We are not told to
seek wisdom and folly; we are urged to find wisdom in the common
and the simple, and are sharply warned against calling anybody a fool.

In such a life the only rewards are those which come through the good will and understanding of others: these rewards are very great, but the life itself is not justified by them. There is only a series of actions, of detachment from those actions, and of coming around to the new beginning. In this new beginning there is the continual freshness of a world newly created, where nothing has been done and where everything is therefore still possible, so that the innocence of a new birth is preserved until death. For death, the Gospel tells us, is the last of our new beginnings: it is not the opposite of life, but only the opposite of birth, until we reach it, when it becomes birth, and in our last and greatest act of renunciation we find that all things have been made anew.

27

Stanley Llewellyn Osborne

5 May 1971

Honorary degree citation. From the typescript in NFF, 1988, box 4, file h.

Mr. Vice-Chancellor:

Stanley Osborne is one of our own graduates, both of Victoria and Emmanuel Colleges. After being graduated from Emmanuel, he studied music, and earned a doctorate in music, going on later to earn a second doctorate in theology. He entered the ministry of the United Church, and after the usual number of assistantships and pastorates, he became principal of the Ontario Ladies' College,[1] a post he filled for twenty years. He took on an exuberant Victorian building and several generations of students, at least a few of whom, private schools being what they are, must have been nearly as complicated as the architecture. A good many of his graduates came to Victoria, and we at the College acquired a good deal of respect for the academic and social standards that he and Mrs. Osborne maintained there, even into an era in which the word "ladies" has become simply the vocative case of "females."

This achievement alone would be fully worthy of recognition by the present convocation. But there was still more to come. It is remarked by Aldous Huxley that the things that happen to people are things that are like them, and perhaps Dr. Osborne's double training in theology and music was an unconscious preparation for what is so far the culminating point of his career. A committee was formed to revise the United Church Hymnary, and Dr. Osborne, who is among other things a member of the International Fellowship for Research in Hymnology and a member of the Consultation on Ecumenical Hymnody of North America, was the obvious person to be secretary of it. That was about the last thing that was obvious in the work of that committee, which laboured mightily for two years, only to scrap much of what it had done and start again with a committee from the Anglican Church of Canada to produce a hymnal to be used by both churches. Once again, Dr. Osborne was the inevitable secretary of the joint committee.

I was an advisory member of this committee myself, though unable to be actively associated with it in its later phase, and I got a glimpse of the kind of work that being secretary of such a committee would involve. Several hundred hymnbooks had to be investigated, and their contents catalogued. A careful record had to be kept of the status of each hymn, for the committee had many changes of mood as well as direction, and hymns went in and out like the reputations of rock bands or the tenures of college presidents. A careful record also had to be kept of the condition the hymn was in, for most hymns had to be operated on for some kind of surgery, mainly the removal of vestigial theological or literary archaisms. Tactful letters had to be written to most of those who had responded to appeals to send in hymns about the perils of travel or the joys of marriage. Speaking of marriage, there were also the endless difficulties in getting the right tunes to go with the words, especially new words. In the final version there are at least two tunes of Dr. Osborne's composition, accepted by a committee which was extremely tough with contributions from its own members. Some members of the committee were outraged by the omission of "Dare to be a Daniel," others by the omission of a hymn of St. Thomas Aquinas. I managed a bit of outrage myself occasionally: in my opinion two of the greatest hymns ever written are Blake's "Jerusalem" and Luther's "Ein Feste Burg," and there were proposals to throw out both. (They stayed in.) Costs had to be considered, and those considerations reduced the number of hymns included by about two hundred, which meant starting the status cycle all over again. Finally as the tremendous task drew to a close there were copyright permissions: speculators who had bought up rights from absent-minded composers, saintly and rapacious widows, purveyors of mod hits demanding royalties that would have taken up to twenty per cent of the entire proceeds of the book. All this meant a special trip to England and many hours of delicate diplomacy.

In classical music, at least, composition is the art of reaching a full close, an instant of harmony after twenty minutes or so of dissonance. Dr. Osborne's work as secretary has been composition in this sense: he has steered his way through the involved counterpoint of ecumenical charity, and has now, with the book complete and accepted by both churches, attained his moment of final concord. The trouble with music is, as many a tired concert-goer has discovered, that as soon as a close of this kind has been reached, another movement is apt to start. Dr. Osborne, having retired from Ontario Ladies' College in 1968 in order to devote himself entirely to this committee, must now spend much time travelling around the country exhibiting the new hymnbook to congregations *a mari usque ad mare*. It is therefore not only for past and present services that we honour him tonight, but for future ones as well. At present, in any case, his career represents a most distinguished contribution to the United Church of Canada, to the two largest Protestant churches of Canada, and through them to the whole people of God.

QUIBUS DE CAUSIS, PRAECLARISSIME CANCELLARIE, PRAESENTO TIBI STANLEY LLEWELLYN OSBORNE, POSTULANS UT EUM ADMITTAS IN GRADUM DOCTORIS LITTERARUM SACRARUM, HONORIS CAUSA.

28

The Leap in the Dark

12 December 1971

Advent sermon preached in the Victoria College Chapel. From the typescript in NFF, 1988, box 4, file d. Published in RW, 256–63. The text Frye quotes at the beginning is taken from The Modern Reader's Bible, *ed. Richard G. Moulton (New York: Macmillan, 1935), with "trode" changed to "stood" in the last line.*

In the Book of the Wisdom of Solomon, chapter 18, verses 14 to 16, we read:

> For while peaceful silence enwrapped all things, and night in her own swiftness was in mid course, thine all-powerful word leaped from heaven out of the royal throne, a stern warrior, into the midst of the doomed land, bearing as a sharp sword thine unfeigned commandment. And standing it filled all things with death; and while it touched the heaven, it stood upon the earth.

Obviously, I should begin by explaining why I have chosen so curious a text for an Advent sermon. The Book of Wisdom begins by talking about the knowledge of nature under the governance of God that the wise man enjoys. But as it proceeds, it increasingly treats wisdom as something existential, something that acts and intervenes in history, usually in a revolutionary direction. So the conception of wisdom here, as in all other books of wisdom in the Hebrew tradition, tends to shift from *Sophia* to *Logos*, from the understanding of the objective world to the sense of a divine power entering the world and changing it. The latter part of the book is an allegorical commentary on the Exodus from Egypt, the central action of all history from the author's point of view, and this text deals with the events accompanying the Exodus itself: the Passover, the slaughter of the Egyptian firstborn, and the final separation of Israel from Egypt. Later, the Gospels tell the story of the life of Christ in relation to the Exodus story also: his birth corresponds to the birth of Moses, his baptism to the crossing of the Red Sea, and so on. Hence this text is the closest we get, in anything before the New Testament, to the famous Nativity passage in Luke: "And there were in the same country shepherds abiding in the field, keeping watch over their flock by night" [2:8].

Of course the gentle, idyllic, pastoral Luke, who has so conquered our imaginations and won our hearts, takes a very different tone from the text I just read. The Christian poets who have made so much of the instant of peace in the reign of Augustus, when the gates of the temple of Janus were closed, indicating the stopping of all war at the moment that the Prince of Peace was born, have followed Luke in surrounding the birth of Christ with an atmosphere of hushed tranquillity. But there are other versions of the Nativity that remind us the Word of God is a sword as well as an instrument of peace; that it divides families and destroys kingdoms. There are three accounts of the birth of the Messiah in the New Testament. One is in Matthew, who has the wise men; one is in Luke, who has the shepherds; the third, which may well be the earliest of the three, is in the twelfth chapter of Revelation, and describes how a terrified woman gave birth to the Messiah in the wilderness, and how a dragon stood before her ready to devour the child as soon as it was born.

Christian painters have given us impressive pictures of kings, with their long retinues of soldiers and slaves and attendants, bearing rich gifts to the Christ Child. But Matthew says nothing about any kings: he says only that certain "wise men" came to Bethlehem to inquire about the birth of a divine child, and slipped out of the country in secret to avoid being murdered by Herod [2:1–12]. There were a good many murders and massacres in Herod's reign, and one of them has been immortalized as the "Slaughter of the Innocents," which accompanied the birth of Christ. The story was that Herod's own son perished in that massacre, and that when the news of it was brought to the emperor Augustus, he remarked (referring to the fact that Herod, though not a Jew, made a great point of observing the Jewish dietary laws) that it was obviously much safer to be Herod's pig than Herod's son.

As for Augustus himself, even if there was a moment of peace in his reign, it was only a peace of exhaustion after a terrible series of civil wars, each with its purges for the losing side. A few years after the birth of Christ, Roman legions were cut to pieces in the German forest, a reminder that the tribes beyond the frontiers of the empire were still watching, and waiting for their time to come. And while there may have been peace in the technical sense of an absence of military campaigns, there was certainly no intermission in the misery of the poor. When Luke begins his account of the Nativity with a decree by Augustus that all the world should be taxed, we should realize that such a decree fell with a crushing weight on the poor that we can hardly conceive of today, for all the complaining we may do about our taxes. A large part of the slave population of the empire was recruited from those who could not pay their exorbitant taxes, any more than they could repay loans bearing anywhere from thirty to fifty per cent interest. Blood, terror, misery, humiliation, were just as much an inseparable part of that first Christmas as Bangla Desh and Cambodia are an inseparable part of this one.

That is why, in the calendar of the church, Christmas is preceded by Advent, a sombre, brooding, foreboding season, carrying with it a sense of menace and the threat to life. As most tragedies remind us, success and prosperity are apt to engender illusion rather than reality, and in the Bible peace and freedom are usually referred to as a state either in the past, as in the lesson from Job (29) which was read this evening, or in the future, as in the lesson from Paul (Colossians 3). A place of blood and terror is not the only place where God can be found, but it is the only kind of place where God can be born. For God can only be born in the context of God's wrath. The wrath of God is not some senile ghost throwing a tantrum in the sky: the wrath of God is the revelation to man of the hell that man has made of his life on this earth. When we speak of the death of Christ as appeasing or atoning for the wrath of the Father, we mean that the death of Christ on the cross makes it possible for man to see a few other things besides hell. But the normal response to the birth of God is fear, as William Blake has said:

> But when they find the frowning Babe
> Terror strikes thro the region wide
> They cry the Babe the Babe is Born
> And flee away on Every side.[1]

Still, Advent is followed by Christmas sooner or later, and so we come to the question, How did Christmas get into Christianity? It is a puzzling and still unsolved question. In the first place, the birth stories of the Gospels are relatively late: the earliest Gospels, Mark and John, begin their accounts with the baptism of Christ as an adult. And, in sharp contrast to the Passion, which is carefully dated to coincide with the Jewish feast of the Passover, there is no indication in the New Testament about the time of the physical birth of Christ. Christianity seems to have been content to take over the winter solstice festival from other religions, from the birthday of the sun in Mithraism and the like. If so, it is the only major feature of Christianity that has been drawn from a source outside the Biblical tradition.

This fact has had both a negative and a positive result. The positive result is that Christmas represents a point of contact between Christianity and other faiths. The negative result, which is naturally much more obvious, is that Christmas has always been essentially a secular festival, on which Christianity has never established much more than, so to speak, squatter's rights. And with the present development of society, the primitive fear of the darkening of the world, of the light of the sun going out perhaps for good, which was a central element in the original winter solstice festival, has of course disappeared. It has been succeeded by the hysterical anxiety of an overproductive society, wondering whether the stimulus of Christmas shopping will keep the cycle of retail trade turning for one more year. In such an environment it is hard to bring back the feeling of the original festival, even in non-Christian forms. It is easy to see a light in the darkness, and when we do, we normally greet it with joy and affection. But it is not so easy to see a genuine light in a world of glitter, of reflections from millions of shiny metallic surfaces.

The ideology of the secular Christmas, in its present form, is a Victoria-and-Albert German Romantic affair, reflecting the culture of Dickens novels, of large parent-centred families, of the penny-postage reform, of the wedding marches of Mendelssohn and Wagner. And while of course all ideology in advertising points to something that no longer exists, if it ever did, there may now be too great a gap with the culture of the anti-novel, the bellowing of rock music, and the disintegration of both the family and the postal service. In a society where the reuniting of a big happy family is the starting point of neurosis rather than of festivity, perhaps an extensive restructuring of Christmas ideology may be necessary if it is to survive.

The present secular Christmas is, in any case, really a New Year festival, with Santa Claus representing the spirit of the Old Year and the New one hazily identified with the Christ child. The identification is not pressed, because that would lead to the unwelcome inference that the birth of Christ and the death of Santa Claus are the same event. Once we accept the identity of God with man, the principle that God works in man only under the limitations of the human situation and that divinity in man is to be associated with suffering and endurance rather than with prosperity—once we accept this, it is all over with the benevolent Providence who showers goodies on his beloved middle class and will get around to the less fortunate parts of mankind somewhat later; who, in the words of the National Anthem, will bless us and our symbols, but will confound the politics and frustrate the knavish tricks of everybody else. That God is dead, except, of course, that he never was alive.

This brings us to the positive feature of Christmas, the community it establishes between Christianity and other faiths. There is a genuine community of feeling with the Roman Saturnalia, the December festival in which masters waited on their slaves in commemoration of the Golden Age of equality symbolized by Saturn, a dumb, helpless ritual which said symbolically that the system of slavery on which Roman society was based was all wrong. There is a community with the Jewish festival of Hanukkah, the festival of lights in commemoration of the dedicating of the temple of a faith that has endured for two thousand years without its temple. There is a community with Yule and other ancestors of our secular Christmas, as enjoyed by a society which, however sentimental and gregarious, still has much genuine good will and a genuine longing for peace on earth.

The primary virtues of Christianity have always been defined as faith, hope, and love. Faith is the adherence to a specific community: it is what defines us as Christians or Jews or Moslems or Marxists, and hence there is an exclusive element in it. Because it is the power that forms a community, it is a tremendously efficient power: it is what accomplishes all the major achievements in the world. One of Mao Tse-Tung's speeches uses a fable about a man who wished to move a mountain that was in front of him, but could move only a shovelful of earth or so at a time.[2] He said, however, that there were his children, his grandchildren, and their children to his remotest descendants, and that sooner or later the mountain would be moved. His devotion so impressed his god that he woke up one morning to find the mountain gone. Mao explains that of course the real God is the organized will of the masses. One understands the identification of divine and human will; one appreciates the echo of the Christian principle that faith can remove mountains. The trouble is that it is only in certain very rare and special contexts that there is any real correlation between divine and human will. Man spends most of his time behaving like the psychotic ape that he also is. And even the virtue of faith, powerful as it is, can still lead in the wrong direction, towards hatred instead of love, because of the element of exclusiveness in it.

The faith that is perverted into hatred is a faith that is neither accepted nor recognized by God, or so we are told in the Gospels. "Then will I profess unto them, I never knew you" [Matthew 7:23]. Christian faith is in no better a situation than any other. Christian faith produced the civilization of Christendom, which reigned supreme in the Western world from the Atlantic to the Caucasus for many centuries, and is still one of the greatest forces of the contemporary world. But while Christendom is a colossal achievement, once we think of all its intolerance, its persecutions, its "religious" wars, its bigotry, it is clear that it too is still not the Kingdom of God that Jesus spoke of.

The real point of contact between Christianity and the rest of the world that is symbolized by Christmas is one of hope. Hope without love is ineffectual, just as faith without love is intolerant. But hope is what divides those who see the leap in the dark as the end of things from those who see it also as a new beginning. In Dostoevsky's *The Brothers Karamazov*, one of the brothers, Ivan, relates a series of incidents illustrating the greatest cruelty and misery in the Russia of his time to another brother, Alyosha [bk. 5, chap. 4]. These incidents prove to Ivan that God does not and cannot exist; precisely the same incidents prove to Alyosha that he does and must exist. I am concerned here, however, not with the existence of God, but with the existence of hope. It is hope, and often nothing more than hope, that divides the Ivans of the world from the Alyoshas, and, as Dante saw, it is hope that those who take up permanent residence in hell must first of all abandon.

The last part of our text reads, "while it touched the heaven, it stood upon the earth." When I was watching the moon expeditions of 1969, it seemed to me that the greatest moment was not the actual landing on the moon, but previously, two expeditions before that, when the crew went round to the dark side of the moon, and what they called the "good earth" disappeared from view. At that point they began reciting the Christian hymn with which the book of Genesis opens. They were the first men who were unable to see the earth from which they had sprung, and in reciting this hymn they established the principle that the real giant step for mankind must be taken on that earth. The really significant events of human life are hidden from view when they occur. Egyptian history knows nothing of any Exodus; Roman history knows nothing of the birth of Christ; 1971 knows nothing of whatever spiritual reality is taking shape now. It is not difficult to see the destroying angel of the Book of Wisdom's vision, what with war in the Near East, war in the Middle East, war in the Far East, America, the champion of democracy, losing its leadership, our own country threatened with collapse. There is nothing new in such forebodings of disaster; they have been essentially the picture the world has presented for the last four or five thousand years, long before the time of Christ. But there is still a difference between seeing only that and seeing in it the eclipsing shadow of a power that is still fighting for us. It is the latter vision that turns the darkness of Advent into the festival of blazing lights, the lights which are the glory of a God who is also Man, who is continually born and continually dying, and yet remains unborn and beyond the reach of death.

29

Wisdom and Knowledge

7 September 1973

Sermon preached in St. Thomas Aquinas Chapel at the Newman Centre, the Roman Catholic centre at the University of Toronto. From the typescript in NFF, 1988, box 4, file kk. Printed in RW, 263–8.

The lesson read by the president comes from the book called Ecclesiasticus, or the Wisdom of Jesus Ben Sirach, chapter 43, which belongs to a large group of writings called wisdom literature. The Bible does not say much about knowledge, but it does have a good deal to say about wisdom, and consequently about folly. In the earliest wisdom literature the normal unit of communication is the proverb. The proverb is usually addressed to ordinary people, without great advantage of birth or wealth, and what it counsels is above all prudence. Whether we find it in the Old Testament, in Greek or Egyptian culture, or in modern times in Benjamin Franklin's *Poor Richard's Almanac*, the message of the proverb is much the same: watch out, be careful, stick to the middle way, don't overdo anything. In this conception of wisdom, the wise are the conservatives who follow the tried and tested formulas of behaviour; the fools are the radicals who think an old fallacy is a new revelation.

Such a view of wisdom leads directly to the religion of Job's three friends. Those who conform to the recognized code will be happy and prosperous; those who do not will end up in the breadline. True, this fails to happen far more often than it happens. The rule of the world is that the unscrupulous, who are thrown on their own resources, are much more likely to be successful, even happy, than the righteous. But that only proves that the ways of God are deeply mysterious. This conception of wisdom is not the most inspiring vision of life, but it does have the advantage of attaching oneself to society. If we do what has always been done, our actions have the dignity of tradition behind them; if we do what is done around us, our actions have the authority of the community behind them. The wise man is thus a representative of a larger human body, and ultimately the whole human race comes to a focus in him.

By the time we get to the Sermon on the Mount the recommended code of behaviour is very different in emphasis. Here it is associated with excess rather than with caution and restraint, with paradoxes about turning the other cheek to enemies and giving up a cloak when only a coat is demanded [Matthew 5:39–40]. It is not enough merely to refrain from theft and murder: one should have a positive enthusiasm about human life and the sharing of goods. Further, it is explicitly said that the just and the unjust get the same amount of sun and rain [45].

The passage in Ecclesiasticus gives us an attractive picture of wisdom: it does talk, quite specifically, about knowledge also, the knowledge of the heavenly bodies and the cycle of nature. But what the author mainly stresses is the wonder, the delight, the excitement of knowing. He dwells on snow and hoarfrost and ice, because those are rare occurrences in the country in which he is writing, and he treasures them as precious experiences. It is this emphasis on the pleasure and desire of knowledge that places what he says in wisdom literature. The world is not just there for him: the world is sublime and it is beautiful, and its beauty and sublimity are part of its reality.

We conquer knowledge by forced marches; we learn more and more as we go on, and find that there is an oddly quantitative element in it. We even try to measure the amount of it, in examinations and similarly unreliable measuring instruments. Yet, in relation to all there is to be known, the difference between great learning and great ignorance is still very slight, and this is a fact that may lead either to disillusionment or to exuberance. Sir Isaac Newton is said to have remarked near the end of his life that however he may have appeared to the world, he seemed to himself like a child playing with pebbles on a beach, while the great ocean of truth lay undiscovered before him.[1] I do not think this remark expressed either false modesty or world weariness. I think what it expressed was a sense of exhilaration in coming to the end of a great effort, and so back to a beginning again, a point where everything has yet to be known. One finds that the ultimate aim in some long and complex effort of knowledge, such as writing a book, is not really to accomplish something by writing it. The ultimate aim rather is to get rid of it, for the sake of that instant of breathless innocence before one starts the next book, the instant when all the possibilities of knowledge are still before one. The bankruptcy of knowledge is one of the most genuine and tangible rewards of knowledge.

Knowledge is of the actual: it has a certainty which is confirmed by reason, by experience, and by experiment. Wisdom is rather of the potential: it faces Newton's ocean, confronting unspecified situations, exposed wholly to the still undiscovered. Such a document as the Sermon on the Mount suggests wisdom, but not necessarily knowledge. Again, knowledge is primarily related to the known: in giving a man a university appointment, for example, the first questions are, What does he know and how much of it does he know? Only after that do we begin to think of him as a person. Wisdom cannot be tested or measured in this way, and seems to be related primarily to the person who is thought to have it, or to be where it is. Knowledge is of nature and of the objective world, but the author of the Book of Job stresses the impossibility of finding wisdom anywhere in nature. "The depth saith, It is not in me: and the sea saith, It is not with me" [28:14].

Nobody, not even Christ himself, can think of himself as a wise man, much less speak of himself in such terms. The Bible is quite clear that anyone who considers himself wise has already proved himself to be a fool. The reason is not hard to grasp. Knowledge is what you have; wisdom is what others may find in you. Strictly speaking, there is no such thing as a wise man, just as, strictly speaking, there is no such thing as a great man. There are only sources of wisdom, and they are extremely unpredictable. The implication is that your relation to others may be more truly yourself than anything that you may have squirrelled away inside you.

This is an age of wonder drugs and panaceas of all kinds, so it is not surprising that there should be a widespread belief that education is a cure for all social evils. But while there are many benefits in the diffusion of knowledge, the moral improvement of society is not one of them. Education makes a bad man more dangerous; it does not make him a better man. Naturally a good deal of disillusionment results from discovering this. I often think of the verse in the Book of the Wisdom of Solomon: "God hath granted me to speak as I would, and to conceive as is meet for the things that are given me" [7:15]. Whoever wrote that was thinking of his intelligence in terms of service, not in terms of posses-

sion, and because he thought in those terms, freedom becomes an inseparable part of what he says. He must say what he believes to be true,
whatever the opposition to his saying it, because he is responsible for
conveying something that does not originate with himself. Similarly,
there has been great bewilderment expressed over the fact that, for
instance, Nazi commandants of extermination camps were often highly
cultivated men with a taste for Mozart. The people who ran extermination camps did so because they had persuaded themselves that certain
kinds of people were inherently inferior to other kinds. It is possible for
an educated man to believe this, because knowledge, in itself, creates
elites and hierarchies; experts find themselves strategic places in society
and dominate those who are ill-informed. The source of wisdom, in contrast, may be a penniless hermit in India or, like Jesus himself, a vagrant
with nowhere to lay his head. Once again, when we think in terms of
service rather than possession, equality, along with freedom, becomes
essential; in this context we must live in a world where everybody is on
the same level, with the same rights and the same duties.

Knowledge is a personal possession, but in itself it is impersonal. History is what happened, not what we think should have happened; science is what is there, not what we'd prefer to see there. Yet the author of
Ecclesiasticus thinks of the sublime and beautiful elements in nature as
expressions of a personality. The sublimity of the storm reminds him of
the majesty of God, the height of heaven, of the sovereignty of God. This
in itself is a feeling which could lead to superstition: it's a sunny day;
God must be in a good mood; or, a volcano has erupted; the gods must
be angry. But this author doesn't in the least sound as though he were
floundering in that quagmire. He is speaking, of course, as a poet rather
than as a scientist, and, as poets habitually do, he sees in nature symbols
of what Martin Buber calls "Thou." In nature itself everything is "It." It
is very natural to worship the rising sun at dawn, but when the sun
becomes a blast furnace ninety million miles off, it may be as impressive
as ever, but it ceases to be adorable. So our author is raising the question
of what kind of reality the poets are talking about.

It is notable that poets have constantly insisted that they did not feel
like the originators of their poems, but rather that their minds were simply places where something was happening to words. The poet, says
Keats, has no identity;[2] his mind is a thoroughfare to be trodden by
images and impressions. T.S. Eliot compares the poet's mind to a cata-
lyst that is present at, without taking part in, a chemical reaction.[3] We

can call this the unconscious or inspiration or whatever vague abstraction we choose, but whatever we call it, it seems to be a sense of being a medium or transmitter of poetry rather than a possessor of it.

The basis of knowledge is the individual: I know, you know, he or she knows. The basis of wisdom is the community; it is what others may get from us, either because of what we say or, much more frequently, in spite of what we say. The next step is that of the poet Rimbaud, who remarks that one should not say "je pense," but rather "on me pense."[4] The point is not that "I think"; the point is rather that somebody or something is thinking with me. Rimbaud is expressing the kind of experience that the great mystics struggle for, the moment the Upanishads express in the formula "Thou art that,"[5] the moment when "I know" goes into reverse and becomes something more like "I am known." This is a tentative sense of a total scheme of things, which can be grasped only by an infinite mind, yet a scheme of things where we belong and find our own place and our own identity. Such phrases as these are not assumptions or hypotheses, much less definitions: they are attempts to put into words feelings which, while they express a sense of complete certainty and conviction, are always in themselves expendable.

This is of course what Paul is talking about when he says that we now know in part, but that there is a state of being where we know even as we are (now) known [1 Corinthians 13:12]. For Paul, it follows that the process we call death is the highest adventure of the questing spirit, where we go from knowledge to what would be more accurately called revelation; where we come to the end of all things for ourselves and therefore come around to the beginning again, the beginning of life within the power that can make all things new.

30

On Christmas

December 1973

From the undated typescript with holograph corrections in NFF, 1992, box 3, file 1, dated by internal evidence. Frye's diary notes a service in the Victoria College Chapel on Sunday, 2 December of this year. The typescript pages are unnumbered and each ends at the end of a paragraph (even when this involves leaving blank space on the page), so that the order of pages is not certain. In this typescript, Frye marked the places where he intended to insert a quotation by the notation (Q): these quotations have been supplied editorially where possible, and are indicated to be such by their inclusion in the text in square brackets.

There is no indication in the New Testament of the time of year when Jesus was born, and the infancy narratives in Matthew and Luke are relatively late. The earlier Gospels, Mark and John, begin with the Baptism, which became the main festival, outside Easter, in the Eastern churches. The Western churches seem to have introduced Christmas because of a feeling that the natural birth of Christ should be emphasized, to counteract a feeling that Jesus was not a man who was born and died, but a kind of ghost who manifested himself for a time and then disappeared. We don't know why the church decided on December 25, but it looks as though Christianity, for once, was adopting something outside the Biblical tradition. Almost every people in the ancient world had some kind of festival at the winter solstice, the time of year when the nights are longest, when some kind of primitive fear emerges that the sun might go out altogether if not encouraged by a ritual of lights and fires. In the great rival religion of Mithraism, which stretched from Persia to Scotland, the chief festival was the birthday of the "unconquered sun" on

December 22, and northern Europe had its "Yule," when a great log was ceremonially set burning.

In the church calendar Christmas is preceded by four weeks of Advent, a sombre, brooding season of the gathering powers of darkness.[1] The infancy stories grow, in part, out of the Exodus story of the Passover, when the Angel of Death was let loose in Egypt and the Israelites held their first Passover standing up and in haste, ready for a quick and silent departure. This feeling recurs in the infancy stories with the account of the slaughter of the innocents, the flight of the Holy Family to Egypt, and the stealthy departure of the wise men. The book in the Apocrypha called the Book of Wisdom describes the time of the first Passover thus:

> [For while all things were in quiet silence, and that night was in the midst of her swift course,
>   Thine Almighty word leaped down from heaven out of thy royal thone, as a fierce man of war into the midst of a land of destruction,
>   And brought thine unfeigned commandment as a sharp sword, and standing up filled all things with death; and it touched the heaven, but it stood upon the earth. (Wisdom of Solomon 18:14–16)]

This is the starting point of the tradition that Christ was born at midnight, just as he was crucified at noon. Besides the two infancy stories, there is a third account of the birth of the Messiah in the New Testament, in Revelation 12, a much more obviously mythical account, and this too preserves the sense of blood and terror and menace in the Christmas story:

> [And there appeared a great wonder in heaven; a woman clothed with the sun, and the moon under her feet, and upon her head a crown of twelve stars:
>   And she being with child cried, travailing in birth, and pained to be delivered.
>   And there appeared another wonder in heaven; and behold a great red dragon, having seven heads and ten horns, and seven crowns upon his heads.
>   And his tail drew the third part of the stars of heaven, and did cast them to the earth: and the dragon stood before the woman which was ready to be delivered, for to devour her child as soon as it was born.

And she brought forth a man child, who was to rule all nations with a rod of iron: and her child was caught up unto God, and to his throne.

And the woman fled into the wilderness, where she hath a place prepared of God, that they should feed her there a thousand two hundred and threescore days. (Revelation 12:1–6)]

W.H. Auden's radio drama, *For the Time Being*, also called *A Christmas Oratorio*, begins with a section called Advent, where the growing power of darkness is linked to the exhaustion of the Roman Empire and the fact that even at the height of its power the barbarians who will eventually destroy it are gathering on the frontiers. The parallels between the time of Christ's birth and our own time emerge very clearly:

[Darkness and snow descend;
The clock on the mantlepiece
Has nothing to recommend,
Nor does the face in the glass
Appear nobler than our own
As darkness and snow descend
On all personality.
Huge crowds mumble—"Alas,
Our angers do not increase,
Love is not what she used to be";
Portly Caesar yawns—"I know";
He falls asleep on his throne,
They shuffle off through the snow:
Darkness and snow descend. (pt. 1, ll. 1–14)]

In Blake's *Introduction* to the *Songs of Experience*, the poet, who is also a prophet, calls to the earth to stop turning away into the dark, and remain in the light, which is also here as well as the darkness. Blake's poem may not sound much like an Advent poem, but it is one.

[O Earth O Earth return!
Arise from out the dewy grass;
Night is worn,
And the morn
Rises from the slumberous mass.

Turn away no more:
Why wilt thou turn away
The starry floor
The watry shore
Is giv'n thee till the break of day.][2]

Robert Southwell was a Jesuit priest in the England of Elizabeth I, who was arrested in 1592 and spent the last three years of his life in prison. He was examined thirteen times, generally with torture, and finally hanged. So there wasn't much about the other side of the Christmas season of peace and good will that he didn't know.[3]

James Reaney's *A Suit of Nettles* is a series of twelve eclogues, one for each month of the year, in which the speakers are geese. Naturally for geese the Christmas season is the time of death, when they get their heads chopped off to provide Christmas for other people. So the only suggestion that the geese might have Christmas feelings of their own has to come out at the end of the November eclogue:

[MOPSUS:
A sun, a moon, a crowd of stars,
A calendar nor clock is he
    By whom I start my year.
He is most like a sun for he
Makes his beholders into suns,
    Shadowless and timeless.
At the winter sunstill some say
He dared be born; on darkest day
    A babe of seven hours
He crushed the four proud and great directions
Into the four corners of his small cradle.
He made it what time of year he pleased, changed
Snow into grass and gave to all such powers.][4]

Of the two accounts of the birth of Christ, Luke gives us a pastoral account. He has the manger with its ox and ass, the shepherds on the hillside. Matthew gives us a more urban story, with wise men bringing costly gifts, and has Jesus born in a house. In later legend Matthew's wise men became three kings, one of whom is traditionally black. For although Matthew says "east," the wise men seem to have even more to do with the south. They are symbolically repeating the journey of the Queen of Sheba, the queen of the south as Jesus calls her [Matthew 12:42], to King Solomon; gold, frankincense, and myrrh are primarily products of Africa, and coming from Africa they would have to go through Egypt, repeating the journey of the Israelites who were guided to the Promised Land in the night by a pillar of fire.

But what the wise men really symbolize in the Christmas story is, I think, the universality of the story—in other words, symbolically they come from all points of the compass. The poet Robert Graves has a poem called *To Juan at the Winter Solstice*, which begins by saying that poetry has only one story to tell: I don't much care for his version of it, but I agree that poetry ultimately tells only one story, and that the winter solstice is one of the times when it gets told. Thus Virgil, a pagan poet writing in 40 B.C., produces a poem which for centuries was taken to be an unconscious prophecy of the birth of Christ. Modern critics, who of course know exactly what was going on in Virgil's mind in 40 B.C., assure us that he was merely congratulating a friend on the birth of a son. Well, here's the poem, or part of it, in a nineteenth-century translation by Calverley, and I think you will agree that it is very curious language to use if that were all Virgil was talking about:

> [Come are those last days that the Sybil sang:
> The ages' mighty march begins anew.
> Now comes the virgin, Saturn reigns again:
> Now from high heaven descends a wondrous race.
> Thou on the newborn babe—who first shall end
> That age of iron, bid a golden dawn
> Upon the broad world—chaste Lucina, smile:
> Now thy Apollo reigns.]⁵

The Roman equivalent of Christmas was a festival called the Saturnalia, held in December in honour of the Golden Age, or reign of Saturn, which Virgil refers to. The Golden Age was a period of complete social equality, and the main feature of the Saturnalia was a period of liberty given to slaves, who sat at table while their masters waited on them. The Saturnalia was a ritual which said symbolically that the master–slave relationship on which the Roman Empire was based was all wrong.

Christmas is conventionally a season of jollity and good will, but it is also the season of neurosis, loneliness, the gibbering of accusing memories and the wearing of uncomfortable social masks that don't fit. As I well remember from my administrative days, it is a period when somebody in the academic community is likely to attempt suicide, though fortunately not often with much enthusiasm. The usual model of Christmas in our minds is a cosy, cuddly, Dickensian Christmas which is not very close to conditions of life in 1973. It is an exclusive feast; we withdraw inside our families and write cheques for the organizations that look after those who are colder and hungrier. But the feeling of exclusiveness bothers us more than we realize. The powers of darkness that gather in Advent are also the powers of tyranny and exploitation, of the arrogance of privilege, of the spirit of the first Christmas when the hotels were so full that a pregnant woman very near her time was forced to spend the night in a stable.

In the Bible the sense of society righting its balance, of the poor and oppressed coming into their own, is often symbolized by the story of a barren woman bearing a son late in life. One of the people to whom this happened was Hannah, the mother of Samuel, who sings a song that contains the verse: [The Lord maketh poor, and maketh rich: he bringeth low, and lifteth up (1 Samuel 2:7)]. This verse is the basis for the verse in the Magnificat that you just read: [He hath put down the mighty from their seats, and exalted them of low degree (Luke 1:52)].

There have always been two sides to the Christmas story, and they are an emotional contrast. One is the sense of quiet, of the world coming to a full stop in its course, of peace descending for one breathless instant at midnight under the stars. This feeling finds its focus in the vision of the mother and the child, the mother who is in some mysterious way virgin, bride, and sister as well as mother, the closed garden of the Song of Songs in which the wind of the Holy Spirit moves to create the newborn God.[6]

The Jewish parallel to Christmas is the feast of the dedication of the temple, called Hanukkah. In the persecution of the Jews by Antiochus of Syria, the temple had been defiled by having a statue of a heathen god placed in the Holy of Holies. For the Jews this was the ultimate triumph of the dark powers, which they called, in the King James translation, "the abomination of desolation" [Matthew 24:15; Mark 13:14]. The persecution provoked the rebellion of the Maccabees, and the success of that rebellion led in turn to the rededication of the temple, on the 25th of the winter month Chislev. The 25th of Chislev is not the 25th of December, but the coincidence of numbers is interesting. The feast of the

dedication was primarily a festival of lights. Something keeps reminding us the dark powers of the heathen gods had been chased away by
the light.[7] We read in 1 Maccabees:

[They made also new holy vessels, and into the temple they brought the
candlestick, and the altar of burnt offerings, and of incense, and the table.

And upon the altar they burned incense, and the lamps that were upon
the candlestick they lighted, that they might give light in the temple. . . .

Look, at what time and what day the heathen had profaned it, even in
that was it dedicated with songs, and citherns, and harps, and cymbals.

Then all the people fell upon their faces, worshipping and praising the
God of heaven, who had given them good success.

And so they kept the dedication of the altar eight days, and offered burnt
offerings with gladness, and sacrificed the sacrifice of deliverance and
praise. . . .

Thus was there very great gladness among the people, for that the
reproach of the heathen was put away. (1 Maccabees 4:49–50, 54–6, 58)]

We notice too how prominent in the Gospels the theme of the cleansing
of the temple is: in the Gospel of John it is one of the first things Jesus
does. The apocalyptic aspect of this festival is picked up in the Book of
Revelation:

[And I saw no temple therein: for the Lord God Almighty and the Lamb are
the temple of it.

And the city had no need of the sun, neither of the moon, to shine in it:
for the glory of God did lighten it, and the Lamb of God is the light thereof.

And the nations of them which are saved shall walk in the light of it: and
the kings of the earth do bring their glory and honour into it.

And the gates of it shall not be shut at all by day: for there shall be no
night there.

And they shall bring the glory and honour of the nations into it.

And there shall in no wise enter into it any thing that defileth, neither
whatsoever worketh abomination, or maketh a lie: but they which are written in the Lamb's book of life. (Revelation 21:22–7)]

31

Wedding of Patricia Russell
and Andrew Binnie

2 March 1974

Service in Victoria College Chapel. From the typescript in NFF, 1988, box 5, file f. Patricia Russell and Andrew Binnie were both former students and good friends of Frye, and the Fryes were godparents to their son James. Frye himself was responsible for the choice of extracts in this service.

We are gathered in the presence of God to join this man and this woman in marriage. Marriage is an honourable estate, instituted by God to manifest that love without which there is no genuine human life. What the will of God has decreed, the laws of man have accepted as a binding contract. Thus marriage cannot be taken lightly or casually, and you who are present have shown that you realize this by coming here. It is a part of this marriage, as of all others, that anyone who believes that he knows of any real impediment to it should be permitted to speak now, and now only. . . . Those who are undertaking it are also reminded that a marriage blessed by God, that is, a marriage which is a genuine marriage, can be entered upon only by those who understand that it is an essential part of their inheritance as children of God, equal in dignity, each of infinite worth in his sight.

Our Father and giver of all grace: send thy blessing upon these thy children, whom we bless in thy name: sanctify the covenant which they are about to make, that they may come to know the gifts reserved for those who love: the peace that is above our peace, the joy that is beyond our joys, the wisdom that comes from body and mind at once, the wisdom of the spiritual body of our risen Lord.

[Ceremony]

Hear the words of Jesus concerning marriage:

> He which made them at the beginning made them male and female, and
> said, For this cause shall a man leave father and mother, and shall cleave to
> his wife: and they twain shall be one flesh. [Matthew 19:4–5]

Hear the words of the Apostle concerning love:

> Love suffereth long, and is kind; love envieth not; love vaunteth not itself, is
> not puffed up, doth not behave itself unseemly, seeketh not her own, is not
> easily provoked, thinketh no evil; rejoiceth not in iniquity, but rejoiceth in
> the truth; beareth all things, believeth all things, hopeth all things, endureth
> all things. [1 Corinthians 13:4–7][1]

Hear the words of the Holy Spirit concerning the commitment to love:

> Set me as a seal upon thine heart, as a seal upon thine arm: for love is strong
> as death. . . . Many waters cannot quench love, neither can the floods drown
> it: if a man would give all the substance of his house for love, it would
> utterly be contemned. [Song of Solomon 8:6–7]

> And Ruth said, Intreat me not to leave thee, or to return from following
> after thee: for whither thou goest, I will go; and where thou lodgest, I will
> lodge: thy people shall be my people, and thy God my God. [Ruth 1:16]

Hear also John Milton:

> What is [marriage] then but that desire which God put into Adam in Para-
> dise, . . . the desire and longing to put off an unkindly solitariness by unit-
> ing another body, but not without a fit soul to his, in the cheerful society of
> wedlock? Which if it were so needful before the fall, when man was much
> more perfect in himself, how much more is it needful now against all the
> sorrows and casualties of this life, to have an intimate and speaking help, a
> ready and reviving associate in marriage?[2]
> All ingenuous men will see that the dignity and blessing of marriage is

placed rather in the mutual enjoyment of that which the wanting soul need-
fully seeks.

Which divinely sorts with that which in effect Moses tells us, that Love
was the son of Loneliness, begot in Paradise by that sociable and helpful
aptitude which God implanted between man and woman toward each
other.[3]

[Hear also William Blake:

> I cry, Love! Love! Love! happy happy Love! free as the mountain wind!
> Can that be Love, that drinks another as a sponge drinks water?
> How can one joy absorb another? are not different joys
> Holy, eternal, infinite! and each joy is a Love.
> Does the sun walk in glorious raiment on the secret floor
> Where the cold miser spreads his gold? . . .
>   . . . does not that mild beam blot
> The bat, the owl, the glowing tyger, and the king of night.
> The sea fowl takes the wintry blast for a cov'ring to her limbs:
> And trees and birds and beasts and men behold their eternal joy.
> Arise you little glancing wings, and sing your infant joy!
> Arise and drink your bliss, for every thing that lives is holy!][4]

The peace of God possess your souls and minds, and the power of
Christ, whose love for us brought him to the terrors of death, and who
by his victory over death made one body and blood of all the peoples of
the earth, shield and protect you throughout life and beyond.

32

Substance and Evidence

17 November 1974

Sermon preached in the Memorial Church, Harvard University, on the text of Hebrews 11:1. From the typescript in NFF, 1988, box 5, file a. Published in RW, 268–75.

The author of the letter to the Hebrews tells us that "faith is the substance of things hoped for, the evidence of things not seen." This sounds like a definition of faith, but I don't think it is one: I think this author would know that definitions, for the most part, are a quite mistaken way of trying to get things clear. What he's done is to make a statement that outlines a general area, and somewhere inside that area we can find what he means by faith. We notice that he links faith with hope when he calls faith the substance of things hoped for, and this reminds us again that Paul speaks of three supreme virtues: faith, hope, and love [1 Corinthians 13:13]. Paul did not write this letter to the Hebrews, but the two authors are thinking within the same kind of structure.

The Christian church insisted for many centuries that faith, hope, and love were what it called "theological" virtues: they were not natural to man, the church said, but were dependent on a knowledge of Christianity. I can hardly imagine anyone saying today that faith, hope, and love can't really be understood or practised outside the Christian tradition. But the other thing the church said was true: faith, hope, and love are not natural to man. We're not born loving: we're born sentimental and gregarious, and vociferously demanding to be loved. We're not born with hope: we're born with an instinct for survival. And we're certainly not born with faith: we're born credulous, gullible, and superstitious.

It's credulity that we mean when we say we're taking "on faith" whatever we accept without question. William James spoke of a "will to believe," and he said of it that we try to believe as much as we can. Again, he was talking about a will to credulity. We all come to points in our lives when we feel that we need to believe in something beyond the world of our senses and reason, not necessarily something religious, but something with serious values in it, like democracy or social revolution or liberty. But, nine times out of ten, whenever we come to such a point we go straight back to our childhood, and we look for the kind of security and protection that we had, or thought we had, when we were told things by somebody we trusted at that time, like a parent or teacher.

I once knew a clergyman who was asked what he thought of the Jonah and the whale story. He answered that if the Bible had said Jonah had swallowed the whale he would still believe it. He seems to have felt that, whether the whale swallowed Jonah or Jonah the whale, there were special virtues attached to, and special rewards waiting for, the reader who was prepared to swallow both. This is typical of what we so often call faith: an attitude that's essentially passive, and holds to an accepted authority. If it conflicts with everything that our reason and senses tell us, so much the better: that just shows how strong the faith is. Faith of this kind operates in all areas, not just in religion. I've known left-wingers who steadily maintained that there was no terrorism in Stalin's Russia, or if there was it was all for the best. And I've known right-wingers who maintained that the late Joseph McCarthy never victimized an innocent person, or if he did it was all for the best. The more their views were contradicted by the plainest evidence, the harder they clung to them. I've known students who believed that at the time of Noah's flood, God made a special miracle to destroy the fish, who of course couldn't be drowned. And I've known other students who rejected everything in their religious tradition, but were genuinely shocked if I expressed any reservations at all about astrology. This kind of faith is not a virtue: it's a mental disease.

What does our author mean when he says that faith is the substance of things hoped for? The word he uses for substance is *hypostasis*, which means lying underneath, like a foundation. It has a derived meaning of trust or confidence, and Paul uses the word in that sense, but in a very different context [2 Corinthians 11:17]. You can find modern Bibles that translate it that way here, and say "faith is the assurance of things hoped for" [RSV]. But that just takes us around in a circle, and reduces faith to wishful thinking. The King James Bible is right, as it generally is in such matters: faith is the substance, that is, the essential nature, the primary reality, the actualization, of what we hope for.

The point is that there are two kinds of reality. There's the reality of what's there, and the reality of what we make out of what's there. There's the reality of the external world that's given us at birth, the world we can't help knowing, the solid world we keep bumping into. But the reality of cities and gardens and books and pictures is different. Here is something that doesn't exist at all to begin with, but is brought into existence by the energy or creative power of man. I think it's this second kind of reality, the kind we make ourselves, that our author is talking about. If we think of a painter painting a picture, we come closer to the kind of thing he means. The picture is the substance of what the painter hoped for. He probably hoped for a better picture. We all hope for better things than we achieve. But faith is the realization, the bringing into being, of what we do achieve.

It's true that we use the words "faith" and "belief" in all sorts of confusing ways. For example, I may say, "I believe Boston is in the state of Massachusetts," because I'm an academic, and I hate to admit that I know anything for a fact. Or I may say, "I believe Mr. Nixon was right in resigning the office of president," although what I'm expressing is not a belief but an opinion. Sloppy language of this kind makes it hard to understand a writer like the author of Hebrews, who uses words with great precision. Knowledge and opinion are not what he means by faith. He means a strenuous effort of the whole personality, and this effort, for him, is the extending and the fulfilment of reason and sense experience, not a denial of them.

If I'm right, then faith is not anything we say we believe, or that we think we believe, or that we believe we believe. What we really believe is what our actions show that we believe. Faith is what we actualize in our lives, and any belief that's not an axiom of practical life is useless mental lumber. A man may believe in nothing but his own ability to cheat and lie, but his life will still be the product of his faith, no less than the life of a saint. But as soon as we understand that the basis of our belief is what we really do, we're confronted with the challenge of freedom. If we believe only in things like getting along or doing what we're told or just surviving, then the less we think about our beliefs the better. But if we're trying to live a serious life, with things like love and responsibility and service to society in it, we have to try to clarify and articulate our beliefs. We may even have to change our lives to conform with beliefs that we respect and want for ourselves.

The basis of this kind of faith is hope, and hope and faith are related much as wish is to will. We start with some vision in our minds of a better state of things than we know. We can't be doctors without some vision of what good health can do for human life, or teachers without some vision of what knowledge and wisdom can do, or social workers without some vision of what better housing or greater freedom from racial prejudice could do. We may be unconscious of having such a vision, or we may know that we have it and dislike talking about it, but it's there all the same. Our faith is what we do to help bring this vision into the world. Whatever we do will fall short of what we hope for, but the important thing is not to lose the hope, or the clarity of the vision that hope produces.

And just as hope is the beginning of faith, so love is the end of it. Let us think, for example, of a Christian and a Moslem, facing each other in one of the Crusades. Neither of them knows the first thing about the other man's religion, but they're both convinced that it is utterly and damnably wrong; they are even prepared to die for that conviction. There must be something the matter with a faith that expresses itself as a desire to kill somebody who doesn't share it. A profoundly Christian writer, Jonathan Swift, remarked that men have just enough religion to make them hate, but not enough to make them love one another.[1] To which we may add that those who have no religion at all don't seem to hate any the less on that account. The general principle here is that whatever reflects any credit on humanity is always attached to something else that's silly or vicious. As Jesus ben Sirach, the author of Ecclesiasticus, says: "What race is worthy of honour? The human race. What race is unworthy of honour? The human race" [10:19, RSV].

It's very important to realize that when we do profess or articulate a faith of any kind, what we're really doing is attaching ourselves to a specific community. Christian beliefs attach us to a Christian community; democratic beliefs make us want to live in a democracy, and so on. What faith should do is to help create a community in which every individual loves those who are closest to him, or what Jesus calls his neighbours. From there his love radiates out into good will and tolerance, which might be called love at a distance, love for those we don't know, or for those in other communities. Confronted with a variety of serious faiths—Christian, Jewish, Marxist, Buddhist, and so many others—our first impulse may be to say that only one of these can be right, and the rest must be wrong, unless, which seems more likely, that all are more or less wrong. But what do we know about rights and wrongs in such matters? All we know is that if one man's faith is better than another's, it is so only because more spiritual energy has gone into living it.

This brings us to the second thing that our author says, which is that faith is the *elenchos*, the proof or evidence, of what is not seen. We hear a good deal about the invisible and unseen world in religious writing, and we often get the feeling that somehow the invisible world is considered to be much better, more congenial to sensitive and subtle people like ourselves. Speaking with contempt of the merely material world seems to be one of the privileges of having a middle-class income. But New Testament writers have no snobbery of this kind. Neither do they associate the invisible or unseen world with the dark, with anything that's really mysterious or unknown. They think of it rather as something they can't see but know to exist. Now if we try to think of things that we can't see but know to exist, the first thing we think of is the air. And in the Bible nearly everything that's said about the spiritual world seems to be said in some kind of metaphor taken from air. The Spirit of God means the breath of God, and is symbolized by the wind. The prophets and other sacred writers, we say, were inspired; that is, they breathed in air.

I think this metaphor of air is very significant in the Bible. I think it means that the invisible world is not thought of as a higher order of things, but that it is, like the air, a medium for the visible world. We see the world because we can't see the air; similarly, the works of our faith are visible because the source of faith is not. If we could see the air, we'd be in a dense fog, in a world that had no direction and no location and no shape. The Old Testament lesson this morning was from the Book of Ecclesiastes, which was written by a shrewd, humorous, tough-minded writer whose theme is, "vanity of vanities; all is vanity" [1:2]. The word we translate as "vanity" actually means fog, mist, vapour, and it's his symbol for the material world as such, the world in which we experience everything but create nothing. In his book he tries to show us how to live through the days of our vanity, that is, how to find our way through the fog. He warns us that a lot of the things that are most worth doing will vanish into that fog: we have to be prepared for this, and do them anyway.

He gives us this warning because in any serious life, the questions will often arise: Why am I doing this? Why bother? Why do hard things when other people get away with doing easy things? Such questions are part of the voice of doubt, the voice that says, All you really know about the world is that you're going to die, and that nothing you do stays where it is. The people who think of faith as uncritical acceptance usually tell us that doubt is the enemy of faith, that it's something to be fought down and silenced, that if you ever have a doubt you should persuade yourself that you didn't really have it.

I don't agree with this at all. I don't think doubt is the enemy of faith: I think doubt is the fertilizing principle of faith. To doubt the value of everything we're doing is only common sense. The voice of doubt *is* the voice of common sense: if anything at all is true, the vision of doubt is true. The only thing is that it may not be the whole truth. But without constant doubt, faith has nothing to define itself against. It's the same with the other unnatural virtues. Despair is the contrary of hope, but those who have known despair, from the author of the Book of Job to writers of our own day, the people who have looked into the face of nothingness and have seen that nothingness is what there is: they are the people who can tell us about hope. The human body is a solid object, but most of it is water: faith is most likely to be a solid organic unity when it's full of doubts and suspended judgments. Tennyson speaks, in a famous passage, of believing where we cannot prove.[2] But it is more characteristic of the spiritual life to prove where we cannot believe, to bring something creative out of our lives that everybody, including ourselves, thinks is probably nonsense.

So far I've been discussing faith in largely humanistic and secular terms, and, of course, the author of Hebrews is not thinking in secular terms. That's the real crux of what he means by the evidence of things not seen. He thinks of a revelation that begins with the statement that in the beginning God made heaven and earth, and he feels that God demands from man the kind of creative response that his own example has set. He argues that it's only when God himself has become visible as a human life that man can take on his full responsibilities. One implication of his argument is that the world that God made is not the world we are living in now. We get our knowledge of the world we live in from our five senses, and every so often we realize that our senses are self-protecting devices: they're designed mainly not to admit reality but to filter it out. We have reason, but we use most of our reason to rationalize doing unreasonable things. That's why we have to rely so much on hunch and impulse, on drives that come to us from out of the unknown and propel us toward something else that's also unknown. As we see, we're back to the notion of faith that we started with, as accepting something beyond what our reason and senses tell us. This notion, we can now see, has a core of truth in it: it's in the application of the idea that we so often go wrong.

What happens if we try to explore this unknown world, explore it, that is, with a clear mind, and without using any drugs? I think we find that it's rather like what the drugs tell us about, in a very muddled and confused way. That is, I think we find that it separates into two worlds, the worlds of the good and the bad trips, one a world of benevolence, goodness, serenity, and peace; the other a world of horror and cruelty and pointless and purposeless malice. In other words, real life, in the long run, is either life within the love of God or life under the wrath of God. The wrath of God is not some senile ghost throwing a tantrum in the sky. The wrath of God is the revelation, to man, of the kind of hell that man has made, and still can make, of his own life in this world. And the love of God is not some fussy parental projection running our lives for us and snooping into everything we do. The love of God is the revelation, to man, that he can, if he tries, find something at the centre of his life that is not only immortal but invulnerable.

33

Memorial Service for
Mrs. Jean Haddow

20 November 1979

*From the typescript in NFF, 1988, box 47, file 2. Mrs. Haddow was the Fryes'
next-door neighbour at 125 Clifton Road. The readings from the Bible are from
the Authorized Version, but Frye has omitted wordings inappropriate to the
occasion. Each omission and alteration is indicated in an endnote.*

[Readings]

Hear the Apostle Paul concerning death and life:

> Now is Christ risen from the dead, and become the firstfruits of them that
> slept. For since by man came death, by man came also the resurrection of
> the dead. . . . So when this corruptible shall have put on incorruption, and
> this mortal shall have put on immortality, then shall be brought to pass the
> saying that is written, Death is swallowed up in victory. O death, where is
> thy sting? O grave, where is thy victory? The sting of death is sin; and the
> strength of sin is the law. But thanks be to God, which giveth us the victory
> through out Lord Jesus Christ. (1 Corinthians 15[:20–1, 54–7])

Hear the vision of John the Divine in Patmos:

> And I saw a new heaven and a new earth: for the first heaven and the first
> earth were passed away; and there was no more sea. And I John saw the
> holy city, new Jerusalem, coming down from God out of heaven, prepared
> as a bride adorned for her husband. And I heard a great voice out of heaven
> saying, Behold, the tabernacle of God is with men, and he will dwell with

them, and they shall be his people, and God himself shall be with them, and be their God. (Revelation 21[:1–3])

Hear the Psalmist:

Lord, thou hast been our dwelling place in all generations.

Before the mountains were brought forth, or ever thou hadst formed the earth and the world, even from everlasting to everlasting, thou art God. . . .

For a thousand years in thy sight are but as yesterday when it is past, and as a watch in the night. . . .

So teach us to number our days, that we may apply our hearts unto wisdom. . . .

Make us glad according to the days wherein thou hast afflicted us, and the years wherein we have seen evil.

Let thy work appear unto thy servants, and thy glory unto their children.

And let the beauty of the Lord our God be upon us: and establish thou the work of our hands upon us; yea, the work of our hands establish thou it. (Psalm 90[:1–2, 4, 12, 15–17])

Hear the Book of Wisdom:

The souls of the righteous are in the hand of God. For God made not death: neither hath he pleasure in the destruction of the living. For he created all things, that they might have their being: and the generations of the world are wholesome; there is no poison or destruction in them; neither is there a kingdom of death upon the earth. For God created man to be immortal, and made him to be an image of his own eternity. (Wisdom of Solomon 1 [3:1, 1:13–14, 2:23])[1]

Hear the vision of Esdras:

And therefore I say unto you . . . that hear and understand, look for your Shepherd, he shall give you everlasting rest; for he is nigh at hand. . . . Be ready to the reward of the kingdom, for the everlasting light shall shine upon you. . . . Flee the shadow of this world, receive the joyfulness of your glory. . . . O receive the gift that is given you, and be glad, giving thanks unto him that hath called you to the heavenly kingdom. Arise up and stand, behold the number of those that be sealed in the feast of the Lord; which are departed from the shadow of the world, and have received glorious garments of the Lord. (2 Esdras 2[:34–9])²

Hear the insight imparted to Plato:

Then is musical education of the first importance, because rhythm and harmony enter most powerfully into the inner recesses of the soul and lay forcible hands upon it, bearing grace with them, and so filling with grace one who is rightly trained. We shall not become musical until we can recognize the forms of the good. For music can end only with the love of the beautiful. (*Republic*, 3.12 [401d–e])³

Hear the proverbs of King Lemuel:

Who can praise a virtuous woman? for her price is far above rubies. Strength and dignity are her clothing; and she shall rejoice in the time to come. She openeth her mouth with wisdom; and in her tongue is the law of kindness. She looketh well to the ways of her household; her children call her blessed, and her husband praiseth her. Give her of the fruit of her hands; and let her own works praise her in the gates. (Proverbs 31[:10, 25–7, 28, 31])⁴

[Prayers]

Our watching Father, we thank thee that, as those whom we have loved in this world pass from us, so doth thy communion of saints grow, as those who have served thee become one with thee. So may it be with us also, as we draw nearer to the time when our hope changes to vision, and the mystery of death becomes the revelation of life.

O Holy Spirit of love and life, thou dost cherish and foster all things that live, from the moment of creation until now, and from now until the end of time. Thou hast never lost one who has lived in thee, and in that security we rest our faith.

Our Saviour and Redeemer, we are gathered to do honour to one of thy servants who has departed for the city of light which is thy home, and is now hers. Wherefore in all tranquillity of mind we commit her body to the dust and her soul to thy power and love. Of thy love we know that it casteth out fear, and that we can love only because thou hast first loved us. Of thy power we know that thou canst change our

bodies into the likeness of thy glorious body, whereby thou canst subdue all things unto thyself.

[The Lord's Prayer]

[Benediction]

The peace of the Lord of the Resurrection and the Conqueror of death be
with you all.

Amen.

34

A Breath of Fresh Air

23 March 1980

From Deer Park Church Magazine, *June 1980, 1–3. Five typescripts are in NFF, 1988, box 47, file 4. Originally given as a sermon in Metropolitan United Church at the baccalaureate service for the graduating classes of Victoria and Emmanuel Colleges.*

[I myself also am a mortal man, like to all, and the offspring of him that was first made of the earth. . . .

For all men have one entrance into life, and the like going out.

Wherefore I prayed, and understanding was given me: I called upon God, and the spirit of wisdom came to me. . . .

I loved her above health and beauty, and chose to have her instead of light: for the light that cometh from her never goeth out.

All good things together came to me with her, and innumerable riches in her hands.

And I rejoiced in them all, because wisdom goeth before them: and I knew not that she was the mother of them.

I learned diligently, and do communicate her liberally: I do not hide her riches.

For she is a treasure unto men that never faileth: which they that use become the friends of God, being commended for the gifts that come from learning.

God hath granted me to speak as I would, and to conceive as is meet for the things that are given me: because it is he that leadeth unto wisdom, and directeth the wise.] (Wisdom of Solomon 7:1, 6–7, 10–15)

[There was a man of the Pharisees, named Nicodemus, a ruler of the Jews:

The same came to Jesus by night, and said unto him, Rabbi, we know that thou art a teacher come from God: for no man can do these miracles that thou doest, except God be with him.

Jesus answered and said unto him, Verily, verily, I say unto thee, Except a man be born again, he cannot see the kingdom of God.

Nicodemus saith unto him, How can a man be born when he is old? can he enter a second time into his mother's womb, and be born?

Jesus answered, Verily, verily, I say unto thee, Except a man be born of water and of the Spirit, he cannot enter into the kingdom of God.

That which is born of the flesh is flesh; and that which is born of the Spirit is spirit.

Marvel not that I said unto thee, Ye must be born again.

The wind bloweth where it listeth, and thou hearest the sound thereof, but canst not tell whence it cometh, and whither it goeth: so is everyone that is born of the Spirit.] (John 3:1–8)

The Old Testament lesson that I chose for today comes from the Book of Wisdom in the Apocrypha, where the author identifies himself with the legendary King Solomon. He wasn't King Solomon: he lived many centuries later than that weak and extravagant horse trader, but I'm going to call him Solomon because he needs a name. Solomon, then, says that all of us, including kings who get a reputation for wisdom, are born as squalling babies, little pellets of ego, confronted with a huge and frightening world. We have to keep fighting for our balance and sanity in this world, but we can't trust our egos to fight for us. The impulses and resentments and desires that keep boiling inside us also keep taking us over and pretending that they are what we really are, and that what they think they want is what we really want. To "do as we like" usually means getting pushed around by inner impulses that we don't understand, and don't know the origin of. When we go to school, we find that what we mainly know about the world is that it doesn't respond to our desires. Our advance in knowledge is pitifully slow, but our advance in ignorance, in our awareness of what we don't know, grows like Jack's beanstalk. Hence all the bored and sulky expressions we see in schoolrooms.

Most people who get as far as university have adjusted to this, and find the pursuit of knowledge fascinating and exhilarating. That's usually because we've already taken, even if unconsciously, the first great step from knowledge to wisdom. How do we get our knowledge? From what other people tell us, in lectures or books. And how do we verify our knowledge? Through other people's agreement with it. What is real about our minds, apparently, is what unites us with other minds. When we understand this, we stop being isolated egos and become members of a community, a community where intelligence and imagination have a real and constant function. For many, I hope the great majority, the years we spend in a community of knowledge at university are very rich and satisfying years. Yet I have known far too many who have got discouraged and dropped out or felt bitter about college afterwards: I have even known attempts at suicide, one or two of them successful. Not one of these, in my experience, was the result of deficient intelligence: every one was simply a clouding over of what should have been a buoyant and hopeful vision of life.

One reason for this is that the sense of a community of knowledge isn't always strong enough to pull us out of the prison of the ego. Perhaps in the course of our studies we have realized that we know things mainly by putting mental constructs on them. Most of what we know is our own mental construct staring back at us, and most of what isn't that is an impenetrable mystery. That's why Paul speaks of ordinary knowledge as a riddle in a mirror [1 Corinthians 13:12]. We translate that as "in a glass darkly," but I imagine that Paul is thinking of a polished metal mirror, where you see hardly anything at all. What society thinks it knows is at best limited and conditioned, at worst silly and superstitious. Solomon says we have to take one jump beyond the human community: there is still a difference between truth and opinion, and when we feel, however vaguely, that we have a glimpse of truth we also feel that we're in touch with a single mind, an infinite mind that comprehends all nature. Solomon identifies this infinite mind with God: many today would hesitate to call it God and yet feel the pull of the same experience. The scientist Erwin Schrödinger, after spending his life studying subatomic physics, came to the conclusion that "consciousness is a singular of which the plural is unknown."[1] Whether he was right or wrong, he was making much the same journey that Solomon had made before him.

For about three centuries before and three centuries after Christ, many thinkers, including Solomon and the author of John's Gospel, kept struggling with two intuitions. One was that all minds are one mind or consciousness or reason—Logos, as they usually called it. The other was that the observed or objective world, the order of nature, was inseparable from the mental world that observes it. Their speculations were still full of metaphor, and they expressed this by talking about fire, air, water, and earth, the elements of nature as they believed them to be, as though they were alive and identical with the Logos. Heraclitus calls the Logos a dry light; the Stoics called it a fire, and spoke of human minds as seeds or fertilizing sparks of Logos.[2] John says that the Logos became flesh in a specific person [1:14]. And in the third chapter of his Gospel Jesus, the Logos become flesh, is telling Nicodemus that everybody is born of the flesh, but must be also born of water and wind. When Nicodemus says he doesn't understand, Jesus insists that he's talking about matters of experience that can be verified in experience. "We speak of what we know," he says, "and bear witness to what we have seen" [3:11, RSV].

The conversation with Nicodemus seems to me appropriate for a baccalaureate address, because it is one of the few places in the Gospels where Jesus is shown dealing directly with the imaginative needs of an educated person. Nicodemus is a cultivated, intelligent, tolerant member of the Sanhedrin or Jewish Council who is fascinated by Jesus, and wants him to have at the very least a fair hearing. The thing which is most difficult for Nicodemus to do is precisely what he is being challenged to do: to turn around and look his own cultural conditioning in the face, and see how much of it is really for him. Like many men in such situations, he pretends to be stupider than he is. "Can a man re-enter his mother's womb and be reborn?" he asks. Jesus explains that he does not mean reincarnation: he is talking about escaping from a womb, not going back into it again, and Nicodemus' womb is the body of assumptions he acts on without examining. In the next chapter of John we see Jesus talking to a woman of Samaria. In Nicodemus' world, pious Jews do not talk to Samaritans, and a holy man does not enter into casual conversation with a strange woman—certainly not if he knows that she has had five husbands and is shacking up with a sixth. Yet later on we find Nicodemus helping to take Jesus' body down from the cross, so he must have realized at some point that there was more to this reborn world than irresponsible paradox.

The King James Bible represents Jesus as saying: "the wind bloweth where it listeth . . . so is everyone that is born of the Spirit." But in the Greek text the words "wind" and "spirit" are the same. "The wind blows where it likes . . . that's what everyone is like who is born of the wind." Let's try to understand John's own metaphorical language, and not stray off into doctrines elaborated centuries later. Why does Jesus say we have to be born of water and wind? Well, for one thing, the career of Jesus himself began when he was baptized with water and a wind descended on him. So water refers partly to baptism, but more important is the symbolism of water that makes baptism significant. Water is a metaphor for cleansing. And cleansing in turn is a metaphor for freedom. But the wind is free because it's totally identified with itself: no gust of wind can be separated from the surrounding air.

Jesus is taking what Solomon says a step further. To enter a world of freedom where the intellect and imagination can function, we have to become a clean wind, a breath of fresh air. He doesn't say born again; he says born another, from above. Let's explore that metaphor a little. It suggests two levels of life. One is an underground world of roots, a world of darkness and shadows and illusion, where we advance an inch at a time, competing, looking for soft spots, circumventing real resistance, keeping our balance by doing what is done in that world. Above it is a daylight world of space and colour and outline, where water flows and air blows freely.

When we think of things we can't see but know to exist, the first thing we think of is the air. We can't see the air: if we could we could see nothing else. One of the functions of the invisible air is to make the visible world visible. Those born of the wind are invisible and transparent, but that doesn't mean that they're ghosts, or that we're in some kind of Platonic world of thought-forms. It means that their egos have vanished: they're not there as obstacles any more, but have become what the author of Hebrews calls a cloud of witnesses [12:1], making it possible for us to see a real world and breathe its fresh air.

This world of air and light is what Jesus calls the kingdom of heaven. It is a world of the spontaneous freedom, the independent power of action, which the image of the wind suggests. No such power is possible except on a basis of love, and the New Testament constantly insists that love and freedom are the same thing. A pagan writer living about fifty years later than John, Maximus Tyrius, remarks that barbarians have no love because they have no freedom [*Dialogues*, 26.2]. Well, never mind about barbarians: it's just as true for us that whatever threatens or curtails our freedom also increases the amount of hatred and suspicion in society. To fight for freedom is also to fight against hatred: if we set up a counter-hatred we also set up a new tyranny. Without love there is no power to act, only to react, to respond to someone else's threats or aggressions.

So wisdom leads to love, and love leads to power, and power takes us back to wisdom again. In the Psalm we read today we get a glimpse of God's power as the Psalmist thinks of it. For him God's power, like his wisdom and his love, is full of gaiety and joyousness and exuberance, an infinite outpouring of energy. Power, wisdom, and love: these three are all aspects of the same thing, and none of them exists apart from the others. Power without wisdom and love is not power: it is only the ability to destroy. Wisdom without power or love is not wisdom, only rationalizing. Love without wisdom or power is not love, only a rutting season. This schizophrenia is what makes up the world shown us by newspapers and television, the world of the cliché and prejudice and arrogance that is born of the flesh. The New Testament tells us that there is another world that makes considerably more sense, and that this other world is not up in the sky or waiting for us after death, but is directly in front of us. It is in fact the same world as the newspaper and television world, and we are living in it when we open our eyes and stop holding our breath.

35

Baccalaureate Service (I)

29 March 1981

From the typescript in NFF, 1988, box 47, file 4.

Commissioning

When we were born we were sent forth from the presence of God, to manifest that presence by life. The presence remains with us until we are called back into it at death. It is closer to us than the air we breathe. The end of the knowledge with which you have been entrusted is to become aware of that presence. No knowledge that does not lead to such awareness is genuine knowledge.

Benediction

The blessing of the one and only God, in his three persons of power, wisdom, and fellowship, be and abide with us.

36

Funeral Service for Jean Gunn

16 November 1983

From the typescript in NFF, 1988, box 47, file 5. Jean Gunn had worked as a secretary for the English department, chiefly at Victoria College, from 1974 until her death. This service included a reading from Psalm 139 by Julian Patrick and a eulogy by Denton Fox, as well as the readings and prayers by Frye reproduced here. The wording used in the Bible readings is not precisely that of either the Authorized Version or the Revised Standard Version.

[Introductory Verses]

God did not make death, nor does he take pleasure in the destruction of the living. He created all things, that they might attain to their full being: the generative forces of the world are wholesome, and there is no poison of destruction in them. Neither is there any kingdom of death upon the earth, for rightness is immortal. [Wisdom of Solomon 1:13–15]

Seeing then that we have such hope, we use great plainness of speech. At this day the veil is on our minds, but when we turn to the Lord, the veil is taken away. Where the Spirit of the Lord is, there is liberty; and we all, with unveiled face reflecting the glory of the Lord, are changed into the same image from glory to glory. [2 Corinthians 3:12, 15–18]

Every good gift and every perfect gift is from above, and comes down from the Father of lights, with whom is no variableness, neither shadow of turning. Of his own will he brought us forth by the word of truth, that we should be a kind of firstfruits of his creatures. [James 1:17–18]

For now is Christ risen from the dead, and become the first-fruits of them that slept. Since by man came death, by man came also the resurrection of the dead. As in Adam all die, even so in Christ shall all be made alive. For he must reign, till he has put all enemies under his feet. The last enemy that shall be destroyed is death. [1 Corinthians 15:20–2, 25–6]

[Readings]

Because Jean Gunn was so closely associated with the study and teaching of literature, it seems appropriate to let the poets speak for us, as well as to us, on this occasion. They are, respectively, Henry Vaughan, Wallace Stevens, Emily Dickinson, and Margaret Avison.

> He that hath found some fledg'd birds nest, may know
> 　　At first sight, if the bird be flown;
> But what fair Well, or Grove he sings in now,
> 　　That is to him unknown.
>
> And yet, as Angels in some brighter dreams
> 　　Call to the soul, when man doth sleep:
> So some strange thoughts transcend our wonted themes,
> 　　And into glory peep.
>
> If a star were confin'd into a Tomb
> 　　Her captive flames must needs burn there;
> But when the hand that locked her up, gives room,
> 　　She'll shine through all the sphere.[1]

> But she that says good-by losing in self
> The sense of self, rosed out of prestiges
> Of rose, stood tall in self not symbol, quick
>
> And potent, an influence felt instead of seen.
> She spoke with backward gestures of her hand.
> She held men closely with discovery, . . .
>
> It was not her look but a knowledge that she had.
> She was a self that knew, an inner thing,
> Subtler than look's declaiming, although she moved
>
> With a sad splendor, beyond artifice,

Impassioned by the knowledge that she had,
There on the edges of oblivion.

O exhalation, O fling without a sleeve
And motion outward, reddened and resolved
From sight, in the silence that follows her last word.[2]

A World made penniless by that departure
Of minor fabrics begs
But sustenance is of the spirit
The Gods but Dregs[3]

The largeness of mourning,
grief for the known face,
shed an aptitude
for nothing unless certitude.

Words are too many. In this place
loss is torn—
a vividness
lost, out of the sun.

Another's eyes
look now, and say,
one stone-dead face
lived, is, will be:

saw those in prison first,
rose, spoke with his
lost friends,
ate honeycomb, and fish.

Though no words but his
speak, in that airlessness,
who hears them is
roused to the utterance

& who trusts him in this
learns all, past time: a voice
no deafness drowns, at last
Love, a face.[4]

[Hymn]

Jean Gunn and her family want this to be a service of affirmation, and in that spirit we will sing what is perhaps the most powerfully affirmative hymn in the English language, the poem of William Blake known as "Jerusalem," which is no. 157 in your hymnbooks.

[Closing and Benediction]

May the peace of God, who conquered death and brought life into the common day, who is the way for us who walk in darkness, whose light of creation touches us with its living fire, whose Word is the sword of wisdom, whose spirit is unremitting love, unite us in the community that has no barriers, and make his presence known to us now and always.

Amen.

37

Baccalaureate Service (II)

14 April 1985

From the typescript in NFF, 1988, box 49, file 3.

Commissioning—Benediction

Let us serve the mind of God with honest reasoning, with tested evidence, with impartial judgment, with respect for all creative gifts.

Let us serve the spirit of God by working for peace on earth, for good will and tolerance, for fulfilling the dignity of all human beings.

Let us strive for the courage to succeed without arrogance and to fail without despair.

Let us listen to the wise man who would have us rejoice in each one of our years, however many or few, and however frequent the darker days.

Let us abide, now and always, in the presence of the light that created our minds, the love that created our souls, and the peace that so greatly transcends us, the peace that none the less we hope to share.

38

The Dialectic of Belief and Vision

3 December 1985

From Shenandoah, *29, no. 3 (1989): 47–64. Reprinted in* MM, *93–107. A typescript with corrections is in NFF, 1991, box 38, file 5, and clean copies in NFF, 1988, box 49, file 1. Originally delivered as a lecture at the School of Continuing Studies at the University of Toronto, in the series "Religion in the Modern World."*

I

I apologize for a somewhat forbidding title, which was extracted from me in a hurry, and I hope most of the argument will lie down in pleasanter pastures. I am continuing the debate with myself that I started in my book *The Great Code*, which was a tentative exploring of the question: what place does the creative imagination, and the kind of response that we make to a work of literature, have in the study of religion in general, or of the text of the Bible in particular? As I have said in that book and elsewhere, the Bible is as literary as it can be without actually being literature, and hence the response to literature must be in some degree a model of the response to the Bible. I am not denying that there would be other models, including those more familiar to the theologian, the pastor, or the historical critic. But the imaginative model is a genuine and relevant one, too little considered by either literary or religious scholars, at least until very recently.

If one turns from literature to the waste land of critical theory, one finds that the Bible is obviously relevant to nearly all the major issues that criticism is concerned with, and throws a quizzical light on its currently fashionable doctrines, including the doctrine that there aren't and shouldn't be any doctrines. In the course of making a few suggestions here, I hope I can recycle such old and tired words as "faith" and "vision" to fit some kind of critical context. A predecessor of mine in this series of lectures, Dr. Wilfred Cantwell Smith, has distinguished the terms "belief" and "faith" in a recent book, *Faith and Belief*. I think I understand the importance of the distinction, but have room here only for the crudest form of it. "Belief" to me refers to a state of mind, "faith" to its expression in action.

Whenever we read anything, literary or not, we are following a narrative movement, starting at the upper left-hand corner of the first page and gradually working our way down to the lower right-hand corner of the last page. After that, there comes a second effort of attention, the effort of understanding what one has been reading as a whole. This effort has of course been accumulating during the reading, but cannot be adequately expressed until all the words are in. Two sets of metaphors get entangled with this approach. One is the metaphor of hearing and seeing. We "listen to" the words as they come past us one after the other, and then, we say, we "see" what it all means. The other set are metaphors of time and space. We read sequentially, moving in time from one word to the next; we understand what we have read in a simultaneous (*Gestalt*) pattern, in conceptual space as it were. For the first stage, there are conventions that what the poet is uttering is not words but music, the art that most obviously moves in time, and that the prose writer is actually speaking. For the second stage, the word "structure" has entered criticism largely because it is a metaphor drawn from the stationary or visual arts, notably architecture.

Such metaphors have produced many confusions in literary theory, which I think remain confusions, even if my attempts to indicate what they are may be thought oversimplified. In Marshall McLuhan, for example, the book is equated with the linear process of reading, and the electronic media are associated with the total or simultaneous vision. This account of the matter overlooks the fact that the book has to be understood as well as read, and that it patiently waits around, repeating the same words however often it is consulted, until its readers proceed from the linear stage of attention to the next one. The electronic media, more particularly television, greatly foreshorten the linear process, but still they do require us to follow a narrative as well as make an effort at apprehension, which means in practice that many television programmes make a strong immediate impression and are soon forgotten afterwards. McLuhan came to understand this very quickly, and warned us constantly about the dangers of "media fallout," the panic caused by the impact of sense impressions that our minds have not been adequately prepared to receive. But in the meantime he had been ground up in a public relations blender and was unable to correct, or even modify, his absurd popular reputation as the man who said that the book was obsolete.

In the work of Jacques Derrida, and still more in that of his American followers, there is an opposite extreme of emphasis on writing, the *écriture* to which Derrida gives a special meaning.[1] According to this school, most if not all philosophers are engaged in a gigantic conspiracy to use writing as a means of abusing writing. The philosopher's model is one of speaking orally to a group of disciples, and he uses writing as a necessary evil, a substitute for a speaking voice and a visible presence. There is a very complex theory here that I have no time to do justice to, but it seems to me that its kernel is a metaphor and a convention taken in the wrong context. For one thing, prose, which all philosophers now use, is based on writing, and oral speech is associative in rhythm. Oral speech often enters into the design of prose in order to informalize it, but prose remains radically a written medium, a form of *écriture*, whatever the author wants it to be or says it is. It is the written structure, not the speaker's presence, to which the response is made: the speaking presence is a conventional pretence. We may compare the parallel convention I just referred to, of the poet's pretence that he is really producing song, or music, rather than words. The epilogue to Milton's *Lycidas* tells us that the narrator has been simultaneously singing and playing a wind instrument. This would be a most impressive feat to watch, but something tells us that if we pursue the matter further convention and metaphor will lead us astray.

The metaphorical use of "structure" has also led to confusion. It is often said or assumed that the effort to understand a work of literature as a whole is really seeking the destruction of that work, as once something has been completely understood there is nothing left of it. But the notion that one has attained such understanding is always an illusion. There certainly are structures in words that can be dispensed with after we have understood them, but the classics of literature are not among them. If what we have read is on the level of Plato or Dante or Shakespeare, our first efforts of structural understanding will be inadequate and immature, but we continue to make further efforts. This continuity of efforts may go on all through our lives, if we are professionally concerned with literature or philosophy. Even then understanding it never becomes definitive: we grow, but the *Republic* or the *Purgatorio* or *King Lear* do not shrink. The work itself has acquired a history: it has picked up centuries of former readers, and brings something of their reading down to us as a part of its own meaning. It will also go on into the future, so that definitive understanding at any stage is not even theoretically possible. Every such work adumbrates something of the paradox of incarnation, the enclosing of the infinite in a finite form. Some literary critics mention this analogy in order to deny or attack.it, on the ground that it makes them nervous, but it is still a datum of critical experience.

One reason why the metaphors of hearing and seeing enter into this aspect of criticism so persistently is that in some areas hearing and seeing become actual sense experiences. One such area is religious ritual. One thinks of the collect of the mass followed by the elevation of the Host; of the words spoken in the mystery religions followed by the exhibition of a visual emblem—at Eleusis, apparently, a reaped ear of corn—and similarly in other contexts. Zen Buddhism has a legend that after the Buddha had preached a sermon, he held up a golden flower, the only member of the audience who got the point being, of course, the founder of Zen. Zen appears to be, or include, a technique of becoming "enlightened" (another visual metaphor) by evading the preliminary address to the ear—an obvious reason for its popularity in the West in the age of television. Going back to metaphor, one thinks also of the climax of the Book of Job, when Job says: "I have heard of thee by the hearing of the ear: but now mine eye seeth thee" [42:5].

In reading a work of literature, no process of belief, in the ordinary sense, is involved. What is involved is a continuous process of acceptance. We accept every word given us in the text without question (unless we are textual editors), and withhold our response until the end. Literature differs from descriptive or factual verbal structures in the degree of emphasis it places on this postponing of response. There are also different degrees of response within literature. A response to a novel of Trollope or George Eliot would include some consideration of the way it illustrates the life and social conditions of its time, but to *Alice in Wonderland* or Rider Haggard's *She* there would be little response of that kind.

If, on the other hand, we are reading a newspaper, the acceptance of what we read is continuously involved with tentative reactions of belief, positive or negative. This item may well be true; this next one may be a rumour; a third one may be slanted by rhetoric and partisanship. Whether such news stories are "true" or only made up is a primary issue, and so we continually compare what we read with what we guess or have read elsewhere about situations in the world outside the newspaper. The fact that no clear or unambiguous "truth" in such matters is possible makes the degrees of approximate truth attainable all the more important.

These differing reactions emerge clearly in the confusions over the phrase "literal meaning." Traditionally, literal meaning has applied to the newspaper type of reaction, where the acceptance of the words is accompanied by some belief or disbelief in their substantial relation to historical events or doctrines. But a body of words cannot be literally anything but a body of words, and literal meaning seems to me to apply only to the sense of a verbal structure in itself, not to its correspondence to something outside itself. In reading the Bible we find ourselves following a verbal structure intensely metaphorical in its language and full of events that seem to have no counterpart in actual history or in ordinary experience. For Samson's feats with a jaw-bone, for Jonah's maritime adventures, for Elisha's accomplishments in magic, for Jesus' feeding five thousand with five loaves and two fishes, afterwards gathering up the fragments that nothing might be lost, it seems clear that the literary model of acceptance is better than the newspaper model of tentative belief for the appropriate response. The postponing of commitment until after the linear stage of acceptance seems to me to be one of the things that Paul is referring to when he speaks of the analogy or proportion of faith (Romans 12:6).

In the era when science was embryonic and objectors were silenced by secular authority, the elements in the Bible that contradict ordinary reason and sense experience were less problematic. If faith fulfilled sense experience and reason, well and good; if it violated them, so much the better: God would approve of the sacrifice of the intellect involved, and would attach special merit to accepting the incredible as factual. Of course in some contexts there is a good deal to be said for Tertullian's axiom, "I believe because it is absurd and inept,"[2] because that stretches the mind to accommodate paradox, and resists the drift to narcissism in all habitual mental processes. But in the twentieth century a totally uncritical response is bound to create a latent hysteria in the believer's mind, leaving an impression that there are aspects of his mind that do not agree with much of what he says he believes, but that they are being internally shouted down or rationalized into silence.

In the more extroverted "literalists" one may see hysteria in the staring glazed eyes, the loud overconfident voice, the forced heartiness, that accompany so much expression of conviction on this level. In more introverted and speculative types there is a high rate of intellectual mortality: a "crisis of faith" frequently occurs sooner or later, and a crisis of faith is normally followed by the total loss of it. I pass over the more pathological and racist forms of such attitudes, merely saying that hysteria, by insisting that an inner state of mind is united when it is actually divided, is bound to project its frustrations sooner or later on some outward scapegoat who symbolizes the objecting inner self. The assertion "I believe that" is not simply meaningless but actively dangerous when we still don't know who "I" is or what "that" is.

Belief of this sort has no way of distinguishing what one believes from what one thinks or believes one believes, the same confusion that led Don Quixote into so many sad predicaments. I have often noticed that a man's beliefs are not revealed by any profession of faith, however sincere, but by what his actions show that he believes. In this respect practically everyone has a belief of some kind, if it is only belief in the importance of one's own interests. Faith, then, is whatever consistency one's behaviour exhibits throughout one's life, and one's lifestyle is the continuous revelation of one's real faith. And faith, even the most limited or antisocial kind, must be powered by some kind of vision. One who believes only in the importance of his own interests will still have some rudimentary vision of what he thinks those interests are. To use terms that have been extensively employed ever since Hegel, faith is the continuous struggle of a time-bound man to pursue the *for itself* which is the burden brought into the world by consciousness.[3] Vision is focused on an aspect of a model world which is the *in itself*, a model that is ineffective if separated from the *for itself*.

Perhaps we are now in a position to confront the definition of faith in the New Testament. The Epistle to the Hebrews tells us that faith is the *hypostasis* of the hoped for and the *elenchos* of things not seen [11:1]. *Hypostasis* is among other things a Greek philosophical term of which the Latin counterpart is *substantia*, and the Vulgate so renders the word, followed by the 1611 Bible, which says "substance." Modern translations usually render it as "assurance," because Paul uses the word in this sense. But Paul is not the author of Hebrews, and "substance" seems to me closer to what is meant here (see also Hebrews 1:3). The believer is being told that he has got something, not being reassured that he is eventually going to get it. Similarly, the word *elenchos* is usually rendered "proof" or "evidence," and commentators often explain that this refers to the inward certainty that requires no external confirmation. But this seems oversubjective, and "proof of the unseen" is an awkward expression. Something like "manifestation" or visible form seems closer to the context. I have often noted that the Bible shows relatively little interest in the invisible world as a separate order; it tends to regard the invisible as the medium for the visible, much as the invisible air makes it possible for us to see anything at all. The author of Hebrews in fact goes on to say this a verse or two later.

Again, if faith is the substance of the "hoped for" (*elpizomenon*), faith and hope, two of the three great theological virtues named by Paul [1 Corinthians 13:13], are essentially connected. It is impossible to separate hope from a visionary quality; hope is not a mere subjective yearning but the construction of a model or ideal in the mind that our actions move toward realizing. "Fear and Hope are Vision," said Blake.[4] Everyone with any social function has some model community in his mind in the light of which he does his job, such as a community of better health for the doctor, of clearer judgment for the teacher, of fewer wrecked and wasted lives for the social worker. The model so constructed is a myth or fiction, and in normal minds it is known to be a fiction. That does not make it unreal; what happens is rather an interchange of reality and illusion in the mind. Most of what we call objective reality is a human construct left over from yesterday; much of this could do with improvement, and the model that hope affords shows up a good deal of this construct as both undesirable and removable, and to that extent unreal. The touchstone of reality is the fictional model vision. The Epistle of James talks about "works" as the complement of faith [2:14–26], but it seems to me a better metaphor to regard faith and hope, belief and vision, as the parents of which works are the offspring.

Faith, then, as distinct from professed faith, is the activity of realizing a visionary model in the mind suggested by hope. I am aware that this collides directly with the traditional view, in which the visionary model of faith is the professed faith, the Apostles' Creed or what not. I shall give my reasons in a moment for thinking that this self-enclosed conception of faith is inadequate, but what concerns us just now is the need for two elements, a programme of work and a model to work from. Belief without vision, the ordering of one's life without a clear notion of what it should be ordered to, soon breaks down, within religious bodies, into anxieties over secondary moral issues. When we talk with some members of those bodies, we find all too often that anxieties over liquor, contraception, divorce, dietary ordinances, absence from church, and the like have blotted out most of the religious horizon for them. Parallel forms of blindness are found in the secular world, such as that of the politician who has forgotten what his party ever stood for in the effort to circumvent the intrigues that surround him. Vision without belief produces what the philosopher Sartre calls, very accurately, "bad faith."[5] This is as a rule the contemplation of a timeless body of truth *in* itself, with none of the limitations of a specific temporal and historical conditioning *for* oneself taken into account. No human being is in a position to gain any benefit from that kind of vision, and the truths such a vision express soon shrivel into platitudes, which are true only because they are too vague to be opposed.

I think that creeds and dogmatic formulations of faith, however important they have been historically and however much modernized in vocabulary, are written in the wrong language for the twentieth century. It so happens that the Bible suggests, in its structure, what the more appropriate language is, but to understand this we have to return to the distinction between preliminary hearing and final seeing that we began with. According to the opening of Genesis, God placed in Eden every tree that was pleasant to sight, and evidently made himself visually available to unfallen humanity. After that comes the fall and the plunging of the human race into history. Here there is no difficulty about hearing the voice of a speaking God, either directly or through his prophets, but any suggestion that God has actually been seen is surrounded by editorial euphemisms and expurgations. With the coming of Jesus in the Gospels visibility is attached to the Godhead, but it is a curiously disguised visibility: the Gospels make it clear that most people in Jesus' vicinity, including the disciples themselves, were confused about many of the things they experienced. Like their descendants down to our own time, they were obsessed about what was happening historically and getting nowhere, and so overlooking the unique importance of what was happening mythically. The transition from hearing to seeing, however, and from time and history to something beyond both, is achieved in the final apocalypse, the account of a Second Coming when, it is promised, "every eye shall see him" [Revelation 1:7].

What the apocalypse proves to be is not a summary of Biblical doctrines or even a summary of its historical narrative. It is primarily a vision of a body of imagery, where the images of every category of being—divine, angelic, paradisal, human, animal, vegetable, and inorganic—are all identified with the body of Christ. That means that all the images are metaphorically related, metaphor being expressed as a statement of identity, in the form "this is that." Whatever is not part of the body of Christ forms a demonic shadow, a parody of the apocalyptic vision in a context of evil and tyranny. This ultimate separation of vision from shadow, the heaven-world and the hell-world, is alluded to in the Gospel parables as a separation that human society cannot attain to in a world of time, but will see as the revelation that comes with the ending of time. Meanwhile, every unreality that the vision of hope in the mind perceives in the world around us is part of an apocalyptic judgment on that world.

The unwillingness of so many religious temperaments to try to grasp the reality of a revelation in any but doctrinal terms recurs in a number of religious communions. It accounts for the divergence in emphasis between, say, the Talmudic and Kabbalistic traditions in Judaism, the scholastic and mystical developments in medieval Catholicism, a parallel difference in Islamic thought, and the Calvinist and Anabaptist traditions in Protestantism. The Reformation was founded on the doctrine of justification through faith, but conceiving faith as something to be expressed in the language of creed or thesis minimized the visionary element in it. We notice that Calvin could make very little of the Book of Revelation in his Biblical commentaries; in spite of its dense texture of allusions to the Old Testament, the quality of its language eluded him. I have now to try to put that language into its cultural context.

II

Every human society is surrounded by a cultural envelope of traditions, beliefs, rituals, customs, and laws. Man cannot live directly in nature; without this envelope he is more vulnerable than a snail without its shell. The cultural envelope is usually called an ideology, which is adequate enough for fairly advanced societies. But ideology suggests the language of thesis and proposition, and hence a basis for argument. Every thesis contains its opposite, and every ideology sooner or later acquires a militant and aggressive quality. Eventually we realize that all ideologies are primarily rationalizations of authority, whether existing or fossilized. They defend our religious beliefs from heresies, our social loyalties from other nations—especially, in our day, nations with different economies—our class structure against revolution or counter-revolution.

It has always been my contention that ideologies are secondary and derived expressions of social concern, and that what they are derived from is mythology. To me a myth is first of all a *mythos*, a story or narrative, and what societies do first of all is make up stories. Myths differ from other types of primitive stories, such as folk tales, not in their structure but in a peculiar importance they have for the society that produces them. They tell a society what it is felt that that society needs to know about its religion, its history, its law and custom, its class structure, and to some degree, although a myth is not a proto-science, its environment. That is, mythology generally comes to a society already in some form of ideology. But then the cultural influences diverge: ideology drifts toward the thesis-language of law, philosophy, and theology; mythology, as an interlocking body of stories, is directly recreated only by literature. A story, unlike a proposition, cannot be refuted or argued about.

What a myth expresses, I think, so far as we can get it disentangled from its ideological developments, is human concern on its primary level. Primary human concerns are those common to the whole human race: concerns over food, sex, shelter, and survival: a freedom without anarchy, a social order without slavery, a happiness without misery. I would not be understood as saying that mythology is concerned only with wish-fulfilment fantasies. On the contrary, what it expresses, nine-tenths of the time, is anxiety over the frustration of those wishes. The dying god myth explored by Frazer, for example, fits into a hundred disparate societies in a hundred disparate ways, though the myth itself is intelligible all over the world as a part of man's concern with the food supply. But the concern inherent in the myth is expressed in many remarkably repulsive stories and rituals, which can sometimes, as in Aztec Mexico, extend to a kind of cultural mass suicide.

It is mainly because of the predominance of anxiety in mythology that, all through history, these primary concerns have had to give way to the secondary demands of ideologies. We want to survive, but we go to war; we want freedom, but live in societies committed to slavery or exploitation; we want happiness, but somehow come to terms with a happiness that depends on the slavery of others. At present human society exhibits a number of ideologies in an adversarial relation to one another. In the twentieth century there are still a great many people, in all parts of the world, including this part, who would think it highly desirable to go to war to smash someone else's ideology. They are restrained only by the reflection that, in an age of nuclear weapons and pollution cutting down the supply of breathable air and drinkable water, we cannot afford such gestures any more. It is, in other words, only in our own day that we seem to have reached a point where we can see that primary concerns must at last become primary, or else.

Literature, like the mythology from which it descends, expresses primary concern, but it may express it positively in romantic fantasy or negatively in irony and satire, and in our day irony and satire strongly predominate. Further, while the great writers of literature understand that they are committed to mythology, it is inevitable, when the theory of criticism is so confused and so dominated by ideologies, that many writers should also be confused about how their social function operates and what their authority as writers is based on. Hence their myths all too often emerge in the perverted form of obsolete or discredited ideologies. Examples are W.B. Yeats, Ezra Pound, and D.H. Lawrence, all of them great writers with much essential to say about the human condition, all of them apt to turn into cranks or fanatics when their myths decline into ideology. Here is one of the terrible final fragments of Ezra Pound's *Cantos*, written after the wrecking of his life had finally begun to erode his belief in the value of what he had done:

> M'amour, m'amour
>   what do I love and
>   where are you?
> That I lost my center
>   fighting the world.
> The dreams clash
>   and are shattered—
> and that I tried to make a paradiso
>   terrestre.

What, we may ask, does the vision of an earthly paradise have to do with the extraordinary *mélange* of Confucian philosophy, social credit, Provençal poetry, the economic policies of John Adams, the history of

Renaissance princes, and hundreds of other things that make up the pastiche of the *Cantos*? The meaning of the passage is quite clear in the mythological context of poetry. The "center" of a poet is the body of what he loves, or what Blake calls his emanation.[6] Searching for this centre, which he has lost sight of in his ideological turmoils, this poet realizes, among the shattered fragments of his dreams, that he had once wanted to express the central mythological vision of the earthly paradise. Myth has to do, we said, with primary concerns, with the food supply, the restoring of sex to love (as distinct from exploiting the genital machinery), with the building of dwelling places for living people, for the gods, and for the dead. But the limit of the mythological vision is not the achievable but the conceivable; it provides a context for these concerns in which nature is infinitely closer to humanity, and human beings to one another, than we have ever experienced in history.

The ideological imagination, though it may accept the vision of unfallen humanity as a traditional mythological datum, cannot incorporate it into its orbit of thinking. It cannot go behind Adam after his fall, struggling to extract a living from an alienated nature, his link with his creator fatally impaired, his lethally feuding family going off to found cities and start more feuds. As long as this vision of ideological man stays within the traditional religious and mythological framework, something of the original myths may cling to it. But now, when the struggle with nature seems to have reached a plateau of independence, and divine origin seems more and more irrelevant even to those who accept it, we are finally achieving a clarified view of what ideological man is. We may now see him as a crazy Oedipus obsessed by two overmastering impulses: one to murder his father God, the other to rape his mother Nature. By "his father" I mean the source of his life, whether we call it God or not.

If there is any substance in this argument, one thing is clear: in the contemporary world of ideological deadlock, the worst thing we can do is to try to "demythologize" anything, in or outside religion. I see it as the essential task of the literary critic to distinguish ideology from myth, to help reconstitute a myth as a language, and to put literature in its proper cultural place as the central link of communication between society and the vision of its primary concerns. Every ideology, because it is or includes the rationalizing of a claim to social authority, tries to get itself established as the right or "orthodox" one. In our day there is an obvious need for an ecumenical source of power that will cut across all these claims, and it seems equally obvious that one must look for such a power source within the visionary aspect of these ideologies, the aspect that links them with mythology. It is only mythology, I feel, that can really express the vision of hope, the hope that is focused on a more abundant life for us all, not the hope of finally refuting the arguments of Moslems or Marxists.

Ideology is argumentative, but a dogmatic basis for ideology renders it impervious to argument, and creates in the world not so much iron curtains as a series of unbreachable Maginot lines. Certain forms of academic religious ideology are more flexible than this, in the sense that they understand how propositions contain their opposites. In learned journals concerned with religion one finds that thinkers who have repudiated all religious connections (Marx, Freud, Heidegger, Nietzsche, for example) seem to be quite as useful and are certainly as frequently referred to as the accredited theologians. But one wonders if this is not partly because there is as yet no political "crunch" in this field. One should not overlook the importance of ecumenical movements either, but they again are subject to the same difficulty as the United Nations and parallel secular assemblies, of being aggregates of sovereign bodies whose delegates are likely to be recalled if they seem about to infringe on that sovereignty. Meanwhile, no literary critic can be in doubt about the intolerance of secular ideologies to myth, considering the very large number of twentieth-century writers who have been driven into silence, exile, imprisonment, suicide, or judicial murder by ideology-obsessed governments.

One large gap in our argument remains—at least one that I can see. I have tried to explain why I think it essential to separate faith from professed faith, and to conceive of genuine faith as a continuous sequence of committed actions guided by a vision. I also said that vision without belief leads to Sartre's "bad faith," the contemplation of objective *in itself*, an unchanging reality that we are not and never can be a part of. In a culture where mythology is largely ignored except for works of disinterested imagination, how is it possible to connect such a mythology to any kind of active faith? Here again I think we have to look at the structure of the Bible for a clue.

At the beginning of the Bible, we said, we have the contrast between the mythical vision of an earthly paradise, and the subsequent vision of man alienated from his God and from nature, subject to sin and death, and about to begin the history that Byron calls the devil's scripture.[7] We said that it took the mythological imagination of the poet to recreate the paradisal vision, whether positively, as in Eliot's rose garden or Yeats's Byzantium,[8] or ironically and elegiacally, as in Dostoevsky's *Dream of a Ridiculous Man*. One feature that we notice about the Eden story is that nature, the external environment, is not simply regenerate but seems to be identified with the humanity that lives within it. All the animals are brought to the "adam" to be named; the trees are pleasant to sight and good for food. The element in experience that we call aesthetic, the ability to see the world around us as beautiful, is not here purely in the eye of the beholder, but is an objective fact as well. The world makes human sense, but there is nothing of the fallacy of trying to reduce the beautiful to the functional; there is rather that sense of purposiveness without purpose that Kant recognized as central to beauty.[9]

Again, the Old Testament word for God, "Elohim," with its plural form, however assimilated to a strict monotheism, seems still to contain a slight sense of plurality in the godhead. Certainly there seem to be other spiritual beings than man whom God addresses, and Milton, in *Paradise Lost*, not only has an angel paying a social call on Adam and Eve but makes Adam say to Eve, with all the accumulated wisdom of being her senior by half an hour or so,

> Millions of spiritual creatures walk the earth
> Unseen, both when we wake and when we sleep. [bk. 4, ll. 677–8]

The great imaginative power of the gods of pagan polytheism lay in the fact that they suggested a relation of identity between a personality and an aspect of nature: there were sea-gods, sun-gods, earth-gods or goddesses, and the like. We feel that the unfallen state included some sense of identity with nature, and that to recover or attain such a state would be to return to it, or, as Emily Dickinson says,

> He will refund us finally
> Our confiscated gods.[10]

But it is the other end of the Bible that I want particularly to look at now. One gap between mythological and ideological imagination I have placed as the point of the fall, where the beginning of history separates from a state of being which is clearly not historical. We see already that myth is not second-hand history, though it sometimes uses historical material to transpose a remote past into a present that confronts the reader directly. At the other end of the Bible, the ideological imagination conceives in the immediate future a millennium, the inaugurating of a Messianic kingdom when justice and peace will spread across the earth. The dream of this imminent kingdom seems to be all over the New Testament, and as the years passed and it failed to materialize it changed into an indefinitely postponed future event. Here again the mythological imagination deals not with a millennium but with an apocalypse, a total transformation of reality which has no more direct connection with the future than the Eden story has with the past, but confronts us with the imperious invitation to drink of its water of life.

The apocalypse, we suggested, was a vast metaphorical structure in which all categories of reality, or what was later called the chain of being, are identified with the body of the Messiah. The golden city which is the New Jerusalem, the trees and rivers of Eden, the final union of bridegroom and bride, are all there, and much besides. The metaphor, which, we said, normally comes to us as a statement of identity of the "this is that, A is B" type, develops out of a phase of consciousness where there is as yet no consistent sense of the separation of subject and object, but rather the easy mingling of personal and natural presence that we find in the god. In literature, the metaphor is the commonest of all verbal figures, so common that perhaps it is part of the function of literature to keep the metaphorical habit of thinking in identities alive. And yet in literature as we know it there are no "real" identities; all literary metaphors are verbal associations only. In literature we may say something like

> Now is the winter of our discontent
> Made glorious summer by this son of York, [*Richard III*, 1.1.1–2]

which, in literature, means, "it is *as though* our discontent were a winter, and the House of York a summer sun." Everyone knows that such metaphors mean nothing at all in the actual world.

But in the Bible the conception of *word* is greatly extended from spoken or written language, and perhaps the metaphorical structure in the Bible can be extended also, moving back to recapture some of the existential force that the metaphor once suggested. No one can read far in, for example, mystical literature without feeling the urgency of the question of whether there is an identity of the kind that the verbal metaphor suggests but does not assert. In fact some sense of ultimate identity, of the kind implicit in the Hindu formula "thou art that,"[11] seems to lie behind nearly all the profoundest religious feelings and experiences, whatever the actual religion, even when the ideological censor forbids its expression as a doctrine.

It is perhaps unnecessary to add that two things happen at the next stage in this development of imaginative identity. One is that Paul's third great virtue, *agape* or love, makes its appearance, not as a third virtue but as the only virtue there is. Outside its orbit, faith and hope are not necessarily virtues at all; the same machinery of action conforming to a model vision goes into operation when we are embezzling funds or murdering our spouses. The other is that the sense of initiative reverses itself. So far we have spoken only of what the human subject is trying to do, but we soon realize that at a certain point we enter into a vaster operation where human personality and will are still present, but where the self-begotten activity no longer seems to be the only, or even the essentially, active power. The initiative is now usually seen to come, not from some unreachable *in itself* world, but from an infinitely active personality that both enters us and eludes us. To go further than this would require another paper that I am not qualified to write. I stop with saying that pursuing the dialectic of belief and vision until they merge seems to be the first step on the ladder that Jacob saw in the "dreadful place" of the *mysterium tremendum*, the mystery that is really a revelation, and mysterious only because its revelation has no end.

39

To Come to Light

5 October 1986

From Frye's No Uncertain Sounds *(Toronto: Chartres Books, 1988), 31–7. Excerpts published as "The Dedicated Mind" in* Vic Report, *15 (Winter 1986– 87): 12–13. The dedication, to his late wife Helen, reads: "In memoriam/ H.K.F./1910–1986." Originally given as a Thanksgiving address at the 150th anniversary of the founding of Victoria College. In this address, the Biblical quotations are taken from the Revised Standard Version unless otherwise indicated.*

> For there is nothing hid, except to be made manifest; nor is anything secret, except to come to light. (Mark 4:22)

Mark's verse occurs four times in the synoptic Gospels, and Luke, who quotes it twice, adds the clause: "What you have whispered in private rooms shall be proclaimed upon the housetops" [12:3]. At the time and place of the New Testament, there were various cults claiming a special knowledge of mysteries to be revealed to initiates. According to this text, the Gospel doesn't reveal a special knowledge so much as an expanding of vision, one that makes a new kind of sense of whatever genuine knowledge we already have. I say genuine knowledge, because we remember that Adam and Eve were forbidden the knowledge of good and evil that went along with their loss of innocence. What they got was a repressive morality founded on a sexual neurosis. That knowledge was forbidden because it is not a genuine knowledge of anything, even of good and evil.

What is proclaimed from the housetops, on the other hand, carries with it the liberty to know and imagine: it offers unlimited access to the treasures of the intellect that the Biblical wisdom literature talks about. A proclamation like this can't be separated from whatever is proclaimed in a classroom or a research paper or a book of poems, or anywhere that an intelligible view of the world is being seriously looked for. The wisdom books tell us that knowledge is the road to wisdom, and that wisdom is one of the most serious goals in life. At the same time it's constantly associated with the highest kind of pleasure. The Book of Proverbs speaks of wisdom as "playing" throughout the earth;[1] the Book of Wisdom itself says that in the friendship of wisdom there is "pure delight" [8:18].

In ordinary speech we distinguish work and play: work is energy used for a further end in view; play is energy used for its own sake. Often enough work is drudgery and play a killing of time: that makes all the more important those aspects of life in which work and play are close together, or become the same thing. If you look at what we associate with the word "play" you can see what I mean. We "play" the piano or tennis, or actors put on a "play," and to do such playing well takes a lot of work. But work looks very different when some end in play is visible. For one thing, play is freedom: if we practise the piano we are setting ourselves free to play it. So play, freedom, wisdom, and all work directed toward these things, point most clearly to what human life should be like.

The assimilating of work and play is very clear in a university, where students are mature enough to see that the work of obtaining knowledge leads directly into an enlarging of outlook, the free play of an awakened mind. A century ago the philosopher Nietzsche, even though he was writing from a point of view very different from our Gospel text, also spoke of a "joyful knowledge," and ridiculed those who thought of the intellect as, in his words, "a clumsy, gloomy, creaking machine, difficult to start."[2] Naturally, the world is full of people who hate everything the university stands for, especially when they suspect that some pleasure may be involved. Dictatorships try to suppress the critical intelligence wherever they can; our own society is profoundly and perversely anti-intellectual; some religious groups think that only a blind faith can see clearly. All such attitudes are dangerous to civilized life and abhorrent to the Gospel.

There is a curious feature in what the New Testament says of the effect of the Gospel on the mind. Paul sometimes speaks of Christ as a whole of which we are the parts: everyone who relates oneself to Christ lives within the body of Christ, like cells within our bodies [1 Corinthians 12:12–13]. At other times he speaks of "Christ in me," where the individual Paul is a whole of which Christ is a part [Galatians 2:20]. This double perspective meets us in a lot of human situations, not necessarily Christian ones. There are times when we feel that we are part of a larger body—greater than we know, as the poet says[3]—and that our individual selves are not lost but fulfilled in that body. Such feelings may be rare or brief, but they are not illusions, even though they may often be projected on things that turn out to be illusions. No religion can dispense with this part-of-a-whole feeling, nor could anyone devote one's life to a serious cause without it. On the other hand, we live in a whole-with-a-part life most of the time: in day to day experience we have to keep on being separate individuals. But for the best kind of life we need to carry something around within us that can turn us inside out at any moment.

The university, once again, gives the clearest example of what I mean. Undergraduates are parts of which the university is the whole; after graduation they are individuals again, and their university experiences have become a part of them. What brings alumni back to reunions is not nostalgia, even if it includes that: it is important to recall a time in one's life when work and play were much the same thing, and when one could directly watch human intelligence turning the vast machinery of human knowledge and creative power. Not that undergraduates live with that intensity of vision, but they sometimes know that it is there, and they know it more clearly after they get their degrees. There is no irony whatever in saying that the memory of one's experience as a student is more real than the experience itself.

A hundred and fifty years is not so old as universities go: the other college that succeeded in graduating me, Merton College in Oxford, is 720 years old. But the last century and a half, even the last half-century, has gone through a quite bewildering amount of history. At the time of Victoria's centenary, in 1936, in the midst of the Depression, there was a great deal of talk about economic "systems." A lot of people, not all of them students by any means, then believed that the capitalist system would evolve or revolutionize into a socialist system, which was assumed to be not only more efficient but morally superior.

I seldom hear people talking about "systems" with any confidence now. The world today is in so deeply revolutionary a state that all systems, whatever they're called, are equally on the defensive, trying to prevent further change. Nobody knows what form such a world will settle into, or even whether the word "settle" describes what it will do. Ten years ago there was a rush by security-minded students into what seemed at the time safe professions, medicine, law, engineering, computer science. But now many students have stopped doing that and are simply studying what most interests them, whether it is calculus or Classics, biology or Buddhism. We often say that in so uncertain a time it is the trained mind that has the best chance of survival, but it's precisely one's specific training that may go out of date. The mind best fitted for survival in any world is the mind that has discovered how knowledge can be joyful, leading to the friendship with wisdom that is pure delight, and is ready to tackle any kind of knowledge with clarity of perception and intentness of will. I should call such a mind not a trained but a dedicated mind, and any business or profession would be lucky to have one.

When Victoria was founded there was a widespread feeling that a university could be religious or secular, but not both. Cardinal Newman wrote a classic defence of this view: for him, the university had in the long run to become either a function of the church or a mere finishing school for a privileged class. In the United States there was an opposite emphasis on the separation of church and state that gave public support only to secular universities. There was also the small group of Methodist clergymen who met at Ancaster in 1829 and passed a resolution to set up an academy in Upper Canada, which would be church-related but emphatically not sectarian. There followed, in course of time, the federation with the University of Toronto that was joined by Trinity and St. Michael's. Federation is based on a principle that is better adapted to present-day conditions than Newman's view of the church or the American view of the state. This is the principle that a contrast or opposition between the religious and the secular, the sacred and the profane, does not work any more, if it ever did. Everything in religion has its secular aspect, and everything in secular life has religious implications, however ignored or undefined they may be.

In a world like ours differences in faith are much less important than agreement in charity. Faith, or the rejection of faith, often revolves around the question, "Why would a good God permit so much evil and suffering?" Charity starts with the question, "Why do we permit so much evil and suffering?" and that is a question on which all men and women of good will can act instead of arguing in circles.

In moments of despair or bereavement or horror, we find ourselves staring blankly into an unresponding emptiness, utterly frustrated by its indifference. We come from the unknown at birth, and we rejoin it at death with all our questions about it unanswered. Sometimes we wonder whether humanity is capable of living in any world at all where consciousness is really a function of life. In a century of nuclear bombs and a pollution that threatens even the supply of air to breathe and water to drink, the human race often seems like a kind of crazy Oedipus, obsessed by the desire to kill his father God and rape his mother Nature. By father and mother I mean the spiritual and physical origins of humanity, whether we accept the sexual metaphors or not.

This impression of a mindless universe is one that we get from certain aspects of nature. As long as we feel alone with a world of natural objects, where everything is an "it," whatever is conscious will be an ego or "I," and human society a collection of egos. Nature, not being conscious, doesn't care whether we have any knowledge or not: we, so far as we are merely egos, care about knowledge only as a way of getting one step ahead of the next person. Such a society is what the Bible means by the Tower of Babel: a world where people either do not understand us or are simply distorted echoes of ourselves. Nations in this kind of world become hysterically hostile, piling up weapons with a kind of lethargic panic, yet half fascinated too by the thought of the destruction their release would cause. The arts and sciences do what they can to make better sense of things, but a Tower of Babel society can use art and science only for exploitation, whether of other human beings or of nature.

Let us look back at our text, which sets the manifest against the hidden, the proclaimed against the secret, the light against the darkness. It is obviously talking about some kind of community, growing out of the teachings of Jesus to his disciples, which is thought of as a social force making for goodness and wisdom. The closer we approach such goals, the further we get from this dreary society of egos. Clearly, no one can say "I am wise and good" without strongly suggesting that one is nothing of the kind. "Wise" and "good" are words that cannot possibly end any sentence starting with "I am." Even Jesus, we remember, resented being addressed as "Good Master" [Matthew 19:16, AV]. As for wisdom, William Blake said that wisdom would result from a fool's persisting in folly,[4] and Paul says something very similar [1 Corinthians 3:18]. And the more we actually know, the less inclined we are to use metaphors about seizing or grasping or possessing truth. The truth that makes one free must be shared: it cannot be owned.

However, even within a church or a university, to say nothing of a nation or a political party, our lives are still ego-ridden, still full of fear and aggressiveness. No actual community of human beings can break the deadlock of a world where there are only separated subjects and unconscious objects. That is why the New Testament is constantly bringing before us the word "spirit," a third force which it identifies both with God and with the kind of understanding it wants us to develop about God. In all languages relevant to the Bible the words for spirit are closely related to the words for air and breath. It is not hard to see why. Taking in air is the body's primary concern from the moment of birth onward. The Spirit of the Bible is to the conscious world what the air is to the physical world. In the physical world, the things we see are visible only because the air is invisible. For the corresponding reason, the Spirit has to be invisible to consciousness, but is none the less a personal presence, personal as we are, present as everything around us is.

This personal presence may be thought of as the unity of God, and addressed as "you" or "thou," a consciousness not of ourselves, though it includes ourselves, and not nature, though it unites us with nature. Within the Spirit of God is the human community that our text is concerned with, particularized in what the author of Hebrews calls a cloud of witnesses [12:1]. These witnesses, for us at this moment, would include those who have kept the university together in the past. If we are or try to be a continuing part of this body of witnesses, the Spirit still does not speak to us, but waits patiently until it can speak through us. If the world of the Spirit were outside us only, it could not be known; if it were inside us only, it could not be real. Like the air, it keeps continually crossing the middle partition between without and within. The Spirit of God is also identified with love, a word that means perhaps too many things in English and is too easily sentimentalized. Fear causes people to build walls against each other, and love knocks them down. But the love of the Spirit is too deeply concerned about our freedom of will, and about the wisdom we gain from experience, to make any newspaper headlines on its own account. Anything that would move in on human life and run things for our benefit would be simply the knowledge of good and evil over again.

We may remember the chapel windows in the college building, with the portrait of Isaac Newton accompanied by his famous remark that he felt like a child playing with pebbles on a beach with an undiscovered ocean still in front of him.[5] But the ocean has no wish to remain undiscovered. The longing to know and create is deeply entrenched in the human mind, but when we pursue knowledge or creation we begin to feel something else moving beyond the control of our wills. Some of us at that point will become frightened at the prospect of doing without the sedating drugs of habit. Others may realize that this is the movement of a Spirit who, we are told, does not shrink from searching all things, even the deep things of God [1 Corinthians 2:10, AV].

Even when we do realize it, we usually carry too much baggage of emotional confusion, social prejudice, and personal worry to follow it very far. These distractions come mainly from what Newton was really talking about, the immense disproportion between all that there is to be known and the swiftness of the passing of life. We choose an anniversary like this to get free of time for a moment, when we can remember without being trapped in the past, and expect, plan, or hope without being trapped in the future. And we conclude this part of our celebration with a religious service to remind ourselves that, although much of our life is rooted in the anxiety of time, in other words the fear of death, the continuity of knowledge and wisdom that has brought us here together is rooted in love, a love that is not only as strong as death [Song of Solomon 8:6], but able to cast out its fear.

Concluding Prayer

As we rededicate ourselves to the aims we have tried to keep before us, we ask for your acceptance of what we offer in faith and love, first to you, then to the world.

We ask also for your help in seeing your Spirit in the world and in ourselves, your Word in our understanding, and our common descent from you in our dealings with one another.

It is part of our hope, as your servants, that the colleges of Victoria University, along with other universities, may continue into the future performing their task of teaching and learning. Of what lies beyond in that future, we ask nothing, only that within the span of our own time each of us may see our salvation and depart in peace.

40

On Lent

23 March 1988

From the retyped version, on his secretary Jane Widdicombe's disk, of a type-script with holograph corrections in NFF, 1991, box 39, file 6; dated by disk date and by an entry in Frye's daybook. This was a sermon given at a Lenten service in the Victoria College Chapel.

Lent, like Christmas, is far older than Christianity. The word itself comes from an Old English word meaning spring, and it goes back to the time when human societies committed themselves to agriculture and had to depend on grain crops for their food. It is probably even older than that, but it can at least be traced to a time of anxiety for the burial of the seed in the ground. Ezra Pound remarks that there seem to be two kinds of people: the people who think that sexual and other forms of licence are good for the crops and those who think they are bad for the crops.[1] The latter group are in control during Lent and the former during the carnival that precedes it. The Lenten mood is the one pre-ferred by most religious establishments, and extended periods of fasting and sexual abstinence help to keep the faithful subdued in other reli-gions as well, as in the fast of Ramadan in Islamic countries. So the primitive basis of Lent is an anxiety connected with the food supply, and survives in customs of "giving things up for Lent." There is no harm in abstaining, say, from eating chocolates during Lent, especially if one is overweight anyway, but such forms of semi-religious observance hardly get up to the level that Christianity is concerned with.

For Christianity, Lent is a kind of extended Good Friday, a period of meditation on the Passion of Christ and his descent into death and hell. The Christian Church forbade the eating of meat in Lent for much the same reason that it forbade it on Friday, the day of the Crucifixion. Lent is also a memorial of what is described in the synoptic Gospels as the temptation of Christ. According to Mark, Jesus withdrew into the wilderness for a period of forty days immediately following his baptism and recognition by his Father as the Son of God. Mark says only that he was with the wild beasts and that angels ministered to him, but Matthew and Luke give us an encounter with the devil and the rejection of a series of temptations. At every period, then, Lent has fitted into some pattern of withdrawal, death, or burial, to be followed by a new life represented in the Gospels by Easter.

John Milton (one of our culture-heroes at Victoria) has a poem on the temptation, *Paradise Regained*, in which he presents the temptation as a kind of withdrawal from the world, during which Jesus clarifies his mind about his mission as the Messiah. He is not allowed to clarify it alone: he is distracted by a struggle with Satan, so he is really also descending into hell, or at least Satan's kingdom. Satan keeps reminding Jesus that he is destined for great things, but has reached a mature age and has as yet done nothing. He proposes, first, that Jesus become a world conqueror, then that he become emperor of Rome, then the greatest of Greek philosophers. By rejecting all this, Jesus does find out something about his real destiny in the world. He is in the world but must not be of it; he must reject every atom of worldly power and wisdom before he can start redeeming that world.

Milton makes it clear that the most agonizing part of Jesus' struggle with Satan is the fact that his relation with his Father is temporarily suspended and he has to fight on his own. Satan in Milton is trying to repeat with Jesus his success with Adam and Eve, and keeps insisting: don't wait; grab your chance; opportunity once passed up never comes back. Behind what he says is the voice of a profound pagan wisdom. *Carpe diem*; seize the day; live while you can, as intensely as you can; it's a pity to die when you've never really lived.

Thus far Milton. The positive side of what Jesus does, the withdrawal of his mind from everything the world has to offer, is, unlikely as it sounds, an act of leisure, or would be if there were no Satan. Leisure in this context is the opposite of laziness or inactivity; it is a period of total concentration on the work of the mind. This pattern of beginning with detaching the mind from action is incorporated into the Christian calendar, where we begin the week with a day of leisure instead of ending it with a day of rest. It is also incorporated into the life of every university student, when he or she decides to postpone entering on most of the active responsibilities of life in favour of a period of study, training, and mental clarification. Aristotle reminds us that the word "school" comes from *scholê*, leisure.[2]

Ideally, leisure should be a pleasant period of quiet, with nothing to distract us. In practice, human life being what it is, it is usually just the reverse. The elements of temptation and distraction are always there: in fact, most of us think of our leisure time as the time when we choose our distractions. None of us is born with the maturity and self-discipline to live a life of leisure, to fight down all irrelevant thoughts, to banish all the self-nagging guilt feelings, broodings over the past and worries over the future. We have to develop that maturity through struggle. Not many of us now think of the enemy of leisure as an objective personal devil; for the most part we feel that the devil we have to fight is inside us and a part of us, something brought in with our genetic codes. In any case, as another poet, T.S. Eliot, says, the Word in the desert is most beset by voices of temptation.[3]

We keep going largely by pretending that we are individuals, and that when we say "I" we are speaking of ourselves as unified conscious beings. Actually we are about as unified as the Parliament in Ottawa. We watch a small child in a tantrum, and we realize that when it says "I want," the "I" is one of a hundred impulses, which will vanish in a moment and be replaced by another "I" that says it wants something else. Human behaviour in this area is almost entirely the behaviour of grown-up children, and that is why periods of leisure are so crucially important. Whatever we do in our leisure, the leisure itself is a matter of quieting down the conflict of impulses, of getting all forms of awareness, intellectual, emotional, sensational, imaginative, to work with one another instead of each trying to seize control of the will. At a certain point a new kind of awareness comes into being, and we begin to know what it is to be a real individual, something who really can say "I."

What we should give up for Lent is not a minor self-indulgence that we resume on Easter morning, but the far more profound self-indulgence of the spirit that in the Christian tradition is called pride. This state is the habitual use of the will by an aggressive consciousness that never listens to anything except its own decisions. It is the opposite attitude to that required of a student, who must constantly be listening for other voices. These are normally the voices that convey information in the arts and sciences, but sometimes we may become aware of a much more deeply buried voice. Psalm 46 contains a verse usually translated "Be still, and know that I am God" [10]. The Greek or Septuagint text of this Psalm renders "be still" as *scholásate*, which is the word *scholê* again, and means something like "have leisure; take your time; react like a student." Here we are listening to a voice that, as Elijah found in the cave, cannot be heard in the earthquake and fire [1 Kings 19:11–12]. If it is heard, we find ourselves awake in a very different kind of Easter morning, in a world with an empty tomb beside us and a new life around us where all Lents have been swept into the illusions of the past.

41

Baccalaureate Service (III)

10 April 1988

From the typescript in NFF, 1991, box 34, file 4.

Commissioning

The knowledge that has been entrusted to you is the food of the spirit. It must be shared with others; if hoarded for yourselves it will spoil. With the knowledge you have, you will often feel as though you had to feed thousands with only five loaves and two fish, but still what you have must be shared.

The knowledge that you can have is inexhaustible, and what is inexhaustible is benevolent. The knowledge that you cannot have is of the riddles of birth and death, of our future destiny and the purposes of God. Here there is no knowledge, but illusions that restrict freedom and limit hope. Accept the mystery behind knowledge: it is not darkness but shadow.

Benediction

May the presence of God consecrate our studies and transmute their elements. May what we offer in ignorance be accepted in providence. May the reverence for God's creation, which all arts and sciences express, grow in us and unite there with his will to create all things new.

42

Baccalaureate Service (IV)

9 April 1989

From the typescript in NFF, 1991, box 34, file 4.

Commissioning

Let your approach to knowledge be without fear, for God wills to reveal himself, and his revelation is mysterious only because it is infinite.

Let your approach to the world be without anger, for God cannot be invoked by bigotry or hatred; he cannot be touched by blasphemy; and his providence can never be seen in the context of human folly.

Let your approach to your life revolve around love, for love is not a virtue among others but the only virtue there is.

Benediction

May the vision of the world of the spirit that God made and saw to be good remain with us as the object and the refuge of knowledge. May we look neither to past nor future, but to the presence of that world, and enter its kingdom, where there is friendship without violation, and welcome without distinctions.

43

Undated Prayers

From the undated typescripts with holograph corrections in NFF, 1992, box 3, file 1. Frye's varying capitalization of words for the Deity such as "Thou" has not been regularized in these short prayers, which evidently date from different periods in Frye's life. No. 8 is annotated at the bottom, "(on Hebrews 4–5)," and no. 13 is annotated, "Prayers/Freshman Chapel Service."

1 Prayer for Baccalaureate Service

Thou art the Eternal Father in Heaven, and we approach thee in the doubts and confusions of our own nature, for of ourselves we know thee only as the unknown God. We seek for thee everywhere: we try to find thee in our own reason, our own affections, our own anxieties, but we cannot by searching find thee out: everywhere there is only the vast shadow of ourselves. We may not come to thee, but thou hast come to us: thou who in the burning bush before Moses gavest thyself a name and a local habitation, and a role in the history of mankind. We may not limit or confine thee; but thou hast confined thyself, and because of that we know that our lives, which have no meaning for us, have meaning for thee. Under the image of Fatherhood thou hast united all men in a free and equal brotherhood, where there is no respect of persons and no gods in our own image besides thee. Through thy word we know that the mystery beyond space is holy; that the life beyond time is happy, that reality itself is our Father, and that wherever we go we are still in our own home.

Thou art the Eternal Son of God: thou didst make thyself of no account in order that human life might be united with thee. We may lose our lives in noble causes, but we cannot save them: all salvation is from thee. When thou didst come to man an invisible shudder passed through the world: armies lost their will to fight; philosophers searched in despair for their lost wisdom; prophecies failed and oracles fell silent. So it is with us now, for thy word is a two-edged sword: when we do great deeds without charity, we are no further removed from death: and when we call upon thy name without charity, we increase our own hatred and fear. Thou wert both teacher and heretic, and where thou art, good humour and understanding drive out intolerance. Thou wert the prophet of Jew and Gentile, and where thou art, there is no distinction of colour or race. Thou wert not subdued by Pilate or Herod, though a hideous death awaited thee; and where thou art, there is the courage to fight oppression.

Thou art the Eternal Spirit which descended on the apostles at Pentecost, and gave them broken fragments of a wisdom not of their own, the magician's power to heal, the oracle's knowledge of mysteries, that they might proclaim thy word in strange tongues. So hast thou been to us in our schools and universities, sanctifying the beauty of the arts, the discipline of science, the equity of our relations with one another. Through thee and the power of thy Spirit we know that our studies have been blessed by thee, that whatsoever things are of good report are touched with thy nature, that whatever makes us truly human, in reason or feeling or imagination, is from thee. We ask that thy peace, which is not of this world, will descend and be present among these of thy children who have been our students, and who now go from our charge into their own lives. Many of them will know thee and grow in thy grace; many of them may not call upon thee by name and yet will strive to do thy will. Help them to grow in the depth of knowledge which is wisdom, the bride of thy creation, and in the depth of feeling which is love, that what has proceeded from thee may return to thee, and that they may know as they have been known.

2

Our Father, Creator of all Being, we thank thee that thou hast called to thyself thy faithful servant, now united to thee in that bright and eternal body which is the city of everlasting light.

Our Saviour and Redeemer, who hast shared with us the suffering of death, the horror of loneliness, and the pain of separation, we praise thee for thy victory over death and hell. Set our footsteps on the way of the pathway to life which thy servant has now trodden to the end, and enlighten our vision in the darkness that does not comprehend thy light.

O Spirit of the living God, who at the creation gavest us a life in which there was not yet death, preserve in us that sense of fellowship in which all those who are united through thee are at one.

Father, Son, and Spirit, we may not look into the mysteries of death: we know only that it is well with all thy servants, and we have no grief save only for ourselves.

3

Our Saviour and Redeemer, who art the source of all compassion, our world is ignorant, and needs Thy Word; it is sick, and needs Thy healing power. When Thou didst come to men an invisible shudder passed through the world: armies lost their will to fight; philosophers searched in despair for their lost wisdom; prophecies failed and oracles fell silent. So it is with us now, when we have done great deeds without charity, but are no further removed from death: now when our people are apprehensive and our leaders falter in indecision, we listen for Thy counsel of peace to men of good will. Thou art both Master and Servant, and where Thou art, there is the spirit of liberty. Thou art no respecter of persons, and where Thou art, all men are equal. Thou wert both teacher and heretic, and where Thou art, good humour and understanding drive out intolerance. Thou wert the prophet of Jew and Gentile, whose disciple baptized the Ethiopian [Acts 8:26–39], and where Thou art, we are all one, with no distinction of colour or race. Thou wert not subdued by Pilate or Herod, though a hideous death awaited Thee; and where Thou art, there is the courage to fight oppression. Through Thee, natural affection becomes the spirit of love, and through Thee, service to others finds its own reward.

We ask that thy peace, which is not of this world, which we may experience but can never comprehend, will descend and be present among these of thy children who have been our students, and who now go from our charge into their own lives. Many of them will know thee and grow in thy grace; many of them will not call upon thee and yet will strive to do thy will. Help them to grow in the depth of knowledge

which is wisdom, in the depth of feeling which is love, that they may
enter into thy Holy Spirit, who has given us a life that can never be
taken away.

4

Our Saviour and Redeemer, we turn to thee in a world in which we can
neither live nor die, where we fear to die only because we fear to live,
where the desire of life struggles with the desire not to be. We are exas-
perated by thy miracles of healing, for we wish to remain sick; we wish
to give full rein to our aggressions and passions; we wish to imagine the
vain things that reflect our own lusts. We cannot speak frankly to one
another: we resent and misunderstand and conceal hidden meanings,
for each of us is locked in the prison of his own darkness, not compre-
hending the light. In this world we can have no community, for each of
us would be sole master, and mould the whole world in his own likeness. Help us to understand the folly of our own existence, to see that
we are of one body in thee, and that we do not exist except in thy unity.
Thou hast delivered us from a life in which we stumble forward into
an unknown future in which the only certain thing is death; thou hast
called us into a world of peace and joy and equality. To reach thy world
we must consume the substance of our vain imaginings; must put away
the desire to injure those who differ from us, to proclaim our virtues in
the face of others whom we ought rather to serve, to rouse those nearest
us to acts of cruelty and greed. To reach thy world we must do all in our
power to destroy the world in which we live: sustain us in the destruction of idols and the annihilation of evil. What keeps us apart is our own
illusion; what unites us is reality, but there is no reality except in thy
presence, which is now and forever.

5

Our Saviour and Redeemer, Thou who art the Word of God, Thou hast
given us our talents of reason and desire; it is Thy will that we should
increase in wisdom and knowledge, in the sense of beauty which manifests the holiness of Thy presence. For Thou hast forbidden us no
knowledge except the knowledge of sin; we know only what Thou dost
know in us; our science is Thy awareness of Thy creation; our art is Thy
commanding voice within us. We thank Thee that we are so often

reduced to doubt, for our real doubts are of ourselves and not of Thee; we thank Thee that we are so often reduced to ignorance, for Thou art infinite, and we may always begin a new day with Thee, with all Thy world still before us. We thank Thee that we cannot by searching find Thee out, for Thou dost guide our search, and art the beginning of a knowledge of which there can be no end. And we thank Thee for our knowledge of death, for in that knowledge is the germ of eternity, the mustard-seed grain of faith which in the power of Thy word may become the Tree of Life in us.

6

Our Saviour and Redeemer, we know that Thou art here, for we feel Thy presence; when we do not recognize Thee, we do not recognize ourselves. We have forgotten our name, our home, and our inheritance; we have lost even the memory of having sold our birthright. We are known by Thee, but we may not know Thee, for we now see in a riddle. Thy world seems to us very small, and hidden away in our depths like a pearl of great price; but all around us stretches the broad highway of useless and futile endeavour that leads us to the grave. Our way is a way of frustrations that deepen to anxieties, of anxieties that deepen to panic and despair; illusions beset us on all sides, and before us is the supreme illusion of death. Beyond that we cannot see, except by Thy eyes. Thou art the creator of the world, but this is not Thy world, for Thy creation was good, and had no death for its end. Thou didst come to us to show us our real world again; at the trumpet of Thy victory the walls of death fell with a crash, and the veil over the world was torn apart. May we turn again to Thy world within us, and see it again as that greater world, the continuing city of which life and death are only the ruins, the city that needs no sun nor moon for light, where there is no longer a divine creator and a human creature, but only Thy presence, Thou who art the eternal reality of God and Man.

7

Our Saviour and Redeemer, we are here to seek the light of the understanding, to foster and cherish what is thy image in us. Thou hast taught us that knowledge is not wisdom, but an interpretation of wisdom, that wisdom is not the research of science or the imagination of art, but a person, and that that person is thyself. Thou art wisdom, the Logos which was from all eternity, and which is God. And our wisdom is ourselves, that in us which cannot die, that in us which is also thyself. We seek thee in the pride of achievement and in the misery of terror; we ascribe our own moods to thee, call thee now compassionate and now wrathful. But thou art always the same, the eternal being of ourselves, the spirit to whom we return when our bodies are dust, and all the works of our hands lie in ruins. Thou art the truth that we strive to seek, and the truth that it is worth our lives to die defending, and whenever we know that we know, it is thyself in us that knows. Deliver us from the false gods that promise us prosperity, and the flattery of an approving conscience; that provide us with the luxuries of hatred for our fellow men and of indifference to the poverty and want of others. Thou who art the world's whole joy and light; thou who carried that light through a hideous death into the depths of hell: to thee we turn in the words of thy prayer . . .

8

Our Saviour and Redeemer, to follow thee is to live the life given us to our furthest human reach. In the symbol of the priest thou hast shown us the total dedication, the total commitment, the total concentration on thy purpose required of us. We who attempt that dedication will constantly fail, will fall short even of our own standards, yet by attempting it we are thy believers, and as thy believers we are thy priests. Faith in thee is not a mystery but a revelation: we who are called to be students are required to test our faith by our intelligence, to see it as a fulfilling and not a contradiction of reason, to understand that the world thou hast revealed to us is not another world, but this world as it is seen by that wisdom which was before the works of old.

As Melchizedek was without father or mother or descent, as thou didst command us to leave our parents to follow thee, so we understand how we must break with our surroundings, how we must leave our prejudices, the sheltering walls of our childhood, our trust in the vaguely good, the dimly seen ideal. There was no shelter in thy life from manger to rock-cut tomb; nowhere to lay thy head, nowhere to find unwavering faith or continuous vision. Thou didst participate in the humiliation and agony of man, in all his fears and temptations, in his terror of the dark that is begotten of his ignorance of what is there, in his fierce partisan loyalties and hatreds. And because of this we know that we may not choose whom we may love, that the society of thy chosen is not only those who are like ourselves. To follow thee is to pass, as thou didst pass, through obedience to freedom, and the terror of freedom, with its awful responsibilities, seems to us in our bondage more fearful than hell. Yet thou didst achieve the greatest of all human triumphs, the triumph over death and sin, and on the other side of our dark valley lies the heaven of thy victory, the heaven which is our earth, formed by thy Word which makes all things new.

9 .

Our Saviour and Redeemer: in thy Gospel we meet thee face to face, in all the blinding simplicity of thy revelation. For we have created gods in the image of our own pride. We have adored thee under the metaphors of our tyrannies; in our desire to be more than human, we have turned to everything in thee that is beyond our reach. We speak of thy sovereign power, but in our minds is an idol of cruelty, mystery, and terror: we ascribe kingdom and glory to thee, but we must have kingdom and glory on our terms, the lust to dominate and the will to hurt. In all this we have forgotten thee, in whom God and Man are one, and in whom man is not the lord but the servant of men. Thou hast taught us that we are what we give, and not what we take at the expense of others. In the society which is thy body all are free, for thou hast delivered us from the law; all are equal, for thou art no respecter of persons; all are brothers and neighbours, linked to each other by bonds of compassion. We continue to make wars and to justify our own righteousness, but we know that we are condemned in thy eyes; we give aid to the poor and wretched in a spirit of contempt and arrogance, and therefore give nothing to thee. We are deeply ashamed of thee, for thy love for all men wounds our security: there is no one to whom we may feel superior in thy presence. In any crisis we will forsake and deny thee, as thy original disciples did; we cannot endure the sight of thy cross, with its reproach to our selfishness and fear. Our lives are absurd and alienated: we make this a merit in ourselves and a fault in thee; our idols betray us and lead us to disaster, and we say that thou art dead. Yet may thy gentleness and the unending patience of thy Gospel lead us back to thy city of light, where kingship is in service, power in compassion, and glory in bearing another's burdens. For in our love for others the image of our love is reflected back to us, and it is the image of thee, who art the manhood of man.

10

O Lord our God, thou hast revealed thyself as a Father, as a Son, and as the Spirit of love and community. Thou hast revealed thy kingdom to us, not as a distant fairyland city of golden streets and fresh waters, but as our own home, as thy residence within us, as the power that binds us to other men. We call to thee from the troubled dream of history, with the voices of false prophets sounding in our ears, proclaiming victories which are no victories, denouncing enemies who are no enemies, urging us to destroy our lives on the altars of evil gods. Wherever we go we are still in the prison of our own captivity; whatever we do we are still in the madhouse of our own desires. Bring us the key of promise, that we may see how we are self-imprisoned, that we may see other men, not as trees walking [Mark 8:24], but as our own brothers, as little worthy as ourselves of thy love, yet encompassed in it as we are. Renew thy covenant within us, the covenant of the dead, the living, and the unborn. For our fathers were thine, and our children will be thine, and even in our captivity we know that we also are among thy sons and heirs.

For we are captives in the city of destruction, the harlot city that drinks the blood of the saints and martyrs, the city whose rulers dream of glory, of gaining the whole world, and yet end as beasts. We await thy word to return to our own place, to rebuild thy temple, to join in worship with those whom Thou hast commanded us to love. Thy temple is not made with hands, neither was it forty years in building; it was destroyed and raised up in three days. All around us are the ruins of heathen cruelty, the despoiled sanctuary of thy presence; we feel abandoned by thee; we say thou art dead; for we can see only what is destroyed; yet thy temple is here, and we have only to enter it. Awaken us that we may dispel the nightmare of time, the wrecks of oppression and folly, the broken towers that we have tried to create. May we awaken in our own home, the home which is thy presence within us. We know that the good world created by thee is here; we know that the victory over death has been won: we may not see these things, yet give us thy vision, that we may see by these things, that the resurrection and life may become our sun, which we may not look at, but in the light of which we see.

11

Our Saviour and Redeemer, thy poets and prophets have seen thee high and lifted up, enthroned on mountain tops, in the clouds, in the serene cold of space. But with thee there is no space: thou art present wherever there is awareness of thee. Wherever there is an act of love and charity, an effort to redress the wrongs of our neighbours, an honest attempt to know and to understand, there thy enthroned triumph is, and its glory fills our lives. Martyrs have died in that glory; the wise have come from the ends of the earth to see it; the simple have known its radiance in poverty and sorrow. In thy service there is no failure; thy servants are not crushed by the malicious and bigoted; thy prophets are not silenced by the voice of fear; thy wisdom is not darkened by our folly. For with thee there is no time: there are no lost causes to be abandoned, no past to annihilate all thy works of love, no future to revive the ancient powers of darkness. There is only thy presence, where, as all suffering is a part of thy death on the cross, so all actions performed by thy will in the light of thy wisdom are a part of thy Resurrection, thy victory over death and hell which was once and for all.

Thou hast given us our minds and talents, and we dedicate them again to thee that the first fruits of our offering as students may be thine. We are often tempted to bury our talents: the world counsels us to be silent in evil times, to make use of our reason to defend its own terror and cruelty, to study the great disciplines of art and science for the sake of our own aggressions, our desire not to be our brother's keeper. For the world is terrified of silence and study: it knows that in the calm mind thy presence appears: it runs from thee shrieking with all its legions of devils. But we know that thy light cannot be concealed, that thy presence is not in the thunder and lightning and fire but in the small and still voice of truth, of peace, and of wisdom. Sanctify our talents that our minds may re-echo thy praise which resounds from the beauty of nature and the great works of love and intellect.

12

Our Saviour and Redeemer, thou art our only deliverance from the prison of hate and fear that we have built for ourselves. For we hate, or think that we hate, whatever seems a menace to our pitiful security. We hate those of different race or social class; we hate those whose vision of thy kingdom is not ours, forgetting that they too may live in thee and that thy father's house has many mansions. We hate because we fear, and what we fear is our own loneliness, the dryness of spirit in which walls of partition shut us off from others. At thy touch these walls fall down; thou art the fulfilment of our dreams of love and freedom, where the lover is one with his beloved and the citizen one with his neighbour. All our fear and hatred of others is founded on our fear and hatred of ourselves; we are sick with self-contempt and with the irony and absurdity of our lives, where nothing lives but what will die. We cherish our possessions as though they were immortal, and we do not see that whatever we possess in hate has already turned to dust. Deliver us from the selfish self, which we must kill before it kills us. Create in us a new hatred, a hatred not of people but of sin and evil, a hatred of tyranny and arrogance and pride and meanness, of the hypocrisy that clothes our will to conquer and destroy in the garments of superior righteousness. Create in us a new self-love, the love of thyself in us which unites us to others, not only as neighbours but as part of ourselves. Create in us a healthy and self-respecting fear, the fear of thee which begins wisdom, the sense of awe and reverence for thy tremendous mystery which comes as revelation to us, thy word which descends in tongues of flame, now as in ages past, which opens new horizons in our knowledge and new perspectives in our understanding. So we may attain a glimpse of thy city where there is no distinction of creator and creature, where there are no men but only man, and where thou art that man, one with God in eternity, yet one with us in the mirage of time.

13

Our Saviour and Redeemer: we have sought thee by the reason and by the will; we have sought thee in the causes of the philosophers, in the trances of the mystic, in drugs and in madness, in all mysteries where knowledge ends. We have sought thy image in our conquerors and tyrants: we have made thee the embodiment of our own fears, our desire to be master, to punish, to revenge ourselves and to condemn. We have sought thee in the solitude of mountains, on the loneliness of the sea, in the silence of the desert: we have looked up to the stars to find thee in the infinite distance; we have searched for the beginning of life to find thy creation: to find thy living presence we have wandered in all the labyrinths of the dead. We have taken the thunder for thy voice and the lightning for thy appearance; we have tried to confine thee in circles of stones, in temples and churches, in sealed books, in syllogisms and definitions. When our pleasures are gratified, we call it thy providence; when they are frustrated, we call it thy affliction. All that we have sought is of thee, yet nowhere can we find thee: at every turn we find only the idols of our own creation.

But thou hast also sought us: thou hast revealed thyself as a father who loves his children, as a son who died for us, as a spirit who unites us. Thou art the father who guards the persecuted and the ridiculed, who made us all of one blood, who has forbidden us pride, contempt, and hatred, who commands us to love, to sympathize, and to serve. Thou art the Son of Man who in his youth visited the wise men of his land, hearing them and asking them questions; thou art the Teacher who taught in the figures of poetry, in the categories of reason, in the examples of history, in the calm detachment of science, and who was able to say to Pilate: in secret have I said nothing. Thou art the spirit who spoke by the prophets, who still works in us to seek the truth, who gives us the courage to face that truth, however unwelcome. We need not try to justify thee in our search for knowledge, for in the search itself thou art justified, and thy mysterious ways are illuminated in every aspect of love and of wisdom.

And so we come at this time to lay our minds on thy altar of sacrifice. If we learn only for our own sakes, we shall learn nothing of thy compassion; if we are lazy and distracted, we can know nothing of thy unceasing watchfulness; if we are troubled about many things, we may lose the better part. We may not know thee, but thou art the source and the love of knowledge; we cannot reach thee by reason, but our reason is thy gift; we may not see thee at any time, but thou art the immortal spirit that sees.

May our vision be thy vision in us.

14

Our Saviour and Redeemer, we bring to thee thine own gift of reason, of the awareness of the world in which we live and the knowledge of it which we may acquire. As all our knowledge is thine, so we offer it to thee, for its only merit is in thy acceptance of it. Without thee, all the world disclosed to our waking minds is terrible and meaningless. Our knowledge of nature is knowledge of a hostile world, a world without pity and without hope, with no answering intelligence but only a mind-less mechanism. Our knowledge of one another is suspicion and mis-trust; all the news of what our fellow men do is for us a cause for alarm. Even the beauty which we create is filled with idolatry: we seek in our own creations a refuge from terror, and find none. Therefore we turn to thee, in whom all knowledge is fulfilled and all beauty revealed. With thee nature is no desert of infinite space, but our own home, a garden of living water and healing trees, a city of light and revelation. With thee there is no black nor white, no privileged or underprivileged, but only the people of the earth made of one blood, redeemed by one blood, united in a single body which is thine. Within thee is our being; all our real knowledge is thy knowledge within us; without thee all is illusion. We confess unto thee that we know no God: for all the gods we know are idols, and live only so long as we breathe life into them. We confess unto thee that we know no man, for man is a creature of a day, an ani-mated dust that will return to the dust. Thou alone art God; thou alone art man. Within thee is an eternity free of all the tempests of time and space; without thee all is waste and void, and darkness upon the deep.

15

Our Saviour and Redeemer, we call to Thee from a fear-haunted twi-light, from the caves of our ignorance and the darkness of our sin. We continually make for ourselves gods out of the dark: gods of lust and cruelty and terror; gods of oppression and contempt for our fellow man; ironic gods who sit aloft and mock at our plight; gods of a gloomy and inexorable fate; gods of the logic of circumstance; gods that beckon us to war and misery and death. We have worshipped these miserable crea-tures in ignorance and fear; when they fail us we curse and revile them, but Thee we despised and rejected, and put Thee to a shameful death. For Thou wert the light, and our darkness cannot comprehend Thee. Our false gods we may worship but can never love; but we may love Thee, for Thou art love; we may unfailingly bless and praise Thee, for all good comes from Thee, all help and understanding, all remedies for the diseases of pride. Out of all the works of Thy creation Thou hast con-cerned Thyself with man; hast redeemed him and given him life; and out of the gratitude and joy that Thine own understanding in us reveals to us, we may say to Thee in the words of Thy prayer . . .

16

Our Saviour and Redeemer, we speak to Thee in Thy hearing, for Thou art very near to us; but Thou art within us, and we are turned away from Thee. And because we are indifferent to Thee we are indifferent to others: indifferent to wars, if they kill only strangers, indifferent to famine and misery and suffering, if we are not hurt. When we see cruelty or oppression, we pass by on the other side; if Thou were to be released to us, we would call for Barabbas. For that terrible saying of Caiaphas is constantly in our hearts, that it is expedient that a man should die for the people; in our contempt and despair of life we constantly seek for victims, and would despise and ridicule Thee for bringing us more abundant life. When among men Thou wert alone, with a loneliness we cannot comprehend; alone among publicans and sinners; alone in feasts and in synagogues; alone when Thy disciples slept in Gethsemane and forsook Thee and fled from the cross. But in that solitude was the presence of eternity, the world of light and joy and peace where there are no longer strangers, but members of one body.

Notes

Introduction

1 For an informed account of NF in the context of the two colleges, Victoria and Emmanuel, that constitute Victoria University, and for the relation of Victoria to the larger federated University of Toronto, see the introduction by Goldwin French and Jean O'Grady to *Northrop Frye's Writings on Education*, forthcoming in CW (2000). For a perceptive examination of NF's reticence, by someone who worked closely with him over a period of ten years and co-taught with him in the legendary Bible course, see Margaret Burgess, "The Resistance to Religion: Anxieties Surrounding the Spiritual Dimensions of Frye's Thought; or, Investigations into the Fear of Enlightenment," in *The Legacy of Northrop Frye*, ed. Alvin A. Lee and Robert D. Denham (Toronto: University of Toronto Press, 1994), 59–75.

2 To perform a legal marriage service in Ontario the individual officiating must be licensed by the province. NF was an ordained minister of the United Church of Canada but, not having the duties of a regular pastorate, never applied for a licence to marry. At the request of students, however, he did play an important role in the conduct of an unknown number of weddings while a licensed minister performed the legally binding part of the proceedings.

3 This contribution, the sections "Tenets of Modern Culture" and "Literature," will be included in a later volume of CW, *Northrop Frye on Twentieth-Century Culture*. In NFF, 1991, box 58, file 8, is a communication sent by NF to the commission; it consists of a copy of his August 1947 *Canadian Forum* review entitled "Toynbee and Spengler" (also to be included in the above CW volume), followed by a "Postscript" which seems to suggest that it might form part of the final report and gives further thoughts on the church and history. These were not used in the printed version.

4 In *The Double Vision*, in the context of a highly critical account of the historical roles played by both Catholicism and Protestantism, NF says that the

388 Notes to pages xxi–xxxv

movement begun by the Reformation "did achieve one major victory: the gradual spread through the Western world of the principle of separation of church and state."

5 The notes in this edition indicate a wide range of theological and philosophical texts known to NF, as well as literary ones.

6 When referring to the human race generically, NF regularly says "man" or "mankind." We use "humankind" or "human beings" except when quoting NF directly, despite his comment on his use of the phrase "man's consciousness" (no. 12, n. 17).

7 For a fuller discussion of NF in relation to patristic exegesis see my two articles: "Old English Poetry: Mediaeval Exegesis and Modern Criticism," in *Studies in the Literary Imagination* (ed. Hugh Keenan [Atlanta: Georgia State University Press]), 8, no. 2 (1975): 47–73 (rpt. in *Typology and English Medieval Literature* [New York: AMS Press, 1992], 43–70); and "Towards a Language of Love and Freedom: Frye Deciphers the Great Code," *English Studies in Canada*, 12, no. 2 (1986): 124–37.

8 Barth learned the term *das Ganz Andere* (*totaliter aliter*) from Rudolf Otto (1869–1937), the Protestant theologian and philosopher who wrote *The Idea of the Holy* (*Das Heilige*, 1919), on the concept of the Numinous as the subject of religion. But Barth greatly changed the idea from what it meant in the work of Otto, who was an ecumenically minded scholar of comparative religion interested in bringing together adherents of all the world's religious faiths.

9 Robert D. Denham, "The Religious Base of Northrop Frye's Criticism," *Christianity and Literature*, 41 (1992): 247; also *SE*, xxiv.

10 Information about Line in the Victoria University Archives is sparse but it is clear that for part of his career he taught concurrently at both colleges. This was not an unusual arrangement. The bulk of his work over the years was at Emmanuel.

11 The United Church is one of Canada's largest Protestant denominations. It was created in 1925 when the Methodist and Congregational churches and a large part of the Presbyterian church joined together. NF and his family were part of the Methodist tradition. See the introduction to *Northrop Frye's Writings on Education*.

12 See *Northrop Frye's Late Notebooks, 1982–1990: Architecture of the Spiritual World*, ed. Robert D. Denham, CW, 5–6 (Toronto: University of Toronto Press, forthcoming, 2000).

13 See the introduction and headnotes to the Emmanuel College essays in *SE*; also the numerous references (indexed) to Edmund Blunden, NF's tutor at Oxford, in *The Correspondence of Northrop Frye and Helen Kemp, 1932–1939*, CW, 1–2 (Toronto: University of Toronto Press, 1996), vol. 2.

14 See the following: Michael Dolzani, "The Book of the Dead: A Skeleton Key to Northrop Frye's Notebooks," in *Rereading Frye: The Published and Unpublished Works*, ed. David Boyd and Imre Salusinszky (Toronto: University of

Toronto Press, 1999), 19–38; *Northrop Frye's Late Notebooks, 1982–1990; The "Third Book" Notebooks of Northrop Frye*, ed. Michael Dolzani (forthcoming in CW).

1. *Pistis* and *Mythos*

1 In most of this paragraph NF is referring to *Poetics*, 9. The idea in his last sentence may also be implicit there, but there is more direct support for it elsewhere in the *Poetics*. For Aristotle, precise observation of the actual describable world is the reference point with which poets begin, however far they move from it in attaching "impossibilities to a description of real things"; see the discussion of mimetic representations of people in action (chap. 2), the account of mimesis itself (chap. 4), and the description of metaphor (chaps. 21 and 22).
2 The phrase is from William Blake's annotations surrounding his engraving of the Laocoön, in *The Poetry and Prose of William Blake*, ed. David V. Erdman and Harold Bloom (Garden City, N.Y.: Doubleday, 1965), 271.

2. History and Myth in the Bible

1 William Butler Yeats, "The Celtic Element in Literature," *Writings on Irish Folklore, Legend and Myth* (Harmondsworth, England: Penguin, 1993), 199.
2 T.S. Eliot, *After Strange Gods: A Primer of Modern Heresy* (London: Faber and Faber, 1934), 46.
3 See Franz Cumont, *Astrology and Religion among the Greeks and Romans* (New York: Dover, 1963), 48–9, 104–5. (In GC [97, 240], NF gives this reference when making the same comment.)
4 In GC (200, 243), NF cites Flavius Josephus, *Contra Apion*, 2.15, as the source of his judgment.
5 See 1 Kings 20 and 22, in which Ahab defeats the Syrians.
6 Heinrich Schliemann's original account in German (1874) was quickly translated into English; see *Troy and Its Remains*, ed. Philip Smith (New York: Blom, 1875), esp. 344–6.
7 Immanuel Velikovsky, *Worlds in Collision* (New York: Doubleday, 1950), 39–46, 233.
8 The last sentence of Edward Gibbon, *Decline and Fall of the Roman Empire*, refers to this experience; see also *The Memoirs of the Life of Edward Gibbon*, ed. George Birkbeck Hill (London: Methuen, 1900), 167.
9 Luke 10:37; the AV text reads "go and do thou likewise."
10 *Midsummer Night's Dream*, 5.1.7–8. NF's substitution of "lawyer" for the word "lunatic" in Shakespeare's text is odd, admitting of no easy explanation, unless it is simply a joke. The substitution is in the original typescript and is not commented on there in NF's holograph annotations; the anomaly

is repeated in the published version and goes unmentioned by the editor of that volume in his discussion of the NF paper in the foreword.

11 Beginning with Rudolph Karl Bultmann: see his "New Testament and Mythology," in *Kerygma and Myth: A Theological Debate*, ed. Hans Weiner Bartsch, trans. Reginald H. Fuller (London: SPCK [Society for the Propagation of Christian Knowledge], 1953), 1–44.

12 See no. 1, n. 2.

13 The religious injunction *credo quia impossible* (I believe because it is impossible) is attributed to Tertullian; cf. his *De Carne Christi*, sec. 5, ll. 24–6.

14 In GC (5, 236), NF cites *The New Science of Giambattista Vico*, trans. Thomas Goddard Bergin and Max Fisch (Ithaca, N.Y.: Cornell University Press, 1968), par. 401 ff. (pp. 127 ff.).

15 James Joyce, *Ulysses* (New York: Random House, 1934), 35.

16 T.S. Eliot, *Little Gidding*, in *The Complete Poems and Plays, 1909–1950* (New York: Harcourt, Brace, 1952), pt. 5, ll. 21–2.

3. The Meaning of Recreation: Humanism in Society

1 John Robins, chair of the English department, 1938–52.

2 See Ferdinand de Saussure, *Course in General Linguistics*, trans. Roy Harris (London: Duckworth, 1983), 77.

3 *The New Science of Giambattista Vico*, 397–415, 140–53, 171 (pars. 1046–96, 423–55, 504). For the concept of the *ricorso* subsequently mentioned, see no. 2, n. 14, above.

4 See "The Creation Epic," trans. E.A. Speiser, in *Ancient Near Eastern Texts Relating to the Old Testament*, ed. James B. Pritchard, 3rd ed. (Princeton: Princeton University Press, 1969), 60–72.

5 René Descartes, *A Discourse on Method*, trans. John Veitch (London: Dent, 1912), 27.

6 See Roman Jakobson and Morris Halle, *Fundamentals of Language* ('s-Gravenhage: Mouton, 1956), 76–82, (pt. 2).

7 John Henry Newman, *Apologia Pro Vita Sua*, ed. Dwight Culler (Boston: Houghton Mifflin, 1956), 30.

8 Northrop Frye, "The Renaissance of Books," *Visible Language*, 7 (Summer 1974): 240.

9 In GC (18), NF remarks that Erasmus's words appear in the Latin translation appended to his edition of the Greek New Testament; a note directs the reader to Roland H. Bainton, *Erasmus of Christendom* (New York: Charles Scribner's Sons, 1969), chap. 6, (p. 140).

10 Goethe, *Faust: A Tragedy*, trans. Walter Arndt, ed. Cyrus Hamlin (New York: Norton, 1976), 30, (pt. 1, ll. 1224–37).

11 See *Elizabethan Critical Essays*, ed. Gregory Smith, vol. 2 (Oxford: Clarendon Press, 1904): George Puttenham, "The Arte of English Poesie," 6; Thomas

Lodge, "Defence of Poetry," 74; Philip Sidney, "An Apology for Poetry," 151; and John Harington, "A Brief Apology for Poetry," 207.

12 P.B. Shelley, *A Defence of Poetry*, ed. John E. Jordan (Indianapolis: Bobbs-Merrill, 1965), 80.

13 Sidney, "An Apology for Poetry," 158. The phrase *ut pictura poesis* is taken from Horace, *Ars Poetica*, l. 361.

14 Harold Bloom, *The Anxiety of Influence* (London: Oxford University Press, 1973).

15 Introduced by Saussure, *Course in General Linguistics*, 79–98, (chap. 3).

16 Robert Grant, "O Worship the King," hymn no. 21 in *The Hymnary of the United Church of Canada* (1930).

17 See his poem, *Spiritual Canticle*, passim.

18 "Jerusalem; The Emanation of the Giant Albion," in *The Poetry and Prose of William Blake*, 229, (pl. 77).

4. Creation and Recreation

1 Karl Barth, *The Doctrine of Creation*, vol. 3 of *Church Dogmatics*, ed. G.W. Bromiley and T.F. Torrance, trans. J.W. Edwards et al. (Edinburgh: T. and T. Clark, 1958), pt. 1, 15.

2 [William] Wordsworth, *The Tables Turned*, [l.] 16. [NF]

3 *The New Science of Giambattista Vico*, trans. Bergin and Fisch (1968), sec. 331, [pp. 96–7]. [NF]

4 *An Introduction to Metaphysics*, trans. Manheim (1959). [NF]. This reference appears to be mistaken. The term appears in Heidegger's *Being and Time*, trans. John Macquarrie and Edward Robinson (New York: Harper and Row, 1962), 223, (1:v).

5 [Introduction to] Apollodorus, *The Library* (Loeb trans., [Cambridge, Mass.: Harvard University Press,] 1921), [1:xxvii]. [NF]

6 Max Müller, *Lectures on the Science of Language*, 5th ed. (London: Longmans, 1866), 1:12.

7 Matthew Arnold, *To a Friend*, l. 7.

8 *Northrop Frye on Culture and Literature: A Collection of Review Essays*, ed. Robert D. Denham (Chicago: University of Chicago Press, 1978).

9 Cf. Wallace Stevens, *The Necessary Angel* ([New York: Knopf,] 1951), 174. [NF]

10 Oscar Wilde, "The Critic as Artist," in *Literary Criticism of Oscar Wilde*, ed. Stanley Weintraub (Lincoln: University of Nebraska Press, 1968), 200.

11 Emily Dickinson, *Letters* ([Cambridge, Mass.:] Belknap Press, 1958), 2:576. [NF]

12 James Joyce, *Ulysses* (New York: Random House, 1934), 35. [NF]

13 Mary Wollstonecraft Shelley, note to Percy Bysshe Shelley, *Prometheus Unbound*, in *The Complete Poetical Works*, ed. Thomas Hutchinson (London: Oxford University Press, 1945), 271.

14 Jacques Lacan, *The Language of the Self*, trans. [Anthony] Wilden ([Baltimore: Johns Hopkins University Press,] 1968), 18. [NF]

15 Oscar Wilde, "The Soul of Man under Socialism," in *De Profundis and Other Writings* (Harmondsworth, England: Penguin, 1973), 34.

16 Walter Pater, *The Renaissance: Studies in Art and Poetry* (New York: New American Library, 1959), 159.

17 [From] *The Green Box*, trans. [George Heard] Hamilton ([New Haven: The Readymade Press,] 1957). [NF]. N.p.; item no. 13.

18 See Thomas Hardy's *God-Forgotten*.

19 *Burnt Norton*, [l.] 67. [NF]

20 See Bernard of Clairvaux's *Sermons on the Song of Songs*, and the *Spiritual Canticle* of St. John of the Cross.

21 Samuel Butler, *Life and Habit*, chap. 7. [NF]. The passage is in chap. 8 of the new ed. (London: Fifield, 1910), 134, which is in NF's library.

22 T.S. Eliot, *The Family Reunion*, in *Complete Poems and Plays, 1909–1950* (New York: Harcourt, Brace, 1952), 234.

23 The story of the fall of Satan is not mainly Milton's invention, but figures in a host of patristic texts, as NF was (partially?) aware (see 122–3, 125, 150, 152, and 153; see also 539n. 35 to his 1950 ed., *John Milton: "Paradise Lost" and Selected Poetry and Prose*). See also 154 for the belief that NF was perhaps reacting against.

24 *Paradise Lost*, bk. 1, l. 741. [NF]

25 Augustine, *Confessions*, [trans. E.B. Pusey (London: Dent, 1932), 260–1], bk. [11, chap.] 12. [NF]

26 Cf. James Ussher, *The Annals of the World Deduced from the Origin of Time* (London, 1658), 1.

27 Augustine, *Confessions*, 283, (bk. 12).

28 Jacques Lacan, *Écrits: A Selection*, trans. Alan Sheridan (New York: Norton, 1977), 281 ff.

29 Robert Graves, *To Juan at the Winter Solstice*, [l.] 9. [NF]

30 The phrase is in sec. 29 of the *Timaeus*. The translation "likely story" is by H.D.P. Lee, *Timaeus* (Harmondsworth, England: Penguin Books, 1965), 41; Jowett uses the phrase "the tale which is probable" in *The Dialogues of Plato*, 2:13.

31 Michael Wigglesworth, *The Day of Doom*, stanzas 172–81. [NF]. In *The Poems of Michael Wigglesworth*, ed. Ronald A. Bosco (Lanham, Md.: University Press of America, 1989), 53–6.

32 Sir Thomas Browne, *Religio Medici*, pt. 1. [NF]. In *Religio Medici*, ed. W.A. Greenhill (London: Macmillan, 1950), 29, (pt. 1, sec. 16).

33 See Pope Clement I, *The Recognitions of Clement: or the Travels of Peter*, vol. 5 of *Primitive Christianity Revived*, trans. William Whitston (London: 1712), 254, (bk. 7, sec. 13).

34 [George] Puttenham, ["The Arte of English Poesie," in] *Elizabethan Critical Essays*, ed. Gregory Smith [London: Oxford University Press, 1904], 2:188. [NF]. NF has modernized the Elizabethan spelling.

35 William Paley, *Natural Theology: or, Evidences of the Existence and Attributes of the Deity* (London: R. Faulder, 1802), 1 ff.; Samuel Butler, *Erewhon*, in *Erewhon; Erewhon Revisited* (London: Dent, 1932), 45, (chap. 7); Swift, *Gulliver's Travels*, in *The Prose Works of Jonathan Swift*, ed. Herbert Davis (Oxford: Basil Blackwell, 1941), 11:19.

36 [Karl Frederick] Klinck, ed., *Literary History of Canada* ([Toronto: University of Toronto Press,] 1965), 130 (actually Lower Canada). [NF]. The rider in Lower Canada was Bishop George Jehoshaphat Mountain of the Church of England, on a trip to his church's mission in Prince Rupert's Land.

37 1 Enoch, sec. 54. [NF]. In *Apocrypha and Pseudepigrapha of the Old Testament*, ed. R.H. Charles (Oxford: Clarendon Press, 1913), 2:221.

38 [G.W.F.] Hegel, *Phenomenology of Spirit* [trans. A.V. Miller, ed. J.N. Findlay (Oxford: Clarendon Press, 1977)], sec. 774, [p. 467]. [NF]

39 *Popol Vuh: The Sacred Book of the Ancient Quiche Maya*, ([trans. Delia Goetz and Sylvanus G. Morley (Norman: University of Oklahoma Press,)] 1950), 82 ff. [NF]

40 Edmund Burke, *Appeal from [the] New to [the] Old Whigs*. [NF]. In *Works* (London: Oxford University Press, 1906–7), 5:101.

41 John Milton, "Of Education," in *The Works of John Milton* (New York: Columbia University Press, 1931), 4:277.

42 [Philip] Sidney, ["An Apology for Poetry," in] Gregory Smith, ed., *Elizabethan Critical Essays*, 1:156. [NF]

43 W.B. Yeats, *A Vision* (New York: Macmillan, 1956), 68.

44 Dante, *Paradiso*, canto 33, [l. 86]. [NF]. NF here replaces the usual English rendering of the Italian word *volume* as "volume" with "word."

45 W.H. Auden, *For the Time Being* (London: Faber and Faber, 1945), 107.

46 Martin Heidegger, *Introduction to Metaphysics*, trans. Ralph Manheim (Garden City, N.Y.: Doubleday, 1961), 1.

47 James Warren Jones (1931–78), known as Jim Jones, was a cult leader who led a band of followers from the People's Temple in San Francisco to a commune in Guyana. When investigated for possible abuses of authority, he instigated a mass murder-suicide in which 913 cultists died.

48 William Blake, *A Vision of the Last Judgment*, in *Poetry and Prose of William Blake*, 548.

49 See [Erich] Auerbach, *Scenes from the Drama of European Literature* ([Glouster, Mass.: Peter Smith,] 1973). The essay on "Figura," 11–76, is practically indispensable. [NF]

50 In his *Thus Spake Zarathustra*, passim.

51 *Paradise Lost*, in *The Works of John Milton*, 2:389, (bk. 12, l. 303).

52 Ibid., 399, (bk. 12, l. 587).

53 John Milton, *Tetrachordon*, in *The Complete Prose Works* (New Haven: Yale University Press, 1953), 2:636–7.

54 John Bertram Phillips, *Letters to Young Churches: A Translation of the New Testament Epistles* (London: Geoffrey Bles, 1947), 58.

55 See no. 3, n. 16.

56 Friedrich Nietzsche, *The Gay Science*, trans. Walter Kaufmann (New York: Random House, 1974), 167, 181–2, (bk. 3, secs. 108, 125).

57 Alfred North Whitehead, *Science and the Modern World* (Cambridge: Cambridge University Press, 1938), 64, (chap. 3).

58 Martin Heidegger, *Poetry, Language, Thought*, trans. [Albert] Hofstadter ([New York: Harper and Row,] 1975), 198. [NF]

59 Revelation 14:6. [NF]. See Blake's *The Everlasting Gospel*, in *Poetry and Prose of William Blake*, 510–16.

5. The Double Mirror

1 Jacques Derrida, *Of Grammatology*, trans. Gayatri Chakravorty Spivak (Baltimore: Johns Hopkins University Press, 1976), 10 ff.

2 See no. 2, n. 11.

3 See no. 3, n. 13.

4 Nietzsche, *The Gay Science*, 168, (bk. 3, sec. 109).

5 See no. 4, n. 53.

6 Marshall McLuhan, *War and Peace in the Global Village*, coordinated by Jerome Agel (New York: McGraw-Hill, 1968), 59.

6. Repetitions of Jacob's Dream

1 Cf. Herodotus, *History*, bk. 1, sec. 181, describing a Babylonian temple.

2 See E.A. Wallace Budge, *The Gods of the Egyptians* (1904; rpt. New York: Dover, 1969), 2:116–17.

3 See emblems 9 and 10 of *For the Sexes: The Gates of Paradise* (previously entitled *For Children: The Gates of Paradise*) in *The Poetry and Prose of William Blake*, 261–2.

4 Thomas Browne, *Religio Medici*, 55, (pt. 1, sec. 33).

5 Geoffrey Chaucer, *The House of Fame*, in *The Complete Works of Geoffrey Chaucer*, Student's Cambridge Edition, ed. F.N. Robinson (Boston: Houghton Mifflin, 1933), 339, (l. 731). NF uses modernized spelling.

6 See no. 4, n. 41.

7 *The Kingdom of God*, in *Complete Poetical Works of Francis Thompson* (New York: Modern Library, 1919), 357.

7. The Bride from the Strange Land

1 On the Book of Ruth see particularly Robert Alter, *The Art of Biblical Narrative* (New York: Basic Books, 1981), esp. 58–60; Jan Wojcik, "Improvising Rules in the Book of Ruth," *PMLA*, 100 (1985): 145–53; D.F. Rauber, "The Book of Ruth," in *Literary Interpretations of Biblical Narratives*, ed. Kenneth R.R. Gros Louis et al. (Nashville: Abingdon Press, 1974), 163–76; Katharine Doob Sakenfeld, "Loyalty and Love: The Language of Human Interconnections in the Hebrew Bible," *Michigan Quarterly Review*, 22 (1983): 190–204. [NF]
2 Quoted from *The Works of Flavius Josephus*, trans. William Whiston (Edinburgh, 1828), 150. [NF]
3 Letter to Tom Keats, 9 July 1818, *The Letters of John Keats, 1814–1821*, ed. H.E. Rollins (Cambridge, Mass.: Harvard University Press, 1958), 1:320. [NF]
4 James Joyce, *Finnegans Wake* (New York: Viking Press, 1939; rpt. 1966), 257. [NF] ·
5 John Milton, Sonnet IX: *Lady, that in the prime of earliest youth*, in *Poems*, ed. John Carey and Alistair Fowler (London: Longmans, 1968), 287–8. [NF]
6 In *A Jest of God* (1966) and *The Stone Angel* (1964).
7 Christina Rossetti, *Poetical Works*, ed. W.M. Rossetti (London: Macmillan, 1904), 383. [NF]
8 Goethe, "Hebräer," in "Noten und Abhandlungen zu besseren Verständnisz des West-östlichen Divans," *Goethes Werke*, Hamburger Ausgabe, 10th ed. (Munich: C.H. Beck, 1981), 2:128–9.
9 W.E. Staples, "The Book of Ruth," *American Journal of Semitic Languages and Literatures*, 53 (1937): 145–57. [NF]

8. The Mythical Approach to Creation

1 See no. 3, n. 10.
2 Leon Trotsky, *Literature and Revolution* (Ann Arbor: University of Michigan Press, 1960), 183.
3 D.H. Lawrence, *Fantasia of the Unconscious* (London: Martin Secker, 1923), 76.
4 See *Apocrypha and Pseudepigrapha of the Old Testament*, 2:191–2.
5 See no. 4, n. 32.
6 *Religio Medici*, 39, (pt. 1, sec. 22).
7 Voltaire, "Chaîne des Êtres Crées," in *Philosophical Dictionary*, ed. and trans. Theodore Besterman (Harmondsworth, England: Penguin Books, 1972), 107–9.
8 *The Bride's Tragedy*, in *Plays and Poems of Thomas Lovell Beddoes*, ed. H.W. Donner (London: Routledge and Kegan Paul, 1950), 33, (act 2, scene 6).
9 Emily Dickinson, *Because that you are going*, in *The Poems of Emily Dickinson*,

ed. Thomas H. Johnson (Cambridge, Mass.: Belknap Press, 1958), 3:875–6.

10 T.S. Eliot, *Burnt Norton*, sec. 2, l. 19.

9. Crime and Sin in the Bible

1 Alexis de Tocqueville published his analysis of American society in 1835 and 1840. See his *Democracy in America*, ed. Phillips Bradley, 2 vols. (New York: Knopf, 1945). [NF]

2 The Quebec Act (1774) re-established French civil law as the law of Quebec, counteracting a royal proclamation by King George III (1763) which had imposed English civil and criminal law on the colony. Quebec Act 1774 (UK) R[evised] S[tatutes of] C[anada] 1985, app. 2, no. 2. [NF]

3 William Blackstone, *Commentaries on the Laws of England* (Boston: Beacon Press, 1962), 4:59. [NF]

4 See for example *The Odyssey*, 3.51 ff.; 7.201 ff. See also Henri Hubert and Marcel Mauss, *Sacrifice: Its Nature and Function* (Chicago: University of Chicago Press, 1964), 37. [NF]

5 See John Stuart Mill, "On Liberty" (1859), in *Collected Works of John Stuart Mill*, vol. 18, *Essays on Politics and Society*, ed. John M. Robson (Toronto: University of Toronto Press, 1977), 213–310. [NF]

6 Hammurabi was King of Babylon from 1792–1750 B.C., and the code (a record of 282 of his decisions) represents the most complete extant account of Babylonian laws. Perhaps best known for its principle of restitution, the *lex talionis* (i.e., an eye for an eye, a tooth for a tooth), its resemblance to the Mosaic code—see Stanley A. Cook, *The Law of Moses and the Code of Hammurabi* (London: Adam and Charles Black, 1903)—is apparent. The correspondence, once viewed as evidence of the dependency of the Mosaic code on that of Hammurabi, is now attributed to a common source. [NF]

7 Sophocles' tragedy dates back to 441 B.C. A modern translation can be found in *Antigone*, trans. Richard E. Braun (London: Oxford University Press, 1973). [NF]

8 W.S. Gilbert and Arthur Sullivan, *The Mikado, or, The Town of Titipu*, in *The Complete Plays of Gilbert and Sullivan* (New York: Modern Library, 1936), 348. [NF]

9 Milton's primary argument is found in "The Doctrine and Discipline of Divorce" (first published in 1643). See *The Works of John Milton*, vol. 3, pt. 2 (New York: Columbia University Press, 1931). [NF]

10 The two key passages are Deuteronomy 24:1 (which describes a "certificate of divorce" in the Mosaic code) and Matthew 5:32 (part of the Sermon on the Mount, in which Jesus explicitly contradicts the passage from Deuteronomy). [NF]

11 Marcel Aymé, *La Grâce*, in *Le Vin de Paris* (Paris: Gallimard, 1947), 79–96. [NF]

12 Hugo Grotius's (1583–1645) most influential work on the law of nations was *De jure Belli ac Pacis* (1625). A translation is found in *The Rights of War and Peace*, trans. A.C. Campbell (New York: M. Walter Dunne, 1901). [NF]

13 See chap. 3 of Maine's *Ancient Law* (London: Dent, 1917), 26–42, in which Maine argues that the Romans sought to create a jurisdiction covering non-Romans which featured only the laws common to several legal systems or codes, and thus somehow "natural" or given. [NF]

14 "An Appeal from the New to the Old Whigs" (1791), in *The Works of the Right Honourable Edmund Burke* (London: Rivington, 1826), 6:218. [NF]. See no. 4, n. 40, for a more accessible source.

15 "A Mask Presented at Ludlow Castle, 1634," in *The Works of John Milton*, vol. 1, pt. 1 (New York: Columbia University Press, 1931), 85–123. [NF]

16 For a modern translation, see Longus, *Daphnis & Chloe*, trans. George Thornely (London: Heinemann, 1916). [NF]

10. The Bible and English Literature

1 In *The Old Testament Pseudepigrapha*, ed. James H. Charlesworth (New York: Doubleday, 1985), 2:457.

2 See no. 8, n. 4, above.

3 See no. 8, n. 3.

4 Browne, *Religio Medici*, 29, (sec. 16).

5 See "The Creation Epic," in *Ancient Near Eastern Texts*, 67, and no. 3, n. 4, above.

6 Bernard Shaw, *Man and Superman*, in *The Complete Plays of Bernard Shaw* (London: Oldhams Press, 1937), 376, (act 3).

11. On the Bible

1 See no. 3, n. 10.

2 *The Poems of Emily Dickinson*, 3:892.

3 See no. 2, n. 13.

4 See no. 4, n. 3.

5 See no. 2, n. 11.

12. The Double Vision

1 Letter to Thomas Butts (22 November 1802), in *The Letters of William Blake*, ed. Geoffrey Keynes, 3rd ed. (Oxford: Clarendon Press, 1980), 44.

2 The United Church of Canada was formed in 1925 by union of the Presbyterian, Methodist, and Congregational churches of Canada. It is Canada's largest Protestant church. [NF]

3 *Quotations from Chairman Mao Tse-Tung*, ed. Lin Piao (Peking: Foreign Language Press, 1967), 61.

4 *Thoughts on Various Subjects*, in *The Prose Works of Jonathan Swift*, ed. Herbert Davis (Oxford: Basil Blackwell, 1939–68), 1:242.

5 Richard Dawkins, *The Selfish Gene* (1976). [NF]

6 See n. 25.

7 [Alfred, Lord Tennyson, *Ulysses*, l. 18; Wallace Stevens,] *Theory*, in *Collected Poems* ([New York: Knopf,] 1954), 86. [NF]

8 See particularly I.A. Richards, *Coleridge on Imagination* [Bloomington: Indiana University Press, 1960]; (rpt. 1960 with comments by Kathleen Coburn), 98. [NF]

9 Ivor Shapiro, "The Benefit of the Doubt," *Saturday Night*, 105, no. 3 (April 1990): 32–40.

10 William Wordsworth, *Peter Bell—A Tale*, ll. 248–50.

11 Letter to Paul Demeny (15 May 1871), in Arthur Rimbaud, *Complete Works*, trans. Paul Schmidt (New York: Harper and Row, 1975), 102.

12 A.N. Whitehead, *Science and the Modern World* (Cambridge: Cambridge University Press, 1938), 72.

13 See no. 4, n. 3.

14 Petr Kropotkin, *Mutual Aid: A Factor of Evolution* (Harmondsworth, England: Penguin Books, 1939), 24, (chap. 1).

15 M. Arnold, "Wordsworth," in *Poetry and Criticism of Matthew Arnold*, ed. Dwight Culler (Boston: Houghton Mifflin, 1961), 33.

16 See *Sophist*, 266c. Or NF may be thinking of *Phaedo*, 60e, where Socrates dreams he is being told to practise the arts, as he does when awake.

17 The English language, in its illogical unwisdom, established the convention many centuries ago that "man" means "men and women" and "mankind" humanity. Other languages preserve the same conventions. In my view it is better to let such vestigial constructions fossilize rather than to attempt the pedantries of a uniform "common language." The fossilizing process does take place: we no longer think of a "Quaker" as a hysteric or of "Christmas" as a mass. Again, it is a distrust of metaphorical thinking that is involved. A seldom noticed aspect of this question is the language of pietistic hymns, one of which begins: "Safe in the arms of Jesus, / Safe on his gentle breast." The essential religious feeling here is that the risen Christ, at least, is quite as female as male. [NF]

18 *Culture and Anarchy*, in *Poetry and Criticism of Matthew Arnold*, 468, (pt. 4).

19 William Morris, *Hopes and Fears for Art* (London: Ellis and White, 1882), 108.

20 [Immanuel] Kant, *Critique of Judgment*, trans. J.H. Bernard ([New York: Hafner,] 1966), sec. 58, [pp. 192–6]. [NF]. [Cf. also sec. 10.]

21 The Blake quotation is from *The French Revolution* [l. 189]; the Wallace Stevens one from *So-and-So Reclining on Her Couch*, in *Collected Poems*, 296. [NF]

22 *September 1, 1939*, in *The English Auden: Poems, Essays and Dramatic Writings, 1927–1939* (London: Faber and Faber, 1977), 246. The stanza containing this line was edited out of later editions of the poem, including the one in NF's library.

23 *Milton*, pl. 30; also *Jerusalem*, pl. 48.

24 *Inversnaid*, l. 16.

25 See *Phenomenology of Spirit*, by G.W.F. Hegel, trans. and ed. by Miller and Findlay 1977, sec. 177, [p. 110]. For the "substance is subject" above see sec. 18, [p. 10], and for the "unhappy consciousness" earlier, sec. 206, [p. 126]. [NF]. [This note was mistakenly keyed, in the printed text, to the "substance is subject" section.]

26 Keats, *Ode on a Grecian Urn*, stanza 5.

27 See Josephus, *Antiquities of the Jews*, 18.8. [NF]

28 I am aware that this distinction between "create" and "make" does not exist in ordinary language, but the distinction is quite as important as though it did. [NF]

29 In fact, as NF himself notes elsewhere (see p. 55–6, above, and *GC*, 71), Augustine says precisely the opposite, attributing the remark to somebody else:
See, I answer him that asketh, "What did God before He made heaven and earth?" I answer, not as one is said to have done merrily, (eluding the pressure of the question,) "He was preparing a hell, (saith he) for pryers into mysteries." . . . I boldly say, "that before God made heaven and earth, He did not make any thing." (*Confessions*, trans E.B. Pusey, 260–1)

30 J. Layard's account of Malekulan mythology is well summarized in G.R. Levy, *The Gate of Horn* ([London: Faber and Faber,] 1948), 152 ff. [NF]

31 See *The Presocratics*, ed. Philip Wheelwright ([New York: Odyssey Press,] 1966), 53. [NF]

32 Edmund Burke, *Reflections on the Revolution in France*, in *Works*, 4:106.

33 Burke, *An Appeal from the New to the Old Whigs*, in *Works*, 5:96.

34 Hobbes, *Leviathan* (London: Dent, 1914), 89, (pt. 2, chap. 17).

35 See no. 4, n. 56.

36 William James, *Pragmatism* (New York: Longmans, Green, 1907), 12–13.

37 See no. 2, n. 15.

38 *The Order of Things: An Archeology of the Human Sciences* (New York: Vintage Books, 1973), 263.

39 *Burnt Norton*, pt. 2, l. 44.

40 Mircea Eliade, *The Sacred and the Profane* ([trans. Willard R. Trask (New York: Harcourt, Brace,)] 1959), 68 ff. [NF]

41 Henri Frankfort, *Ancient Egyptian Religion* ([New York: Harper and Row,] 1961), 102 ff. [NF]

42 *Time Regained,* in *Remembrance of Things Past,* trans. C.K. Scott Moncrieff, Terence Kilmartin, and Andreas Mayor (London: Chatto and Windus, 1981), 3:215, (chap. 3).

43 *The Eighteenth Brumaire of Louis Bonaparte,* in Karl Marx and Friedrich Engels, *Basic Writings on Politics and Philosophy,* ed. Lewis S. Feuer (New York: Anchor Books, 1959), 320.

44 S.T. Coleridge, *Conciones ad Populum:* "On the Present War" [in *Coleridge: Select Poetry and Prose,* ed. Stephen Potter (London: Nonesuch Press, 1953), 141]. [NF]

45 Joachim of Fiore, *The Book of Concordance,* trans. E. Randolf Daniel, in *Apocalyptic Spirituality: Treatises and Letters of Lactantius, Adso of Montier-en-der, Joachim of Fiore, the Franciscan Spirituals, Savonarola,* trans. and with an introduction by Bernard McGinn; preface by Marjorie Reeves (New York: Paulist Press, 1979), esp. 124, 130, (bk. 2, pt. 1, chaps. 4 and 9).

46 *An Horatian Ode upon Cromwel's* [sic] *Return From Ireland,* ll. 40–4.

47 Dante Alighieri, "Letter to Can Grande" and "The Four Levels of Interpretation" (from the *Convivio,* 2.1), in *Literary Criticism of Dante Alighieri,* trans. and ed. Robert S. Hallen (Lincoln: University of Nebraska Press, 1973), 95–114.

48 William Anderson, *Dante the Maker* ([London: Routledge,] 1980), 347. [NF]. The son was Pietro Alighieri.

49 Dylan Thomas, *A Refusal to Mourn the Death,* [*by Fire, of a Child in London,*] [last line]. [NF]

50 Browne, *Religio Medici,* 18, (pt. 1, sec. 9).

51 The life of Plotinus by his disciple Porphyry begins with the statement that Plotinus was ashamed of being in the body. [NF]

52 Milton, *De Doctrina Christiana.* [NF]. In *Works of John Milton,* vol. 16; the general idea occurs on pp. 149, 197, 265. For use of the phrase "rule of charity" see, e.g., *Tetrachordon,* in *Works,* 4:85.

53 *The Lichtenberg Reader,* ed. and trans. Franz H. Mautner and Henry Hatfield (Boston: Beacon Press, 1959), 64.

54 *Collected Poems* [i.e., *The Poems of Emily Dickinson*], ed. Thomas H. Johnston [poem no.] 1317, [p. 911]. [NF]

55 See "To Come to Light," item no. 39, below, p. 363.

56 The line "to purify the dialect of the tribe," in Eliot's *Little Gidding* [pt. 2, l. 74] is derived from Mallarmé's *Le tombeau d'Edgar Poe* [*Œuvres complètes* (Paris: Gallimard, 1945), 70]. [NF]

57 David Bohm, *Wholeness and the Implicate Order* ([London: Routledge and Kegan Paul,] 1980), chap. 7. [NF]

16. Merry Christmas?

1 In *The Works of Charles Dickens in 36 Volumes* (New York: Charles Scribner's Sons, 1911), 18:28–9.

2 The references are to the war between nationalists and Communists in China, factional strife connected with the partition and independence of India, and terrorism in Palestine after the UN's decision to create a Jewish state.

19. The Church: Its Relation to Society

1 "Reason of Church-government Urg'd against Prelaty," in *Complete Prose Works of John Milton*, 1:760–1.
2 See Arnold Toynbee, *A Study of History*, passim.
3 J.S. Mill, [*Considerations on*] *Representative Government*, in *Utilitarianism, Liberty, and Representative Government* (London: Dent, 1931), 256–75, (chap. 7).
4 John Newman, *Essay on the Development of Christian Doctrine* (1845).
5 See no. 3, n. 5.
6 Trofim Denisovich Lysenko, "Address by Academician T.D. Lysenko on the Situation in Biological Science," in *The Situation in Biological Science: Proceedings of the Lenin Academy of Agricultural Sciences of the U.S.S.R.: July 31–August 7, 1948* (Moscow: Foreign Languages Publishing House, 1949), 11–50.
7 John, Baron Acton, Letter to Mandell Creighton, in Louise Creighton, *Life and Letters of Mandell Creighton* (London: Longmans, Green, 1904), 1:372.
8 Lewis Carroll, *Alice's Adventures in Wonderland*, chap. 1.
9 *The Works of John Ruskin*, ed. E.T. Cook and Alexander Wedderburn (London: George Allen, 1903–12), 17:38.

20. Man and the Sabbath

1 Charles William Merton Hart, "Industrial Relations Research and Social Theory," *Canadian Journal of Economics and Political Science*, 15 (1949): 67–8.

21. The Analogy of Democracy

1 See Dean Acheson, "United States Policy toward Asia" (speech of 15 March 1950), in *Department of State Bulletin*, 22, no. 560 (27 March 1950): 472.
2 See no. 2, n. 15.
3 *You ask me, why, tho' ill at ease*, ll. 11–12.
4 See no. 12, n. 32.
5 "Am I my brother's keeper?" [Genesis 4:9].
6 See no. 3, n. 5.

23. Baccalaureate Sermon

1 *Report of the Commission to Study the Development of Graduate Programmes in Ontario Universities* (1966), chaired by J.W.T. Spinks, 49.

2 See *The Presocratics*, ed. Philip Wheelwright, 71.

3 The remark, uttered shortly before his death, is quoted by Sir David Brewster in his *Memoires of the Life, Writings, and Discoveries of Sir Isaac Newton*, 2nd ed. (Edinburgh: Edmonston and Douglas, 1860), 2:331, (chap. 27). NF shortens Newton's words a little.

26. Sermon in Merton College Chapel

1 In Dickens's *David Copperfield*.

2 Albert Camus, *The Myth of Sisyphus and Other Essays*, trans. Justin O'Brien (New York: Vintage Books, 1955), 91.

27. Stanley Llewellyn Osborne

1 The Ontario Ladies' College was a private boarding and day school for girls founded in 1874 in Whitby, Ont., under the aegis of the Methodist church; the church affiliation was continued by the United Church.

28. The Leap in the Dark

1 Blake, *The Mental Traveller*, ll. 93–6.

2 "The Foolish Old Man Who Removed the Mountains," speech of 11 June 1945 to the Seventh National Congress of the Communist Party of China, in *Selected Works of Mao Tse-Tung* (Oxford: Pergamon Press, 1967), 3:272.

29. Wisdom and Knowledge

1 See no. 23, n. 3.

2 Letter to Richard Woodhouse (27 October 1818), in *The Letters of John Keats*, 4th ed., ed. Maurice Buxton Forman (London: Oxford University Press, 1952), 227.

3 "Tradition and the Individual Talent," in *The Sacred Wood* (London: Methuen, 1960), 54.

4 Letter to Georges Izambard (13 May 1871), in *Lettres de la vie littéraire d'Arthur Rimbaud*, ed. Jean-Marie Carré (Paris: Gallimard, 1990), 39.

5 See esp. "Chandogya Upanishad," in *The Principal Upanishads*, ed. S. Radhakrishnan (London: Allen and Unwin, 1953), 458.

30. On Christmas

1 NF has written "12 days" above "powers of darkness" in the typescript.

2 There is no "Q" here, but it seems likely that NF quoted stanzas 3 and 4 of the *Introduction*.

3 It seems likely that, in addition to the biographical facts mentioned, NF is alluding to Southwell's poem *The Burning Babe*, in which the newborn infant Christ on the night of his nativity experiences the torments of his crucifixion. Although there is no "Q" at this point in the typescript, NF may have quoted the poem.

4 The passage quoted is spoken by the detached philosopher goose Mopsus, and is the only speech by one of the farm geese in the November eclogue. It is in the December eclogue, immediately following, that the Christmas feelings of the other geese are expressed, as the "Day of wrath and terror" comes on them. See James Reaney, *A Suit of Nettles* (Toronto: Macmillan, 1958), 52–4.

5 C.S. Calverley, Virgil's *Fourth Eclogue*, in *Translations into English and Latin*, 3rd ed. (London: George Bell and Sons, 1886), 114.

6 At this point NF has interlined the phrase "Read ten poems." Speculation about the poems NF may have read aloud is probably not useful, but readers are referred to the references to the Song of Songs in *GC*, 107–8, 140–2, and 154–6, to bride(s) imagery in *WP*, 202–3, 206, 209, 213, 221, 224, 227, and also to garden–body metaphors in the latter book, 191, 196–200, 202, and 216.

7 "Something keeps reminding us" is added in NF's handwriting above the typewritten text.

31. Wedding of Patricia Russell and Andrew Binnie

1 The AV has "charity" in this quotation, where NF has "love." In this and other quotations cited here, NF has run the verses of the AV together.

2 "The Doctrine and Discipline of Divorce," in *The Works of John Milton*, 3:396, (bk. 1, chap. 4). NF modernizes spelling.

3 Ibid., 398.

4 Blake, *Visions of the Daughters of Albion*, pl. 7, ll. 16–17; pl. 5, ll. 5–6; pl. 7, l. 30; pl. 8, l. 1; pl. 8, ll. 4–6, 8–10. The square brackets are in the original typescript.

32. Substance and Evidence

1 See no. 12, n. 4.

2 Tennyson, Prologue to *In Memoriam*, l. 4.

33. Memorial Service for Mrs. Jean Haddow

1 NF omits "But" at the beginning of 3:1, and also the second half of the verse, "and there shall no torment touch them." In the third sentence of the quota-

tion he changes the AV "were healthful" to "are wholesome"; in the next
clauses of the same sentence he slightly alters the AV's "and there is no poison of destruction in them; nor the kingdom of death."

2 The words omitted at the first ellipsis are "O ye heathen"; at the second,
"that shall come in the end of the world"; at the third, "for evermore"; and at
the fourth, "I testify my Saviour openly."

3 NF paraphrases rather than quotes directly the last part of this extract.

4 In citing verse 10 here, NF changes the AV "Who can find a virtuous
woman?" to "Who can praise a virtuous woman?" The Hebrew verb *matsa*
means "find," not "praise." The occasion of a memorial tribute to a specific
woman is the evident reason for the change. In citing verse 25 he makes a
semantically less abrupt change of the AV "strength and honour" to
"strength and dignity." The Hebrew noun *hadar* "honour," "beauty," or
"majesty" can mean "dignity." He also changes "time" to "the time." In his
reading of verses 27 to the end of the chapter, again guided by the occasion,
NF omits as much as he quotes.

34. A Breath of Fresh Air

1 Cf. Erwin Schrödinger, "Seek for the Road," in *My View of the World*, trans.
Cecily Hastings (Cambridge: Cambridge University Press, 1964), 34.

2 For a discussion of Heraclitus' view of the Logos as light, see Philip Wheelwright, *Heraclitus* (Princeton: Princeton University Press, 1959), 25. For the
cosmic fire of the Stoics, see ibid., 50.

36. Funeral Service for Jean Gunn

1 Henry Vaughan, 17th century, *They Are All Gone into the World of Light*[!]
[ll. 21–32]. [NF]

2 Wallace Stevens, *The Owl in the Sarcophagus* [stanza 5, ll. 1–6, 10–18].
[NF]

3 Emily Dickinson, Quatraine. [NF]. I.e., poem no. 1623 in *The Poems of Emily
Dickinson*, ed. Thomas H. Johnson.

4 Margaret Avison, *In Truth* [ll. 7–10, 22–25, 30–45] from *The Dumbfounding*.
[NF]

38. The Dialectic of Belief and Vision

1 See his book *Of Grammatology*.

2 See no. 2, n. 13.

3 For the term, see Hegel, *Phenomenology of Spirit*, 72–5, (sec. a.2.119–23).

4 *For the Sexes: The Gates of Paradise*, emblem 13.

5 Jean-Paul Sartre, "Bad Faith," in *Being and Nothingness*, trans. Hazel E. Barnes (New York: Philosophical Library, 1956), 57–70, (chap. 2).

6 See, e.g., *Jerusalem: The Emanation of the Giant Albion*, pl. 71.

7 George Gordon, Lord Byron, *The Vision of Judgment*, ll. 688–9.

8 See Eliot's *Burnt Norton*; and Yeats's *Sailing to Byzantium*.

9 See no. 12, n. 20.

10 See no. 8, n. 9.

11 See no. 29, n. 5.

39. To Come to Light

1 NF is here adopting the Vulgate's translation of Proverbs 8:31, as explained in *GC*, 125.

2 Nietzsche, *The Gay Science*, 257, (bk. 4, sec. 327). "Joyful knowledge" is a frequent translation of Nietzsche's title, *Die Fröhliche Wissenschaft*.

3 Wordsworth, *The River Duddon*, Sonnet XXXIV, l. 14.

4 William Blake, *The Marriage of Heaven and Hell*, Proverbs of Hell, l. 18.

5 See no. 23, n. 3.

40. On Lent

1 Ezra Pound, *Make It New* (1934); rpt. in *The Literary Essays of Ezra Pound*, ed. T.S. Eliot (New York: New Directions, 1935), 83.

2 The primary meaning of the Greek word *scholê* is of course "leisure." There are several passages in Aristotle, however, in which the context clearly demands that the word or its derivatives must mean "school" and "scholarship"—e.g., *Politics*, 1313b.3, 1323b.39. It was hardly necessary for Aristotle to point out the etymological connection, since the words are identical, and NF appears to be remembering his usage rather than his actual statement. (We are indebted to Wallace McLeod for this information.)

3 T.S. Eliot, *Burnt Norton*, pt. 5, ll. 19–20.

Emendations

80/29–30	changd, even as in ancient times? *for* chang'd, even as in ancient time? [Erdman edition]
89/23	or contexts *for* or context
92/23	as a ziggurat *for* as ziggurat
95/27	Walter Hilton's *for* John Hilton's
97/29	for the sake of *for* for sake of
98/26	scheme of things *for* scene of things
99/22–3	*Phenomenology of Spirit for Phenomenology of the Spirit*
100/38	walking *for* talking
103/37	Pitched betwixt *for* Pitched between
111/11	*Le livre de Ruth for Introduction au livre de Ruth*
113/34–5	with her [Naomi] *for* with her Naomi
119/21–2	this has been the traditional . . . too *for* this has also been the traditional . . . too
121/38	Of Fish *for* of fishes
128/35	'Tis but one *for* There's but one
132/26	The myth asserts *for* The myth, also, asserts
135/36	chapter 34 *for* chapter 31
138/1	source of crime *for* sources of crime
145/36	we perform with *for* we undergo with
148/8–9	a seed, the enfolded form *for* a seed, the unfolded form [as in next sentence; presumably the tape was misheard]
148/33	that consists of *for* the consists of
150/16–17	or . . . was ever intended *for* and . . . was never intended
150/21	proto-science *for* proto of science
151/14	living beings *for* livings beings
151/18	Of Fish *for* of fishes
151/21	brought them unto Adam to see *for* brought all the animals to the adam to be named, to see [AV]
152/36	human society *for* human quality
153/7	as they affect *for* as it affects
153/19–20	and into George Macdonald's very remarkable nineteenth-century story *for* and to George Macdonald's nineteenth-century very remarkable story
154/16	a kind of *for* kind of
162/11	illusion *for* illusions
162/24	adventure *for* adventures
191/29	[NF's note was mistakenly keyed to 191/18]
192/18–19	our views both of the relations of human beings to one another and of the relation of the human *for* our view of the relation both of human beings to one another and of the relation of the human [cf. TS]
194/27	*Phenomenology of Spirit for Phenomenology of the Spirit*

197/22–3	complimented . . . on *for* complimented . . . in
202/5	application of *for* application to [as in TS and on a tape of the lecture]
204/33	of the classifying systems *for* of classifying systems
207/21–2	as horrible in results as their Fascist counterparts *for* as horrible in their results as in their fascist counterparts
226/16	(1 Kings 20:23) *for* (1 Kings 20:24)
226/39	(2 Kings 2:24) *for* (2 Kings 2:23)
241/1	problem *for* problems
241/3	at college *for* at colleges
246/5	with the lifting *for* with lifting
254/21	as an individual *for* as the individual [NF's correction]
254/39	social order *for* social worker [NF's correction]
258/18	impact on society *for* impact of society
264/38	such a revolution *for* much a revolution
273/1	more . . . than *for* more . . . that
274/19	it is based *for* is is based
288/15	or representation of *for* of representation of
291/39	in itself *for* it itself
300/7–8	in the same country . . . in the field *for* in that same country . . . in the fields [AV]
303/34	wished *for* wishes
304/12	profess *for* confess [AV]
308/37	and to conceive *for* and conceive [AV]
314/10–11	of the Christmas *for* of Christmas
319/7	they twain *for* they [AV]
319/13	rejoiceth not in iniquity *for* rejoiceth not in unrighteousness [AV]
319/21–2	if a man would give all the substance of his house for love, it would utterly be contemned *for* if a man would give the substance of his house for love, he would be utterly contemned [AV]
319/24	And Ruth said, Intreat me *for* Then said Ruth: entreat me [AV]
319/25–6	and where thou lodgest, I will lodge: thy people shall be my people *for* where thou lodgest, I will lodge; thy people are my people [AV]
319/31	the desire and longing to put off *for* the desire to put off
319/32	but not without a fit soul *for* with a fit soul
324/28–9	worthy . . . unworthy *for* most worthy . . . most unworthy [RSV]
328/11	risen *for* arisen [AV]
329/13	wherein thou hast afflicted us *for* of our affliction [AV]
335/35	everyone that is born *for* everyone born
341/9	fabrics begs *for* systems begs
358/29	by this son *for* by the sun [Riverside Shakespeare]
360/14	What you have whispered *for* What is whispered [RSV]
371/15	Accept the mystery behind knowledge: it is not *for* Accept the mys-

tery behind knowledge, but illusions that restrict freedom and limit
hope. Accept the mystery behind knowledge: it is not [line appears
to have been repeated]

381/21–2   may be thine. We are often tempted [an illegible sentence, interlined between these two sentences, has been omitted]

393/15   *Phenomenology of Spirit* for *Phenomenology of the Spirit*
404/30   *The Owl in the Sarcophagus* for *The Owl and the Sarcophagus*

Index

City of God, 255, 265

Classic, meaning of, 42–3, 90, 123, 209, 346–7

Claudel, Paul (1868–1955): *Introduction au "livre de Ruth"* (1938), 111

Claudius I (Tiberius Claudius Drusus Nero Germanicus) (10 B.C.–A.D. 54), 216

Clement I, Pope (1st. century A.D.): *The Recognitions of Clement*, 60

Cold War, 170, 171, 172–3, 266

Coleridge, Samuel Taylor (1772–1834), 120, 180, 212

Colossians, Epistle of Paul to, 301

Comedy, 49, 89, 107–8, 188; as Bible's shape, 3, 15

Communion, 289

Communism, 101, 168–9, 172, 262, 264, 266, 270

Comte, Auguste (1798–1857), 211, 262

Concern: primary, 178, 185, 187, 190–1, 212; primary and secondary, 144–5, 169–71, 353–6; spiritual primary vs. secondary, 171–3, 196

Conditioning, social or cultural, 37, 232–3, 335

Constable, John (1776–1837), 40

Constitutions, written and unwritten, 133–5

Conventions, social, 282–3

Cook, Stanley A. (1873–1949), 396

Copernicus, Nicolas (1473–1543), 61

Corinthians, Epistles of Paul to, 175, 197, 235, 260, 272, 310, 321, 322, 364, 366; on Christ, 362; on faith, hope, and charity, 321, 350; on language, 80, 160, 177; on love, 76–7, 90, 164, 289; readings from, 319, 328, 339, 340; on spiritual body, 176, 194; translation of, 221–2, 334

Council of Trent, 173

Counter-Reformation, 174

Creation: and beginning of time, 199; divine and human, 35–6, 41, 60–1, 66, 151, 287

– human: in the arts and culture, 36–43, 45–7, 67–70, 189, 323; includes criticism, 196–7; as social vision, 43–5, 47–51, 81–2;

– myth of, 13; in the Bible (Priestly and Jahwist accounts), 47–8, 52–3, 55, 56, 57–9, 62, 63, 66–7, 79, 119–32 passim, 148–57 passim, 163, 205; in Christian tradition, 63–6; in Mayan culture, 63; NF on, xvii, xxii, xxiv–xxx; in *Paradise Lost*, 74; two types of (sky-father and earth-mother), 53–7, 59

Crime, 133, 135, 138–42, 146

Criticism, 191, 196–7, 209–10; Biblical, 33–4; higher, 18

– literary: applied to Bible, 17–19; learns from Bible, 83, 87–90, 344–5; task of, 355–6; and text, 75

Cromwell, Oliver (1599–1658), 217, 220

Cross, 202, 379, 381

Crucifixion, 202, 225, 368

Cuchulain, 10

Culture, 186; as envelope, 37–8, 47, 352; as freedom, 276; as recreation, 67–70; and social conditions, 42, 188

Cyclical patterns, 24, 54, 59–60, 167–71, 199–200, 202, 206, 212

Cyrus the Great (d. 529 B.C.), 215

Dagon, 226

Danae, 92, 96, 156

Daniel, Book of, 15, 126, 252

Dante Alighieri (1265–1321), 3, 30, 65–6, 78, 126, 304, 346; on interpretation, 222; *De Monarchia*, 219; *Inferno*, 65, 99–100, 129, 257; *Paradiso*, 65, 67, 94, 111, 165, 181,

Frazer, Sir James George (1854–1941),
38, 39, 114–15, 353; *Folklore in the
Old Testament* (1918), 115; *The
Golden Bough* (1907–15), 115–17
Freedom: charter of, 88–9, 228; Christian, 262, 265, 267, 276; and habit,
208; individual and social, 137, 254,
256, 258–9, 276; Jesus on, 336; and
language, 88–9; Milton on, 66, 99,
129; and play, 361; as political goal,
169, 170, 273; as primary concern,
145, 170, 171; resistance to, 45
French Revolution, 98, 127, 141, 204
Freshmen, 239–43 passim
Freud, Sigmund (1856–1939), 41, 62,
68, 176, 189, 201, 356
Freudianism, 132, 233
Frye, Herman Northrop (1912–91):
his evangelical background, 156; on
hymnbook committee, 297; as minister, xix–xxi; on his moments of
enlightenment, 210; *Creation and
Recreation* (1980), xxiv–xxx;
*Northrop Frye on Culture and Litera-
ture* (1978), 39
– *The Double Vision* (1991): argument
of, xxiv–xxxvii; occasion of,
xviii–xix, xxx–xxxiv, 166–7
– *The Great Code* (1981), 123–4, 147,
344; relation to shorter works,
xvii–xviii, xxiv, xxx, 166
– *Words with Power* (1990): Frye on,
xxxi, 147; relation to shorter works,
xvii–xviii, 166
Fuller, Richard Buckminister (1895–
1983): *I Seem to Be a Verb* (1970), 79
Fundamentalism, religious, 175
Future: anxiety about, 198–9, 235, 252,
281–5; fixation on, 205–6, 207; as
present, 210; vision of, 43–5, 146

Galatians, Epistle to, 140, 229, 362

Galileo (1564–1642), 56
Garden symbol, 57
Gaskell, Elizabeth Cleghorn (1810–
65): *Ruth* (1853), 112
Genesis, Book of, 15, 89, 105, 106, 109,
226, 228, 229; on Jacob, 91, 101, 165,
230; proper critical approach to, 18;
on Tower of Babel, 93
– Creation myth in: xxvi–xxvii, 47,
48, 55, 57, 62, 63, 79, 119, 120–32
passim, 148–57 passim, 163, 189–90;
and fall, 139
Genghis Khan (ca. 1162–1227), 220
George VI (1895–1952), 271
Germany, 256, 302
Gibbon, Edward (1737–94): *Decline
and Fall of the Roman Empire*
(1776–88), 14, 16, 32, 206
Gilbert, Sir William Schwenck
(1836–1911): and Sir Arthur
Seymour Sullivan (1842–1900): *The
Mikado* (1885), 140
Gilgamesh, Epic of (ca. 1200–1000
B.C.), 52
Gnostics, 218
God: as creator, xxv, xxviii, xxx, 7, 36,
47, 48, 55, 60, 63, 119, 122, 125–6,
150, 151, 197, 199; and crime and
sin, 135, 136–8; death of, 8, 79, 83;
and Job, 71; and love, 94, 164; and
metonymic language, 27, 78; of Old
Testament, 11–12, 226–33 passim,
357; relation to man, 7, 107, 186,
193, 235, 286, 326; science and, 184,
185; as spirit, 182, 213, 365; and suffering, 229–30, 232, 233, 363; and
temporal rulers, 203, 214, 216, 217,
223, 255–6; as truth, 334; wrath of,
232, 301, 327. *See also* Word
gods: development of, 214–18; nature
of, 102, 118, 203, 357
Goethe, Johann Wolfgang von (1749–